Civil Society and the Reform of Finance

Efforts to resolve the recent financial crisis have obscured a more deeply rooted financialization crisis that impacts not only the market economy but also the vital civic and moral traditions that support it. This book reveals the cultural influence of finance in reshaping the foundations of American civil society and proposes a return to certain "first principles" of the Republic to restore the nation's economic vision.

This book demonstrates how funding concerns and financial incentives "revalue" faith traditions, educational institutions, nonprofit organizations, and even the nation's healthcare system in ways that are eroding the diversity of American culture. These changes also undermine the ethical framework of both democratic government and the free market system. While financial influence has diminished the value of civil society, this book proposes that revitalized intermediary institutions still offer the best path forward in restoring the financial sector and, more broadly, enriching the American competitive ethic toward development of a more virtuous economy.

The book is written for an academic and professional audience, offering a blueprint for the involvement of civil society with government in providing more communally integrated oversight that could contribute to a genuine democratization of finance.

Charles McDaniel, Jr. is Assistant Professor in the Interdisciplinary Core Program of Baylor University's Honors College, USA. He is also the Book Review Editor for the *Journal of Church and State*.

Routledge Critical Studies in Finance and Stability

Edited by Jan Toporowski

School of Oriental and African Studies, University of London, UK

The 2007–8 Banking Crash has induced a major and wide-ranging discussion on the subject of financial (in)stability and a need to revaluate theory and policy. The response of policy-makers to the crisis has been to refocus fiscal and monetary policy on financial stabilization and reconstruction. However, this has been done with only vague ideas of bank recapitalisation and 'Keynesian' reflation aroused by the exigencies of the crisis, rather than the application of any systematic theory or theories of financial instability.

Routledge Critical Studies in Finance and Stability covers a range of issues in the area of finance including instability, systemic failure, financial macroeconomics in the vein of Hyman P. Minsky, Ben Bernanke and Mark Gertler, central bank operations, financial regulation, developing countries and financial crises, new portfolio theory, and New International Monetary and Financial Architecture.

1 **Banking Systems in the Crisis**
The faces of liberal capitalism
Edited by Sue Konzelmann and Marc Fovargue-Davies

2 **Post-Keynesian Views of the Crisis and its Remedies**
Edited by Óscar Dejuán Asenjo, Eladio Febrero Paños and Jorge Uxo Gonzalez

3 **The Rise and Fall of Money Manager Capitalism**
Minsky's half century from World War Two to the Great Recession
Eric Tymoigne and L. Randall Wray

4 **Cycles, Growth and the Great Recession**
Edited by Annalisa Cristini, Steven M. Fazzari, Edward Greenberg and Riccardo Leoni

5 **Liquidity Preference and Monetary Economies**
Fernando J. Cardim de Carvalho

6 **Civil Society and the Reform of Finance**
Taming capital, reclaiming virtue
Charles McDaniel, Jr.

Civil Society and the Reform of Finance

Taming capital, reclaiming virtue

Charles McDaniel, Jr.

Routledge
Taylor & Francis Group
LONDON AND NEW YORK

First published 2016
by Routledge
2 Park Square, Milton Park, Abingdon, Oxon OX14 4RN

and by Routledge
711 Third Avenue, New York, NY 10017

Routledge is an imprint of the Taylor & Francis Group, an informa business

British Library Cataloguing in Publication Data
A catalogue record for this book is available from the British Library

Library of Congress Cataloging in Publication Data
McDaniel, Charles, Jr.
Civil society and the reform of finance: taming capital, reclaiming virtue/ Charles McDaniel, Jr.
pages cm
Includes bibliographical references and index.
1. Finance–Moral and ethical aspects–United States. 2. Financial institutions–United States. 3. Civil society–United States. I. Title.
HG181.M374 2015
332.0973–dc23 2015002313

ISBN: 978-1-138-88569-1 (hbk)
ISBN: 978-1-315-71526-1 (ebk)

Typeset in Times New Roman
by Wearset Ltd, Boldon, Tyne and Wear

For Angus, Hambone, and "Mr. Fred," who helped me to see life in a whole 'nother way!

Contents

Acknowledgments

A book with an interdisciplinary approach to its subject requires an eclectic group from which to draw its resources. I have been fortunate in that regard. The diverse contributions of colleagues, students, business professionals, theologians, ethicists, and others with whom I have had countless conversations on the ethics of the financial system have inspired the material that follows.

Because of an aging memory (never particularly robust to begin with), I am at a loss to recall all the contributions, but certain individuals have given much time and intellectual energy to this project and deserve special mention. My colleague and friend, Dr. Les Ballard, whose diligence and attention to detail is extraordinary, was instrumental in helping me refine the manuscript. Les spent many late nights catching too many flaws in my writing and argumentation; he deserves some kind of medal. My former student, Dresden McGregor, joined the "team" after taking my capstone class in 2013 and contributed in countless ways up to the very day I submitted the manuscript to Routledge. Her keen eye for getting to the pith of arguments is a gift that will benefit her own work for many years to come. Another former student, Vance Woods, was willing to venture beyond his comfort zone in providing insights on a subject that, as will be seen, can be highly intimidating. Two other students, Anthony Severin and Cole Short, are moving on to bigger and better things, but they provided many imaginative ideas as well as important resources to help make the arguments that follow.

Several colleagues provided both insight and inspiration and deserve to be mentioned. Dr. Michael Stegemoller of Baylor University's Finance Department chaired a conference session in which I presented many of the ideas found in Chapters 2 and 3, and his refreshingly holistic disciplinary perspective shaped my thinking. Also, a team of Bible scholars and theologians—Marvin Chaney, Roger Nam, Ellen Davis, Neill Elliot, Diana Swancutt, and Ron Simkins—offered unique perspectives that greatly informed the materials in Chapter 8. Thanks to Richard Horsley of the University of Massachusetts Boston for not only putting together the session but offering much inspiration through his many years of research and writing in reminding us all that Biblical and theological perspectives on economics and finance are critically needed. I also learned much from countless conversations with my colleague and good friend, Dr. Sam Perry, concerning the "materiality of discourse" that contributed to Chapter 7. These expressions of appreciation undoubtedly leave out other important contributors to whom I apologize but am no less grateful.

1 Introduction

On a conference call with reporters and financial analysts in March 2012, JPMorgan Chase (JPM) CEO Jamie Dimon found himself apologizing for his company's "errors, sloppiness and bad judgment" stemming from a multi-billion-dollar trading loss in the credit derivatives market attributed largely to the actions of the so-called "London Whale," Bruno Iksil. Investigators uncovered evidence that led to JPM being fined around $920 million and two of its bankers being charged with conspiracy, wire fraud, and filing false reports with the Securities and Exchange Commission (SEC) even as the "Whale," because of his cooperation with authorities, was not charged.

Only two years earlier, Dimon had appeared before the Financial Crisis Inquiry Commission, lauding his company's performance in 2008 and 2009, the most challenging years of the crisis. At that time, he stated that along with its conservative accounting approach, JPM's decisions to not "unduly leverage" its capital and to maintain high-quality standards for investment enabled the company to remain strong and even to aid resolution of the financial mess by acquiring Bear Stearns and buying the assets of Washington Mutual.[1] JPM was perceived not merely as a survivor of financial calamity but as an exemplar of financial integrity.

So it was both ironic and embarrassing that the company thought to have weathered the maelstrom best, now had to assume the position of many of its competitors, appealing for public forgiveness and ensuring that all appropriate steps had been taken to prevent such losses in the future. Economist Paul Krugman was inspired to quote Yogi Berra that "it's déjà vu all over again" in suggesting the company's troubles demonstrated that few if any lessons were learned from the crisis commonly recognized as the most serious since the Great Depression.[2] Indeed, JPM's major transaction loss in 2012 was, in certain ways, more alarming than the losses leading to the initial crisis because it signaled that what many have suspected is true: the factors motivating risky behavior by large banks and investment companies have changed little. That it occurred during what turned out to be a profitable quarter for the company also reaffirmed the perception that giant financial firms can make money in spite of themselves.

Dimon's mea culpa hardly came as a shock to an American public already desensitized to financial mismanagement and rogue trading. After evidence surfaced of undisciplined acts that contributed to the crisis, the idea was that such "aberrant" behaviors could be controlled by tightening the regulatory noose and making the operations of financial institutions more transparent. Subsequent disclosures of the power of individual traders to jeopardize major markets, however, demonstrated that the need for institutional reform, so apparent in the lack of oversight that led to earlier abuses, had gone unheeded. Worse, it suggested the temptation to engage in risky practices that effectively used taxpayers as the ultimate insurance was more entrenched than originally thought. Dimon had earlier criticized the "Volcker Rule," designed to prevent the kinds of trading that precipitated the crisis, for its "mind-numbing complexity" even as it was revealed that his company engaged in the kind of risky investment practices the regulation was designed to restrict. While Dimon was correct about the inherent complexity in "postcrisis" attempts at regulatory reform, his criticism, which suggested the impossibility for regulators to distinguish hedging from proprietary trading, begs the question whether the industry is evolving beyond the capabilities of regulatory regimes altogether.[3] Regardless, the sad reality is that Americans are no longer surprised to learn of new financial scandals and have little expectation that those involved will pay for any transgressions, presuming that transgressions even can be discerned. What *is* truly shocking are changes that have flown largely beneath the radar but have far more serious implications for cultural, not simply economic, wellbeing. Evidence suggests financial influence, and in some cases corruption, reaches deep into American civil society—the network of nonprofit and voluntary associations that perform a critical mediating function between citizens and large institutions and are crucial to the development of both individual and social ethics. This book contends that the "financialization of American civil society" presents a more serious challenge than the recent financial calamity to the nation's long-term stability. In fact, the intensive effort to deal with the financial crisis appears to have further obscured a more deeply rooted "financialization crisis," one that has been building over decades and one that expanded regulation or even ethical reform of the financial sector cannot resolve.

Financialization refers to the continuous movement of capital from the production of real goods and services to the financial sector and the increasing dominance of financial values and interests in all institutions. It is a broad cultural phenomenon involving value changes that impact democratic capitalism's social and ethical structure. Financialization of the economy has negative consequences for macroeconomic stability and income distribution, among other effects; the financialization of "society," and especially that of civil society, has far more alarming implications for the continuation of the American experiment. It poses fundamental questions that require the involvement of ethicists, philosophers, educators, and religious leaders, who must locate appropriate forums for addressing the cultural effects of changes in finance, including the depersonalization of exchange, the distancing of owners from assets, and the growing divide in financial literacy.

More than systemic risk crept in undetected during the turmoil; these events exposed the global economy's vulnerability to the ethical integrity of key market players, many of whom failed the test. Despite the extensive development of administrative systems in both public and private spheres designed to support the financial economy, it appears more dependent on the personal ethics of individuals—including both executives and mid-tier workers in key technical positions—than ever before. These revelations suggest that even as finance has been characterized as failing the broader culture through fraudulent practices and rogue trading, the reverse may also be true. Traditional institutional supports that provide the moral framework for development may be failing to supply adequate ethical guidance necessary for a dynamic new financial industry in which moral quandaries proliferate alongside "innovative" products.

One reason for this systemic failure is that the same dynamism that challenges individual ethics also strains those institutions responsible for social and moral stability. Financial concerns are altering both the missions and values of religious groups, voluntary associations, and nonprofit organizations that help form citizens for self-government and protect them against exploitation by large impersonal establishments, both public and private. By reshaping civil society, financialization potentially undermines the cultural layer that supports the development of a virtuous citizenry. It is the consummate financial Catch-22: finance's incursions into civil society destabilize organizations that provide the moral framework for democratic governance and the market economy even as the methods and instruments it inspires place greater responsibility on individual virtue. The constant push for innovation in finance and the industry's importance to overall economic health seems only to heighten that exposure.

Recent scandals have revealed how the expansion of financial instruments beyond the comprehension of many market participants has negative cultural effects. These instruments and their associated techniques magnify information asymmetries, leading to an odd combination of market concentration within the financial industry and atomization of the financial marketplace, further widening the distribution of wealth and disenfranchising segments of society. In addition, resignation to the growing impossibility of "average investors" knowing what they own in any real sense due to the layers of financial interests and instruments involved in the investment process has the effect of alienating them from the cultural outcomes of economic behavior. The question is how to go about restoring and redeploying civil society to regain some of the responsibility for development that has been given over to dynamic new forms of investment.

A glaring example of finance's influence on civil society was revealed in 2014 with hedge fund mogul William Ackman's attempt to take down the Herbalife Company, a manufacturer and distributor of nutritional supplements. Ackman, the head of Pershing Capital Square Management LP, shorted Herbalife stock—a practice in which an investor "borrows" stock to sell with the obligation to buy back the shares in the future, anticipating the share price will go down—in what was effectively a $1 billion bet on the company's failure. Alluding to Herbalife as a "pyramid scheme" that targets minorities, Ackman vowed to use his vast resources and fight "to the end of the earth" to expose the company's practices, substantiating this claim by hiring political lobbyists and

PR firms to help accomplish his objective. In light of his activities, the *New York Times* stated that the "attempt to bring ruin to one company, is a novel one, fusing the financial markets with the political system."[4]

However, it is not only the political system that Ackman is using, and that is the more troubling relevance here. Ackman also deployed an extensive network of media companies and nonprofit advocacy organizations to advance his cause. As part of his mobilization against Herbalife, he has paid around $130,000 to civic groups such as the Hispanic Federation and National Consumers League to get them to lobby Congress and also to solicit their help in locating "victims," for which toll-free numbers were set up.[5] These groups sent letters that contained virtually identical language to their constituencies, which sought out those who may have been duped by the "abusive pyramid scheme" after being lobbied by Ackman's organization. Additionally, there is now evidence that Herbalife has outspent the Ackman campaign in this public relations war by contributing not only to political lobbying firms but also to groups such as the United States Hispanic Leadership Institute, a nonprofit committed to "non-partisan civic engagement."[6]

The point is not whether Herbalife is or is not a pyramid scheme or even whether Ackman is a civic-minded CEO or self-interested cad. It is rather that financial interests increasingly hold sway even over nonprofit, social service organizations formed to advance the public interest. Monetary inducements today are highly influential in those very institutions that are supposed to balance progress by offsetting vested political and economic interests. In this case, one powerful investor is determined to expose a company's presumed wrongdoing, using his immense resources to turn the outcome of a primarily financial transaction in his favor and co-opting civic groups in the process. And the company targeted has adopted similar tactics in a bidding war for the services of ostensibly nonpartisan organizations. Perhaps Herbalife will be revealed as a scam and Ackman will be vindicated, but the larger point is that public advocacy and community service organizations are being incentivized to take sides in financial "contests" between for-profit entities. This campaign crosses a boundary that has significant cultural implications should such practices become widespread.

One might counter with the argument that the Ackman-Herbalife controversy is an extreme case of financial influence. From the perspective of this book, however, that valid criticism highlights an even larger problem: the potential damage from the extension of big money into the civic realm and the need for American citizens to act to prevent it. The Supreme Court's decision in *McCutcheon* v. *Federal Election Commission* (2014), which struck down restrictions on "aggregate" giving by contributors to election campaigns while upholding limits on giving to individual campaigns, stimulated a vigorous public debate and became the fodder of late-night talk shows. Observing the new rules allowing donors to write virtually unlimited checks in limited increments, comedian Jon Stewart quipped, "the last great hope of preserving our democracy from the corrupting influence of money is carpal tunnel syndrome."[7] Where citizens are less likely to perceive financial influence is in the subtle changes in the values and relationships of civil society organizations, and likewise in the myriad decisions made in boardrooms and administrative departments that are often compelled to emphasize financial interests over mission.

Evidence will show how financial decision-making criteria increasingly "crowd out" others even in nonprofit, social service organizations. In many cases, a definite wall no longer separates the functions of for-profit from nonprofit organizations. Institutional homogenization is an underemphasized but significant byproduct of the financialization phenomenon. Finance is not portrayed as a malevolent force in this process; it serves merely as an efficient vehicle for capital formation and transference that facilitates, with similar efficiency, the potential reconstruction of social values. What particularly should concern Americans is the expansiveness and nuance of the means by which the financialization of civil society has occurred. Changes in the American competitive ethic are influencing many institutions to emphasize immediate financial concerns over issues that often are fundamental to these organizations' identities.

Just as scholars such as Robert Putnam have provided evidence showing that television and other forms of entertainment increasingly distract individuals from participation in civil society,[8] this book reveals an analogous form of "institutional distraction." Religious, educational, and social service organizations have become less focused on their missions and more invested in activities that affect their financial wellbeing. The combination of individual and institutional distraction is ominous for American civil society, and it amplifies the warnings of notable philosophers and economists who have warned that capitalism ultimately will exhaust its own moral resources.

While the ethical consequences of intensifying financial pressures are most easily observed in the banking and investment industries, other events of less monetary but greater cultural significance than rogue trading or creative accounting reveal the potential damage of finance's rising hegemony. Nongovernmental organizations (NGOs), preoccupied with budgetary concerns, are forced into cuts that are certain to impair services. Nonprofit healthcare organizations behave like for-profit entities, streamlining operations to solicit the investment attention of profit-seeking national healthcare systems. In other cases, healthcare nonprofits simply relocate to more affluent areas, chasing the insured and fleeing the indigent care needs of their communities and leading to what has been described as "medical white flight."[9]

Religious groups sometimes treat adherents as "clients," partnering with financial firms to market investment services. In some extreme situations, these groups act recklessly or even deceptively in attempts to further the interests of leaders or the organizations themselves at the expense of their members. Cases such as the New Birth Missionary Church in Atlanta, where members eventually sued the Church to recoup investment losses, or the Baptist Foundation of Arizona, whose leaders constructed an elaborate Ponzi scheme based on Arizona real estate that caused investors to lose $570 million, demonstrate the "religious" allure of finance.[10]

These troubling developments for civil society are not limited to the United States. In the UK, the clerical pension fund of the Church of England suffered major losses because of wildly speculative practices. According to pension consultant John Ralfe, the Church "just decided to go double or quits at the casino"[11] by investing in hedge funds and other volatile instruments. When the pension fund's losses became public, Church officials attempted to justify investments in hedge funds even though certain Anglican theologians had criticized the practice of short-selling (a common practice of hedge funds) as perpetrated by "bank robbers and asset strippers."[12] Anglican leaders rationalized their actions with an ecclesiastical take on "the ends justify the means," offering the statement: "Maximizing the returns on our investment portfolios is an essential part of delivering our foundations' missions, for the benefit of society."[13] In other words, even "sacred" institutions must at times engage in practices that may challenge their theological principles in efforts to achieve a greater good.

Examples like the aforementioned are increasingly common. Organizations, even those with primarily religious and social service missions, are becoming desensitized to potential conflicts between their professed values and their financial practices. As Randy Martin observes, "the present invitation to live by finance—which has survived the fizzled boom—is still being extended to players beyond the corporate world."[14] Many of those players find their once-privileged places in civil society threatened by a largely unperceived yet reckless *social* experiment driven by the radical expansion of finance.

The threat posed by financialization has been enabled by a curious ideal that formed surreptitiously in the American consciousness: the belief that a market economy can be separated from those social and moral structures traditionally thought to support it. Trust in the ethical resilience of the market system has encouraged inattention to those institutional supports essential to harmonizing material and moral development. It also contributes to a myopic focus on reason and technique in problem resolution. Technical reform of the financial system itself, however, tends to address the symptoms of reckless or unethical action rather than the root causes, just as it tends to expose the unintended consequences to government intervention. The Dodd–Frank Wall Street Reform and Consumer Protection Act and other efforts to "fix the financial system" have been largely mechanical attempts to put the economy back on track after its recent derailment, without considering the cultural implications of new financial techniques or potential moral hazards associated with reforms themselves.

A significant social cost of financialization posited here is that it collapses the nation's value pluralism and its traditionally inclusive view of progress into a singular obsession with "return." In addition, it seems to signal other changes in American society:

- The great material expansion from the period of industrialization through the late-twentieth century is waning, leading to more parasitic forms of money making;

- The broad expansion of wealth that inspired the American Dream has stalled and, based on income trends, shows no near-term sign of recovery;
- The American imagination is fading—we are running out of ideas for development beyond electronic gadgetry and novel ways of repackaging assets; and
- The "Protestant Ethic" that ostensibly fueled the American economic miracle is in decline; industriousness in production and frugality in consumption have effectively reversed such that we are skimming-the-cream of past productivity.[15]

Despite the pessimistic tone of previous comments, many of the morally vitalizing qualities of the American economic system remain in place. Entrepreneurialism still thrives in certain segments of the economy, as do many socially responsible corporations that recognize obligations beyond maximizing return to shareholders. Nonetheless, the processes of financialization amplify those less-than-virtuous qualities of capitalism as it has evolved—impersonal transacting, widening of information asymmetries, the distancing of owners from assets, and the attenuating of reputation as an effective criterion for market decision making—even as they encroach upon institutions traditionally relied upon to humanize the system. Many books have been written on finance to address technical factors that are presumed to have contributed to recent crises and to provide policy recommendations for their resolution. The approach here is to assess the broader cultural implications of financialization, observing how it reshapes social relations and influences ethics even as it accentuates market volatility and distributes wealth in ways that may or may not conform to the desires of American citizens.

Financialization: what it is and what it represents

The literature on financialization's economic effects is substantial. Previous works by such authors as Greta Krippner, Thomas Palley, and Gerald Epstein have discussed ubiquitous overleveraging, alterations in wealth distribution, volatility in stock and commodity markets, and the drain of resources from the production of real goods and services brought about by the explosion of the financial sector. Even theologians and religious leaders have weighed in on the displacement of real production by purely financial activity, though they typically have provided little definition to differentiate between the two. This critical omission suggests that conventional forms of financial intermediation can be easily distinguished from financial activity as an end in itself.[16] Given the proliferation of new financial tools, however, that assumption no longer holds. Some recent innovations seem to have reoriented finance to its own purposes rather than enabling it to better serve society. This view of a growing separation between the financial sector and the real economy is commonly cited as evidence of financialization's harm.

Scholars have offered such a variety of definitions for financialization that arriving at a precise interpretation of this phenomenon is virtually impossible.

Some have offered broad descriptions, such as economist Thomas Palley's observation that financialization is "the process whereby financial markets, financial institutions, and financial elites gain greater influence over economic policy and economic outcomes," or the Marxist Rudolf Hilferding's timeless definition of financialization as the "ascendency of the rentier class," describing how it elevates the role of investor over that of entrepreneur.[17] UCLA finance professor Greta Krippner offers a more pragmatic definition: "a pattern of accumulation in which profit making occurs increasingly through financial channels rather than through trade and commodity production"; Gerald Epstein sees it as the "increasing role of financial motives, financial markets, financial actors and financial institutions in the operation of the domestic and international economies."[18] Among more expansive definitions of financialization, O'Boyle, Solari, and Marangoni describe how economic agents in a global climate of individual freedom and deregulation

> increasingly are avowing a way of thinking that measures economic performance in financial terms, especially short-term profits and return on investment, often to the exclusion of other considerations such as employment security, environmental protection, workplace safety, corporate governance, and living wages, not to mention world poverty, hunger, and disease.[19]

This dominance of a financial way of thinking and its displacement of other values and forms of reasoning are critical aspects of financialization that will be emphasized throughout this book.

The multiplicity of definitions offered by scholars and analysts has failed to detect one of financialization's most serious consequences: Financialization dislocates financial activity from the value-expression function of a market economy. The narrow focus on return and the ability to distance investors and their values from the assets they hold through impersonal, complex methods, lessening the emphasis on stewardship in favor of profit, is perhaps its most insidious quality. Moreover, the processes of financialization appear to have accommodated this "need" of a mass, modern economy with little reflection on the changes in social relationships and moral values that accompany them.

Also troubling is that financialization seems to challenge certain assumptions about the morality of the market. The rising complexity of the financial sector calls into question the idea that self-interested action in market contexts naturally reinforces ethical behavior. Participants must be able to connect actions and consequences to determine what constitutes moral conduct in the marketplace; but the frenetic activity fueled by financialization blurs such connections. The novelty and rapidity with which choices inundate both consumer and investor compromises their ability to make prudent decisions consistent with their values. In other cases, algorithms replace the need for investor choice altogether. Investment today often is a game involving models and graphs used to predict trends in asset prices rather than channeling capital to uses consistent with the investor's values or social vision. Even mundane business dealings often involve technical details that eclipse the understanding of transacting parties. A "simple" mortgage refinance involves dozens of financial and legal documents, some of which are beyond the comprehension of the homeowners engaging in these transactions.

Financial illiteracy of the general population compounds this problem. Statistics demonstrating the depth of financial illiteracy among citizens of developed nations illustrate the major challenges ahead in achieving a financially educated population. In the United States, for example, 55 percent of adults and 66 percent of the country's high school students lack basic comprehension of concepts such as inflation and interest rates.[20] In Britain, a Market and Opinion Research Institute (MORI) survey in 2004 "demonstrates the inability of most British consumers to perform elementary [financial] calculations and highlights a distinct problem about the misplaced confidence of the higher socio-economic groups in their own ability to make choices."[21] In other words, those *believing* they are financially literate may pose as much of a problem as those who are demonstrably illiterate because the former appear willing to act on those beliefs, with potential negative outcomes resulting from inadequate or inaccurate knowledge. Even worse, the municipal bankruptcy of Birmingham, Alabama, and the massive debts incurred by Milan, Italy, in derivative financing transactions demonstrate that even governments and institutional investors may be less knowledgeable than they believe, especially in the face of rapid financial innovation.

The insatiable desire for novelty in investment that has attended financialization amplifies uncertainty and contributes to instability by continually expanding the unknowns. Complexity also becomes an enemy of virtue where it obscures the consequences of one's actions beyond a very narrow field of vision. Its depth of penetration in finance leads Steven Schwarcz, a law professor whose research focuses on finance, to conclude that "solving problems of financial complexity may well be the ultimate twenty-first century market goal."[22] Continual growth in financial complexity is part of the "new normality." Martin observes that financialization "insinuates an orientation toward accounting and risk management into all domains of life."[23] The limited resources (in particular, "time") available to address financial issues means that they will continue to demand more from individuals simply to stay current with changes in the industry. That "investment" necessarily will come at the expense of other activities that contribute to the full development of the human person, and it is likely to stress disproportionately those already struggling to keep their heads above water. The imperative to maintain a financially educated culture thus not only poses an increasing challenge; it also threatens to expand the already significant divide between those with the financial knowledge to compete and those without, if it cannot be accomplished with some degree of social symmetry.

Banks and investment firms have the upper hand in this environment. As witnessed in scandals like that involving Merrill Lynch in 2008, some companies appear to have few qualms in using customer information to make proprietary trades for their own benefit, even as they often charge customers cryptic, undisclosed fees.[24] In the financialized society, the ease with which one can conceal deceptive behavior makes it easy to exploit others. Chung-Hua Shen and Hsiang-Lin Chih provide substantial evidence showing investment banks (IBs) that make stock recommendations are "net buyers" of the stocks they present to clients before recommending them and then become "net sellers" of those stocks after making their recommendations, whereas nonrecommending IBs do not demonstrate this behavior.[25] The Shen-Chih study empirically reinforces a growing perception that financial firms leverage their clients for proprietary gains.

Goldman Sachs' record $550 million settlement with the Securities and Exchange Commission demonstrates exposure on the other side of these deals. The company was fined for misrepresenting the risks of subprime mortgage-based collateralized debt obligations (CDOs) that it marketed to municipalities and other entities.[26] Financialization encourages this kind of precarious, ethically questionable dealing by pressuring all parties to accept new tools and a new mentality demanded by a rapidly changing industry. Participants are compelled to "adapt or fail," regardless of knowledge limitations or ethical concerns.

Present conditions did not emerge in a vacuum. Emil Røyrvik has observed how financialization came about "as a major capitalist response to a crisis in the social relationships of Fordism,"[27] the form of industrial growth that characterized the "long boom" beginning at the end of World War II and extending to the 1970s. Characterized by the mass production and consumption of standardized products that greatly enhanced the material welfare of many Americans, this economic transformation also precipitated major social changes: rapid growth in wage scales, increases in pension and health insurance obligations, and other benefits that, in combination with declining birth rates, began to push the system beyond its limits. Increased international competition in the same period led to declines in corporate earnings. Accented by the OPEC oil embargo, these declines resulted in the "stagflationary recession" during the Carter administration that extended to the first term of Ronald Reagan.[28] Neither American companies nor state entities could sustain the rapid increase in wages and benefits being doled out in the Fordist era, and some scholars believe that what has been described here as financialization resulted primarily from attempts to preserve twentieth-century economic gains through financial deregulation and the development of a "finance conception of the firm."[29] American corporations in manufacturing, electronics, and other industries turned to their investment and credit divisions in seeking profits, deemphasizing traditional lines of business and transforming the landscape of the American economy.

The social maladies associated with Fordism were confirmed by fiscal problems in the city most closely associated with it. Detroit's bankruptcy in 2013 demonstrated that the desperate turn to finance in the attempt to preserve gains brought about by industrialization could have disastrous consequences.[30] In a rather morbid analogy, columnist George Will compared Detroit's problems to the parasitic Ichneumon that lays its eggs inside a living caterpillar, its larvae feeding on their host while being careful to avoid vital organs so as to keep the caterpillar alive. The difference, Will observed, is that Detroit had no such natural instinct. Rather than "keeping its host alive" through fiscally responsible policies, it engaged in a

> double delusion: Magic would rescue the city (consult the Bible, the bit about the multiplication of loaves and fishes) or Washington would deem Detroit, as it recently did some banks and two of the three Detroit-based automobile companies, "too big to fail."[31]

Neither has occurred, of course. The greater lesson of Detroit—once the fourth largest city in the U.S., whose population has shriveled to less than it was in 1950[32]—is that it is far from alone in its faith in magic and/or federal largesse to overcome its fiscal problems. Camden, Birmingham, and Harrisburg are among some 641 municipalities that declared bankruptcy between the creation of Chapter 9 (the code covering municipal bankruptcy) in 1937 and July of 2012, but that number is heavily backloaded with a dramatic escalation of defaults in the last five years.[33]

Innovation in finance presents continual challenges to ethics because of its alluring potential to ease persistent fiscal problems, often at much greater risk. The dire straits of American cities have made the "magic of finance" an attractive option to officials who see no other way of balancing the books; if a city manager or comptroller can perform some accounting trick or financial sleight of hand and defer dealing with seemingly intractable conundrums, she would be a fool not to seize the chance and instead take the political hit for inaction in a climate where risky financial practices have become acceptable. This siren's song appeals not only to business corporations and government entities but also to churches, schools, NGOs, civic organizations, and other groups that are critical to cultural development. As will be seen, however, there have been significant functional costs to those organizations that most contribute to social cohesion and moral development: some have experienced fiscal impairment from financial mismanagement while others have undergone "mission drift" as financial concerns come to dominate core values.

A changing competitive ethos

The explosion of finance over the past couple of decades has extended its influence well beyond the sector itself and impacted the very ways in which we compete. A significant danger posed by the concentrations in market power and the further widening of wealth divisions that have attended financialization is that society is becoming desensitized to changing norms of competition, as demonstrated by Facebook's 2012 IPO ("initial public offering"). Industry analysts cautioned "average investors" against taking part in the stock offering because large institutions would be given priority. Morgan Stanley, the principal underwriting investment bank for the IPO, made the initial determinations of who could buy shares, placing its largest and most influential clients at the top of the list. Max Wolff, a stock analyst who weighed in on the event, stated that "the

IPO allocation is an elite lottery system, where people who don't need to win are invited to play"; moreover, the system gives the elites "a chance to deliberate and evaluate the assets, and then the general public comes in for the feeding frenzy."[34] The apparent contradiction between the process by which Facebook stock was offered to the public and the values of our system of "democratic" capitalism went largely unnoticed. Analysts made matter-of-fact statements warning the little people to stay away or get burned. Considering the enormity of this event, relatively few challenged the methods by which it was conducted as a violation of the level playing field that many believe fundamental to the American way of life.

The process of initial public offerings—much like the development of derivatives and other "financial weapons of mass destruction," as Warren Buffett once described them—appears beyond the grasp of the American people. Mastery of finance today, whether through privileged trading access or knowledge of financial models and instruments, yields tremendous power; yet many would contend it has contributed to the rather shaky ride of the past few years. Today's "quants"—mathematicians, physicists, computer scientists and other statistical types who found their way to Wall Street for the purpose of devising complex financial models—are the "Master Blasters" of the financial world. Likewise, the impersonalized, computer-based trading of esoteric products their methods facilitate forms the backbone of contemporary investment, expanding novelty at the expense of stability.

Regarding the recent turmoil, one might question whether organizations caught in the intricacies of innovative finance understood their portfolios well enough to take responsible action, or whether the industry fell victim to a herd mentality that led, lemming-like, to great leaps of faith in the system's resilience. The ethical implications of either answer are significant. Financialization is implicated in this respect because it spawns a kind of competition that is rather valueless. It eases commodification through indiscriminate and accelerated capital flows, offering less opportunity for reflection on the ultimate purposes of capital. Similarly, the distancing of investors from assets acquired creates the likelihood of "unintended investment." And this form of competition extends beyond firms. To the extent that individual investors are content to point-and-click the direction of their capital based on price movements in unknown companies and assets, they buy into the "derivative mentality" that has consumed the institutional investment and banking communities, making economic development as a whole increasingly directionless.

A troubling aspect of the recent crisis that points to a change in the American competitive ethic was revealed in the apparent "rationality" of actions that led to massive failures in the industry. While many are convinced that ethical lapses were a major factor, the logic behind most trading techniques that contributed to the crisis and subsequent recession seem rational even if, at times, they were employed excessively. Much of what has been misperceived as Wall Street corruption has been subsequently revealed as reasonable responses to changing market conditions in a highly competitive industry. Computer-based trading and the desire of investment firms to position their computers as close to exchange servers as possible to gain nanosecond advantage over competitors is an entirely rational, profit-centered motivation. Similarly, derivatives are not simply tools for speculation; they can be important defense mechanisms employed by firms to hedge against possible negative contingencies in the market. These instruments enable price-risk to be separated from underlying assets and traded separately to allow more efficient distribution of the risks to investment. Furthermore, the growth of mortgage-backed securities (MBSs) was predictable, even inevitable, given their origination through the Government National Mortgage Association (Ginnie Mae) in 1970 and the spread of information technology that made them easily implementable.[35] But these observations beg the question of whether rational, self-interested action in complex, concentrated industries like finance can jeopardize the economy as a whole. It also might be asked whether, in the face of rising financial complexity and pressures to adapt to new standards of competition, rationality has come to be equated with morality in market behavior.

Where else was the financial industry to go concerning these and other developments given the acceleration of competition in American culture generally and, in particular, the demand for innovation in the competition for profits? Brilliant minds from the nation's best business schools have been pouring into the offices of Wall Street firms for decades and charged with the onerous task of distinguishing themselves among equally gifted and driven individuals. Not to press the bounds of competition, intellectually and even ethically, likely would mean failure for those who had invested heavily in their educations. And for their firms to expect less of them would mean the irrational proposition of companies' "self-limiting" potential returns in a market where profit maximization is considered essential to survival. Despite the apparent rationality of much trading behavior that had negative effects, the underlying problems leading to recent crises were more ethical than mechanical, yet changes to the nation's competitive ethos have made them difficult to recognize. These are not ethical issues in the sense of Bernie Madoff's bilking of billions from his investors. That was an individual transgression involving overt illegality rather than cultural or systemic corruption. The moral problem that afflicts the American economy is far more subtle and has progressed in stages of alteration to our competitive ethic. Those changes have whittled away the idea that moral development in market contexts requires discernible connection between work performed and value contributed, between capital invested and return received, and other linkages vital not only to market ethics but also to proper functioning of the market system.

Capitalism, to some extent, always has struggled to maintain such connections. Extreme reliance on the price system for measures of value led Frank Knight to offer a classic description of the disjunction between the two: "the final results diverge notoriously from the ethical standards actually held. No one contends that a bottle of old wine is ethically worth as much as a barrel of flour, or a fantastic evening wrap for some potentate's mistress as much as a substantial dwelling-house, though such relative prices are not unusual."[36] Divergence between price and value only has grown since Knight's observation. Financialization further strains the pricing system to the point that many Americans no longer think of price, especially as determined in financial markets, as an expression of value. In this sense, the financial economy as it has evolved poses no *unique* problem; rather, it further loosens critical relationships necessary for synching values and market outcomes and limits the ability to discern where slippage occurs.

Ignoring this disjunction is no longer feasible because moral failings now appear a principal source of our material problems. It is not simply the market (broadly conceived) that is ethically reifying. Instead, it is specific characteristics of the market as institution—personalism and transparency in transacting, for example—that give the market its ethically ennobling qualities. Economic conservatives commonly recognize "freedom" as a necessary condition for moral behavior in the market; where choices are coerced, true moral action cannot take place. The argument is similar here: the ability to discern market conditions and engage others in the free exchange of commodities that can be *known with relative certainty* is equally necessary to support capitalism's morally affirming qualities. Yet when moral deficiencies are found to impact market outcomes, the standard answer is to update and expand the regulatory system while minimally addressing the information constraints, competitive incentives, and virtue deficiencies that often make regulation an ineffectual option.

Whatever additional regulatory changes are enacted, the evidence from recent scandals insists that the need to address virtue remains. No regulatory system is capable of corralling an industry with an incentive structure that rewards the expansion of information asymmetry and lack of transparency in trading. While institutional controls and enhanced oversight are important, personal integrity formed with the aid of religious and moral traditions remains the first line of defense in preserving a sense of financial justice for the reason that innovation will always outpace regulation. There are two goods in that realization: first, it establishes an imperative to re-personalize the industry in ways that help ensure financial relationships are truly human ones. Second, it insinuates a "virtue approach" to present problems that is likely to have positive effects beyond the financial realm.

Resolution of the moral problem that has been revealed requires reorientation of both individuals and enterprises from treating ethics as rules that establish impediments to progress to the view that "ethical progress"—the development of both institutional ethics and individual virtue—can have significant economic benefits. While some may doubt that an emphasis on virtue can ever eclipse the profit motive in financial relationships, there can be little doubt that if such an approach were successful, it would have far-reaching effects. In the encyclical *Caritas in Veritate*, Benedict XVI called attention to the need "to launch financial initiatives in which the humanitarian dimension predominates" and for financial professionals to "rediscover the genuinely ethical foundation of their activity, so as not to abuse the sophisticated instruments which can serve to betray the interests of savers." Many contemporary problems are traceable to a competitive ethic that has evolved so as to discount religious, ethical, and other measures of social health in favor of rational gauges of productivity and return. To address present problems with technical corrections while avoiding reflection on foundational issues buys into the narrowly materialist conception of progress that feeds financialization. It also ignores the need for development of a "civil economy"—one founded upon personal exchange and supported by moral institutions that are attuned as much to spiritual and social development as to material progress. A civil economy requires deliberation on what constitutes real production and how finance might be re-conceptualized such that it fosters social relationships and promotes the stewardship of assets to identifiable ends consistent with participant values. This effort will necessarily engage individual virtue, for "*development is impossible without upright men and women, without financiers and politicians whose consciences are finely attuned to the requirements of the common good.*"[37]

Financialization, civil society, and the need for a new regulatory paradigm

It is at least possible that financialization has inspired some good developments along with the bad. While acknowledging the negatives, business ethicist John Boatright contends that "most people in modern society appreciate the benefits financialization has brought and accept the loss of some of the more humane aspects of *Gemeinschaft* with its richer web of relationships, and communal support systems." That loss, according to Boatright, "has been offset ... by the greater material wellbeing and security and the empowerment of individuals that financialization has made possible."[38] He goes on to list insurance, pensions, and other forms of "risk-pooling" as preferential "to the kind of improvidence that relies on community support."[39] A tradeoff of relational forms of communal security for mass forms of pecuniary security is implicit in the financialized society. The programs of risk-pooling Boatright observes, however, appear increasingly less secure given evidence of insolvent pension funds, declining entitlement programs, and persistent unemployment with limited compensation benefits.

Another significant social cost associated with financialization is that it has transformed the "transaction," once used to represent and facilitate social relationships, to an end in itself for purposes of wealth creation. According to Paul Dembinski, "financialization involves large-scale exploitation of relationships for transactional purposes," and "when relationships are established merely for transactional purposes, we are dealing with a clear inversion of ends and means."[40] Financialization has arrived through a confluence of forces—economic, technological and, it is argued here, social and moral—that have broken down traditional restraints and enabled abstract representations of wealth to achieve legitimacy. It has also softened resistance to the kind of mega-firm market structure that arrived with the Industrial Revolution by implicitly advancing the idea that large institutions are a natural part of the financial industry and necessary to manipulate vast quantities of capital, often taking massive risks in the process. And these big firms inevitably are accompanied by potentially intrusive big data. However appropriate these conditions may be for economic development (a question beyond the scope of this book), they expose limitations to the potential for virtue development in the modern financial economy.

The arrival of financialization threatens more than just the comforts of personal relationships forged in a local economy or the peace of mind afforded by one's mortgage being held for the duration by the same institution. By constantly stressing the urgency of economic stability, the financialized society gives inadequate attention to the pluralism that provides ultimate stability in any system of representative government and free markets. In addition, both the vigor and variety of American civil society are being challenged by the growing hegemony of finance itself. This is not a power grab by financial titans or the imposition of the state's will on the people. It is a value transformation that carves away at the nation's most vital resources—its religious institutions, civic organizations, and voluntary associations—and, in the process, erodes civic virtues.

Just as with financialization, countless definitions have been offered for civil society such that there is confusion as to its meaning. For purposes of this book, a definition provided by the World Bank is especially helpful: "the wide array of non-governmental and not-for-profit organizations that have a presence in public life, expressing the interests and values of their members or others, based on ethical, cultural, political, scientific, religious or philanthropic considerations."[41] Importantly, from a functional perspective, civil society is the *sine qua non* for any social order based on liberty, but that is true as much with respect to the economic as the political establishments of free societies. That statement may seem odd to those who see certain economic institutions as providing a critical mediating function between citizens and their government. Often that is the case. However, when large, impersonal markets develop and potentially exploitative forms of competition emerge in critical industries with the sanction of the state, citizens require intermediate institutions to buffer them from establishments in the "political-economic" order, not simply from government alone.

As an example, in 2012 the London Interbank Offered Rate (Libor) scandal rocked the credit world with charges of collusion among major banks for the purpose of fixing benchmark rates that are the basis for determining interest rates on mortgages, credit cards, and other instruments. The Libor rates determine interest charges on trillions of dollars in loans worldwide, and the banks that participate in this process effectively "set" rates by submitting their estimated costs of capital in the interbank loan market—the approximate rates each bank is charged to borrow funds from other banks—for multiple currencies and loan maturities. These estimates are then put through an averaging process to determine Libor rates.[42] In 2012, there were charges of fraud and collusion among member ("panel") banks and Barclays and the Royal Bank of Scotland were among five institutions that agreed to large settlements and experienced the resignations of top officials because of the scandal. A trader for the Dutch Rabobank Group NV also pled guilty to rate manipulation.[43]

The Libor scandal will suggest to some the need for greater government oversight of this critical function, which is difficult because the banks involved span national boundaries, creating jurisdictional complications. Others have suggested the need for a market-based process in establishing the Libor rates where information is derived from actual transactions, but this idea has been called impractical because not all panel banks consistently borrow funds in all currencies and at different maturities, thus requiring "estimation."[44] On the other hand, more socially reputable and inclusive answers to such system "imperfections" may better involve civil society in ways that are less coercive and more consistent with a stable and just system of democratic capitalism. Greater involvement of nonprofit, civic-minded groups in conjunction with professional organizations can provide broader perspectives on industry structure and practices, improving transparency in the regulatory process. Equally important, structures to address financial problems that draw more heavily on civil society would engage citizens in ways such that more people are invested in the system, building social capital. Carolyn Hodges Persell observes that healthy societies require spreading critical social responsibilities among different sectors. She notes that "the three major arenas in modern societies—economy, state, and especially civil society—offer somewhat distinct conceptions of social justice, or normative orders, based on their dominant values."[45] Those values are themselves somewhat interdependent and, at times, values in one domain can come to dominate those of the others. Yet while interdependence exists, there is also a definite hierarchy in the normative structure of robust modern societies because civil society serves as the foundational "value cache" for the political and economic spheres. Politics and economics become mechanical in the atomistic relations of financialized culture; civil society remains the dynamic, socially and morally formative structure for both individual and institutional development. Moreover, it gives pluralistic societies teleological purpose by preserving balance among disparate visions. Persell notes that a society's sense of social justice depends on strong and "competing" expressions coming from the three arenas: "If one or more spheres are weak, social justice may not be debated or even considered, and relative advantage or sheer power will dominate the actions taken."[46] And when norms and values forged in either political or economic systems feed back into and distort institutions of civil society, they have the potential of redirecting the culture to their own ends.

The United States is faced with accomplishing a persistent challenge to "empires" in history: in a context of great political pressure to continually increase the level of economic growth, it must re-discipline and deleverage individuals and institutions by establishing the parameters of real production and reducing forms of credit that have caused cultural damage. Kevin Phillips, writing about this phenomenon in *American Theocracy* (2006), sees patterns in the decline of Western empires—the Hapsburg, Dutch, and British empires specifically—similar to that found in the U.S. today.[47] Phillips offers a quotation from historian Brooks Adams on how economic instincts change as civilizations evolve, a more complete version of which is provided here:

> In proportion as movement accelerates societies consolidate, and as societies consolidate they pass through a profound intellectual change. Energy ceases to find vent through the imagination, and takes the form of capital; hence as civilizations advance, the imaginative temperament tends to disappear, while the economic instinct is fostered, and thus substantially new varieties of men come to possess the world.[48]

The "new varieties of men" who today possess new forms of capital—and thus the world—are altering the rules of competition in their industries and, presumably, influencing the ethics of the wider society. Moreover, this is occurring despite attempts in both industry and government to maintain transparency in business relations and to preserve fairness in exchange such that markets allow creativity to "find vent through the imagination." Imagination still thrives in certain areas, yet too much imagination has been spent on manipulating abstract capital to generate short-term rewards for the few at the expense of generating real capital to support a long-term vision for the many.

Reflection on the damage inflicted by a relatively small number of traders and the lingering perception of an out-of-control financial sector accents the threat described above and appears to signal the unraveling of what might be called "Weber's bargain." In addition to his landmark theories on Protestantism's ethical contribution to the market system and the rationalization of Western culture in *The Protestant Ethic and the Spirit of Capitalism*, German sociologist Max Weber was one of the first to explore the social effects of bureaucracy. While acknowledging its dispiriting effects, Weber predicted the rise of an efficient and enduring order of specialists in which "mechanism—in contrast to the feudal order based on personal loyalty—is easily made to work for anybody who knows how to gain control over it."[49] The cost of this society's rationalization for Weber is "disenchantment" in which "no mysterious incalculable forces … come into play" but rather humankind becomes convinced of its ability to "master all things by calculation."[50] George Armstrong Kelly, discussing Weber's relevance to the American religious consciousness, has written that "until fairly recently, most Americans imagined transcendent, conceivably magical properties in their enterprise" in which the nation's unique Providence "could embrace Weberian calculation and still remain free, open, and enchanted."[51] Financialization is the principal disenchanting force of contemporary civilization, extending its rationalism and bureaucracy while giving the appearance of enhancing security and stabilizing the economy through the distribution of risk. Instead of stability, however, bureaucratic administration and reckless behavior seem to be growing simultaneously. Instability appears to have increased alongside innovation in finance; consumers and investors are subject to bureaucratic, depersonalizing systems even as they pay the price for the ethical shortcomings of creative traders with doubtful commitments whose firms seem unable, or unwilling, to control them. The combination of these forces seems only to heighten the potential for state intervention and tends to promote the formation of a financial technocracy.

It is not only individual ethics that has been tested by financial innovation. Organizations of all kinds have been caught up in the frenzy to play the high-risk, often radically leveraged games of creative finance in efforts to improve their survival chances. Colleges and universities take on high levels of risk with their endowments.[52] Many nonprofit, community service organizations act in ways that defy the name, feeling intense competitive pressures in industries where, theoretically, competition should take a back seat to social vision. Governments have gambled with employee pensions out of fear that they can keep up neither with future obligations nor with the innovative investment methods of peer institutions, which effectively establish a baseline of competition. A financially inspired determinism has been building over decades that, as will be seen in Chapter 3, seems to be re-charting Friedrich Hayek's "road to serfdom."

Assumptions by liberals on how financial reform should proceed typically involve government and the need to fill in the regulatory potholes. Conservatives often counter that freeing the private sector from excessive oversight would better enable the market to adjust, eliminating inefficient producers and punishing those who would cheat. Unfortunately, the processes of financialization impair policy proposals from both sides of the debate. On the one hand, government becomes an even less viable enforcement option because regulators are challenged by the ever-quickening pace of innovation, which often leads either to confused inaction or draconian solutions with collateral damage. On the other hand, the market is limited in its ability to "self-correct" because information asymmetries in finance continue to expand as more intricate products are devised to differentiate firms' investment strategies and practices which are, in the increasing absence of hard capital, their assets.

Financial complexity and its demand for specialists contribute to regulatory confusion.[53] Financialization, in one sense, represents the extent to which specialization has splintered American culture, demonstrating the possibility of an industry becoming so technical and inaccessible as to be able to define value independently of the society in which it exists. The connection Aristotle made between praxis and moral development, in particular, is relevant to contemporary finance's ability to dissociate money-making practices from the moral development of those who practice them. Richard Nielsen believes that "Aristotle can be interpreted as suggesting that the purpose of business activity/praxis is to create wealth in a way that makes the manager a better person and the world a better place."[54] The financialization of society has greatly muddled connections necessary to make financial managers better people just as it seems to have harmed the ability of the financial industry to make the world a better place.

The good news is that there are means for lessening financial influence in civil society and, in turn, involving intermediate organizations more heavily in redirecting the financial system to more humane ends. "Definancializing" this cultural sector to the extent possible to achieve genuinely "disinterested" institutions, which some social thinkers addressed in subsequent chapters believe essential to a moral economy, enables greater opportunities for the ethical development of citizens. It also offers possibilities for sharing some oversight responsibility between government and civic-minded organizations, reinvesting Americans in their financial system, making potential conflicts of interest more transparent, and possibly even enhancing financial literacy. Greater involvement of civic groups in reform of the financial industry could also work in the direction of a true "democratization" of finance by establishing representative institutions between citizens and large financial interests as well as government.

Re-mastering competition by reimagining the financial economy

The magnitude of problems caused by small groups of people with questionable ethics and access to potent financial tools signals that despite the ability of market mechanisms to instill discipline and the development of regulatory systems designed to harness those less-than-virtuous motivations of our "animal spirits," the human inclination to excess always emerges.[55] Financialization is seen as an enabler by extending financial values and a financial way of thinking to most areas of life even as it inspires development of instruments for the manipulation of capital with amazing proficiency. Yet, from a broader perspective, it may be more helpful to think of financialization as a bellwether signaling the kind of cultural imbalance that portends civilizational decline.

In his 1939 essay "Creative Democracy—The Task Before Us," John Dewey famously noted that "at the present time, the frontier is moral not physical." The frontier of today is, indeed, moral, but it also has become increasingly financial. Dewey referred specifically to the American founding period from his vantage on the continuing Great Depression with the comment: "It is a challenge to do for the critical and complex conditions of today what the men of an earlier day did for simpler conditions."[56] The social and technological complexity associated with financialization has ratcheted up that challenge yet again. There is a critical need to revisit Dewey's observation "that democracy is a personal way of individual life; that it signifies the possession and continual use of certain attitudes, forming personal character and *determining desire and purpose in all relations of life*."[57] Financialization has done much harm to democracy; by accenting economic indirection and obscuring personal responsibility such "desire and purpose" are being lost in what is an essential component of modern life.

The transition to a modern economy has involved considerable sacrifice of social and moral purpose to economic efficiency. Few today target moral development as even a subordinate goal of commercial activity. In fact, most contemporary capitalists are not inspired to "target" anything at all, at least not in a collective sense. The triumph of what Hayek called "subjectivism" in economics and the great twentieth-century material expansion that was presumed to flow from it reinforced that value. However, the recent financial crisis and its perceived ethical origins reveal that the moral content of economic relationships today may impact material outcomes to a greater extent than in less sophisticated eras of development. Such a change suggests the need for greater collective reflection on market morality.

Persistent answers to the problems that have emerged are likely to be found at the convergence of political, economic, and civic life. That means engaging a critical disjunction between economy and morality that has emerged over time and only been amplified by financialization. As E. J. Dionne notes, there is a great need for debate "over what constitutes a moral economy" and "*there is a moral obligation to have that argument in the first place*."[58] In this regard, Americans are out of practice. Indeed, the present generation has had little experience in social debates beyond ideologically divisive issues such as affordable healthcare, border security, and military spending, which offer little insight as to how we should actually "live." We no longer think deeply about the morality of the market despite obvious ethical transgressions of recent years.

Such moral reflection on economic issues is out of step with the contemporary discipline of economics as science. Yet for most of its history, economics was a thoroughly interdisciplinary and normative exercise. Classical philosophers, medieval scholastics, and Enlightenment thinkers all integrated discussions of economy with ethical, religious, and philosophical concepts in debating what *should be* the purpose of commercial activity. Recovering economics as a moral science will require returning to philosophical and theological sources for insights into the nature of value, the purpose of exchange, and the role of virtue in the market. Positivist exercises that capture present economic conditions for the purpose of predicting future events may be critical to getting us through the immediate fiscal quarter, but they do little to envision and shape the next decade. Observing that the Dow dropped because of political instability in Pakistan, or the probable default of the Greek government, or pressures on the international credit system provides no information as to what we can actually *do* to escape the present doldrums of financial determinism.

Effective solutions must engage core issues that get at the very purpose of finance and draw from diverse disciplines for the reason that problems are deeper and more extensive than can been addressed by financial experts and government officials. Challenges to the financial sector thus are challenges to American society as a whole. More broad-based involvement in resolving financial problems insists that the extent of finance's reach, which has been portrayed negatively to this point in the sense that the entire society is being "financialized," can turn positive for the reason of its pervasive influence. Finance might actually become a beachhead for reviving virtue. There is also good news in that the reform movement that is required is consistent with the best traditions of American culture. In addition to vigorous debates among the American Founders concerning the moral foundations of the market economy, various social movements and countless ethicists, theologians, and social thinkers in American history have sought to reaffirm and, in some cases, restore the ethical basis of the American economic system. Most of these reformers have recognized that responsibility for capitalism's moral sustenance cannot fall on markets alone. Just as democracy depends on intermediate institutions to provide for the moral development of citizens as the basis for self-government, so too does market exchange require similar institutions—civic, religious, educational—that are distanced to some extent from the fray of political and economic contingency to provide its moral framework.

The changes proposed in Chapter 8 present a rather radical shift in the regulatory paradigm of a critical American industry, but the growing recognition that simply piling on regulations within the present structure will not work insists that radical change is necessary. In this case, however, it is proposed that "radical" means returning to some implicit and evolved first principles of the American Republic. While most American Founders had no illusions that virtue in the classic sense was workable for the modern republic that was developing in the new world, they sought to establish conditions that would instill a naturally formed "liberal virtue" from the spontaneous interactions of citizens in the freest nation the world has ever known. The virtuous character developed in the intermediate organizations that formed naturally in the space between citizens and their government provided the ethical foundation to support the nation's development. Sadly, the financialized American culture of today has lost that vision. This book seeks to provide a means by which it may be revived.

Notes

1 Jamie Dimon, "JPMorgan Chase Testimony before the Financial Crisis Inquiry Commission," (January 13, 2010); available at http://investor.shareholder.com/jpmorgan-chase/releasedetail.cfm?ReleaseID=437415.
2 Paul Krugman, "Dimon's Déjà Vu Debacle," *New York Times* "Opinion Pages" (May 21, 2012): A23.
3 Hedging involves taking investment positions to offset the risks associated with other investments. Proprietary trading in this context is when a financial firm invests its own resources in the attempt to attain profits for the firm rather than investing client money on their behalf. See Agustino Fontevecchia, "Dimon's Volcker Rule Contradiction: On Hedging, Prop Trading and the London Whale," *Forbes* (June 13, 2012); available at www.forbes.com/sites/afontevecchia/2012/06/13/dimons-volcker-rule-contradiction-on-hedging-prop-trading-and-the-london-whale/.
4 Quoted in Michael S. Schmidt, Eric Lipton, and Alexandra Stevenson, "After Big Bet, Hedge Fund Pulls the Levers of Power: Staking $1Billon That Herbalife will Fail, Then Lobbying to Bring it Down," *New York Times* Business Day (March 9, 2014); available at www.nytimes.com/2014/03/10/business/staking-1-billion-that-herbalife-will-fail-then-ackman-lobbying-to-bring-it-down.html?_r=0.
5 Schmidt, Lipton, and Stevenson, "After Big Bet."
6 Schmidt, Lipton, and Stevenson, "After Big Bet." See also "Ackman outspent by Herbalife in lobbying battle," *Reuters* [with a contribution by *CNBC.com*] (March 10, 2014); available at www.cnbc.com/id/101479247#. The United States Hispanic Leadership Institute website can be located at www.ushli.org/.
7 *The Daily Show*, "Donors Unchained," (April 3, 2014); located at http://thedailyshow.cc.com/videos/74yxyf/donors-unchained.
8 Robert D. Putnam, *Bowling Alone: The Collapse and Revival of American Community* (New York: Simon & Schuster, 2000).
9 "Proposed Round Lake Hospital Draws Protestors from City, as Groups Charge Advocate with 'Medical White Flight,'" *PR Newswire*; available at www.prnewswire.com/news-releases/proposed-round-lake-hospital-draws-protestors-from-city-as-groups-charge-advocate-with-medical-white-flight-57846222.html.
10 Chuck Fager, "Ponzi Payback: Treachery of the Highest Order," *Christianity Today*

46(5) (April 22, 2002): 16; and Nicola Menzie, "Eddie Long Settles with Megachurch Members in Lawsuit Linked to Alleged Ponzi Investor Ephren Taylor," *The Christian Post* (February 6, 2014); located at www.christianpost.com/news/eddie-long-settles-with-megachurch-members-in-lawsuit-linked-to-alleged-ponzi-investor-ephren-taylor-114071/.

11 Quoted in Sam Jones and Norma Cohen, "Pensions: Led Into Temptation," *Financial Times* (*FT.com*) [London] (January 12, 2010); available at www.ft.com/intl/cms/s/0/8e775de8-ff1a-11de-a677–00144feab49a.html#axzz1RoaxHEcQ.

12 Sam Jones, "Hedge Funds Win Church of England Blessing in Reform Fight," *Financial Times* (*FT.com*) [London] (October 7, 2009); available at www.ft.com/intl/cms/s/0/7a31f792-b2aa-11de-b7d2–00144feab49a.html#axzz1RoaxHEcQ. Short-selling is the practice of selling "borrowed" securities with the promise to buy them in the future in anticipation that their market price will fall; thus, those who engage in short-selling profit from the drop in a company's stock valuation.

13 Megan Murphy and Norma Cohen, "Church Preaches Against Bonus Excess," *Financial Times* (*FT.com*) [London] (April 15, 2011); available at www.ft.com/intl/cms/s/0/f2281992–679a-11e0–9138–00144feab49a.html#axzz1RoaxHEcQ.

14 Randy Martin, *Financialization of Daily Life* (Philadelphia: Temple University Press, 2002), 3.

15 Some likely would challenge the last point, citing statistics on gross domestic product or American worker productivity. However, growing resignation to long-term unemployment coupled with the increasing inability of many who are employed to understand what they contribute, distinguishes the present work ethic from the one that contributed to the nation's economic exceptionalism.

16 For example, see Benedict XVI, *Caritas in Veritate* ("*Charity in Truth*") (2009), #21, #40, #65.

17 Thomas I. Palley, "Financialization: What It Is and Why It Matters," Levy Economics Institute, Working Paper no. 525 (December 2007): 2; available at www.levy.org. R. Hilferding, *Finance Capital: A Study in the Latest Phase of Capitalist Development* (London, Routledge and Kegan Paul, [1910] 1981); cited in Greta R. Krippner, "The Financialization of the American Economy," *Socio-Economic Review* (2005) 3: 181.

18 Greta Krippner, "What is Financialization?" mimeo, Department of Sociology, UCLA (2004). Gerald Epstein, "Introduction: Financialization and the World Economy" in *Financialization and the World Economy*, ed. Gerald Epstein (Northhampton, MA: Edward Elgar, 2005), 3.

19 Edward J. O'Boyle, Stefano Solari, and GianDemetrio Marangoni, "Financialization: Critical Assessment Based on Catholic Social Teaching," *International Journal of Social Economics* 37: no. 1 (2010): 4–5.

20 Organization for Economic Co-operation and Development [OECD], "OECD's Financial Education Project," *Financial Market Trends*, no. 87 (2004), p. 224; cited in Ismail Erturk *et al.*, "The Democratization of Finance? Promises, Outcomes and Conditions," *Review of International Political Economy* 14, no. 4 (October 2007): 563.

21 Erturk, *et al.*, "The Democratization of Finance?," 563. MORI is a market research firm in the United Kingdom. The authors offer the following citation for this information: MORI (2004) Research conducted for the Institute of Financial Services (IFS), supplied to the researchers by the IFS. Summary available at: www.ifslearning.com/news/archive/newsreleases 04/mori.htm.

22 Steven L. Schwarcz, "Protecting Financial Markets: Lessons from the Subprime Mortgage Meltdown," *Minnesota Law Review* 93 (2008): 405.

23 Martin, *Financialization of Daily Life*, 43.

24 Ben Protess, "Merrill Lynch Settles S.E.C. Fraud Case," *New York Times* DealB%k (January 25, 2011); available at http://dealbook.nytimes.com/2011/01/25/merrill-settles-s-e-c-fraud-case/?_php=true&_type=blogs&_r=0.

25 Chung-Hua Shen and Hsiang-Lin Chih, "Conflicts of Interest in the Stock Recommendations of Investment Banks and Their Determinants," *Journal of Financial and Quantitative Analysis*, vol. 44, no. 5 (October 2009): 1162–70.

26 Robert Khuzami, Director of the SEC's Division of Enforcement, stated: "This settlement is a stark lesson to Wall Street firms that no product is too complex, and no investor too sophisticated, to avoid a heavy price if a firm violates the fundamental principles of honest treatment and fair dealing." See U. S. Securities and Exchange Commission, "Goldman Sachs to Pay Record $550 Million to Settle SEC Charges Related to Subprime Mortgage CDO"; available at www.sec.gov/news/press/2010/2010–123.htm.

27 Emil Røyrvik, *The Allure of Capitalism: An Ethnography of Management and the Global Economy in Crisis* (New York: Berghahn Books, 2011), 8.

28 Franco Modigliani, "Reagan's Economic Policies: A Critique," *Oxford Economic Papers*, New Series, 40, no. 3 (September 1988): 397–426.

29 Donald Tomaskovic-Devey and Ken-Hou Lin, "Income Dynamics, Economic Rents, and the Financialization of the U.S. Economy," *American Sociological Review* 76, no. 4 (August 2011): 542–8.

30 Growth of specialization in production during the Fordist period might also be seen as a model for specialization in the service industries, including finance, that would follow. In this way, financialization was not only a response to the social stresses arising during Fordism, it also seems to have adopted a kind of mass production mentality in the manipulation of capital.

31 George Will, "Parasites Kill Host City: Detroit Ruined by Unions, Made Worse by Government Bailouts," *Washington Post*; reprinted in the *Waco Tribune Herald* (August 2, 2013); available at www.wacotrib.com/a/parasites-kill-host-city/article_a11d8366–0c94–5f69-b71d-06eeff09c96c.html.

32 Will, "Parasites Kill Host City."

33 Fareed Zakaria, "Why US Cities Are Going Bankrupt," *CNNWorld* (July 20, 2012); available at http://globalpublicsquare.blogs.cnn.com/2012/07/20/why-u-s-cities-are-going-bankrupt/.

34 Quoted in Suzanna Kim, "Facebook's IPO Launches; Should You Buy Stock?" *ABCNews* (May 18, 2012); available at http://abcnews.go.com/Business/facebook-ipo-facebook-fans-chance-company/story?id=16372015.

35 Richard L. Haney, Jr., "An Analysis of Yield Spreads Between Ginnie Mae Pass-Throughs and Aaa Corporate Bonds," *Financial Management* 7, no. 1 (Spring 1978): 17–18.

36 Frank Hyneman Knight, "The Ethics of Competition," in *The Ethics of Competition* (New Brunswick, NJ: Transaction Publishers, 1997), 48.

37 Benedict XVI, *Caritas in Veritate* (2009), #65, #66 (emphasis Benedict's).

38 John Boatright, "Review of Paul H. Dembinski, *Finance: Servant or Deceiver? Financialization at the Crossroads* (Basingstoke: Palgrave Macmillan, 2009)," *Business Ethics Quarterly* 19, no. 3 (July 2009): 463.

39 Boatright, "Review of Paul H. Dembinski, *Finance: Servant or Deceiver?*"

40 Paul H. Dembinski, "Financial Ethics Trapped by Financialization," *Ethikundgesellschaft* 2(2009): 3, 5; available at www.ethik-und-gesellschaft.de/mm/EuG-2–2009_Dembinski.pdf.

41 Quoted in World Economic Forum, *The Future Role of Civil Society*, World Scenario Series (January 2013); available at www3.weforum.org/docs/WEF_FutureRoleCivilSociety_Report_2013.pdf.

42 The Libor system is set up such that between seven and 18 banks are asked to submit estimates of their interest-rate costs for borrowing funds, and a selection and averaging process is used in establishing the benchmark rates. Evidence was obtained through e-mail correspondences and other sources that banks were entering into agreements to misrepresent the information used to set these rates. See Peter Madigan, "Secrets and Libor," *Operational Risk and Regulation* 13:9 (September 2012): 22–5.

43 Michael Calia, "Former Rabobank Trader Pleads Guilty to Libor Manipulation: Takayuki Yagami Admits to One Count of Conspiracy to Commit Wire Fraud and Bank Fraud," *Wall Street Journal Online* (June 11, 2014); available at http://online.wsj.com/articles/former-rabobank-trader-pleads-guilty-to-libor-manipulation-1402497314?tesla=y.
44 Information on the Libor system is available at www.global-rates.com/interest-rates/libor/libor-information.aspx.global-rates.com/interest-rates/libor/libor-information.aspx; accessed on July 14, 2014.
45 Carolyn Hodges Persell, "The Interdependence of Social Justice and Civil Society," *Sociological Forum* 12:2 (1997): 150.
46 Persell, "The Interdependence of Social Justice and Civil Society," 151.
47 Kevin Phillips, *American Theocracy: The Peril and Politics of Radical Religion, Oil, and Borrowed Money in the 21st Century* (New York: Viking, 2006), 218–32.
48 Brooks Adams, from Chapter 10 of *The Law of Civilization and Decay: An Essay on History* (New York: The Macmillan Company, 1896), 297. An abbreviated quotation is provided in Phillips, *American Theocracy*, 301.
49 Max Weber, *From Max Weber: Essays in Sociology*, trans. and ed. by H. H. Gerth and C. Wright Mills (New York: Oxford University Press, 1946), 229.
50 Max Weber, "Science as a Vocation," in *From Max Weber: Essays in Sociology*, trans. and ed. Gerth and Wright Mills, 139.
51 George Armstrong Kelly, "Faith, Freedom, and Disenchantment: Politics and the American Religious Consciousness," *Daedalus*, vol. 111, no. 1 (Winter 1982): 137.
52 Katherine Ryder, "The University Endowment Model: Cracked not Broken," *CNNMoney* (July 12, 2010); available at http://money.cnn.com/2010/07/06/news/economy/university_endowments.fortune/index.htm.
53 The results of allowing competition in this critical industry to spin out of control are dire, as has been witnessed, but the expansion of legislation such as the Dodd–Frank Act presents a similarly nightmarish scenario. As of July 2013, 155 new rules had been completed comprising almost 14,000 pages with another 243 rules yet to be developed. This effort required over 1,000 meetings between regulators and representatives of the big banks. The enormity of the task suggests that the unintended consequences to this exercise in financial regulation may be equally enormous and will require the additional development of rules as those effects are revealed, which will, of course, have their own unintended consequences.
54 Richard P. Nielsen, "High-Leverage Finance Capitalism, the Economic Crisis, Structurally Related Ethics Issues, and Potential Reforms," *Business Ethics Quarterly* 20:2 (April 2010): 299 [2008 Society for Business Ethics Presidential Address].
55 John Maynard Keynes called the animal spirits the "spontaneous urge to action rather than inaction." Robert Shiller and Bruce Akerlof revive Keynes' famous phrase in the context of modern financial problems, stating that the proper role of government should be to enable creativity, but it should also "countervail the excesses that occur because of our animal spirits." See Robert Shiller and Bruce Akerlof, *Animal Spirits: How Human Psychology Drives the Economy and Why it Matters for Global Capitalism* (Princeton, NJ: Princeton University Press, 2009), 9.
56 John Dewey, "Creative Democracy—The Task Before Us" in *John Dewey: The Later Works, 1925–1953, vol. 14: 1939–1941*, ed. Jo Ann Boydston, textual ed. Anne Sharp (Carbondale and Edwardsville, Ill: Southern Illinois University Press, 1988), 225; available at www.faculty.fairfield.edu/faculty/hodgson/Courses/progress/Dewey.pdf; accessed on October 22, 2014.
57 Dewey, "Creative Democracy," 226 (emphasis added).
58 E. J. Dionne, *Souled Out: Reclaiming Faith & Politics After the Religious Right* (Princeton, NJ: Princeton University Press, 2008), 89 (emphasis Dionne's).

Bibliography

Adams, Brooks. "Chapter 10. Spain and India." In *The Law of Civilization and Decay: An Essay on History*, 286–325. New York: The Macmillan Company, 1896.

Benedict XVI. *Caritas in Veritate*, (2009). www.vatican.va/holy_father/benedict_xvi/encyclicals/documents/hf_ben-xvi_enc_20090629_caritas-in-veritate_en.html; accessed on September 10, 2014.

Boatright, John. "Review of Paul H. Dembinski, *Finance: Servant or Deceiver? Financialization at the Crossroads*." *Business Ethics Quarterly* 19, no. 3 (July 2009): 453–64.

Calia, Michael. "Former Rabobank Trader Pleads Guilty to Libor Manipulation: Takayuki Yagami Admits to One Count of Conspiracy to Commit Wire Fraud and Bank Fraud." *Wall Street Journal Online*, June 11, 2014. http://online.wsj.com/articles/former-rabobank-trader-pleads-guilty-to-libor-manipulation-1402497314?tesla=y; accessed on June 11, 2014.

Dembinski, Paul H. "Financial Ethics Trapped by Financialization." *Ethikundgesellschaft* 2, (2009): 1–23. www.ethik-und-gesellschaft.de/mm/EuG-2–2009_Dembinski.pdf; accessed on May 4, 2013.

Dewey, John. "Creative Democracy—The Task Before Us." In *John Dewey: The Later Works, 1925-1953, vol. 14: 1939-1941*, edited by Jo Ann Boydston, textual editor Anne Sharp Carbondale and Edwardsville, Ill: Southern Illinois University Press, 1988.

Dimon, Jamie. "JPMorgan Chase Testimony before the Financial Crisis Inquiry Commission." *JPMorgan Chase & Co.*, January 13, 2010. http://investor.shareholder.com/jpmorganchase/releasedetail.cfm?ReleaseID=437415; accessed on July 22, 2013.

Dionne, E. J. *Souled Out: Reclaiming Faith & Politics After the Religious Right*. Princeton, NJ: Princeton University Press, 2008.

"Donors Unchained." *The Daily Show*. Comedy Central, April 3, 2014. http://thedailyshow.cc.com/videos/74yxyf/donors-unchained; accessed on April 28, 2014.

Epstein, Gerald. "Introduction: Financialization and the World Economy." In *Financialization and the World Economy*, edited by Gerald Epstein, 3–16. Northampton, MA: Edward Elgar, 2005.

Erturk, Ismail, Julie Froud, Sukhdev Johal, Adam Leaver, and Karel Williams. "The Democratization of Finance? Promises, Outcomes and Conditions." *Review of International Political Economy* 14, no. 4 (October 2007): 553–75.

Fager, Chuck. "Ponzi Payback: Treachery of the Highest Order." *Christianity Today* 46, no. 5 (April 22, 2002): 16.

Fontevecchia, Agustino. "Dimon's Volcker Rule Contradiction: On Hedging, Prop Trading and the London Whale." *Forbes*, June 13, 2012. www.forbes.com/sites/afontevecchia/2012/06/13/dimons-volcker-rule-contradiction-on-hedging-prop-trading-and-the-london-whale/; accessed on July 9, 2014.

Haney, Richard L., Jr. "An Analysis of Yield Spreads between Ginnie Mae Pass-Throughs and Aaa Corporate Bonds." *Financial Management* 7, no. 1 (Spring 1978): 17–28.

Hilferding, R. *Finance Capital: A Study in the Latest Phase of Capitalist Development*. London: Routledge and Kegan Paul, [1910] 1981.

Jones, Sam. "Hedge Funds Win Church of England Blessing in Reform Fight." *Financial Times* (*FT.com*). October 7, 2009. www.ft.com/intl/cms/s/0/7a31f792-b2 aa-11de-b7d2-00144feab49a.html#axzz1RoaxHEcQ; accessed on May 21, 2011.

Jones, Sam, and Norma Cohen. "Pensions: Led Into Temptation." *Financial Times* (*FT.com*). January 12, 2010. www.ft.com/intl/cms/s/0/8e775de8-ff1a-11de-a677-00144feab49a.html#axzz1RoaxHEcQ; accessed on May 23, 2011.

Kelly, George Armstrong. "Faith, Freedom, and Disenchantment: Politics and the American Religious Consciousness." *Daedalus* 111, no. 1 (Winter 1982): 127–48.

Kim, Suzanna. "Facebook's IPO Launches; Should You Buy Stock?" *ABCNews*, May 18, 2012. http://abcnews.go.com/Business/facebook-ipo-facebook-fans-chance-company/story?id=16372015; accessed on June 20, 2012.

Knight, Frank Hyneman. "The Ethics of Competition." In *The Ethics of Competition*. New Brunswick, NJ: Transaction Publishers, 1997.

Krippner, Greta R. "The Financialization of the American Economy." *Socio-Economic Review* 3, no. 2 (2005): 173–208.

Krippner, Greta R. "What Is Financialization?" mimeo, Department of Sociology, UCLA, 2004.

Krugman, Paul. "Dimon's Déjà Vu Debacle." *New York Times*, May 21, 2012, sec. A23.

Madigan, Peter. "Secrets and Libor." *Operational Risk and Regulation* 13, no. 9 (September 2012): 22–5.

Martin, Randy. *Financialization of Daily Life*. Philadelphia: Temple University Press, 2002.

Menzie, Nicola. "Eddie Long Settles with Megachurch Members in Lawsuit Linked to Alleged Ponzi Investor Ephren Taylor." *Christian Post*, February 6, 2014. www.christianpost.com/news/eddie-long-settles-with-megachurch-members-in-lawsuit-linked-to-alleged-ponzi-investor-ephren-taylor-114071/; accessed June 7, 2014.

Modigliani, Franco. "Reagan's Economic Policies: A Critique." *Oxford Economic Papers*, New Series, 40, no. 3 (September 1988): 397–426.

Murphy, Megan, and Norma Cohen. "Church Preaches against Bonus Excess." *Financial Times* (*FT.com*). April 15, 2011. www.ft.com/intl/cms/s/0/f2281992-679a-11e0-9138-00144feab49a.html#axzz1RoaxHEcQ; accessed on May 21, 2011.

Nielsen, Richard P. "High-Leverage Finance Capitalism, the Economic Crisis, Structurally Related Ethics Issues, and Potential Reforms." *Business Ethics Quarterly* 20, no. 2 (April 2010): 299–330.

O'Boyle, Edward J., Stefano Solari, and GianDemetrio Marangoni. "Financialization: Critical Assessment Based on Catholic Social Teaching." *International Journal of Social Economics* 37, no. 1 (2010): 4–16.

Organization for Economic Co-operation and Development [OECD]. "OECD's Financial Education Project." *Financial Market Trends* 87 (October 2004): 223–8.

Palley, Thomas I. "Financialization: What It Is and Why It Matters." Working Paper no. 525, Levy Economics Institute, 2007. www.levy.org; accessed on March 22, 2011.

Persell, Carolyn Hodges. "The Interdependence of Social Justice and Civil Society." *Sociological Forum* 12, no. 2 (1997): 149–72.

Phillips, Kevin. *American Theocracy: The Peril and Politics of Radical Religion, Oil, and Borrowed Money in the 21st Century*. New York: Viking, 2006.

PR Newswire. "Proposed Round Lake Hospital Draws Protestors from City, as Groups Charge Advocate with 'Medical White Flight.'" (n.d.); www.prnewswire.com/news-releases/proposed-round-lake-hospital-draws-protestors-from-city-as-groups-charge-advocate-with-medical-white-flight-57846222.html; accessed on May 30, 2014.

Protess, Ben. "Merrill Lynch Settles S.E.C. Fraud Case." *New York Times* DealB%k, January 25, 2011. http://dealbook.nytimes.com/2011/01/25/merrill-settles-s-e-c-fraud-case/?_php=true&_type=blogs&_r=0; accessed on March 17, 2014.

Putnam, Robert D. *Bowling Alone: The Collapse and Revival of American Community*. New York: Simon & Schuster, 2000.

Reuters. "Ackman Outspent by Herbalife in Lobbying Battle." Reuters, *CNBC.com*, March 10, 2014. www.cnbc.com/id/101479247#; accessed on July 9, 2014.

Røyrvik, Emil. *The Allure of Capitalism: An Ethnography of Management and the Global Economy in Crisis*. New York: Berghahn Books, 2011.

Ryder, Katherine. "The University Endowment Model: Cracked Not Broken." *CNN Money*, July 12, 2010. http://money.cnn.com/2010/07/06/news/economy/university_endowments.fortune/index.htm; accessed on September 11, 2013.

Schmidt, Michael S., Eric Lipton, and Alexandra Stevenson. "After Big Bet, Hedge Fund Pulls the Levers of Power: Staking $1 Billon That Herbalife Will Fail, Then Lobbying to Bring It Down." *New York Times* Business Day, March 9, 2014. www.nytimes.com/2014/03/10/business/staking-1-billion-that-herbalife-will-fail-then-ackman-lobbying-to-bring-it-down.html?_r=0; accessed on March 12, 2014.

Schwarcz, Steven L. "Protecting Financial Markets: Lessons from the Subprime Mortgage Meltdown." *Minnesota Law Review* 93, no. 2 (December 2008): 373–406.

Shen, Chung-Hua, and Hsiang-Lin Chih. "Conflicts of Interest in the Stock Recommendations of Investment Banks and Their Determinants." *Journal of Financial and Quantitative Analysis* 44, no. 5 (1149–1171): October, 2009.

Shiller, Robert, and Bruce Akerlof. *Animal Spirits: How Human Psychology Drives the Economy and Why it Matters for Global Capitalism*. Princeton, NJ: Princeton University Press, 2009.

Tomaskovic-Devey, Donald, and Ken-Hou Lin. "Income Dynamics, Economic Rents, and the Financialization of the U.S. Economy." *American Sociological Review* 76, no. 4 (August 2011): 538–59.

U. S. Securities and Exchange Commission. "Goldman Sachs to Pay Record $550 Million to Settle SEC Charges Related to Subprime Mortgage CDO." *Sec.gov*, July 15, 2010. www.sec.gov/news/press/2010/2010-123.htm; accessed on August 14, 2013.

Weber, Max. *From Max Weber: Essays in Sociology*. Edited and translated by H. H. Gerth and C. Wright Mills. New York: Oxford University Press, 1946.

Weber, Max. "Science as a Vocation." *From Max Weber: Essays in Sociology*, edited and translated by H. H. Gerth and C. Wright Mills, 129–46. New York: Oxford University Press, 1946.

Will, George. "Parasites Kill Host City: Detroit Ruined by Unions, Made Worse by Government Bailouts." *Waco Tribune Herald*, August 2, 2013. www.wacotrib.com/a/parasites-kill-host-city/article_a11d8366-0c94-5f69-b71d-06eeff09c96c.html; accessed on June 2, 2014.

World Economic Forum. "The Future Role of Civil Society." World Scenario Series presented at the World Economic Forum, January 2013. www3.weforum.org/docs/WEF_FutureRoleCivilSociety_Report_2013.pdf; accessed on December 18, 2014.

Zakaria, Fareed. "Why US Cities Are Going Bankrupt." *CNNWorld*, July 20, 2012. http://globalpublicsquare.blogs.cnn.com/2012/07/20/why-u-s-cities-are-going-bankrupt/; accessed on September 6, 2013.

2 The technocratic tendencies of contemporary finance

> Seven blunders of the world that lead to violence: wealth without work, pleasure without conscience, knowledge without character, commerce without morality, science without humanity, worship without sacrifice, politics without principle.
>
> Mahatma Gandhi (1869–1948)

The remarkable explosion of information and communication technologies (ICT) over the past half-century has facilitated the development of equally complex financial instruments traded in highly specialized markets. Although some analysts suggest these technologies contributed to the economic instability recently witnessed, others insist that their benefits overcome any destabilizing or dislocating effects. The general rise in living standards enabled by the greater ease in global capital transfers is thought to exceed any negative consequences that accompany financial innovations. What is typically lost in such discussions, however, is the impact of financial technologies on social values and relationships. Greater efficiency in capital flow must be weighed against the nature and composition of growth it supports as well as the value changes and alterations in relationships—owner-asset, creditor-debtor, investor-community, and others—to fully understand its cultural, not only material, effects.

Understanding the history behind recent changes in banking and finance helps frame the social and ethical challenges that accompany them. As an industry, finance has developed over decades to exhibit the characteristics of "technocracy," conventionally defined as a meritocratic system of rule by technical specialists.[1] However, early use of the term did not pertain specifically to finance but rather to the myriad changes that accompanied the Industrial Revolution. On a systemic level, dramatic increases in energy consumption propelled the rapid expansion of new technologies and proliferation of new products at low prices, leading to more efficient production and higher living standards for many. At the same time, demand for skilled labor was markedly reduced. The mass "deskilling" of the labor force then worked in conjunction with the price system to bring about the "technological unemployment" of many, ensuring the persistence of poverty in a society of plenty. This phenomenon as well as other social maladies drew the ire of the "technocrats," such as Howard Scott, Dal Hitchcock, and

Langdon Post, directors of the Continental Committee on Technocracy, who were also among those that insisted a society led by technical specialists could reduce, if not eliminate, unmeritorious wealth distributions that concentrated around coupon pullers and other aristocrats.[2]

William Smyth, who is said to have coined the term "technocracy" in 1919, insisted that it is not the capitalist business manager but rather the scientist and engineer who are capable of harnessing the power of modern invention and directing the organization to its greatest productive potential. To avoid the "mysterious" economics and finance of old, it would be necessary to "initiate Skill economics, economics of our Twentieth Century mechanistically characterized activities—economics of the Scientist, of the Technologist, of the Mechanic, on a nationwide scale."[3] But while Smyth was ebullient over possibilities for enlisting engineers and scientists to the cause of a merit-based, more egalitarian progress, he was also dour concerning managerial finance's implications for wealth creation and distribution. According to Smyth, the economic system of the early 1920s, as well as the financial system that supported it, were leftovers "from an Age of Predatory Autocracy" built upon the businessman's boundless materialism that sought "power, irresponsible and absolute" as its sole object.[4] For the financier, power was attained by achieving the indebtedness of the masses even as he could attain a "respectful awe" afforded in previous ages only to "witch doctors," "soothsayers," and "ecclesiastics."[5] In Smyth's view, this realm of financial wizardry—often mysterious even to the wizards—held the public spellbound such that "financing the enterprise" had become so important that "without its potent magic it would be unsafe, if not impossible, to build a schoolhouse or wage a war."[6]

Much of what Smyth associated with the old financial wizardry that resulted in abstract representations of value and unapproachable jargon understood by a very few is exacerbated by the cryptically scientific finance of today. Reading Smyth's book *Technocracy* in light of recent developments, it seems we have arrived at the worst of all financial worlds. Engineers of finance, in particular the so-called "quants"—mathematical savants from statistics, physics, computer science, and other fields who join Wall Street banks and investment firms to develop complex financial models—have not eliminated wizardry but rather compounded it, making finance more impenetrable than ever. In Smyth's time, financier and engineer represented distinct classes vying for control of the firm. In the new finance, however, those roles have become more functionally interdependent even as they have grown more technically estranged.

In combination with academics and policy analysts who have advocated a "finance-based theory of the corporation,"[7] the new architects of finance forge a deterministic force that no entity seems capable of controlling. In the face of rapid technological change, the state is dependent on these financial engineers for the proper functioning of the economic system, even as it is dependent on its own specialists for regulatory and other functions. This dependency establishes the authority of technocrats whose identities, functions, and powers are unknown to the vast majority of those whose fates they influence. The question is how to balance this dynamic new power structure so as to preserve the description of the American social order as one of "democratic capitalism."

Financial technocracy and the end of Weber's bargain

In his book, *The Quants*, *Wall Street Journal* reporter Scott Patterson offers an insightful look into the changing global financial culture caused by an invasion of quantitative specialists. Often coming from academic disciplines such as mathematics, physics, and computer science, these technicians inspired a revolution in both the philosophy and the mechanics of wealth creation. Despite Warren Buffett's famous caution to "beware of geeks bearing formulas," they were recruited by banks and investment firms from the nation's best universities and research institutions for their ability to craft complex financial models, which ultimately formed the basis of a multi-trillion dollar industry. Through derivatives and other instruments, quantitative specialists have helped transform the financial industry from a largely human network of analysts and traders with all its inherent inefficiencies, mistakes, and communication problems to one based on intricate algorithms and computer networks where machines, not human beings, increasingly run the show.[8]

The idea that people could develop "profitable" mathematical systems with little to no training in economics or finance spread like wildfire. Eventually, this move toward nontraditional investment professionals inspired the brain drain from engineering, computer science, and other fields that has been described as a significant component of financialization. Paul Kedrosky and Dane Stangler, for example, have studied the "entrepreneurial consequences" of this transition and its negative impacts on the quantity and quality of firm formation in the United States. Their research indicates that "the Securities and Commodities Exchanges sub-sector accounted for the twelfth-highest share of science and engineering employment by sub-sector, ahead of semiconductor manufacturing, pharmaceuticals, and telecommunications" by 2006.[9] The obvious implication is that the "real economy" has suffered from the ability of the financial sector to attract the best and the brightest from industry and academia. Moreover, this transformation has fundamentally altered financial professions: the development of structured finance, with its unique personnel requirements, has

> spawned a new breed of highly paid smart graduates well versed in mathematics and calculus but alas, quite divorced from the real world of old-fashioned finance with its putative sixth sense of sniffing out risk through a deep appreciation of human psychology, market sentiment and moral hazards.[10]

The difficulty of accounting for this "sixth sense" in computer models has not hindered their importance to the financial system or the rising influence of those who develop and maintain them.

One problem in deconstructing this technical edifice is that scholars and policy analysts often treat technocracy as a purely political phenomenon. In their analyses, technocrats and government bureaucrats become nearly synonymous. However, modern governance contains far greater subtlety than such rigidly demarcated categories imply. An article published in *The Economist* in 2011, "Technocrats: Minds Like Machines," noted that "full-scale technocratic governments" generally exist only for short periods in "unusual circumstances." However, other institutions that "rule big chunks of public life" and often enjoy constitutional protections are increasingly filled with technical specialists capable of implicitly determining rules of governance.[11] This is especially true in periods like the recent crisis, wherein central banks, along with government-sponsored entities (GSEs) such as Fannie Mae and Freddie Mac, created opportunities for more insidious, persistent forms of technocracy to develop in powerful institutions. *Wall Street Journal* columnist David Wessel observed how the Federal Reserve became "almost a fourth branch of government during the crisis, deciding which financial firms would live and which would die and lending hundreds of billions of dollars and putting taxpayers at risk without having to get congressional approval."[12] Other powerful though less publicly prominent groups have also attained considerable wealth and influence with the rise of finance: Gerald Davis, for example, notes how American academic "consultants" employed to advise Russia in the privatization of its economy became major investors in those institutions they help to privatize, despite contractual restrictions on such investment.[13]

The novelty of this emerging technocratic order calls for redefinition of the concept. Past descriptions of technocracy too often have emphasized "government" specialists chosen for their technical expertise in ways that limit understanding of how, propelled from within a market economy, technology impacts society.[14] A simpler, more straightforward definition of technocracy as "a system of governance in which power accrues to those with technical knowledge" helps more by showing that technocracy need not be either centralized or even intentional. Some who achieve power in a technocratic order may not desire it; their unique skills, even circumstance itself, may vault them into positions of authority. Others, perhaps, are more opportunistic. Technical knowledge of the global financial system can yield tremendous wealth and political influence without need for appointment or election; for example, Alasdair Roberts has shown how "technocrat-guardians" have emerged as a political force during periods in which weaknesses in the popular sovereignty governance of American liberal democracy gave way to the need for greater discipline.

What Roberts calls the "logic of discipline" includes a tactical argument "that the best way to promote the virtues of farsightedness, consistency, and public-spiritedness was to impose constraints on democratic processes, either by foreclosing certain choices entirely (as balanced budget rules do) or by transferring authority over certain choices to specialists who are protected from political interference."[15] A major institution in this transition was the central bank that, in the 1990s, developed research capabilities similar to those of economics departments in tier-one academic institutions. Central bank economists and financial analysts increasingly were graded on a similar scale to academics based on their pursuit of independent research agendas. According to Roberts, this led to the "'scientization' of central banking" and the greater autonomy of the banks; yet it also led to "doctrinal blindness" by disconnecting them from a critical public purpose.[16] Central banks became preoccupied with inflation control and relatively indifferent to "systemic stability," which is arguably more central to their missions, despite growing evidence of the housing market bubble.[17] But not only have central banks emphasized their own agendas at the expense of the public. Through concentrations of power, the financial industry—along with the rising influence of Wall Street technicians and their opaque relationships to government regulators—has denigrated the notion of popular sovereignty and today challenges the ideals of those who advocate the "democratization of finance."

The persistence of nonelected positions in the political economy of industries involving significant public-private cooperation is the lifeblood of technocracy. In the case of finance, government institutions forge relationships with private banks and investment firms in an industry critical to national security, creating an environment in which the state takes on a significant role, at times, in determining which firms survive and which perish. Along with the heightened emphasis on productive efficiency, these conditions predispose regimes toward empowering those with the technical skills to eliminate barriers to capital flow.[18] This structure creates a perfect incubator for technocratic development and helps explain the increasing inclination of the American financial system in that direction. Miguel Angel Centeno suggests that there "may be a certain natural affinity between technocracy and market capitalism" because of "the emphasis both phenomena place on productive efficiency."[19] Emphasis on productive efficiency may also predispose regimes toward empowering those with the technical skills to eliminate barriers to capital flow. These highly proficient technicians may even be able to evade the typical administrative systems and bureaucratic structures that encumber less technically skillful workers in large institutions, especially those where technical knowledge is asymmetric. They may come to be revered for their ability to *work around the system* to achieve results impossible for those who work within it. Sometimes those "results" turn negative. For example, a trader named John Rusnak of Allfirst Financial in Baltimore was granted permission to trade during his vacation period, a practice that goes against company policy because individual trader downtimes are often when colleagues discover improprieties. By the time Rusnak's trading losses were revealed, they totaled some $691 million over a five-year period.[20]

Recent changes in the financial culture may reveal the dissolution of what might be called "Weber's bargain"—classical sociologist Max Weber's theory that, though dispiriting, bureaucratic structures have at least the benefit of taming those "charismatic spirits" that cause instability. Weber saw bureaucracies as enabling the development of specialized administrative functions by objective standards such that the more complexity grows in modern culture, "the more its external supporting apparatus demands the personally detached and strictly objective *expert*."[21] Weber considered charismatic forms of organization unstable; thus, the "good" to bureaucratic development is that it theoretically works to eliminate actions based on "personal, irrational, and emotional elements which escape calculation."[22] As Liz McFall has observed, however, even Weber recognized that "the existence of ideal types does not preclude the blurring of elements in practice."[23] In a kind of "hybrid or institutionalized form,"[24] charisma has persisted alongside the systemization and thorough rationalization of finance.

Sebastian Mallaby's *More Money than God: Hedge Funds and the Making of a New Elite* (2010) traces the development of major charismatic figures in the hedge fund industry over the past 50 years, from "Big Daddy" Alfred Winslow Jones to "The Alchemist" George Soros and "Top Cat" Julian Robertson.[25] These new elites revolutionized finance by breaking the mold of the staid financial executive, wearing esoteric investment and risk strategies as badges of honor and publicly advancing myriad causes that often thrust them into the limelight. Yet alongside these charismatics, financiers continued to believe that mathematical sophistication was bringing ever greater economic stability. The spreading of risk through derivatives and other products was based on the myriad calculations of anonymous mathematicians who believed they were systematically removing the volatility associated with market capitalism. Adaptation to a financial system unconcerned by purpose and dismissive of the social impacts of method was smoothed over by those who insisted that security is accomplished through calculation.

At least within the financial sector, however, recent developments have challenged the surety of calculation. Both the instability and moral ambiguity of the technocratic turn within the financial industry have been evident in the mortgage-backed security (MBS) market. A key premise of many analytical treatments of the latest economic crisis was the claim that the process of securitization actually reduced "systemic risk." In practice, however, the complexity of these instruments grew exponentially in ways that made risk increasingly difficult to assess. Theoretically, the benefit to mortgage securitization—the pooling of individual mortgages into a common security for trading on secondary markets—is that securities enable risk to spread across a larger number of investors and, in the process, enhance the liquidity of a traditionally illiquid asset (the mortgage contract). Securitization also allows those investors to choose among more or less risky bonds associated with mortgage securities. However, few anticipated the speed with which these products would evolve, or that they would generate the kind of frenzy that occurred. Perhaps more importantly, the motivations of key players and the relationships among regulatory authorities, ratings agencies, and private firms became as intricate and difficult to fathom as the instruments themselves. Technology was a significant enabler of this complexity and the risk attendant to it that grew beyond the cognizance of industry analysts.

Securitization and other techniques designed to enhance liquidity pose a number of ethical questions associated with financialized capitalism and technological advance more generally. Buchholz and Rosenthal observe that technology can be subject to "misuse" because of ignorance of its "inherently social and moral dimensions." Moreover, this ignorance corresponds "to the abstraction of technology from the concrete situations in which it operates and from its role in enhancing the fullness and richness of human life."[26] In general, technological developments can have ambiguous cultural consequences (i.e., they may increase or reduce wealth distribution), and they commonly complicate ethical decision making. An example of this in the financial industry involves the push toward computer server "colocation," in which banks and investment firms strategically position their computing facilities in the closest possible proximity to stock and commodity exchange servers to secure nanosecond advantages over competitors. The privatization of exchanges themselves has made this practice especially controversial. In 2005 the New York Stock Exchange reorganized as a publicly traded, for-profit company, which led to the rise of a robust exchange "industry" and brought with it a host of competitors. The N.Y.S.E.'s market share in the stock exchange industry has dropped from around 70 percent of trading among listed stocks in 2006 to around 36 percent in 2011.[27] Privatization of exchanges makes the buying and selling of preferred access to those competitive exchanges not only acceptable but also "necessary"; revenue from the sale of access becomes a means by which exchanges compete. Although the impact of server colocation and other means of enhancing high-speed trading on firm profitability can be significant, to the tune of "millions, if not billions, a year," their implications for market fairness and impact on the allocation of real capital are more nebulous.[28] "Private" exchanges expand the potential for corruption through the bartering of access to them and the possibility that major players will corner the "exchange market" by buying up access rights and infrastructure to exclude rivals. In addition, scholars have shown how high-volume, high-speed trading can play havoc with market valuation; the ability of supercomputers to place and cancel thousands of orders per second in responding to price movements with the potential of yielding big profits also has questionable implications for real assets and the values assigned to them.[29]

Highly controversial in this regard has been the practice of "spoofing," which commonly "involves an effort to fool market participants into believing that large orders for futures contracts exist, to draw them into making trades."[30] Often, traders place orders with the intent of cancelling the orders before trades are executed to fool other traders into action by which the "spoofing" party may profit. High-speed, computer-based trading facilitates such practices through nearly instantaneous processing of enormous volumes of transactions. Such trading can influence market valuation. In this regard, Joe Saluzzi of Themis Trading, LLC, offered a negative assessment of high-speed trading: "Valuation is irrelevant. It's all about just moving price up and down the ladder all day long. Each day is new. Each day starts fresh. So, you have to question the true valuation of the markets now."[31]

Server colocation, high-speed trading, and other practices thus pose significant questions. In these and other areas particular to computerized finance, however, both regulatory policy and cultural change to deal with their consequences lag behind. Meanwhile, scholars note the dramatic impacts of these financial technologies. Nicolas Maystre and David Bicchetti note that derivatives trading came to eclipse physical production by some 20 to 30 times, and that "financial investors" as a percentage of market participation grew from less than 25 percent to more than 85 percent between the 1990s and 2008.[32] The authors also provide data showing increases in trade volume for commodities, approaching 100 times for select commodities between 1996 and 2011, and suggest that automated, high-speed trading has caused price deviations not justified by changes in supply and demand.[33] In short, stock and commodity volatility appear to have increased from the influence of machine-based trading.

Beyond the volatility brought about by automation was a consequence associated with the arrival of the "new finance" announced by Robert Haugen in 1995: the discrediting of the efficient market thesis. This thesis maintains that financial markets exhibit uniformity in the ubiquity and cost of data necessary for responsible investment decisions and that necessary information for market decision making is contained in asset prices.[34] In fact, broad information asymmetries obtain in financial markets that inevitably lead to market "tiering," in which some groups are relegated to lesser (potentially less profitable and riskier) positions vis-à-vis competitors with greater access to information. Collectors of "primary information," such as banks and other large financial firms, will forever be faced with the responsibility to avoid using such information willfully and self-interestedly against others. According to Paul Dembinski, Director of the Observatoire de la Finance in Geneva, Switzerland:

> This "primary" information is used by a whole range of specialized players—ratings agencies, advisers, experts, and so on—to produce secondary information that is explicitly aimed at less professional clients. Organized markets thus only deal in securities that meet the relevant information standards. All other financial assets and contracts are traded "over the counter," between professionals, or aimed at "qualified investors" rather than the general public, who by definition are less knowledgeable and more gullible.[35]

Such market structures are the norm for hedge funds, private equity funds, foreign currency exchanges, and other markets largely off-limits to the average investor. These also tend to be markets that lie beyond public purview, with the potential that systemic risk can develop under the radar, as witnessed in the recent crisis. In one sense, privileged access to these markets helps to protect smaller investors with inadequate resources to play in these high-stakes games. In another equally important sense, however, it limits potential for legitimate market participation and violates the notions of fairness necessary to any system that might be labeled "democratic capitalism." Similarly, while most of the focus on high-tech trading has been on machines and automated processes, analysis has failed to address adequately the ways in which new infrastructure and techniques can dynamically empower uniquely skilled entrepreneurs and workers. These shifts in financial governance are taking place with the public knowing little to nothing about what these workers do or whether functions enhance or detract from market fairness.

Technocratic aspects of contemporary finance further discredit the information efficiency thesis by showing that investors cannot assume the "net good" of ICT in providing more universal, instantaneous access to the information necessary for investment decisions. In some cases, coordination of technological developments among financial firms and exchanges can make information "relatively" more costly to obtain for some market participants, not less. The development of "dark pools," for example, enables large investors to make trades around the major exchanges, thus concealing their transactions, and potentially valuable information, from the wider market.[36] Even as new technologies are implemented that enhance user access to financial information, other technologies are being developed to expand the complexity of products offered, enhance the market power of certain industry players, and obfuscate business relationships. Moreover, in high-speed systems of immense complexity, the calculus that determines asset valuations is commonly inaccessible to the public, and even professional groups like credit rating agencies often have insufficient information or expertise with which to make sound decisions. Scholars have theorized how such information asymmetry and the impressions of unfairness and confusion it inspires can lead to a herd mentality in investment or, in some cases, can cause investors to turn cautious and retreat to the sidelines.[37]

The technocracy-enabling combination of finance and technology may potentially obscure both the inner workings of business relationships and the motivations of individual actors. The combination also threatens to accelerate change beyond the coping mechanisms of regulators and to greatly increase the cost of market-related "assumptions" as those regulators lag behind. Consider, for example, the disastrous assumption that derivative trading, in aggregate, reduces system risk. Together, finance and technology present a number of unique challenges. While both are essential to progress and the stability of the global economic system, they will, in and of themselves, stimulate periods of instability. Likewise, given their specialized language and unique conceptual constructs, only professionals and technicians can interact with them substantively; laymen find their functions largely impenetrable. Both finance and technology are dependent on stores of proprietary knowledge to trigger industry advance. Once firm secrets become known, their value for the innovating company falls precipitously.[38] Although technology's union with finance can greatly privilege possessors of certain knowledge, market forces can just as quickly dissolve those privileges. In this regard, both finance and technology tend to "dictate the market" and are oriented in the direction of exhausting possibilities in their respective realms.[39]

The trajectory of contemporary finance entails that what Adam Greenfield calls "ubiquitous computing" will remain a significant part of financial reality.[40] It remains to be seen whether this phenomenon can "tolerate" traditional industry ethics and support balanced social development alongside financial growth. Financial literacy undoubtedly will become more important to the full participation of citizens in the United States and other developed nations. In this regard and somewhat alarmingly, scholars exploring the language of the British Financial

Services Authority document *Building Financial Capability in the UK* (2004) noted the frequent association of the terms "financially literate" and "citizens," with the implication that the financially *illiterate* may be "excluded from market democracy."[41] The general flourishing of a population depends on both the availability and the intelligibility of financial technologies to persons presently locked out of the system either because of financial illiteracy or insufficient resources. For this to happen, whatever negative consequences for ownership that attend the rise of technocratic finance must be offset. Wharton Business School behavioral finance scholars Olivia Mitchell and Steven Utkus have argued that the financial choices for employees and retirees with 401(k) and individual retirement account (IRA) plans might be simplified to better synchronize the options available with investor capabilities.[42] Even more vividly illustrating the point, a class-action suit brought by employees and retirees against Lockheed Martin for irresponsibly managing one of its 401(k) funds hints that, in some cases, even plan administrators in large corporations may be deficient in navigating the financial marketplace.[43] Given the growth in financial system complexity as a whole, the need for greater simplicity might be extended to encompass investors generally. Simplification of the financial system, however, will be difficult to accomplish in an environment in which complexity itself has become a significant enabler of competitive advantage.

Wall Street Rule via the "Wall Street Rule"

While not a technocracy in a strict political sense, the complex of government agencies and private firms that cannot be allowed to fail demonstrates aspects of technocratic control that extend beyond the industry itself. Actors within this system can influence policy simply by developing sophisticated instruments that make up a significant portion of financial assets. Those policies seemingly necessitate the input of experts from the private sector, as witnessed by the over 2,000 meetings between representatives of major financial institutions and government agencies concerning the Dodd–Frank legislation, as reported by pro-industry reform groups.[44] More fundamentally, the institutional structure of the industry has led managers to reorient operations around the increasing importance of shareholder value, creating what University of Michigan business professor Gerald Davis calls "a Copernican revolution in thinking about the corporation." In this new mindset, the economy no longer revolves around large companies but rather "around financial markets and the signals they generated."[45] This combination of factors has promoted financial specialists to significant positions of influence; these same individuals commonly help determine the rules and standards for the rating and regulation of financial products. Government officials have been forced to respond to the mercurial rise of derivatives as a percentage of total assets in the United States which, despite the destabilizing volatility associated with these contracts in the recent crisis, have continued to grow. For example, the notional amount of derivatives held by federally insured U.S. commercial banks in the second quarter of 2011 was \$249 trillion, 11.6 percent higher than at the same time in 2010 and up 2.2 percent in that quarter alone.[46] Continued growth in products that were at the center of financial breakdown demonstrates the extent to which financial technologies dictate the market and call into question whether adequate governance mechanisms exist to regulate them.

The continued proliferation of certain financial products does not mean that the market understands them adequately to ensure stability. According to Jerry Z. Muller, recent economic setbacks constitute the first "epistemologically-driven depression" in the sense that they appear to have resulted from the "failure of the private and corporate actors to *understand what they were doing*."[47] However, several other scholars, including Arnold Kling, Lucian Bebchuk, and Holger Spamann, have debated extensively over the extent to which recent upheavals indeed result from cognitive failure, and the extent to which moral failure may have played a role. Supporters of the cognitive failure theory believe that financial instability stems from the difficulty of acquiring the knowledge necessary to make appropriate financial decisions in such a complex environment. Those who cite moral failure often note the growing moral hazards of economic relationships in which one party is responsible for furthering the interests of another but has an equal or greater incentive to put its own interests first.[48]

From the perspective of the cognitive/moral failure debate, perhaps the most chilling aspect of crisis revelations was the widespread approval by government officials of "innovative" techniques largely responsible for creating the crisis in the first place, as Kling describes:

> Regulators were aware of the ways that banks were using securitization, agency ratings, off-balance-sheet financing, and credit default swaps to expand mortgage lending while minimizing the capital necessary to back such risks. Like the bankers themselves, the regulators believed that these innovations were making financial intermediation safer and more efficient.[49]

Generational differences within the regulatory structure may play a part here. Brad Katsuyama, the former Royal Bank of Canada trader who helped to expose alleged "market rigging" by high-speed traders that was the focus of Michael Lewis's *Flash Boys*, has described an interesting encounter with the Securities and Exchange Commission (SEC). Katsuyama met with SEC officials to forewarn them of his plan to go to the *Wall Street Journal* with evidence that high-speed traders were buying the ICT and access capacity to "step in front" of other investors and make virtually assured profits at others' expense. The response to his revelation by "younger" SEC staffers shocked Katsuyama. His plan was to help level the playing field, which eventually included developing the exchange IEX that attempts to equalize the speed of transacting among all investors. Young staffers called his idea "unfair" to high-frequency traders (HFT).[50] Katsuyama's presentation to the SEC exposed divisions within its ranks between the young guns who saw HFT as innovative and liquidity-enhancing and older regulators who viewed these high-speed middlemen as skimming profits off the top while offering no value of their own. According to Lewis, the issue largely was decided in favor of high-frequency trading; not coincidentally, Lewis's book references a study conducted by the RBC that has not been released publicly showing that, since 2007, over 200 SEC workers had left the organization for employment either with "high-speed trading firms or the firms that lobbied Washington on their behalf."[51] After the publication of Lewis's book, several industry analysts criticized it publicly, with at least one describing the book's account of HFT as "sensationalized" and "salacious."[52] However, few if any critics have challenged Lewis's description of the basic industry and market structure.

A moral to the Katsuyama story is that the cognitive-moral failure debate will become only more difficult to resolve as technology advances. Kling describes the "moral failure" narrative as soothing to those seeking "clear villains" in the crisis and a straightforward means to its resolution through policy attempts to "reorganize and reinvigorate the regulatory apparatus."[53] Supporters of this narrative see an opportunity to clean up the system, and they look principally to government to save the day. In this paradigm, regulators must stay one step ahead of those talented, highly motivated participants in the financial system, whose ingenuity appears boundless. Hence the problem: the logic of the market dictates that regulators will forever lag behind innovators. Moreover, innovators will develop the instruments and practices through which wealth will be allocated; but, they will be incapable of foreseeing the ways in which continual innovation will strain individual ethics and firm governance. This approach foreordains a perpetual tit-for-tat game between regulators and enterprising professionals with questionable social and moral commitments who will press innovation to its limits to maximize profits, with little regard for systemic risk or the social and moral consequences.

Another problem in sorting through the moral failure-cognitive failure debate lies in the fact that the two arguments are far from mutually exclusive. It could be argued that cognitive limitations resulting from the complexity of the financial system have provided cover against claims of moral failure. Jamie Dimon's testimony before the Senate Banking Committee on June 12, 2012, showed how the intricacies of the financial system help shield executives forced to defend their companies' questionable practices. At one point, the questioning turned to whether or not JPM's investments were intended as a hedge against portfolio risk (a legitimate function for banks) or as investment for profit (which is not allowed according to certain provisions of the proposed Volcker Rule). Dimon offered a response that seemed to implicate system complexity as a defense against implicit accusations of moral failure: "I don't know what the Volcker Rule is. It hasn't been written yet. It's very complicated. It may very well have stopped parts of what this portfolio morphed into."[54] Use of such passive language to describe the intricately designed portfolio of a large bank implies that even it is awash with the tide of financial convolution. Executives likely will continue to retreat into that complexity when called to account for their firms' failures. And, at some level, those explanations will likely ring true to politicians, regulators, and even the public, who must fight their own battles with an intensely financialized economic system that seems to be growing beyond control. Dimon's testimony raises several questions. Was JPM's strategy simply the responsible hedging of portfolio risk, or was it reckless proprietary trading of the kind many believe to have been a cause of the recent crisis?[55] Was it yet another example of financial practices that take advantage of regulatory blind spots, despite obvious connections between such practices and recent crises?

Other activity at JPM went beyond ill-advised trades that resulted in losses. The company was fined $13 billion in 2013 in connection with charges that it made false statements and omitted material facts concerning the sale of $33 billion worth of mortgage bonds to Fannie Mae and Freddie Mac between 2005 and 2007.[56] Industry analysts noted some of the activity that resulted in the fine occurred in Bear Stearns and Washington Mutual before their acquisition by JPM, and thus was largely beyond the purview of JPM's management.[57] Rising confusion concerning the risks to investment, and the potentially unethical or even illegal actions by traders buried deep within the system, would seem to make bank mergers virtual crap shoots from several perspectives.

Certainly, government's promotion of the merger in question, to "save the financial system," offered moral justification for the deal even if it inspired greater industry concentration that some see as problematic. The ethics of proceeding into unchartered financial waters, with the backing of insured deposits or the comfort of a "too big to fail" label, while claiming ignorance when problems arise, shows that the cognitive issue is not easily separated from the moral one. Furthermore, to suggest that the magnitude of the recent crisis has stemmed this tide is to ignore realities in the political economy of the financial sector. In December 2014, the *New York Times* reported that both Democrat and Republican lawmakers were attempting to force a provision into the "catch-all" federal spending bill for 2015 that would do away with the so-called "push out" provision in the Dodd–Frank financial reform law. That provision of the legislation requires major banks to shift derivative trading to subsidiaries whose assets are not backed by the Federal Deposit Insurance Corporation (FDIC).[58] Passage of the new bill would gut provisions of Dodd–Frank designed to eliminate practices that left taxpayers on the hook for speculative trades by large banks.

Lee Sheppard, a contributing editor with *Tax Analyst* Publications, attributes much seemingly endemic corporate indiscretion to what has come to be known as the "Wall Street Rule." According to Sheppard, the "Rule" is a practice in which private equity and other firms with similar fee structures "take aggressive positions, and they figure that if enough of them take an aggressive position, and there's billions at stake, then the IRS is kind of stopped from arguing with them because so much would blow up" if the IRS acted to curb their practices.[59] Acting chief counsel for the IRS, Emily Parker, offers a two-part definition for this unspoken rule:

> the IRS can't attack the tax treatment of a transaction if there is a long-standing and generally accepted understanding of this expected tax treatment,

> and the IRS is deemed to have acquiesced in the tax treatment of a transaction if the dollar amount involved is of a "significant magnitude."[60]

In other words, the Wall Street Rule holds that if enough players in a high-profile industry like private equity are willing to challenge a complex area of regulation in practice, they have relative assurance that government agencies will not step in for fear of larger possible repercussions from regulatory action.

Revelations of ongoing corporate improprieties suggest a financial market in need of greater discipline. The question is what will be the source of that discipline? While industry professionals have often recognized their privileged positions and taken steps in the direction of self-regulation, self-discipline can be highly self-interested. Few seem convinced that additional state regulation will accomplish much, given the process by which Dodd–Frank was constructed and the pending legislation that seeks to dilute it further. That massive trading losses can be attributed to small groups of traders reveals inadequacies in firm governance and the financial system's vulnerability to individual ethics. Yet one may be less concerned with how individual traders involved their companies in risky deals than with how those companies' policies and procedures gave them such leeway in the first place. The answer, again, appears connected to the phenomenon of financialization: the organizational culture of banks and investment firms moved with the times, adapting to bolder attitudes toward risk and continually ramping up expectations of return. Outliers like the "London Whale" were willing to take risks that perhaps others were not; however, a consensus seems to be forming that many parts of these organizations were complicit in ethical transgressions previously attributed to a few. William C. Dudley, president of the New York Federal Reserve Bank, noted in an address at a workshop on "cultural reform" in financial services that despite the loss of public trust and more than $100 billion in fines accruing to the nation's largest banks since 2008, "the pattern of bad behavior did not end with the financial crisis."[61] Dudley points to organizational culture, those "implicit norms that guide behavior in the absence of regulations or compliance rules," and asks "whether the sheer size, complexity and global scope of large financial firms today have left them 'too big to manage.' "[62] Interestingly, he sounds much like Pope Benedict XVI in the encyclical *Caritas in Veritate*, reminding financial firms that their responsibilities to the public extend beyond their obligations to shareholders, clients, and employees.[63]

Wall Street Journal columnist David Weidner believes that the technological revolution in finance may be reinforcing this rogue mentality. He points to a series of botched trades, "flash crashes," and patterns of corrupt behavior that have been aided by automated systems, and he notes findings by investigators that trading specialists "regularly step in front of customers to trade their own accounts."[64] Weidner believes the system has fueled inequalities among traders that inevitably work to the advantage of large firms and their specialists. The lack of trust in the stock market and the volatility inspired by electronic trading suggest that increased technological sophistication may actually have hurt the prospects for more widespread market participation:

> The reality is that electronic trading has turned out to be simply another bill of goods sold by Wall Street to investors. It's not dependable. It's not trustworthy. It's easily manipulated. It hasn't delivered what the industry and the Securities and Exchange Commission assured us it would.[65]

This failure has obvious consequences for long-term economic growth and financial stability. It also has ethical implications, as market participants are constantly presented with new, ethically uncharted situations and constantly pressured to keep up in a frenetic environment propelled by technological innovation. The incentive still exists for banks and other firms to find ways to leverage their investments against society as a whole. In this regard, financialization clearly evinces that narrowness has become the enemy of good. It has created an environment in which rent-seeking is rampant—most participants today seek greater surety to their own gains with little regard for whether the creation of new wealth benefits society. So long as the economy grows and monetary returns continue to build, few will question the system's ability to allocate capital productively even in the face of corporate irresponsibility and fraudulent behavior. Moreover, market concentration in the financial industry, built on multinational banks and investment firms, gives the impression of no other choice.

The somber truth, however, is that *rent-seekers cannot flourish* in the Aristotelian sense of the term. Mastery of financial technique has become a principal means of rent-seeking that, despite the best intentions of any modern-day technocrats in the spirit of Smyth, actually thrives in a system of governance where power accrues to the knowledgeable. Technical experts from for-profit companies often craft the very rules that regulate their firms, thereby spreading de facto governance to players across the public-private sector divide in ways that often evade public knowledge. Ben Domenech uses examples from the electronics and online retail industries to suggest that big government and big corporations often work "in tandem to create a system where corporate rent-seekers can profit from the paternalistic technocratic state."[66] The financial industry is particularly susceptible to such paternalism; as such, the remedies to financial technocracy must involve more than the present combination of regulators and for-profit firms; as will be seen in subsequent chapters, they should also include less self-interested institutions of civil society to the fullest extent possible. At the moment, however, all answers seem focused on once again reviving an old, tired regulatory regime.

Riding the regulation/deregulation wave

With the passage of the Glass–Steagall Act in 1933, Congress made a philosophical statement about the banking function in the American economy. Traditional demand deposits of commercial banking customers were to be kept separate from those funds available to investment bankers, who might be tempted to use them for speculative purposes. Economic justice demanded that a privileged few should not enjoy access to the capital of the many to facilitate their own money-making. In this regard, Congress expressed the wisdom that risk must accrue to those who stand to profit from business dealings and not spread to those who have nothing to gain.

Glass–Steagall thus attempted to dissociate the banking system's obligations to its depositors, with the newfound backing of the FDIC, from any security trading practices of the banks themselves, which were considered significant among the causes of the Great Depression.[67] As the distance from Black Tuesday grew and memories of the Depression era faded, however, appreciation of the need to distinguish between commercial and investment banking eroded, a trend Zingales observes:

> Unlike many other banking regulations, Glass–Steagall had an economic rationale: to prevent commercial banks from exploiting their depositors by dumping on them the bonds of firms that were unable to repay the money they had borrowed from banks. The Glass–Steagall Act's most significant consequence, though, was fragmentation of the banking industry. This fragmentation created divergent interests in different parts of the financial sector, reducing its political power. Over the past three decades, these arrangements were overturned, starting with the progressive deregulation of the banking sector.[68]

Commercial banks began taking advantage of more lax regulation over their investments even before Glass–Steagall's repeal. In 1996, Congress acted to allow banks to generate as much as 25 percent of their income from securities transactions.[69] Over time, people of various political persuasions came to view Glass–Steagall as an antiquated set of restrictions that inhibited growth. Despite the association of Senator Phil Gramm (R-Texas) and other prominent Republicans with the Act's repeal, it was President Bill Clinton, in response to the merger of Citibank and the investment firm Smith-Barney in 1998, who famously noted that the post-Depression legislation was "no longer relevant."

Banks have taken full advantage of more lax rules regarding their investments in derivatives, which continued despite the restrictions applied by Dodd–Frank. A *Forbes* article in 2013 revealed that, despite the role played by derivatives in the recent crisis, American commercial banks and savings associations held derivatives amounting to some $223 trillion in notional value as of the end-of-year 2012, an amount equivalent to more than 14 years' worth of GNP.[70] The latest Congressional effort to overturn the Dodd–Frank restrictions that limit derivative and other security trading among FDIC-backed banking institutions shows the determination of banks to trade with the underwriting of American taxpayers and the considerable political muscle that backs those efforts.

These political initiatives are occurring though many have called for greater restrictions on banking practices and even for the reinstitution of legislation similar to Glass–Steagall, which these now-contentious provisions of Dodd–Frank attempted to accomplish. Sandy Weill, a former head of Citigroup and a major force behind the legislation's repeal in the 1990s, created a firestorm in July 2012 when he suggested that it may be time again to reinstate the division between commercial and investment banks and break up the banking industry to avoid putting taxpayer money at risk, a position that a *Salon.com* columnist described as akin to "Karl Marx embracing the invisible hand."[71] Ironically, others who are often critical of the financial system have countered that such legislation would be ineffectual given the nature of problems that led to the crisis. Michael Lewis observes, for example, that the 1930s legislation would not have prevented the failure of either Bear Stearns or Lehman Brothers, since they were investment banks, and AIG, as an insurance company, was also part of an industry not impacted by Glass–Steagall.[72]

Investment banks have experienced their own forms of deregulation, however, with significant consequences. In 1970, well before the repeal of Glass–Steagall, the New York Stock Exchange did away with a rule that prevented investment banks from selling their stock to the public. This repeal changed the culture of investment banking from one in which partners within firms supplied capital (offering a significant incentive for partners to oversee each other's investment decisions) to one in which public ownership lessened the risk burden of managing partners. According to John L. Campbell, "incorporation and public listing lifted the burden of responsibility from the partners' shoulders and enabled them to take advantage of soaring stock prices. In other words, they could now begin to play with other people's money."[73] And play they did. Development of the "value-at-risk" model (VaR) by quants at J. P. Morgan around 1990 enabled firms of all kinds to take on much greater risks without building their capital bases, trading with a false sense of security as the VaR model became institutionalized in the financial industry. VaR served as a "crutch" that enabled a leveraged investment frenzy.[74] The bankruptcy of Lehman Brothers in 2008 resulted from derivative exposure enabled by the company's reliance on what is actually a suite of statistical models called VaR and its shortcomings in accurately gauging the potential for risk volatility during "quiet markets."[75]

Given the regulation roller-coaster of the financial sector, conservative arguments unsurprisingly tend toward minimizing regulatory dependence. Government oversight and intervention are often unpredictable, as demonstrated by the impact of government-sponsored entities (GSEs), such as the Federal National Mortgage Association and the Federal Home Loan Mortgage Corporation, established for the purpose of implementing national housing policy. Their creation and the pioneering of mortgage securitization—the bundling of many mortgages with difficult-to-assess risk combinations into marketable securities—provided such a shot in the arm to the American housing market that it almost killed the patient. Subprime abounded, and capital flowed freely. Mortgages that historically were managed locally through banks and (formerly) savings and loans were channeled through the secondary market for mortgage securities beyond banks and GSEs to investors in the global market. These changes also encouraged the extension of credit to poorly qualified applicants. John L. Campbell notes: "Fannie and Freddie's move to buy up subprime mortgages institutionalized the congressional will to help people buy homes."[76] Yet it did so in what many would contend was a market-distorting manner. In combination with the Federal Reserve's persistent commitment to low interest rates, structural alterations to the mortgage market started the United States down a path toward pervasive home ownership even as they interjected certain "market imperfections," the consequences of which are still felt today.

These developments resembled past attempts to achieve greater levels of growth with less risk. Economist Victor Zarnowitz notes the rise of consumer and investor confidence based on the belief "that a seismic shift had taken place and great new opportunities were opening up at remarkably low costs and risks"—what Zarnowitz calls the "happy prophecy of a growing recession-free economy." Seeing the first decade of the twenty-first century as similar to both the 1920s and 1950s with respect to its cultural impacts, Zarnowitz offers a few reasons why the most recent "Golden Age" was considered to be more stable and lasting than those preceding: improvements in management techniques, advancements in computer and information technology (CIT), and enhanced inventory management fostered the idea of an enduring prosperity. And, ironically, a concurrent shift from what was considered the more "volatile goods-producing sectors like manufacturing and construction" in favor of service industries, including finance, where deregulation was thought to contribute to economic "stabilization," furthered this perception as well.[77]

Rather than stability, modern finance has too often inspired volatility that seems to result as much from changes in the investment culture as the regulatory framework. On November 13, 2008, hedge fund manager George Soros admitted to Congress that regulators must restrain the excessive, therefore problematic, use of leverage by hedge funds in previous years. According to Soros, however, neither the complexity of financial products nor the ethics of market participants were to blame for the ensuing crisis. Instead, the fault lay with regulators for doing their jobs inadequately. Government is obligated, he claimed, to fill in the regulatory holes that investment professionals looking to get a leg up on their rivals inevitably exploit, suggesting that the nature of financial competition is to press regulatory limits in pursuit of profit. Another fund manager, James Simons of Renaissance Technologies, blamed regulators and rating agencies while avoiding the issue of his own group's possible complicity in the financial mess.[78] The testimonies of these fund managers suggested that dealings forbidden neither by law nor by regulatory policy are not only allowed but called for. This "catch us if you can" mentality seems to have become a financial industry norm.

On the other hand, it is not just particular interest groups but rather the entire culture that has been moving toward greater risk tolerance and overleveraged positions. The collective strength of the enduring prosperity myth influenced an entire generation of financiers, regulators, and countless others toward greater risk, acceptance of high levels of debt, the expansion of banking beyond conventional demand-deposit/lending practices, and the de-emphasis of financial "fundamentals" that had long served as the basis for sound economic growth.

John L. Campbell describes two senses in which government intervention has not allowed financial markets to function properly. First, the abandon with which government agencies, intent on "saving the system," rescued floundering firms has enabled many organizations that should have failed to survive—an antimarket outcome. Second, "a variety of regulatory moves by the state affected how [those firms] were organized and how they performed in the first place," creating incentives toward excessive risk taking.[79] At the same time, it seems that industry concentration overwhelms most any form of government regulation. As long as a few firms control massive amounts of capital and the human resources required to keep innovation ahead of regulation, simply tweaking the regulatory system will have little effect. So the cycle continues: innovative products inspire growth but also foment instability, over which the public demands greater oversight; yet when government takes regulation too far, it risks damaging an industry critical to economic growth.

This delicate balance must be managed even as various players in the industry seek to exploit the inevitable blind spots that form within any regulatory regime. As Dembinski concludes, "government intervention 'socializes losses' and also has the pernicious medium-term effect of encouraging moral hazard type behaviors on behalf of operators who are tempted to take ill-considered risks."[80] Leading to the recent crisis, state housing and monetary policy provided the impetus to a cascade of financial innovation that resulted in present instabilities. However, similar instabilities likely dissuade even many conservative observers from believing that the answer is government's total withdrawal from financial markets. All human institutions are subject to the progressive layering of rules, norms, and practices that inevitably advantage some and disadvantage others. Although government action comes with hazards, inaction in the face of injustice has moral implications all its own. Over the past several decades, the waxing and waning of financial regulation undoubtedly has empowered technical specialists in both public and private spheres, who assess the impact of both regulation and deregulation on their organizations and the wider economy; that fact also portends the continuing accrual of power to those whose technical abilities grant them critical pockets of control within the global economy.

The inadequacy of financial ethics

Technocratic finance has been fueled by the rise of financialization and its shift of wealth and income from traditional segments of real economic production to the financial sector and a corresponding rise in the importance of financial firms, instruments, and values. The challenge posed by this emerging regime is what Peter Emberley, employing terms drawn from Heidegger, Grant, and Ellul, has described as the "self-augmentation of the technological ensemble" where "the diversity and depth of human experience, possibility, and meaning have been relentlessly absorbed within what each has respectively identified as 'technological monism,' 'total functionality,' and 'optimal efficiency.'"[81] The incessant drive toward optimization in the distribution of capital and risk has significant value implications that conform to Albert Borgmann's "device paradigm" theory. Borgmann has shown how the proliferation of technical devices tends to obscure "real" elements of existence and render those immersed in this paradigm unaware of their device dependence.[82]

Tatum extends Borgmann's device paradigm concept to the values-action relationship: "As technology is increasingly embraced as a means of disburdening us from social and bodily engagement with things around us, the devices used also increasingly constrain the means that are available to us for expressing values through action."[83] The value-expression function of investment may have been an initial casualty of our disburdenment as evidenced, ironically, by the emergence of "values-based investing" (VBI) as a distinct genre. VBI developed to enable investors to express ethical values or social goals through investment in ways that extend beyond simple investment for monetary gain. Research has shown that issuance of investment assets in the values-based sector grew 30 to 40 percent between 2013 and 2014, and 83 percent of financial professionals interviewed say they are "interested in investing based on societal or environmental impact."[84] The emergence of this distinct category of investment, however, suggests that "standard" investing has become inherently valueless, or at least become so preoccupied with return that investor values are greatly subordinated. The turn to VBI perhaps reveals a growing and healthy recognition that technology has distanced investors from those real objects of investment, thus limiting value expression in the allocation of capital.

This idea of "asset devaluation" in a moral sense appears somewhat inherent in the nature of computer-based finance. Technical methods of investment insert layers of technique between owner and asset. One of the results of detachment that Horrigan recognizes as having arrived with the "new finance" is that

> investors are not interested in individual firms, and they are not encouraged to engage in any analysis, other than selecting a homemade risk level for a portfolio. They are encouraged, however, to promote volatility of returns at the expense of creditors.[85]

Volatility—in firm valuation, commodity prices, credit ratings, and countless other financial measures—has been associated with financialization and seems to be compounded by the expansion of technology; volatility also arises from the increasing importance of specialists who promote the abstraction or even eradication of the nonnumerical, noncomputable elements of trading.

In his description of technology as the "will-to-knowledge," George Grant suggests that a technologically inspired social trans-valuation has already begun to threaten what Peter Emberley describes as the "eclipse of moral discourse."[86] Without adequate ethical dialogue surrounding the implementation of technology, objects and processes of innovation will supply values of their own making:

> The frequent characterization of technology as itself a neutral instrument at our disposal is inadequate, for technology is part and parcel of the way we

> exist in the world and is inseparably intertwined with the way we know and value the world. Any technology embodies some set of values, and as a technology succeeds within a society, that technology's values will in turn be reinforced. Every technology promotes some values, inhibits others, and bears with its ongoing use its own distinct style.[87]

Horrigan reinforces this point, observing that "positive ideas inevitably become normative ideas when they are promulgated in decision oriented subjects, such as financial management."[88] Technocratic finance embodies its own distinct style and set of values that, absent ethical guidance, will establish the default by which future financial relationships are defined and future financial practices determined.

Unmanageable complexity and the failure to develop ethics adequate to meet the challenges of contemporary finance ensure that market participants will falter. The value of *reputation*, however, on which Adam Smith clearly rested much of his economic theory, no longer represents an adequate deterrent to financial recklessness. Smith outlined his conviction in *Theory of Moral Sentiments* that socialized human nature endowed a person "with an original desire to please, and an original aversion to offend his brethren." Therefore, success "almost always depends upon the favor and good opinions of their neighbors and equals."[89] In short, individuals seek the approbation of others and avoid their scorn. This applies especially to people in the business world:

> A dealer is afraid of losing his character, and is scrupulous in observing every engagement. When a person makes perhaps 20 contracts a day, he cannot gain so much by endeavouring to impose on his neighbors, as the very appearance of a cheat would make him lose. Where people seldom deal with one another, we find that they are somewhat disposed to cheat, because they can gain more by a smart trick than they can lose by the injury which it does their character.[90]

For a banker or investment adviser, this rule implies achieving returns for clients in a reputable fashion with known risk/return relationships and irreproachable transparency. Instead, today's financiers commonly measure reputation in dollars, and success too often has come to mean cheating without getting caught. Technical complexity undoubtedly has influenced the indifference for personal reputation by often enabling an "out" for those accused of ethical wrongdoing. It also appears to have accented an already growing assumption that business and ethics are fundamentally distinct from one another. Kirsten Martin and R. Edward Freeman observe how the "separation thesis"—a dominant assumption in ethics research that business decisions lack moral content and moral decisions lack business content—has been taken to a second level, positing a similar conceptual divide between technology and ethics:

> The implicit assumption with most business ethics authors is that technology and ethics are distinct entities that must be brought back together.

> Technology is simple, separate, and *abstract* from our social system and must be integrated back into the fold—technology is assumed to be a distinct object waiting to either control or be controlled by society. Just as business is treated as distinct and abstract from the values of our community, so, too, is technology.[91]

The authors show that this second level of abstraction, one of technology from ethics, emerges from a contest of dueling determinisms, the social and the technological. The "technological determinism" camp views technology as harmful in that it forces its own values on consumers and investors in an environment in which "opting out" of the system is simply impossible; the "social determinism" camp views technology as value neutral, merely expressing the values of the individuals and institutions that use it.[92] Both positions, however, are equally problematic. The bifurcation of these camps promotes the abstraction of technology from ethics in unique, morally limiting ways. With its alleged value neutrality, the "social determinist" position encourages the belief that technological design has no ethical content capable of challenging the moral frameworks of its users, while the "technological determinist" position holds that "analyzing technology in an ethical context is a *futile* exercise—we just do not have control over the advancement of technology."[93] Thus, ethics and technology become ever more estranged.

The disjunction between technical and moral development grows as new technologies permit more and faster modes of transacting. Antonio Argandoña suggests that "the speed of change hampers ethical learning processes—the speeding up of processes is, in itself, an ethical problem."[94] Even as he insists that the new economy (and presumably the new finance that supports it) requires no "new brand of ethics," Argandoña admits the "change in values that may be caused (or, at least facilitated) by the opportunities created" by technology.[95] Technological change in the financial sector has prompted substantial alterations in our ethical systems, even revision of ethical assumptions regarding the *source* of values. The financialized society increasingly looks to legal rules as "guides" to behavior rather than "boundaries" establishing its limits, as revealed in the testimony of hedge fund managers and the actions of traders. Such "legislated morality" in an industry of rising complexity virtually guarantees the expansion of technocratic control.

Conclusion

The emergent modern technocracy differs greatly from that envisioned by William Smyth, Langdon Post, and other technocrats of the early twentieth century. Wildly utopian and myopic in its own way, "classical" technocracy at least was centered on a meritocratic vision of rewarding those who furthered technological progress for the benefit of society. Extension of the scientific method to social problems and the eventual elimination of the price system, which was to be replaced by the calculations of scientists and engineers, held the key to culturally sustainable progress. Financial wizardry was classical technocracy's sworn enemy; the old-school technocrats despised the financial elite for their gross misallocations of the risks and rewards to human progress, and their ability to subjugate those whose real contributions exceeded their own.

The new financial technocracy is far more subtle and distributed. Yet it also is utopian, if not spurious, in its vision of achieving equal opportunity through financial literacy. Power accrues to those who can create the greatest monetary returns to capital, irrespective of whether that capital is "real" or contributes to the life conditions of fellow citizens. Modern-day technocrats achieve power not by design but by dependency as the products of their imaginations become embedded in a financial system in which failure is unthinkable. Technical wizardry, therefore, is an ally not an enemy. Reputation is of little concern because the modern technocrat's motivation is wealth achieved through opaque methods; his algorithms are kept under lock-and-key for fear either that competition might steal his secrets or altruists might reveal his real worth. Modern technocracy ultimately trusts the continual rise of complexity, with the hope that it grows to the point that reputation can no longer be discerned.

Disregard for reputation in the emerging technocratic system is obviously at variance with one of Adam Smith's prerequisites for a properly functioning market order. The role of reputation that Smith believed essential to preserving virtue in market societies is challenged by complacency in the face of runaway technological and financial development. Complacency erodes intentionality and contributes to social decline. Arden notes how complacency in the face of automation causes the atrophy of manual skills once essential to individual and social function.[96] While technological innovation has "clearly improved many aspects of performance" with major gains in "productivity, efficiency, and quality control," it also has led to a general decline in basic skills like cooking and math.[97] The atrophy of basic skills that Arden observes has implications for ethics as well. If one accepts Aristotle's view of moral virtue as a kind of skill developed through habit, then insofar as automation divorces the individual from ethical decision making, moral discernment may atrophy as well.[98]

The notion that investment choices have little or no moral component has insidious implications for cultural development given the amount of time and resources contemporary Americans devote to investing. In this way, technocratic finance threatens to slam shut the door to human intentionality. As Beth Azar observes: "The more [people] trust a device, the more complacent they become and the less likely they'll notice when something goes wrong."[99] One might suggest a caveat to Azar's theorem in that once something does go wrong, as in the case of the financial system, the ability to uncover the problems and take action is contingent upon understanding the system's inner workings and possessing the agency to effect change. The opaqueness of the financial system was unproblematic so long as its contribution to economic output and stability remained unquestioned. Now the situation has changed, and the groping for solutions continues. The real question is whether such a technologically advanced financial sector can allow for the repersonalization of ownership and the reengagement of investor with the capital and community essential to any moral conceptions of human flourishing. Wealth creation is not the problem; rather, it is the creation of a kind of faux wealth that obviates the need for directed activity—and thus moral development—in the pursuit of wealth. If investors are content to allow computers to splice and dice possessions into smaller and smaller pieces, the granularity of which is determined only by technical capability, then all objects of investment may eventually turn to dust.

Technocracy is best countered by robust, personalized markets that enable consumers and investors to express their values and by those less financially interested institutions of civil society that have traditionally performed prophetic roles in balancing the nation's progress. Succeeding chapters reveal, however, financialization's encroachments on those very establishments needed to counter its effects and prevent the drift toward a technocratic order. Reestablishing virtue in the financial economy means rejecting the idea that finance is a purely technical domain reserved for specialists. Rather, reestablishing virtue in the financial economy means acknowledging finance's social and ethical dimensions and involving the religious groups, civic organizations, and other intermediate associations that traditionally have provided the moral ground for American economic development.

Notes

1 The term "technocracy" has been controversial from the beginning. The American Engineering Council (AEC), in its annual meeting in Washington, DC, in 1933, divorced itself from the radical connotation applied by Howard Scott and the Columbia University technocrats who offered "startling predictions which involve a complete overturn in our economic structure." The AEC insisted that technical change within the existing political and economic structure still had great promise but that "complete replacement of men by the machine is precluded by the law of diminishing returns." See "Organized Engineers Repudiate Technocracy," *Science News-Letter*, vol. 23 (January 28, 1933), 63 [the quotations appear to paraphrase AEC resolutions].

2 Leroy Allen, "Technocracy—A Popular Summary," *Social Science*, vol. 8, no. 2 (April 1933): 175–8.

3 William Henry Smyth, *Technocracy*: *First*, *Second and Third Series*: *Social Universals* (Los Angeles: University of California at Los Angeles, 1921 [Reprint from the Gazette, Berkeley, California]), 41; also Smyth, *Technocracy*, 27.

4 Smyth, *Technocracy*, 12. Smyth stated: "Thus, it is in high degree probable that old fallacies and superstitions still infest and ramify (unsuspected) those activities which deal with life in its more than ordinary complex aspects—religion, philosophy, government, finance." See Smyth, *Technocracy*, 41.

5 Smyth, *Technocracy*, 42.

6 Smyth, *Technocracy*, 42.

7 Gerald F. Davis notes how academics from Harvard, the University of Chicago, and other institutions not only advocated the "finance-based theory of the corporation," they also served as industry consultants and set up hedge funds from which some profited handsomely. Some even invested heavily in Russian financial firms they were "helping to privatize" despite contractual restrictions on such activity. Davis references David McClintick, "How Harvard Lost Russia," *Institutional Investor* (January 13, 2006); in *Managed by the Markets*: *How Finance Re-Shaped America* (New York: Oxford University Press, 2009), 57.

8 Ed Thorp, a former mathematics professor at MIT and UCLA, has been called the "the original quant." In 1969, Thorp founded a firm called Convertible Hedge Associates (CHA), renamed Princeton-Newport Partners in 1974. An Internet article by Ken Kurson discusses Thorp's 1962 book *Beat the Dealer*, in which Thorp describes how his system of card counting in blackjack removes risk from the game and creates positive expected return: in short, Thorp's counting method suggested that it was possible to "beat the house." According to Kurson, Thorp applied what he learned at the blackjack table to finance when he started CHA, which became one of the most successful hedge funds in the United States. For more, see Ken Kurson, "Having an Edge on the Market," (February 2003); available at http://webhome.idirect.com/~blakjack/edthorp.htm on July 5, 2012; and Scott Patterson, " 'The Quants': It Pays To Know Your Wall Street Math"; available at www.npr.org/templates/story/story.php?storyId=123209339.

9 Paul Kedrosky and Dane Stangler, "Financialization and Its Entrepreneurial Consequences," Kauffman Foundation Research Series: Firm Formation and Economic Growth (March 2011): 7; available at www.signallake.com/innovation/financialization032311.pdf.

10 Alok Sheel and Meeta Ganguly, "Rise and Fall of Securitized Structured Finance," *Economic and Political Weekly* (April 19, 2008): 44.

11 "Technocrats: Minds Like Machines," *The Economist* (November 19, 2011); available at www.economist.com/node/21538698.

12 David Wessel, "Economics—Financial Crisis: Inside Dr. Bernanke's E.R.—As Obama Considers Reappointing the Fed Chairman, a Look at How He Took on More Power," *Wall Street Journal*, Eastern edition [New York, N.Y] 18 July 2009: W.3; available via ProQuest ABI Inform.

13 Davis references David McClintick, "How Harvard Lost Russia," in Davis, *Managed by the Markets*, 57.

14 Investopedia offers a typical example: "A form of *government* where decision-makers are chosen for a governing office based on their technical expertise and background" (emphasis added); available at www.investopedia.com/terms/t/technocracy.asp.

15 Alasdair Roberts, *The Logic of Discipline*: *Global Capitalism and the Architecture of Government* (Oxford Scholarship Online, 2010), 14; available at www.oxfordscholarship.com/view/10.1093/acprof:oso/9780195374988.001.0001/acprof-9780195374988.

16 Roberts, *The Logic of Discipline*, 35–6.

17 Roberts, *The Logic of Discipline*, 41.

18 According to Centeno, the complexity of the tasks undertaken by a regime, the legitimation of a regime based on performance criteria, the institutional autonomy of state organizations associated with experts, the stability of the regime, and the position of the regime within a world system all influence the development of a technocratic order. For more, see Miguel Angel Centeno, "The New Leviathan: The Dynamics and Limits of Technocracy," *Theory and Society* 22 (June 1993): 316–17.

19 Centeno, "The New Leviathan," 311. Centeno's definition of technocracy is highly relevant here: "*The administrative and political domination of a society by a state elite and allied institutions that seek to impose a single, exclusive policy paradigm based on the application of instrumentally rational techniques*" (emphasis Centeno's). See Centeno, "The New Leviathan," 314.

20 Bruce Weber, "The Growing Threat of Rogue Trading," London Business School *Business Strategy Review* (September 2011); available at http://bsr.london.edu/blog/post-50/index.html.

21 Max Weber, excerpt from "Bureaucracy," (1925) in *Sociological Theory in the Classical Era: Text and Readings*, eds. Laura Desfor Edles and Scott Appelrouth (Los Angeles: Pine Forge Press, 2010), 217 (emphasis Weber's).

22 Weber, "Bureaucracy," 217.

23 Liz McFall, *Devising Consumption: Cultural Economies of Insurance, Credit, and Spending* (New York: Routledge, 2014), 62.
24 McFall, *Devising Consumption*, 62.
25 Sebastian Mallaby, *More Money than God: Hedge Funds and the Making of a New Elite* (New York: Penguin Press, 2010).
26 Rogene A. Buchholz and Sandra B. Rosenthal, "Technology and Business: Rethinking the Moral Dilemma," *Journal of Business Ethics* vol. 41, no. 1–2 (November–December 2002): 45.
27 Graham Bowley, "The New Speed of Money, Reshaping Markets," *New York Times* (January 1, 2011); available at www.nytimes.com/2011/01/02/business/02speed.html?pagewanted=all&_r=0.
28 CBS News, *Sixty Minutes*, "How Speed Traders are Changing Wall Street," October 11, 2010; available at www.cbsnews.com/8301–18560_162–6936075.html?tag=contentMain;contentBody.
29 Companies are making nine-figure investments in their computer networks to gain microsecond advantages, and the exchanges themselves are leaders. As Bowley notes, "all the exchanges have pushed down their latencies—the fancy word for the less-than-a-blink-of-an-eye that it takes them to complete a trade. Almost each week, it seems, one exchange or another claims a new record." See Bowley, "The New Speed of Money, Reshaping Markets."
30 Peter J. Henning, "'Spoofing,' a New Crime with a Catchy Name," *New York Times* DealB%k (October 6, 2014); available at http://dealbook.nytimes.com/2014/10/06/a-new-crime-with-a-catchy-name-spoofing/.
31 Quoted in CBS News, *Sixty Minutes*, "How Speed Traders are Changing Wall Street."
32 The authors cite A. Silvennoinen and S. Thorp, "Financialization, Crisis and Commodity Correlation Dynamics," Research Paper 267, Quantitative Finance Research Center, University of Technology Sydney, for the volume statistics, and M. W. Masters, "Testimony of Michael W. Masters before the Committee on Homeland Security and Governmental Affairs," United States Senate, (May 20, 2008) for the financial investors statistic. See Nicolas Maystre and David Bicchetti, "The Rise of the Machine: Does High-Frequency Trading Alter Commodity Prices?" *VOX* (April 5, 2012); available at www.voxeu.org /article/are-commodity-derivatives-good-or-bad-new-evidence-high-frequency-data; accessed March 20, 2015.
33 Maystre and Bicchetti, "The Rise of the Machine."
34 Robert Haugen, *The New Finance: The Case Against Efficient Markets* (Upper Saddle River, NJ: Prentice Hall, 1995).
35 Paul H. Dembinski, *Finance: Servant or Deceiver? Financialization at the Crossroads* (New York: Palgrave Macmillan, 2008), 35.
36 Chris Wright, "What Is A Dark Pool And What Does Barclays' Misuse Of It Mean For Bank Shares?" *Forbes* (June 27, 2014); available at www.forbes.com/sites/chriswright/2014/06/27/what-is-a-dark-pool-and-what-does-barclays-misuse-of-them-mean-for-bank-shares/; accessed on January 4, 2014.
37 Interestingly, Erturk, *et al.*, describe an investment climate in which many members of lower socioeconomic groups lack the "calculative competence" to manage their own financial affairs while members of higher groups have "a delusional belief in their own calculative and decision making ability." See Ismail Erturk, Julie Froud, Sukhdev Johal, Adam Leaver, and Karel Williams, "The Democratization of Finance? Promises, Outcomes and Conditions," *Review of International Political Economy* vol. 14, no. 4 (October 2007): 564–5.
38 Paul A. David, "Intellectual Property Institutions and the Panda's Thumb: Patents, Copyrights, and Trade Secrets in Economic Theory and History," in *The Global Dimensions of Intellectual Property Rights in Science and Technology*, eds. Mitchel B. Wallerstein, Mary E. Mogee, and Robin A. Schoen (Washington, DC: National Academy Press, 1993): 32–6.

39 In this respect, technology works toward automation of the last manual process while finance seeks to extract the last penny of profit.
40 Adam Greenfield, "Some Guidelines for the Ethical Development of Ubiquitous Computing," *Philosophical Transactions: Mathematical, Physical and Engineering Sciences* 366, no. 1881 *From Computers to Ubiquitous Computing, by 2020* (October 28, 2008): 3824–30.
41 Erturk, *et al.*, "The Democratization of Finance?" 559.
42 Olivia Mitchell and Steven Utkus, "Lessons from Behavioral Finance for Retirement Plan Design," Pension Research Council Working Paper 2003–2006 (2004): 34–5; available at http://papers.ssrn.com/sol3/papers.cfm?abstract_id=464640&download=yes.
43 Jim Zarroli, "Lockheed Martin Case Puts 401(k) Plans on Trial," *NPR.org* (December 15, 2014); available at www.npr.org/2014/12/15/370794942/lockheed-martin-case-puts-401-k-plans-on-trial.
44 One of these groups, the Sunlight Foundation, provides an excellent breakdown of these meetings at http://sunlightfoundation.com/feature/dodd-frank-3-year/.
45 Davis, *Managed by the Markets*, 34.
46 Comptroller of the Currency Administrator of National Banks, "OCC's Quarterly Report on Bank Trading and Derivatives Activities Second Quarter 2011," Washington, DC (2011), 1; available at www.occ.gov/topics/capital-markets/financial-markets/trading/derivatives/dq211.pdf.
47 Jerry Z. Muller, "Our Epistemological Depression," *AMERICAN*, January 29, 2009, www.american.com/archive/2009/february-2009/our-epistemological-depression; quoted in Arnold Kling, "The Financial Crisis: Moral Failure or Cognitive Failure?" *Harvard Journal of Law and Policy* 33(2): 507.
48 See Muller, "Our Epistemological Depression." See also Lucian A. Bebchuk and Holger Spamann, "Regulating Bankers' Pay," *Georgetown Law Journal* vol. 98, iss. 2 (2010): 255–69.
49 Kling, "The Financial Crisis," 515.
50 Michael Lewis, *Flash Boys: A Wall Street Revolt* (New York: W. W. Norton & Company, Ltd., 2014), 104–6.
51 Lewis, *Flash Boys*, 106.
52 See www.cnbc.com/id/102214298#.
53 Kling, "The Financial Crisis," 518.
54 "JPMorgan Chases' Big Losses, Big Risk; Blip on Radar or Systemic?" [transcript of JPMorgan Chase CEO Jamie Dimon's testimony before the U.S. Senate Banking Committee on June 12, 2012], PBS NewsHour; available at www.pbs.org/newshour/bb/business/jan-june12/jamiedimon_06–13.html.
55 Dennis Kelleher, president of BetterMarkets.com, a nonprofit NGO advocating the reform of Wall Street through greater transparency and heightened financial regulation, described proprietary trading as the situation "when the banks use their money and they swing for the fences with big bets, very high risk, with potential for very big revenue coming in or very big losses." He notes it was this type of trading that led to the 2008 crisis, causing "many of these banks to fail or almost fail." See "JPMorgan Chases' Big Losses."
56 Tom Schoenberg, Dawn Kopecki, Hugh Son, and Dakin Campbell, "JPMorgan Said to Reach Record $13 Billion U.S. Settlement," *Bloomberg.com* (October 20, 2013); available at www.bloomberg.com/news/2013–10–19/jpmorgan-said-to-have-reached-13-billion-u-s-accord.html
57 Banking consultant Bert Ely was interviewed on PBS Newhour and noted that the fine imposed on JPMorgan Chase included action occurring in Bear Stearns and Washington Mutual before acquisition, "so it's important to realize that JPMorgan Chase and its management is not responsible for the total amount of this problem." See "Will JPMorgan's Record Settlement Set Incentive for Better Bank Behavior?"; available at www.pbs.org/newshour/bb/business-july-dec13-jpmorgan_11–19/.

58 Teresa Tritch, "Will Lawmakers Sneak a Gift to Wall Street into the Spending Bill?" *New York Times* (December 9, 2014); available at http://takingnote.blogs.nytimes.com/2014/12/09/will-lawmakers-sneak-a-gift-to-wall-street-into-the-spending-bill/?_r=0.
59 Quoted in National Public Radio, "All Things Considered" (August 28, 2012) [Melissa Block, host]; available at www.npr.org/2012/08/28/160196045/bain-capital-tax-documents-draw-mixed-reaction.
60 Mark Battersby, "Tax Watch: The Wall Street Rule isn't a Rule of Law, the IRS Insists," *Investment News* (October 6, 2006): p. 17; available via LexisNexis at www.lexisnexis.com/hottopics/lnacademic/?verb=sr&csi=224239.
61 William C. Dudley, "Enhancing Financial Stability by Improving Culture in the Financial Services Industry," Remarks at the Workshop on Reforming Culture and Behavior in the Financial Services Industry, Federal Reserve Bank of New York, New York City (October 20, 2014); available at www.newyorkfed.org/newsevents/speeches/2014/dud141020a.html.
62 Dudley, "Enhancing Financial Stability."
63 Dudley, "Enhancing Financial Stability." See also Benedict XVI, *Caritas in Veritate* (2009), #24, #65.
64 David Weidner, "This Wall Street Tech Deal Doomed Investors; Commentary: How Electronic Trading Failed the Marketplace," *Wall Street Journal MarketWatch* (August 7, 2012); available at http://articles.marketwatch.com/2012–08–07/commentary/33061370_1_specialist-firms-specialist-system-floor-specialists.
65 Weidner, "This Wall Street Tech Deal Doomed Investors."
66 Ben Domenech, "Technocrats and Populists: Who Trusts the People?" *Real Clear Politics* (August 13, 2013); available at www.realclearpolitics.com/articles/2013/08/13/ezra_klein_and_technocrats_vs_populists_119588.html.
67 James Rickards, "Repeal of Glass–Steagall Caused the Financial Crisis," *U.S. News & World Report* (August 27, 2012); available at www.usnews.com/opinion/blogs/economic-intelligence/2012/08/27/repeal-of-glass-steagall-caused-the-financial-crisis.
68 Luigi Zingales, *A Capitalism for the People: Recapturing the Lost Genius of American Prosperity* (New York: Basic Books, 2012), 12.
69 Corinne Crawford, "The Repeal of the Glass–Steagall Act and the Current Financial Crisis," *Journal of Business and Economics Research* vol. 9, no. 1 (January 2011): 129.
70 Halah Touryalai, "Risk is Back: America's Big Banks are Knee-Deep in Derivatives," *Forbes* (March 28, 2013); available at www.forbes.com/sites/halahtouryalai/2013/03/28/risk-is-back-americas-big-banks-are-knee-deep-in-derivatives/.
71 Andrew Leonard, "Ex-Citi Chief: Break up the Banks!" (July 25, 2012); available at www.salon.com/2012/07/25/sandy_weill_sees_the_light/
72 Lewis, "Glass–Steagall." The later Bank Holding Company Act of 1956 did declare that bank holding companies could not own subsidiaries that deal in securities and insurance.
73 John L. Campbell, "Neoliberalism in Crisis: Regulatory Roots of the U. S. Financial Meltdown," in *Markets on Trial: The Economic Sociology of the U.S. Financial Crisis: Part B*, eds. Michael Lounsbury and Paul M. Hirsch (Bingley, UK: Emerald Group Publishing Limited, 2010), 83.
74 Joe Nocera, "Risk Mismanagement," *New York Times* (January 2, 2009); available at www.nytimes.com/2009/01/04/magazine/04risk-t.html?pagewanted=all&_r=0.
75 Martin Hutchinson, "How Lehman Brothers' Own Risk Management Strategy May Cause it to Fail," *Money Morning* (September 12, 2008); available at http://moneymorning.com/2008/09/12/lehman-brothers-holdings/.
76 Campbell, "Neoliberalism in Crisis," 73.
77 Victor Zarnowitz, "Theory and History Behind Business Cycles: Are the 1990s The Onset of a Golden Age? National Bureau of Economic Research Working Paper

Series, Working Paper 7010 (March 1999): 2–7; available at www.nber.org/papers/w7010.pdf.

78 See *New York Times* DealB%k, "Hedge Fund Managers Testify Before Congress," (November 13, 2008); available at http://dealbook.nytimes.com/2008/11/13/hedge-fund-managers-set-to-testify-before-congress/.

79 Campbell, "Neoliberalism in Crisis," 71–2.

80 Dembinski, *Finance*: *Servant or Deceiver*, 37.

81 Peter C. Emberley, "Values and Technology: George Grant and our Present Possibilities," *Canadian Journal of Political Science* XXI: 3 (September 1988): 466.

82 Albert Borgmann, "The Moral Complexion of Consumption," *Journal of Consumer Research* vol. 26, no. 4 (March 2000): 420.

83 Tatum adopts Borgmann's terms "disburdening," "engagement," "things," and "devices" as used in Borgmann's book *Technology and the Character of Contemporary Life*: *A Philosophical Inquiry* (Chicago: University of Chicago Press, 1984); in Jesse S. Tatum, "Technology and Values: Getting Beyond the 'Device Paradigm' Impasse," *Science, Technology, & Human Values* 19, no. 1 (Winter 1994): 71.

84 Bianca Flowers, "Values-Based Investing Entices Advisers as Client Demand Grows," *InvestmentNews* October 1, 2014; available at www.investmentnews.com/article/20141001/FREE/141009990/values-based-investing-entices-advisers-as-client-demand-grows.

85 Horrigan states: "Clearly, the world of the New Finance is not a nice place ethically." See James O. Horrigan, "The Ethics of the New Finance," *Journal of Business Ethics* 6 (1987): 107.

86 Emberley, "Values and Technology," 471–2.

87 Buchholz and Rosenthal, "Technology and Business," 49.

88 Horrigan, "The Ethics of the New Finance," 97.

89 Adam Smith, *The Theory of Moral Sentiments* (New York: Cambridge University Press, 2002), 116. Quoted in Jeremy Shearmur and Daniel B. Klein, "Good Conduct in a Great Society: Adam Smith and the Role of Reputation," in *Reputation*: *Studies in the Voluntary Elicitation of Good Conduct* (Ann Arbor, MI: University of Michigan Press, 1997), 29–45.

90 Smith, *Lectures on Jurisprudence*, eds. R. L. Meek, D. D. Raphael, and P. G. Stein (New York: Oxford University Press, 1978), 538–9; quoted in Shearmur and Klein, "Good Conduct in a Great Society," 104.

91 Kirsten E. Martin and R. Edward Freeman, "The Separation of Ethics and Technology in Business," *Journal of Business Ethics* 53, no. 4 (September 2004): 354 (emphasis authors'). The initial separation thesis of business and ethics is found in R. E. Freeman, "Business Ethics at the Millennium," *Business Ethics Quarterly* 10(1) (2000): 169–80.

92 Martin and Freeman cite Daryl Koehn's "Ethics in a Technological Age," *Business and Society Review* 104(1) (1999) as representative of the technological determinism position; in Martin and Freeman, "The Separation of Ethics and Technology in Business," 355; also see R. T. Herschel and P. H. Andrews, "Ethical Implications of Technological Advances on Business Communications," *Journal of Business Communication* 34(2) (1997); in Martin and Freeman, "The Separation of Ethics and Technology in Business," 355–6.

93 Martin and Freeman, "The Separation of Ethics and Technology in Business," 356.

94 Antonio Argandoña, "The New Economy: Ethical Issues," *Journal of Business Ethics* 44 (April 2003): 6.

95 Argandoña, "The New Economy," 6.

96 J. E. Arden, "The Good, the Bad, and the Automatic," *GPSolo* 26(8): 60–1; available via ProQuest ABI Inform.

97 Arden, "The Good, the Bad, and the Automatic."

98 Dembinski sees one consequence of financialization as "ethical alienation" in which

"no one feels responsible for the overall result, but everyone feels an exaggerated technical responsibility for his or her particular segment." See Dembinski, *Finance: Servant or Deceiver*? 155.

99 Beth Azar, "Danger of Automation: It Makes Us Complacent," *APA Monitor* 29, 7 (July 1998): 19, quoted in J. E. Arden, "The Good, the Bad, and the Automatic."

Bibliography

Allen, Leroy. "Technocracy—A Popular Summary." *Social Science* 8, no. 2 (April 1933): 175–88.

Arden, James Ellis. "The Good, the Bad, and the Automatic." *GPSolo* 26, no. 8 (December 2009): 60–1. Available via ProQuest ABI Inform.

Argandoña, Antonio. "The New Economy: Ethical Issues." *Journal of Business Ethics* no. 44 (April 2003): 3–22.

Azar, Beth. "Danger of Automation: It Makes Us Complacent." *APA Monitor* 29, no. 7 (July 1998): 19.

Battersby, Mark. "Tax Watch: The Wall Street Rule Isn't a Rule of Law, the IRS Insists." *Investment News*, October 6, 2006. LexisNexis. www.lexisnexis.com/hottopics/lnacademic/?verb=sr&csi=224239; accessed on August 29, 2012.

Bebchuk, Lucian A., and Holger Spamann. "Regulating Bankers' Pay." *Georgetown Law Journal* 98, no. 2 (2010): 247–87.

Benedict XVI. *Caritas in Veritate*, (2009); available at www.vatican.va/holy_father/benedict_xvi/encyclicals/documents/hf_ben-xvi_enc_20090629_caritas-in-veritate_en.html; accessed on September 10, 2014.

Borgmann, Albert. *Technology and the Character of Contemporary Life: A Philosophical Inquiry*. Chicago: University of Chicago Press, 1984.

Borgmann, Albert. "The Moral Complexion of Consumption." *Journal of Consumer Research* 26, no. 4 (March 2000): 418–22.

Bowley, Graham. "The New Speed of Money, Reshaping Markets." *New York Times*, January 1, 2011. www.nytimes.com/2011/01/02/business/02speed.html?pagewanted=all&_r=0; accessed on December 14, 2014.

Buchholz, Rogene A., and Sandra B. Rosenthal. "Technology and Business: Rethinking the Moral Dilemma." *Journal of Business Ethics* 41, no. 1–2 (November–December 2002): 45–50.

Campbell, John L. "Neoliberalism in Crisis: Regulatory Roots of the U.S. Financial Meltdown." In *Markets on Trial: The Economic Sociology of the U.S. Financial Crisis: Part B*, edited by Michael Lounsbury and Paul M. Hirsch, 65–101. Bingley, UK: Emerald Group Publishing Limited, 2010.

CBS News. "How Speed Traders Are Changing Wall Street." *Sixty Minutes*, October 11, 2010. www.cbsnews.com/8301-18560_162-6936075.html?tag=contentMain;contentBody; accessed on October 5, 2012.

Centeno, Miguel Angel. "The New Leviathan: The Dynamics and Limits of Technocracy." *Theory and Society* 22, no. 3 (June 1993): 307–35.

Comptroller of the Currency Administrator of National Banks. "OCC's Quarterly Report on Bank Trading and Derivatives Activities Second Quarter 2011." Washington, DC: 2011. www.occ.gov/topics/capital-markets/financial-markets/trading/derivatives/dq211.pdf; accessed on October 12, 2012.

Crawford, Corinne. "The Repeal of the Glass–Steagall Act and the Current Financial Crisis." *Journal of Business and Economics Research* 9, no. 1 (January 2011): 127–34.

David, Paul A. "Intellectual Property Institutions and the Panda's Thumb: Patents, Copyrights, and Trade Secrets in Economic Theory and History." In *The Global Dimensions of Intellectual Property Rights in Science and Technology*, edited by Mitchel B. Wallerstein, Mary E. Mogee, and Robin A. Schoen, 19–61. Washington, DC: National Academy Press, 1993.

Davis, Gerald F. *Managed by the Markets: How Finance Re-shaped America*. New York: Oxford University Press, 2009.

Dembinski, Paul H. *Finance: Servant or Deceiver? Financialization at the Crossroads*. New York: Palgrave Macmillan, 2008.

Domenech, Ben. "Technocrats and Populists: Who Trusts the People?" *Real Clear Politics*, August 13, 2013. www.realclearpolitics.com/articles/2013/08/13/ ezra_klein_and_technocrats_vs_populists_119588.html; accessed on December 12, 2014.

Dudley, William C. "Enhancing Financial Stability by Improving Culture in the Financial Services Industry." Remarks at the Workshop on Reforming Culture and Behavior in the Financial Services Industry, Federal Reserve Bank of New York, New York City, October 20, 2014. www.newyorkfed.org/newsevents/speeches/2014/dud141020a.html; accessed on December 12, 2014.

The Economist. "Technocrats: Minds Like Machines." *The Economist*, November 16, 2011. www.economist.com/node/21538698; accessed on October 22, 2014.

Emberley, Peter C. "Values and Technology: George Grant and our Present Possibilities." *Canadian Journal of Political Science* XXI, no. 3 (September 1988): 465–94.

Erturk, Ismail, Julie Froud, Sukhdev Johal, Adam Leaver, and Karel Williams. "The Democratization of Finance? Promises, Outcomes and Conditions." *Review of International Political Economy* 14, no. 4 (October 2007): 553–75.

Flowers, Bianca. "Values-Based Investing Entices Advisers as Client Demand Grows." *InvestmentNews*, October 1, 2014. www.investmentnews.com/article/20141001/FREE/141009990/values-based-investing-entices-advisers-as-client-demand-grows; accessed on December 16, 2014.

Fox, Michelle. "HFT Critic Michael Lewis 'Dead Wrong:' Author." *CNBC.com*, November 24, 2014. www.cnbc.com/id/102214298#.

Freeman, R. Edward. "Business Ethics at the Millennium." *Business Ethics Quarterly* 10, no. 1 (January 2000): 169–80.

Greenfield, Adam. "Some Guidelines for the Ethical Development of Ubiquitous Computing." *Philosophical Transactions: Mathematical, Physical and Engineering Sciences, From Computers to Ubiquitous Computing, by 2020*, no. 1881 (October 28, 2008): 3823–31.

Haugen, Robert. *The New Finance: The Case Against Efficient Markets*. Upper Saddle River, NJ: Prentice Hall, 1995.

Henning, Peter J. "'Spoofing,' a New Crime with a Catchy Name." *New York Times* DealB%k, October 6, 2014. http://dealbook.nytimes.com/2014/10/06/va-new-crime-with-a-catchy-name-spoofing//; accessed on December 12, 2014.

Herschel, R. T., and P. H. Andrews. "Ethical Implications of Technological Advances on Business Communications." *Journal of Business Communication* 34, no. 2 (n.d.): 1997.

Horrigan, James O. "The Ethics of the New Finance." *Journal of Business Ethics* 6, no. 2 (February 1987): 97–110.

Hutchinson, Martin. "How Lehman Brothers' Own Risk Management Strategy May Cause It to Fail." *Money Morning*, September 12, 2008. http://moneymorning.com/2008/09/12/lehman-brothers-holdings/; accessed on December 14, 2014.

Investopedia. "Technocracy." www.investopedia.com/terms/t/technocracy.asp; accessed on December 1, 2014.

Kedrosky, Paul, and Dane Stangler. *Financialization and Its Entrepreneurial Consequences*. Kauffman Foundation Research Series: Firm Formation and Economic Growth. Kauffman Foundation, March 2011. www.signallake.com/innovation/financialization032311.pdf; accessed on June 7, 2011.

Kling, Arnold. "The Financial Crisis: Moral Failure or Cognitive Failure?" *Harvard Journal of Law and Public Policy* 33, no. 2 (Spring 2010): 507–18.

Koehn, Daryl. "Ethics in a Technological Age." *Business and Society Review* 104, no. 1 (Spring 1999): 57–90.

Kurson, Ken. "Having an Edge on the Market." *WebHome.iDirect.com*, February 2003. http://webhome.idirect.com/~blakjack/edthorp.htm.

Leonard, Andrew. "Ex-Citi Chief: Break Up the Banks!" *Salon.com*, July 25, 2012. www.salon.com/2012/07/25/sandy_weill_sees_the_light/; accessed on December 12, 2014.

Lewis, Michael. *Flash Boys: A Wall Street Revolt*. New York: W. W. Norton & Company, Ltd., 2014.

Mallaby, Sebastian. *More Money than God: Hedge Funds and the Making of a New Elite*. New York: Penguin Press, 2010.

Martin, Kirsten E., and R. Edward Freeman. "The Separation of Ethics and Technology in Business." *Journal of Business Ethics* 53, no. 4 (September 2004): 353–64.

Masters, M. W. "Testimony of Michael W. Masters before the Committee on Homeland Security and Governmental Affairs." United States Senate. May 20, 2008.

Maystre, Nicholas, and David Bicchetti. "The Rise of the Machine: Does High-Frequency Trading Alter Commodity Prices?" *VOX*, April 5, 2012. www.voxeu.org/article/are-commodity-derivatives-good-or-bad-new-evidence-high-frequency-data; accessed on March 20, 2015.

McClintick, David. "How Harvard Lost Russia." *Institutional Investor*, January 13, 2006.

McFall, Liz. *Devising Consumption: Cultural Economies of Insurance, Credit, and Spending*. New York: Routledge, 2014.

Mitchell, Olivia, and Steven Utkus. "Lessons from Behavioral Finance for Retirement Plan Design." Pension Research Council Working Paper 2003–2006, Social Science Research Network, 2004. http://papers.ssrn.com/sol3/papers.cfm?abstract_id=464640&download=yes; accessed on December 16, 2014.

Muller, Jerry Z. "Our Epistemological Depression." *AMERICAN*, January 29, 2009. www.american.com/archive/ 2009/february-2009/our-epistemological-depression.

National Public Radio. "All Things Considered." August 28, 2012. www.npr.org/2012/08/28/160196045/bain-capital-tax-documents-draw-mixed-reaction; accessed on August 29, 2012.

New York Times DealB%k. "Hedge Fund Managers Testify before Congress." November 13, 2008. http://dealbook.nytimes.com/2008/11/13/hedge-fund-managers-set-to-testify-before-congress/; accessed on July 23, 2012.

Nocera, Joe. "Risk Mismanagement." *New York Times*, January 2, 2009. www.nytimes.com/2009/01/04/magazine/04risk-t.html?pagewanted=all&_r=0; accessed on December 13, 2014.

"Organized Engineers Repudiate Technocracy." *Science News-Letter* 23, no. 616 (January 28, 1933): 63.

Patterson, Scott. "'The Quants': It Pays To Know Your Wall Street Math." February 1, 2010. www.npr.org/templates/story/story.php?storyId=123209339; accessed on December 14, 2014.

PBS NewsHour. "JPMorgan Chases' Big Losses, Big Risk; Blip on Radar or Systemic?" *PBS.org*, June 13, 2012. www.pbs.org/newshour/bb/business/jan-june12/jamiedimon_06-13.html; accessed on June 27, 2012.

PBS NewsHour. "Will JPMorgan's Record Settlement Set Incentive for Better Bank Behavior?" *PBS.org*, November 19, 2013. www.pbs.org/newshour/bb/business-july-dec13-jpmorgan_11-19/; accessed on December 12, 2014.

Rickards, James. "Repeal of Glass–Steagall Caused the Financial Crisis." *U.S. News & World Report*, August 27, 2012. www.usnews.com/opinion/blogs/economic-intelligence/2012/08/27/repeal-of-glass-steagall-caused-the-financial-crisis; accessed on December 12, 2014.

Roberts, Alasdair. *The Logic of Discipline: Global Capitalism and the Architecture of Government*. New York: Oxford University Press, 2010. www.oxfordscholarship.com/view/10.1093/acprof:oso/ 9780195374988.001.0001/acprof-9780195374988; accessed on December 5, 2014.

Schoenberg, Tom, Dawn Kopecki, Hugh Son, and Dakin Campbell. "JPMorgan Said to Reach Record $13 Billion U.S. Settlement." *Bloomberg.com*, October 20, 2013. www.bloomberg.com/news/2013-10-19/jpmorgan-said-to-have-reached-13-billion-u-s-accord.html; accessed on November 12, 2014.

Shearmur, Jeremy, and Daniel B. Klein. "Good Conduct in the Great Society: Adam Smith and the Role of Reputation." In *Reputation: Studies in the Voluntary Elicitations of Good Conduct*, 29–46. Ann Arbor, MI: University of Michigan Press, 1997.

Sheel, Alok, and Meeta Ganguly. "Rise and Fall of Securitized Structured Finance." *Economic and Political Weekly*, April 19, 2008.

Silvennoinen, Annastiina, and Susan Thorp. "Financialization, Crisis and Commodity Correlation Dynamics." Research Paper 267, University of Technology, Sydney, 2010.

Smith, Adam. *The Theory of Moral Sentiments*. New York: Cambridge University Press, 2002.

Smith, Adam. *Lectures on Jurisprudence*, edited by R. L. Meek, D. D. Raphael, and P. G. Stein New York: Oxford University Press, 1978.

Smyth, William Henry. *Technocracy: First, Second and Third Series: Social Universals*. Los Angeles: University of California at Los Angeles, 1921.

Sunlight Foundation. "What the Banks' Three-Year War on Dodd–Frank Looks Like." *SunlightFoundation.com*, July 22, 2013. http://sunlightfoundation.com/feature/dodd-frank-3-year/; accessed on December 16, 2014.

Tatum, Jesse S. "Technology and Values: Getting beyond the 'Device Paradigm' Impasse." *Science, Technology, & Human Values* 19, no. 1 (Winter 1994): 70–87.

Touryalai, Halah. "Risk Is Back: America's Big Banks Are Knee-Deep in Derivatives." *Forbes*, March 28, 2013. www.forbes.com/sites/halahtouryalai/2013/03/28/risk-is-back-americas-big-banks-are-knee-deep-in-derivatives/; accessed on December 13, 2014.

Tritch, Teresa. "Will Lawmakers Sneak a Gift to Wall Street into the Spending Bill?" *New York Times*, December 9, 2014. http://takingnote.blogs.nytimes.com/2014/12/09/will-lawmakers-sneak-a-gift-to-wall-street-into-the-spending-bill/?_r=0; accessed on December 10, 2014.

Weber, Bruce. "The Growing Threat of Rogue Trading." London Business School *Business Strategy Review* (September 2011); available at http://bsr.london.edu/blog/post-50/index.html; accessed on January 5, 2014.

Weber, Max. Excerpt from "Bureaucracy" (1925). In *Sociological Theory in the Classical Era: Text and Readings*, edited by Laura Desfor Edles and Scott Appelrouth, 212–20. Los Angeles: Pine Forge Press, 2010.

Weidner, David. "This Wall Street Tech Deal Doomed Investors; Commentary: How Electronic Trading Failed the Marketplace." *Wall Street Journal MarketWatch*, August 7, 2012. http://articles.marketwatch.com/2012-08-07/commentary/33061370_1_specialist-firms-specialist-system-floor-specialists; accessed on September 26, 2012.

Wessel, David. "Economics—Financial Crisis: Inside Dr. Bernanke's E.R.—As Obama Considers Reappointing the Fed Chairman, a Look at How He Took on More Power." *Wall Street Journal*. July 18, 2009, sec. W3. Available via ProQuest ABI Inform; accessed on April 4, 2014.

Wright, Chris. "What Is A Dark Pool And What Does Barclays' Misuse Of It Mean For Bank Shares?" *Forbes* (June 27, 2014); available at www.forbes.com/sites/chriswright/2014/06/27/what-is-a-dark-pool-and-what-does-barclays-misuse-of-them-mean-for-bank-shares/; accessed on January 4, 2014.

Zarnowitz, Victor. "Theory and History Behind Business Cycles: Are the 1990s the Onset of a Golden Age?" Working Paper 7010, National Bureau of Economic Research Working Paper Series, 1999. www.nber.org/papers/w7010.pdf; accessed on July 10, 2014.

Zarroli, Jim. "Lockheed Martin Case Puts 401(k) Plans on Trial." *NPR.org*, December 15, 2014. www.npr.org/2014/12/15/370794942/lockheed-martin-case-puts-401-k-plans-on-trial; accessed on December 15, 2014.

Zingales, Luigi. *A Capitalism for the People*: *Recapturing the Lost Genius of American Prosperity*. New York: Basic Books, 2012.

3 An alternate road to serfdom

Technocracy has seen no greater opponent than the Austrian economist Friedrich Hayek. The extent of Hayek's animus toward the technical extremes of "economic science" came across clearly in his banquet speech the night before he was awarded the Nobel Prize for contributions to that field. Hayek announced to a somewhat startled audience that had he been "consulted whether to establish a Nobel Prize in economics," he "should have decidedly advised against it."[1] He believed that such accolades stroked the egos of those experts and technical specialists who too often used their complex methods and tools in the attempt to plan society's development and, in the process, jeopardized freedom. Despite his inability to limit the mathematization of economics and its domination by "technicians," Hayek's work inspired a revolution in economic thinking that impacted policy to a greater degree than it did the academy.

In 1994, fellow Nobel laureate Milton Friedman wrote the introduction to the fiftieth anniversary edition of Hayek's *Road to Serfdom* and therein acknowledged Hayek's contributions, lauding the Austrian as a champion of liberty. Near the end of the introduction, however, Friedman's praiseful tone is dampened by a statement of obvious disappointment: "On both sides of the Atlantic, it is only a little overstated to say that we preach individualism and competitive capitalism, and practice socialism."[2] While Friedman's implication that Americans "practice socialism" was an exaggeration, one might sympathize with his general argument that despite the nation's reputation for rugged individualism and its professed devotion to free market principles, collectivist sentiments will not go away. In the U.S., the implementation of a national healthcare program, seemingly interminable government stimulus actions, and stock purchases in banks and other financial firms designed to "save the economy," mirror the kinds of practices cautioned against by both Hayek and Friedman. Globally, financial problems encourage state involvement in national economies to an extent rarely seen since the "defeat of socialism." This chapter provides an explanation for the persistence of policies that threaten liberty and it describes how financialization has rerouted the road to serfdom that Hayek first charted.

Hayek's influence

Many have considered Hayek's *The Road to Serfdom* a decisive treatise in the struggle between capitalism and socialism; perhaps Friedman's frustration with Western nations for not practicing what they preach stemmed from their failure to apply Hayek's wisdom. Hayek exposed the threat to human liberty posed by socialist philosophy and interventionist governments that thrive in periods of crisis and insist that progress must be "planned." The book would be seminal to the "rebirth" of the free market system that occurred during the Reagan–Thatcher revolution in the last quarter of the twentieth century. Its influence on prominent academics, business leaders, and politicians has been remarkable. American libertarian Ron Paul, Harvard professor Robert Nozick, and former U.S. Supreme Court Chief Justice William Rehnquist have been among those who credited the book as highly influential in forming their worldviews. Former governor and Republican presidential candidate Rick Perry of Texas stated in 2011 that *The Road to Serfdom* helped him arrive at the "understanding that John Maynard Keynes absolutely knew nothing about economics."[3] Presumably, Keynes knew something about economics, the contrary conclusion of a Texas politician notwithstanding. And, of course, Hayek knew something about economics himself. He was awarded the aforementioned Nobel Prize in Economic Sciences (along with Sweden's Gunnar Myrdal) in 1974 for his contribution to the theory of money and business cycles and his work on the "interdependence of economic, social and institutional phenomena."[4] Also impressive was the breadth of Hayek's intellectual pursuits. He was an accomplished polymath, contributing to an array of disciplines from epistemology to psychology.

Despite the acclaim achieved by *The Road to Serfdom* and the legion of Hayek disciples that formed subsequent to its publication, popular discussions of its influence have largely ignored one of the book's central themes. Readers of the book commonly emphasize Hayek's views on the *socialist* threat to freedom while overlooking more subtle aspects of his thought that warn of the danger to *democracies* that "embark on planning," specifically, that those democracies may themselves devolve into oppressive regimes. This dissolution of democratic rule occurs as authority is delegated to specialized interests with technical knowledge that seek to impose their unique plans on society. The impossibility of achieving consensus among these factions, entrusted with an effectively "political" responsibility, increasingly frustrates both the democratic process and the polity. Citizens can then become persuaded that they need a central authority to settle what cannot be decided by those groups vying for power.

Contemporarily, one sees evidence of financialization in the elevation of financial specialists to unprecedented positions of influence. Revelations during the height of the recent crisis that the services of some "quants," whose mathematical models helped destabilize the global financial system, were still much in demand in order to "unwind" the investment morass to which they had contributed, demonstrated society's growing dependence on those Warren Buffet once described as "geeks bearing formulas." The necessary involvement of financial specialists in the reregulation of their industry in the aftermath of the crisis further demonstrates the technocratic tendencies of finance posited in the preceding chapter. In an environment of technical complexity and vast interdependencies, government authority and financial interests inevitably *must* combine in ways that advantage some at the expense of others. The Dodd–Frank Wall Street Reform and Consumer Protection Act created almost 14,000 pages of new rules and prompted over 1,000 meetings between regulators and representatives of the big banks in the period leading up to July 2013.[5] These statistics are offered not to further intrigue but rather to convey that pragmatism demands technical knowledge for the creation of financial regulation, and government officials alone cannot supply that expertise.

Adding to the perception of financial manipulation was the immense power wielded by Federal Reserve Chairman Ben Bernanke, which led *Wall Street Journal* columnist David Wessel to remark that the Fed became "almost a fourth branch of government during the crisis, deciding which financial firms would live and which would die and lending hundreds of billions of dollars and putting taxpayers at risk without having to get congressional approval."[6] This statement is consistent with Hayek's observation that undemocratic control mechanisms prompted by destabilizing forms of *competition* can acclimate citizens to government intervention in markets to restore order. Hayek perceived no conspiracy in such developments. He considered that "we all are in some measure specialists" who believe that we can rationally persuade others as to the wisdom of our visions, and, given the right conditions, the more idealistically inclined would impose their visions through political coercion.[7] This chapter shows that the technocratic tendency of modern financialized society is not only logical, but also consistent with Hayek's view of collectivism, not as some external force imposed against the will of a sovereign people, but as an impulse that arises from within free societies that find it increasingly difficult to manage their freedoms.

Debt and servitude

In proposing financialization as an alternate road to serfdom, the ubiquitous rise of debt, which hamstrings nation-states as much as individuals, seems an obvious place to begin. Economist Thomas Palley contended even before the crisis of 2008 that chronic debt was the "defining feature of financialization in the U.S." The addiction to credit represents a value change in American society that has been underway for some time and chronologically parallels the financialization model described in this book. Palley observed the growth of U.S. credit market debt, from 140 to 328.6 percent of GDP between 1973 and 2005.[8] American economic policy encourages both corporate and household indebtedness: a tax code that treats debt financing more favorably than equity financing offers incentives to corporations, and a consumer base that has been habituated for decades to "get in over their heads" through government-sustained low interest rates.

The persistence of a credit system that too casually encourages future obligations should serve to caution those analysts who speak enthusiastically about the recent rise in retail sales and real estate values. Moreover, student loan debt now totals more than $1 trillion and has eclipsed credit cards as the single largest source of indebtedness.[9] Karen Dynan observed the rise in the median household debt-to-income ratio from 0.14 to 0.61 between 1983 and 2008.[10] Although mortgage debt service payments dropped from a peak of 7.2 percent of personal disposable income in the fourth quarter of 2007 to 4.82 percent in the fourth quarter of 2013,[11] it required a massive number of delinquencies and foreclosures, as well as lender-incentivized refinancing transactions to accomplish that feat. The dip is likely to be temporary if mortgage debt follows the pattern of credit card balances. After declining in 2012, the total amount Americans owe on their credit cards rose by 8 percent or $38.2 billion from 2012 to the last quarter of 2013, with an even larger increase predicted in 2014.[12] The Federal Reserve Board of Governors refuted the claim that the Great Recession that began in 2008 moderated the American debt addiction. Its report on American consumer credit stated that after a recession-based correction that saw consumer debt actually decline through 2010, debt began to rise again from an annual seasonally adjusted rate of 4.1 percent and total level of $2.75 trillion in 2011 to 6.4 percent and $3.13 trillion in February of 2014.[13]

Escalation of debt has been shaped by a marked change in cultural attitudes and supported by an elaborate information infrastructure that feeds the credit fetish. Young Americans have been brought up to expect quick decisions from potential creditors. According to Richard Carter, CEO of Nostrum Group,

> the explosion of Big Data means that alternative lenders have embraced new technologies which use algorithms to determine risk profiles in a matter of minutes and based on a combination of data sources. Everything from an applicant's payment history to social media feeds, demographic data and professional connections can now be brought together to provide a holistic view of an individual and their risk profile. Using Big Data means that a lending decision can be made in minutes.[14]

Credit card companies aggressively market their services, especially to young consumers. Despite passage of the Credit Card Accountability Responsibility and Disclosure Act (CARD Act) of 2009 that requires fuller disclosure of fees and limits some of the more aggressive marketing practices, credit card companies have done little to change their tactics, making college students a principal target of their campaigns.[15] However, the pervasive upsurge in debt tolerance has not been simply a supply-side phenomenon. Debt liberalization has been a collaborative project involving government programs, lending firms, credit rating agencies, and consumers themselves, who have taken advantage of historically unprecedented access to credit to pursue their diverse visions of the American Dream. Whatever its roots, debt now straps individuals in ways that limit freedom (to retire, to travel, to educate children) and even portends intergenerational conflict as Millennials wake up to the massive obligations delegated to them by their predecessors.

The indebtedness of American public institutions is of equal concern, with the federal deficit estimated by the Treasury Department at more than $17 trillion. Recent "good news" consisted in breaking the string of $1 trillion plus annual deficits from 2008 to 2012, with the 2013 shortfall coming in at around $680 billion. This deficit slowdown, however, is projected to be temporary as baby boomer healthcare and retirement obligations continue to grow.[16] Non-federal government institutions also have alarming debt levels. In a December 2011 article, *The Economist* described "the parlous finances of America's state and local governments" as the greatest threat to the country's economic system, in large part due to the increasingly unstable municipal-bond market, estimated at $3.7 trillion.[17] Most notable was the bankruptcy filing of Jefferson County, Alabama, the most populous of the state's counties, which got involved in a derivative-based financing plan and racked up $4.2 billion in debt, much of which was targeted toward infrastructure projects such as sewage system refurbishment. Other municipalities have followed suit. Harrisburg, Pennsylvania filed on October 12, 2011, with a $300 million deficit. Boise County, Idaho, and Central Falls, Rhode Island, were also forced to file for bankruptcy in 2011.[18]

Debt and speculation become joined at the hip in the financialized society as innovative financing plans funnel high-risk credit to government officials who, as discussed in Chapter 2, many times lack knowledge of the risks involved. Those product offerings are appealing because of the growing inability of governments to meet their citizens' needs for basic infrastructure and welfare services. Although some improvement has been made in the financial status of American state and local governments (the National Conference of State Legislatures reported a decline of collective debt among these institutions from $174 billion in 2010 to $91 billion at the start of 2012), future obligations will continue to hamstring governments, likely resulting in the degradation of both physical and social infrastructure.[19]

Palley offers an explanation for the rapid rise of debt and also the explosion of speculative activity that have accompanied financialization: "The fact that the process of financialization was long-running and expansionary in the early and middle stages made it extremely hard to oppose."[20] In other words, people are hardwired to "let the good times roll" without addressing either the social or ethical issues that accompany prosperity, or even considering whether prosperity is sustainable. As growth stalled and financial problems emerged during the recent crisis, many Americans were comforted by past economic performance and the idea that "eventually markets will right themselves." However, as more people perceived that debt and speculative behavior contributed to economic instability, demand increased for official action to return stability. Government intervention appeared increasingly attractive as specialized interests competed "over the heads" of average citizens, achieving "political" power and further destabilizing the situation, just as Hayek would have predicted.

The new financial dynamism, however, makes policy tools that should address problems less reliable and more likely for policies themselves to have what Hayek referred to as "unintended consequences." Palley describes financialization as an unpredictable, evolutionary process that has "major implications" not only for economic activity but also for the econometric modeling upon which much of the system depends.[21] The system as it evolved fed an addiction to debt and the acquiescence to state intervention, based on officials' assessments of the prevailing economic winds. Those assessments were made more difficult to.gauge by the effects of financialization itself. In Hayek's terms, these forces also stimulated the "planning mind" of often well-intentioned but intellectually overmatched "idealists," tempting them to step into the fray to try to save civilization from itself.[22]

These cultural changes caused by the recent crisis persist. Americans have grown accustomed not only to high levels of debt and a widening distribution of income but also to the need for government to perpetually stimulate the economy. The question that remains is how the nation can return to a less financially volatile and state-dependent economy that spreads its rewards more equitably.

A democratic solution?

Yale professor Robert Shiller is among those who propose the "democratization of finance" as a solution to the financial instability and inequity that has emerged in recent decades. Rather than restrict the derivatives that contributed to corporate bankruptcies and the need for government bailouts, Shiller has proposed making similar products available to consumers to enable hedging against fluctuations in housing prices, energy costs, college tuition, and countless other contingencies. In his words, "we need to democratize finance and bring the advantages enjoyed by the clients of Wall Street to the customers of Wal-Mart."[23] The system Shiller envisions would have enabled American homeowners, for example, to engage in derivative contracts that would have facilitated an offsetting payment in the event of the kind of precipitous drop in housing prices that occurred.

One might think that Hayek's unyielding objections to state planning and reputation as a champion of liberty might have inspired similar "democratizing" ideas in response to the socialist challenges of his own day. Instead, he insisted that he had no intention "of making a fetish of democracy."[24] Hayek's political reflections often come as a shock to those who assume, perhaps logically, that in addition to the free market system he would also zealously defend democratic principles. However, Hayek criticized the willingness of democracy's more idealistic proponents to depict it as an end in itself, describing democratic government as "a means, a utilitarian device for safeguarding internal peace and individual freedom. As such it is by no means infallible or certain."[25] Even more ominously, he tendered the possibility that democracy could disintegrate into "a true 'dictatorship of the proletariat'" which, "if it undertook centrally to direct the economic system, would probably destroy personal freedom as completely as any autocracy has ever done."[26] Hayek did recognize that communist dictatorships are more inclined toward arbitrary exercises of power than are capitalist democracies; however, in theory, any system of government that privileges private interests in seeking their own aims at the expense of the society can devolve into arbitrary authority, running roughshod over its people.

If the democratic system is not inherently supportive of individual liberty, then what is? For Hayek, the answer to that straightforward but highly involved question was the "spontaneous order" of a free society guided by a regime of law and a "minimal state."[27] He believed a "fashionable concentration on democracy" as a universal answer to abuses of authority makes people dangerously complacent in believing that the mere existence of democratic structures resolves all questions of who holds power.[28] Hayek detected in the very processes of democratic government an inclination toward control by specialists arising from the growing sophistication of civilization—social, political, technological. Yet he certainly was not of the same mind as William Henry Smyth, his fellow Nobel laureate Gunnar Myrdal, and other purveyors of technocracy that "experts" held the key to economic prosperity and the preservation of liberty.

An analogue might be drawn between Hayek's conception of democratic institutions and his ideal of markets that is consistent with his notion of the spontaneous order as an abstract construction that encompasses individual decision making in many institutional contexts. Democratic institutions and free markets are both means of value expression; in fact, they are the primary means through which a liberal society expresses values. Hayek's conception of "workable" democracy makes the legal system responsible for fairly mediating myriad, often conflicting, values and interests, just as the present financial order makes its regulatory system responsible for doing likewise (e.g., restricting federally insured banks that want to use deposits for risky investments). Also, both systems are imperfect, and, when their value-expression capabilities are constrained, they lose much of their social utility. Markets *can* be remarkable mediators of societal goals and values when free individual choice is permitted, but, just as Hayek observed of democracy, markets have no *inherent* ability to prevent the development of coercive power. That capability depends on many factors: the ease of entry into markets, the ubiquity and accessibility of information, the presence of many competitors, and the degree of concentration in market power, among others.

Hayek's concerns respecting democracy resulted from the perceived inability of the parliamentary process to provide what the people desire and what he considered impossible: a comprehensive plan to reconcile conflicting interests. To those who advocated democratic principles as a panacea, Hayek objected that, as all governments, democracies involve constituencies with differing objectives that seek power. Democracies are challenged with achieving agreement among these specialized groups on an impossible range of issues. Given the imperfections of the political process, some power seekers inevitably use their privileged means to pursue selfish goals at the expense of others, an inherently arbitrary process that infringes on liberty.

Recent events demonstrate that powerful financial interests at times engage in various rent-seeking or collusive behaviors that work against the public interest and even the liberty of citizens. Major banks can manipulate key interest rates and other benchmarks at a significant costs to consumers and businesses. Through either complicity or negligence, those institutions can also allow employees to take excessive risks, putting taxpayers on the hook for the actions of a few. Investment firms have been shown to advise their clients to take trading positions that the firms themselves "bet against" in transactions for their own proprietary purposes, as Merrill Lynch and Credit Suisse were fined for doing in 2011.[29] In such cases, just as Hayek observed, citizens often demand that government act to protect their interests.

The impossibility of a common moral code

Although perceived injustice often leads people to call on government to exert economic control, Hayek thought that a major impetus for state planning arose from the persistent though illusory ideal of a realizable social good or "common good." The idea of working for the "common good" ostensibly represents the possibility of a commonly held moral code, but Hayek believed that such terms "have no sufficiently definite meaning to determine a particular course of action."[30] The vagueness of these concepts, however, does not prevent their promotion by idealists. In *The Road to Serfdom*, Hayek resisted the temptation to judge as good or bad this notion of a common moral code, emphasizing instead the *impossibility of achieving it* in a context of rising pluralism. Civilization is progressing toward a social order free from traditional constraints, and any attempts to resist this development are inevitably coercive. His explanation for this evolution is largely anthropological:

> The rules of which our common moral code consists have progressively become fewer and more general in character. From the primitive man, who was bound by an elaborate ritual in almost every one of his daily activities, who was limited by innumerable taboos, and who could scarcely conceive of doing things in a way different from his fellows, morals have more and more tended to become merely limits circumscribing the sphere within which the individual could behave as he liked. The adoption of a common ethical code comprehensive enough to determine a unitary economic plan would mean a complete reversal of this tendency.[31]

Despite the seeming backwardness of constructing a comprehensive moral system capable of supporting a planned economy, the ideal persists. At some point, however, realization of government ineptitude in accomplishing these goals enters the social consciousness. Hayek quoted British political philosopher Harold J. Laski: "the present parliamentary machine is quite unsuited to pass rapidly a great body of complicated legislation."[32] The ineffectiveness of legislatures lies in their relative lack of expertise. Blame should be cast not on legislators themselves, but on the scope of parliamentary endeavors; the issues on which clear majorities can agree are limited yet "they are not asked to act where they can agree, but to produce *agreement on everything*—the whole direction of the resources of the nation."[33] The conflicting ends of constituents means crafting either a moral code or a comprehensive economic plan by a legislature "makes nonsense" and, in the end, pleases no one.[34]

The limitless, often complex issues on which politicians are asked to legislate causes them to turn for help to more technically competent individuals or specialized agencies. This road, too, is a dead end because it promotes a multiplication of plans to satisfy different interests. In short, it leads to division rather than agreement: "Even if, by this expedient [delegation], a democracy should succeed in planning every sector of economic activity," Hayek writes, "it would still have to face the problem of integrating these separate plans into a unitary whole."[35] The conflicts inspired by delegation and the inability to reconcile different approaches create rising frustration with the legislative function altogether, convincing the people of the need for control by a central authority.

Hayek understood the popular frustration that results from the "impossibility" of the legislative process in complex societies. He also understood that unfair competition and, sometimes, just bad fortune can lead citizens who seek economic justice to call on the state; however, he consistently cautioned against government involvement in such matters beyond establishing a basic system of property rights and some minimum social safety net. To Hayek, this was as much a moral as a social or economic issue, but not "moral" in the idealists' sense of a common code capable of binding citizens around a collective vision, achievable through political channels. Rather, *The Road to Serfdom* is a moral treatise in that it outlines Hayek's understanding of social morality as determined by a perpetual trial-and-error process that allows free individuals to express their ethical as well as material preferences through exchange with others. Any attempts by government to coerce particular outcomes, however well intended through legitimate parliamentary processes, undermine this moral dynamism and threaten liberty.

The slippery slope of constructivism

If the persistent ideal of a collective moral code was the impetus to social planning, the attitude that led to its realization was something Hayek described with a highly charged word: "constructivism." The constructivist mindset centered on the notion that some central authority is more capable of planning progress and acting to achieve it than are free citizens. He believed state intervention disrupts the efficient allocation of resources and enables elites to direct society to their own purposes. For Hayek, constructivist thinking was common to both socialism and "progressive" government programs, like FDR's New Deal. Socialist and "progressive" liberal governments both sought to guide society toward predetermined objectives rather than let a competitive order of free individuals determine the best path to the social good.[36]

Constructivism thrives on the illusions of specialists, both technical experts and special interests—from farmers to craftsmen to efficiency experts—all of whom believe in the rightness of their social visions. Even people on the lower rungs of society are convinced that they can reshape the whole to suit their ideals, through persuasion at first and, failing that, through the coercive action of government.[37] For Hayek, however, the "social good" cannot be achieved through the deliberation of committees or even by way of political compromise, except on certain issues like national defense, because disparate groups define the "good" in ways that inevitably conflict. For most issues faced by ideologically plural societies there are almost as many solutions as there are citizens. The difficulty of aggregating these competing views into a single vision only magnifies the complexities of the political process and exposes the limitations of democratic rule.

Two contradictory forces result from the constructivist ethos and undermine freedom. The popular "agreement that planning is necessary," combined with the increasing "inability of democratic assemblies to produce a plan," can lead to what Hayek called the "cry for an economic dictator" to relieve the chaos.[38] He saw this demand for a single authority capable of resolving competing social visions as a "characteristic stage" in the progression of the planned (and ultimately totalitarian) society:

> It is the essence of the economic problem that the making of an economic plan involves the choice between conflicting or competing ends—different needs of different people. But which ends do so conflict, which will have to be sacrificed if we want to achieve certain others, in short, which are the alternatives between which we must choose, can only be known to those who know all the facts; and only they, the experts, are in a position to decide which of the different ends are to be given preference. It is inevitable that they should impose their scale of preferences on the community for which they plan.[39]

There are contemporary examples, both liberal and conservative, of special interest groups attempting to impose their rather narrow visions on others by political means. On the left, advocates of the Green Movement and People for the American Way often seek enforcement of their goals through political channels, while on the right, the "contract" of Grover Norquist seeks through legal agreements with lawmakers to impose a singular vision of balanced federal budgets as a panacea for cultural ills.[40]

Financial motivations often drive these groups to political involvement, at times stimulating not only conflict but also unlikely alliances. Evidence of this dynamic was seen in political battles over the American Recovery and Reinvestment Act of 2009, which was prompted by the financial crisis and ensuing recession. This legislation was to be the Obama administration's signature effort in restoring integrity to government programs; it contained provisions specifically designed to improve accountability and transparency in the allocation of its funds. Besides rekindling a battle among economists over the wisdom of Keynesian economic policies, however, it also became the focus of attention among hundreds of special interest groups vying for money. The law also received intense criticism from many diverse organizations. The American business community loudly criticized its "Buy American" provisions because of the stringent regulations for acquisition of materials and equipment that applied to government contractors and others who received funds.[41] In October of 2009 the State of Massachusetts Office of the Inspector General "assembled a team of analysts, lawyers, and investigators to initiate a variety of cases aimed at detecting and preventing fraud, waste and abuse in ARRA-funded projects."[42] Other states across the country replicated that effort.

Anticipating the free-for-all of special interest groups, the Obama administration attempted to limit their influence in vying for portions of the almost $800 billion in stimulus money. The administration implemented strict rules on lobbying activity in order to help ensure that funds were used in the best possible ways to facilitate recovery; the restrictions drew criticism. An organization called Citizens for Responsibility and Ethics in Washington (CREW) was among many groups protesting the lobbying rules as limiting free speech. Ironically, CREW was founded by Norm Eisen, the president's chief ethics counsel,[43] illustrating the divisiveness of this complex legislation. The enormous funds at stake precipitated action by hundreds of organizations seeking their pieces of the pie, and these groups often had widely differing ideas concerning what must be done to stimulate the economy.

Hayek viewed attempts to craft legislation involving specialized interests with divergent objectives as a major step down the road to serfdom. In such situations, everyone seemingly has a clear vision of how to solve the "problem," whereas from a Hayekian perspective no one does—all are simply competing for their own interests through political means. In short, as complexity and the plurality of interests expand, democracy falters. Unfortunately, recent attempts at financial reform suggest that similar forces may contribute to continued instability. Various groups, often at cross purposes, were involved in the Dodd–Frank legislation and greatly muddled the final product. For example, the law initially proposed a 20 percent down payment requirement on home purchasers but, at the behest of myriad lobbies (including real estate industry groups and even some low-income housing activists) as well many politicians, regulators eliminated the down payment criterion. The *Washington Post* editorial board called Dodd–Frank's watering-down a "discouraging" demonstration of the "housing lobby's power" and the refusal of regulators to err "on the side of safety."[44]

Technological change often can accent political divisions by expanding special interests. A limitation with Hayek's view of the road to serfdom, however, is that his statements on the cultural implications of technology were inconsistent. He recognized that technology can be a catalyst to the fragmenting of social vision by promoting specialization but, for the most part, he considered this largely a *fait accompli* of modern society and, as a problem, overstated.[45] Hayek refuted, for example, the notion that technological progress can actually stifle competition by limiting participation to those with technical knowledge. He believed this idea to be a chimera derived from the "Marxist doctrine of the 'concentration of industry'" that created a dichotomy "between control of production by private monopolies and direction by the government."[46] This false dilemma was advanced by opponents of competition in order to impose their idealist vision: the omnipotent state.

Hayek's optimism for the freedom-enhancing qualities of competition even in the face of cultural complexity and rapid technological change resulted from his enthusiasm for the price system. "The more complicated the whole," Hayek stated, "the more dependent we become on that division of knowledge between individuals whose separate efforts are coordinated by the impersonal mechanism for transmitting the relevant information known by us as the price system."[47] Local knowledge expressed through the subjective choices of individuals is essential to accurate pricing and thus supportive of market coordination. Ben Jackson observes how Hayek arrived at "one of his most important insights, namely that markets functioned as devices that coordinated knowledge that was otherwise dispersed among different individuals."[48] Anything that restricts local knowledge from exchange or distorts asset pricing disturbs the natural coordination function of the market. Certainly, that disruptor can be government, but it is not necessarily so.

Recent changes in the mortgage market illustrate how accurate pricing and, thus, efficient resource allocation, can be challenged by financial developments. In many cases the "distributed local knowledge" Hayek deemed so important to market function[49] has been abridged by the displacement of local mortgage companies by national (and often online) lenders that have limited familiarity with specific communities. Scholars also have observed how a credit bubble from 1997–2007 supported by growth in mortgage securitization—the common practice of mortgage companies bundling individual mortgages together as a common security in order to trade them on the secondary market—led to an escalation in real housing prices.[50] The expansion of mortgage-backed securities also corresponded to "an enormous failure by the private sector to recognize and adequately price mortgage default risk."[51] The combination of mortgage securitization, relaxed credit requirements, innovative financing models, and laxity by some credit rating agencies all helped create the conditions for the subprime mortgage binge and the crisis that followed. That crisis led to acceptance of government involvement to stabilize markets and, eventually, to rectify perceived injustices as mortgage companies were accused of "foreclosure abuse."[52]

Problems in the mortgage market reveal how market disruptions can result from both government action and private sector developments. They also reinforce Hayek's warnings about government paternalism. Regardless of the source of market disturbances that prompt state interventions, such actions almost inevitably result in unforeseen effects. Gerald P. O'Driscoll notes how Hayek cautioned especially against "countercyclical policy to combat cyclical declines," quoting the Austrian economist concerning the Great Depression from his *Monetary Theory and the Trade Cycle* that to "combat the depression by a forced credit expansion is to attempt to cure the evil by the very means which brought it about."[53] Such policies, as all government interventions, presume an impossible knowledge of cause and effect and, thus, are likely to have unintended consequences.

Overconfidence in the market system

Just as unanticipated outcomes can result from trust in the ability of state agencies to intervene in the economy with the appropriate policies and timing, others argue that overconfidence in the adjustment capabilities of the market, especially in conditions like those of the "new" mortgage market that emerged, can have negative effects. Excess confidence in capitalism's capacity for self-correction is thought to have contributed to a neoliberal attitude that encouraged regulators to look the other way as financial excesses came to light. Robert Prasch believes today's regulatory culture of finance is built on the Hayekian conviction that "market outcomes 'must be' the collective consequence of innumerable useful innovations and successful decisions." It also results from the impossibility of comprehensive regulation, which would depend on a "vast and changing quantity of 'local knowledge.' "[54] A growing awareness of how government actions have exacerbated past economic problems reinforces a hands-off approach, on the assumption that markets eventually adjust and thereby preclude government intervention. Once interventions have occurred, however, there is continuing pressure to sustain government involvement. In this regard, Alan Greenspan's "shocked disbelief"[55] at the failure of the financial system to self-correct was less shocking to some Hayek defenders, who pointed to policies—prolonged periods of artificially low interest rates and state-subsidized home ownership programs, in particular—as causing the housing bubble.[56]

Indeed, more of Hayek's followers should have shuddered during the run-up to the recent chaos. They should have recognized that securitization of otherwise tangible and local assets such as mortgages was leading to the abstraction of asset information into ether. Moreover, they should have become wary when analysts began describing asset prices as "misleading," especially given the critical function of price in Hayek's economic thought. Economist Michael Perelman has observed how the "allure of fictitious capital" distorted asset pricing as a whole and contributed to growing instabilities that are still being worked out of the system.[57]

Hayek was prescient in many ways, though not with respect to the impact of "technique" on modern markets. He may not have envisioned the advent of complex asset-backed securities—facilitated by technical advances—where the value and risk of these instruments can confound even trained financial professionals. And that is even before one considers the willingness of brokerage firms to understate the number of bad assets in the securities they sell, as in the case of Merrill Lynch in 2011.[58] The development of derivative instruments based on complicated algorithms accessible to only a select few would seem to undermine the critical roles of information and price in disciplining behavior, which Hayek saw as essential to properly functioning markets.

Processes associated with financialization can both distort asset pricing and accent information asymmetry, providing greater legitimacy to those who insist that government intervention is necessary to preserve justice in economic relations. Unfortunately, this attitude also makes the threat of serfdom more real. In such conditions, firms seek security by eliminating "unknowns" that often involve forms of coordinated activity with other players. One question arising from Hayek's ideas is whether certain developments in financial markets—including bank mergers, investment firms gaining preferential access to exchange servers, institutional investors receiving trading priority in IPOs, and so forth—can be considered elements of "planning." Industry "coordination," at least, is evident in that financial institutions commonly follow the lead of innovators, and regulators have at times appeared to turn a blind eye to dubious forms of competition. As shown in the last chapter, banking and investment firms, acting in concert, periodically have invoked the "Wall Street Rule" to coerce regulators into inaction.

Hayek's thought fails to account adequately for such behavior. He seems to minimize the importance of market concentration on competition and assumes rather clear divisions between public and private sectors, suggesting that planning is solely a state activity. He did recognize some elasticity in planning, as Peter Boettke and Nicholas Snow recognize with their comment that Hayek "demonstrates that planning could be democratic, but incoherent, or coherent but dictatorial."[59] If only Hayek had added that planning can also be "capitalist," with its coherence determined by factors like market structure, ease of firm entry, and government involvement in industry, then he would have offered a fuller picture of the planning continuum.

Such a picture, however, might have implied the possibility of a middle way that Hayek found unacceptable. In the gray area between government control and true liberty, Hayek perceived a netherworld of inept, inevitably harmful government action where state institutions, convinced of their good intentions, would enact poorly conceived programs that distort markets and throw the system into chaos. The middle way was no way, a route to endless state tinkering in affairs over which it has little knowledge and, thus, to perpetual obstruction of productive behavior and destabilization of the economic system. Hayek stated,

> The close interdependence of all economic phenomena, makes it difficult to stop planning just where we wish and … once the free working of the market is impeded beyond a certain degree, the planner will be forced to extend his controls *until they become all comprehensive.*[60]

In other words, once government embarks on planning, it becomes impossible to stop. This attitude also reinforced clear divisions of function in Hayek's thought among political, legal, and private entities that supported his later views, which many have described as libertarian.[61]

Suppose for a moment, however, that the "functional" line between government and private institutions is less distinct than Hayek surmised. What if a major sector of society, because of its sheer size and technical complexity, has grown beyond the oversight capability of government and has come to wield significant influence within its host society because of the perception that its collapse would be catastrophic? Suppose also that, through consolidation and other means, the major organizations in this industry have forged a significant power bloc capable of exercising control over industry structure, pricing, and even regulation. Furthermore, imagine that the classic oligopoly model of economic behavior holds—that corporations follow each other's moves in relative symmetry. Are the potential "social" consequences of such a system so different from one in which the political establishment "embarks on planning" because democratic institutions have proven inadequate to resolve technical issues? If Hayek's logic has a utopian aspect, one sees it in his confidence that market vigor in the absence of state involvement would naturally level the playing field and prevent the rise of coercive power. With respect to contemporary financial problems, at least some of which appear to have been associated with "deregulation," a different situation has emerged.

After the damage caused by rogue trading and excessive leveraging, government intervened. Surprisingly, government purchases of shares in major banks and the insurance giant AIG, except for minor protests and some public posturing by politicians, were met with relative indifference. Although supporters of federal initiatives observe that the government has divested itself of these holdings at a profit, the perceived "success" of the programs may well portend that future state incursions into the private sector will be met by even less opposition. This interventionist mindset is of the kind Hayek described that leads to serfdom.

Hayek recognized furthermore a critical threshold in "resource control" that, once exceeded, results in state domination over the lives of its citizens. "Although the state controls directly the use of only a large part of the available resources," Hayek wrote, "the effects of its decisions on the remaining part of the economic system become so great that indirectly it controls almost everything."[62] The potent combination of large financial interests and state power seem to reinforce the threat Hayek observed; it matters little if government is acting to tame those interests since its actions have "unintended consequences." In the context of the financialized society's technocratic tendencies discussed in the previous chapter, one might even substitute the word "finance" for Hayek's "the state" in the previous quotation and still find Hayek in agreement.

Some politicians recognize the need for preserving the demos' control over its finances. Senator Elizabeth Warren of Massachusetts has staunchly advocated reenacting the Glass–Steagall legislation that divided commercial from investment banking for more than 60 years. In making the case, she has called public attention to an important fact: the four largest American banks are now 30 percent larger than they were five years ago.[63] This growth of concentration in banking at a time when many called for breaking up the industry reveals not only the considerable clout of financial interests in the U.S. but indicates the willingness of government to facilitate the creation of massive financial firms if officials believe such action can stave off threats to the "system."

That attitude was confirmed by a series of meetings in March 2008 when Secretary of the Treasury Henry Paulson, Fed Chair Ben Bernanke, and the president of the New York Fed, Timothy Geithner, met with the leaders of American finance to facilitate the rescue of AIG, the acquisition of Bear Stearns and Washington Mutual by JPMorgan Chase, and Bank of America's acquisition of Merrill Lynch. Through those actions, the U.S. government helped to determine the banking structure of which Warren is now critical. In light of the financial industry's demonstrated proclivity to excess and the willingness of government to bail out firms "too big to fail" or become involved to stabilize an economy undermined by financial mismanagement or abuses, and one may say with little hyperbole that the financial system indirectly controls almost everything.

"Planning" fills a void

Recent developments in the financial industry indicate the extent to which specialization encourages planning. Those involved, however, are not merely, or even primarily, government bureaucrats. The kind of planning that has evolved undoubtedly includes regulators, but also lobbyists, bank officials, hedge fund managers, high-speed traders, and large investors whose specialized knowledge and interdependency with other participants compels coordination. Those actors "compete" but must also cooperate in certain ways that defy the notion of true market competition. In *Flash Boys*, Michael Lewis described the existence of "dark pools," private stock exchanges designed for large investors and operated by large brokerages that convinced their customers that "*transparency was the enemy*."[64] These unique institutions conceal the trading activities of major players in a way that public exchanges do not so that the wider market cannot react to their moves. Lewis uses the example of Fidelity entering the market to sell a million shares of Microsoft. In the public exchange context, a major trade often involves many transactions that cannot be completed at once, allowing the rest of the market to react. In Lewis's example, it would cause the share price of Microsoft to dip, thus incurring a cost to Fidelity. Inside the dark pool, only the broker and transacting parties have knowledge of trading activity, so Microsoft's stock price could be maintained until the completion of a major trade.[65] Dark pools serve to coordinate financial activity so that big-time players can predict the consequences of their trades and insulate themselves from some of the market volatility associated with public exchanges. In short, dark pools provide greater certainty in investment.

Dark pools and similar institutions develop naturally from a common motivation that philosopher John Dewey observed long ago: the quest for certainty. If one may reduce to a single cause the financial crisis that began in 2008, it was the obsessive desire of investors to find the holy grail of the industry: risk-free investment. Removing government from the equation does not hinder the quest or prevent various interests from attempting to coordinate their activities to enable more certain outcomes. Adam Smith famously noted, "People of the same trade seldom meet together, even for merriment and diversion, but the conversation ends in a conspiracy against the public, or in some contrivance to raise prices."[66] Perhaps Smith's comment need not have mentioned "conspiracy" or referenced the public as a target at all. Businessmen desire greater certainty in their quest for profits regardless of conspiratorial methods; some attempts to achieve it will work against the public interest and may involve "extra-market" methods.

Similarly, consumers and investors desire greater certainty that at times may work against some producers' interests. In a financialized society, all acquire a rent-seeking attitude because of greater volatility and heightened competition. Finance, because of its inherent risks and sophistication, promotes rent-seeking behavior, and its extensive reach makes such activity seem all encompassing. According to Paul Dembinski, director of the Observatoire de la Finance and a professor of the University of Fribourg, finance "is not actually totalitarian, but is certainly 'totalizing.' Its complexity makes it very suitable for division of responsibility, which insulates players from the consequences of their acts."[67] The division of responsibility and the masking of market players and their actions only accent the need for supplemental forms of coordination.

A significant criticism of Hayek is that his dogmatic objections to planning in general seem to neglect the pragmatic need for planning *on some level.* He recognized, of course, that governments as well as private organizations and individuals must plan certain activities. Hayek even understood that, in special cases, planning may benefit the whole:

> It is, for example, at least conceivable that the British automobile industry might be able to supply a car cheaper and better than cars used to be in the United States if everyone in England were made to use the same kind of car or that the use of electricity for all purposes could be made cheaper than coal or gas if everybody could be made to use only electricity.[68]

Thus, in some situations involving "compulsory standardization or the prohibition of variety beyond a certain degree, abundance might be increased in some fields more than sufficiently to compensate for the restriction of choice by the consumer."[69] As a general rule, however, attempts to plan production are woefully misguided and result in inefficiencies that make everyone worse off; moreover, they lead to the centralization of power.

Interestingly, Hayek typically associated those special cases that justify central planning with the need for technological standardization, even though he strongly contested the idea that the advance of technology makes centralized planning inevitable:

> While it is true, of course, that inventions have given us tremendous power, it is absurd to suggest that we must use this power to destroy our most important inheritance: liberty. It does mean, however, that if we want to preserve it, we must guard it more jealously than ever and that we must be prepared to make sacrifices for it. While there is nothing in modern technological developments which forces us toward comprehensive economic planning, there is a great

> deal in them which makes infinitely more dangerous the power a planning authority would possess.[70]

This last argument was decisive for Hayek's belief that the spontaneous order is superior to any sort of planned order, no matter the extent of technological development. He insisted that the inclination to planning is based on a "complete misapprehension" of the way competition functions in society. In fact, "far from being appropriate only to comparatively simple conditions, it is the very complexity of the division of labor under modern conditions which makes competition the *only* method by which such coordination can be adequately brought about."[71] In other words, as coordination needs become more widespread because of social and technical intricacies, the importance of competitive markets grows. Imperfections in those markets such as information asymmetry, however, keep the planning impulse alive as participants seek to overcome the system's limitations.

Planning in practice

In the 1980s, institutional economist John Munkirs advanced his "centralized private sector planning model" (CPSP), which he believed to represent more realistically the role of planning in the field of economics. With this construct, Munkirs attempted to break down a dichotomy that tends to define the economic world as either capitalist and competitive or socialist and centrally planned. This dualism makes too hard and fast a distinction between capitalism and socialism. Just as entrepreneurship often develops in state-run economies, some need for planning arises even in free market economies. Munkirs produced statistics showing critical dependencies in the areas of finance, technology, and administration that revealed how American corporations use planning instruments to coordinate their production and distribution activities. Among the instruments Munkirs identified were "formal and/or legally binding planning instruments"—boards of directors, stocks, and corporate debt (primarily bonds). More informal instruments (numbering in the hundreds) included trustees, transfer agents, and stock registrars whose knowledge of the financial intentions of American corporations made them valuable sources of expertise and enabled them to perform certain coordination functions.[72]

Munkirs noted seven major banks (including J. P. Morgan, Citicorp), four insurance companies (including Prudential, New York Life), and one diversified financial institution (Continental Corporation) on which he gathered statistics to prove these corporations constituted the Central Planning Core (CPC) of the American economy. These CPC corporations might be thought of as a national financial hub. Munkirs described the "interstitial elements" (formal and informal planning instruments and processes) that "bond these institutions into a cohesive and solid structural and functional unit."[73] He provided statistics on governing board "intralocks" within the CPC, in which the same board member sits on more than one CPC board, and also "interlocks" among governing boards, situations in which board members of a non-CPC corporation also sit on the boards of directors of at least one corporation that is part of the CPC. Munkirs noted that, in 1978, for example, 35 percent of General Electric Corporation's board of directors was directly interlocked with the CPC, and 41 percent of Exxon Corporation's board members also sat on the boards of CPC companies. Regarding the Central Planning Core itself, Munkirs also showed that 29 percent of New York Life's board and 39 percent of Continental Corporation's board were intralocked with other corporations within the CPC.[74] Along with others such as stock ownership structures and corporate debt relationships, those linkages effectively represent instruments of coordination important in determining the overall direction and health of the American economy.

Munkirs' objective was not to expose the "evils" of the CPSP system—he saw it as practical necessity more than collusion—but rather to create a more functionally accurate model of the American economy. By fostering "*effective* rational debate and solutions to the country's increasingly disruptive economic problems," he also sought to help break the grip of a damaging ideological divide that limits our economic self-knowledge.[75] The CPSP model suggests that without at least minimal public planning to support industry, private planning self-initiates to fill the void. Munkirs argued that "conscious awareness of these interdependencies would almost automatically contribute to a great deal of intra- and inter-industry coordination and cooperation, that is, to CPSP"; to act otherwise, he said, would be "highly irrational."[76] Munkirs also argued that "structure begets behavior." When coordination among major market players reaches a certain level, the CPSP model more accurately describes the economy than does the perfect competition model of neoclassical economics, despite the fact that the latter provides the theoretical framework for financial models used to support American business and is commonly taught in American business schools.[77]

Other scholars have observed forms of coordination that have developed in American industry. William Lazonick has shown how a major aspect of financialization—that of "maximizing shareholder value"—has become dominant in evaluating corporate performance. Lazonick shows that the extreme emphasis on share price, combined with companies' use of the stock market for "compensation and combination functions," causes financially driven firms across many industries to follow similar patterns, emphasizing debt over equity financing and using stock repurchases to boost share price. Yet, in many cases, according to Lazonick, these policies have curbed innovation and have created instability and inequity in the American economy.[78]

Lazonick's observations are consistent with those of Munkirs: absent "official" planning mechanisms, formal and informal means of private coordination evolve to fill the planning void. Libor is an interesting example because, although it is coordinated through the British Bankers' Association (BBA), its member banks span national boundaries; thus, regulation by a single public entity is virtually impossible.[79] The Libor scandal made news in 2012 when multiple banks were accused of manipulating the benchmark Libor interbank loan rate that impacts interest charges on trillions of dollars in loans worldwide.

Homeowners and other groups initiated class-action lawsuits, and the British megabank Barclays, at the center of the scandal, agreed to a $453 million settlement in the case.[80] Despite Libor's obvious potential for "rigging," market determination of interest rates at which banks loan funds to each other has been considered impractical, though it is now being reevaluated. The Libor method, which involves polling 18 major banks for estimates of their costs of capital in interbank loans, arose out of necessity. The Libor scandal reinforces the idea that "extra-market" attempts at coordination are likely to have unintended, often negative, consequences.

Whatever criticisms one might level against Munkirs' modeling or methodological approach, he offered economics a gift it largely rejected. He implored Congress to commission a detailed study of the American economy, and he encouraged American political leadership to "stop all the self-serving ideological prattle about the Welfare State, Socialism, and Capitalism and, instead, take a long hard look at the economy's dominant structural and functional characteristics."[81] Sadly, Munkirs made little dent in the ideological deadlock between "free markets" and "centralized planning." In retrospect, the failure to heed his call may have been shortsighted. Some have suggested the financial crisis revealed the limitations of economic models based on the unrealistic assumptions of neoclassical theory.[82] Because key figures such as Alan Greenspan placed great trust in mainstream economics and its models, mounting financial problems either went undetected or were considered correctable by market forces and resulting problems arguably were exacerbated.

However regulation is refashioned to account for the problems that have come to light, the regulatory system is likely to remain inadequate because incentives of market players are often difficult to identify and, even when recognized, tend to adjust to changing conditions, often prompting new regulatory dilemmas. This cat-and-mouse method of regulation is likely to be reaffirmed with the recent revelations that high-speed traders are buying faster access in order to jump ahead of other investors and "scalp" profits off the top. Any rules applied to new market phenomena will become the new constraints within which to optimize firm profitability; regulators will forever lag behind traders in this game because of the latter's profit motivation and superior resources. Unrealistic models make growing risk factors and instabilities in the system only more difficult to detect.

Hayek on concentration and regulation

How Hayek would view the role of industry concentration in recent financial crises is uncertain. His thought on monopoly, in general, is less straightforward than many of the other concepts he expounded in *The Road to Serfdom*. Ellen Frankel Paul describes Hayek's views on monopoly as "perhaps the most tangled" of his economic ideas.[83] As noted, Hayek rejected the popular belief that gives rise to regulation: the impotence of competition in technical environments leaves citizens with a choice between "private monopolies and direction by the government." Instead, he believed the root cause for the breakdown of market competition that leads to the "concentration of industry" lies not in technological change but rather in state policy.[84] The promotion of protectionist policies by governments has led to the rise of giant monopolies and their negative effects on competition. To make his case, Hayek uses two examples: (1) Germany beginning around 1878 with the expansion of "cartels and syndicates" that was "systematically fostered by deliberate policy"; and (2) Great Britain in the post-Depression era when government set out to protect its industries by establishing a path toward economic recovery.[85] In both cases, the attempts of states to boost their economies through central coordination and protectionism resulted in the creation of monopolies that damaged competition. Hayek derives from these examples a basic principle: government attempts at industry coordination are impossible and generally detrimental because of the incompleteness of available information and the inability to coordinate timely action by all players. The problem of such coordination, writ large, is the impossibility of socialism.

Hayek also suggests another cause of monopoly in what he called the "universal struggle against competition."[86] He also saw that general hostility as a major motive behind most attempts at regulation. Regarding growing industry concentration in finance and recent calls for reregulation, however, many fault not anticompetitive policies but instead the deregulation of the financial industry, beginning in the 1980s and culminating with the repeal in 1999 of the Glass–Steagall Act, which not only deconstructed the firewall between commercial and investment banks but also enabled insurance companies to engage in securities trading. Little evidence of hostility to competition preceded former Treasury Secretary Lawrence Summers' announcement of "historic legislation" that "would better enable American companies to compete in the new economy."[87] At a time when retirement account balances, along with corporate profits, were surging, most turned a blind eye to questions like that posed by the Federal Reserve Bank of Dallas concerning whether bank mergers were "creating value or destroying competition," when it reported in 1998 that the number of banks in the U.S. dropped from around 14,500 in 1984 to approximately 9,000.[88] Regardless, given Hayek's apprehensions about government attempts to limit concentration, "anticompetitive" action in the form of mergers was not what he was referring to with his comments on "hostility to competition." Rather, Hayek meant a pervasive spirit of "anticompetition" that instigates the movement toward centralized planning.

Senator Warren perhaps has been the most vocal critic by calling for the breakup of large banks that resulted both from deregulation and the emergency acquisitions and mergers deemed necessary by officials to save the economy; Hayek doubtless would be more reluctant. He established strict guidelines regarding the harm necessary to prove allegations of monopolistic activity. Consumer coercion is a necessary feature but is by itself insufficient. The services being "coerced" must also be essential to the consumer's subsistence. "So long as the services of a particular person are not crucial to my existence or the preservation of what I most value," Hayek explained, "the conditions he exacts for rendering these services cannot properly be called 'coercion.'"[89] Monopoly is possible only with "essential commodities." Hayek also gave little weight to the concentration of producers and the size of firms in a given industry when determining what constitutes monopoly. Paul notes that "bigness itself is not a problem" for Hayek; rather, obstacles to entry into the market were his principal concern.[90]

Government incompetence and oppression, as much as any other factors, determined Hayek's resistance to state action against monopolies. In industries such as electricity, gas, and railways where "monopoly is inevitable," he insisted that leaving the individual monopolies in "private hands" (for example, not allowing gas and electricity monopolies to be controlled by one company) is better for the consumer than state control.[91]

As an alternative to government regulation, Hayek recommended that industries regulate themselves by using the legal system to file civil suits against firms that act to squelch competition.[92] This form of "regulation," however, has obvious limitations. Contemporarily, it would allow large firms, especially in highly technical industries, to build defenses with their legal resources in a system that increasingly determines winners and losers through attrition as much as evidence. In the context of the American financial industry, Hayek's "privatized" regulatory paradigm seems inadequate given the pervasiveness of behavior that jeopardized the financial system and still seething public anger over the rarity of indictments from such misdeeds. With its unique combination of technological sophistication, functional specialization, and crucial intermediary role in the overall economy, finance is particularly intimidating.

Hayek likely failed to anticipate how complexity and the structure of industry complicate the determination of when states should act or leave an industry to regulate itself. According to Paul, Hayek "was convinced that the 'rule of law' provides an adequate and clear line beyond which government action is impermissible."[93] Although Hayek placed great emphasis on the rule of law as *the* safeguard against unfair practices, that dependence on law assumed the ability of lawmaking bodies to keep up with changes in technically complex industries like finance. Hayek himself discounted the possibility in those sections of *The Road to Serfdom* in which he wrote about frustrated legislatures turning to "specialists." This presents a subtle, though critical, distinction (and perhaps contradiction) in Hayek's thought: legislators who attempt to engage technical issues must delegate responsibility to specialists whose different designs cannot be reconciled. Therefore, the very law that Hayek sees as crucial to the proper functioning of the spontaneous order becomes deficient by virtue of the process by which it is enacted.

If Hayek overemphasized the role of *government* in planning while underestimating the planning motivations of private interests because of his confidence in the competitive safeguards found in the legal and pricing systems, and, if he also stressed a general hostility toward competition that does not seem evident today, how do we explain that in some ways we appear to be heading down the road

Hayek feared? First, some of Hayek's predictions have come true. Endless conflict has created widespread dysfunction in the legislative process. The political system has been complicated by the maze of special interests, lobbyists, and activist organizations, all of which intend to bring constituent values into the process but ultimately confuse more than clarify. Moreover, the rising technical complexity of issues themselves requires experts to educate legislators on various topics. As a result, industry professionals and nonelected public officials who staff congressional offices, in many cases, must craft the details of legislation—witness the Byzantine construction of the Dodd–Frank legislation. One Senate finance committee staffer complained that the models with which she works and from which she makes recommendations to legislators have become "black boxes" in need of much greater transparency. She states that legislative staffs are bombarded by confusing models and that "modelers owe it to policymakers to show as clearly as possible the key drivers of the models."[94] Thus, it appears policies are being developed based on the results of models that often are not well understood.

One particular case illustrates how market players take advantage of regulatory complexity. In July 2013, a *Bloomberg Businessweek* report described an IRS investigation of Renaissance Technologies, founded by billionaire James Simons, who rechanneled his mathematical genius from the role of Cold War code breaker to hedge fund manager. Renaissance engaged in a technique of buying what are called "basket option contracts" from major banks like Barclays in a way that allowed its $10 billion Medallion Fund to convert the fund's "rapid trading" profits into long-term capital gains, lowering the tax liabilities of investors.[95] The banks bought investment portfolios with the securities that Renaissance fund managers desired to trade and then paid Renaissance to manage the portfolio. The Medallion Fund would then buy a two-year option contract tied to the value of the portfolio, allowing it to report the ownership of only one asset—the option contract. Since the contract was held for longer than one year, investors in the fund could report as long-term gain any income deriving from it. According to Steven Rosenthal, a fellow at the Urban Institute in Washington and former tax attorney, "the profits are just being transmuted, through the alchemy of derivatives, to a preferenced return."[96] Innovative financial tools like derivatives are enabling financial alchemy to flourish, defying conventional forms of regulation and, just as troubling, implying that Hayek's preferred regulatory method—self-regulation—is increasingly unrealistic.

Democratic versus technocratic regulation

Growth in financial complexity presses the question whether socially broad-based forms of regulation can provide an alternative to the present default form: technocratic regulation. Matthew Desmond investigated the possibility of a "democratic" regulatory system and arrived at some interesting conclusions. Desmond began his inquiry by asking a simple but pertinent question: "Are we (the U.S.) stupider than Canada?" He notes that prior to the crisis, many nations, including even the Chinese, thought that Canadians represented financial backwardness.[97] As others were securitizing and lowering reserve requirements, the Canadians were raising them. The result of such financial primitivism? Canada emerged as the "only G7 country to weather the financial crisis without a state bailout of its financial sector."[98] Desmond cites Chrystia Freeland of the *Financial Times*, who had been investigating how Canada stayed dry during a financial tempest that soaked so many. He summarizes Freeland's conclusion concerning Canada's financial integrity with the words "rules and institutions," citing "capital requirements, quality of capital, and leverage ratio" in addition to a regulatory environment that holds bank executives personally responsible for the risks their institutions take. Canadian finance ministers had the gumption to say "no to financial manipulations just as complex and obfuscated as the ones we in the United States said yes to."[99] Importantly, this expansion of financial complexity makes remote the possibility of more democratic forms of regulation.

In *Flash Boys*, Matthew Lewis also affirmed the sanity of Canadians in the midst of the world's destabilizing financial craze by bringing to public attention Brad Katsuyama, a former head trader of the Royal Bank of Canada Capital Markets. Katsuyama played a major role in exposing high-speed traders' (HSTs) "rigging" of financial markets. In the perception of both Lewis and Katsuyama, the mercurial high-speed traders are "scalpers" in that they acquire faster routes along the exchange network to attain a preferential vantage on data transfers between private exchanges and the major exchanges—the New York Stock Exchange, NASDAQ, etc. In fact, a group of investors have filed suit, alleging that the Chicago Mercantile Exchange sold "market data to high-frequency traders, cheating other investors who lacked such access."[100]

Even where data is not sold, the preferential positions of HSTs in the trading network enable them to detect major security trades, initiated often by institutional investors, which one transaction cannot accomplish. With their superior connections, these HSTs step in front of other traders with knowledge that transactions needed to complete a major market move are "on the way" only milliseconds later, allowing them to begin their own transactions with this foreknowledge and secure near guaranteed profits. "Cutting in line" raises the prices of securities in cases of major stock purchases, even if only by a small fraction, but it frees the HSTs to "buy low and sell high" based purely on speed, without needing to analyze what is being traded.[101]

Finance has become, in many cases, a game in which product "innovation" outpaces society's ability to assess its risks and benefits. Speed and complexity create "value" by enhancing the market positions of certain traders and accentuating already substantial information asymmetries. Growing sophistication means fewer players can participate in the game, which leads to greater concentrations of wealth. Major income shifts accompany the trading of assets that, in some cases, cannot be defined with accuracy even by those who trade them. As taxpayers observing from the sidelines witness economic instability and must bail out some of those with the resources to play these high-stakes games, public indignation justifiably rises.

Interesting, with respect to the above, was public criticism that arose regarding the distribution of funds from the Troubled Asset Relief Program (TARP). The funds were intended to spur bank lending and provide capital for mortgage modification and other measures to benefit consumers. Some have charged, however, that intense lobbying enabled the large banks partly responsible for the financial mess to fortify their own positions even as they restricted loan creation, defying a principal purpose of the legislation.[102]

The changing financial culture of the U.S. has enabled new rules and institutions to develop that Canadians notably rejected. Bank mergers and consolidations were buoyed by the Financial Services Modernization Act of 1999, which did away not only with the Glass–Steagall provisions separating commercial from investment banking but also restrictions associated with the 1956 Bank Holding Company Act.[103] The Modernization Act was supported overwhelmingly by both Republicans and Democrats (the Senate vote was 90 to 8 in favor). Senator Phil Gramm (R-Texas) stated, "The world changes, and Congress and the laws have to change with it."[104] There could be a no more Hayekian description of this legislation. Gramm's statement implied that day-to-day exchanges in the spontaneous order determine the *real rules* of financial conduct. Moreover, those changes presuppose little need for collective reflection on either the nation's original economic ideals or how market competition impacts social and moral development. Legislators are left primarily to codify those normative changes forged in the marketplace.

Gramm's statement is also informed by those technocratic aspects of the financial system revealed in the previous chapter. Perhaps the most telling evidence of the move toward technocracy is the form of regulation presently taking shape. It is crafted not from a national vision of what the people desire from the financial system but rather from agreement among experts who set the rules by which the players (including many of those same experts) play the game. This structure limits the ability of many to understand, participate in, and benefit from the financial system, leading to divisions in wealth and general discontent with a critical component of the economy. K. Sabeel Rahman observes that the "expert-driven and rational" approach to financial regulation leads to a problem in that the regulatory ethos "obscures the reality of the normative disputes underlying seemingly technical policy questions."[105] According to Desmond, this reality means that contemporary society is revisiting a problem that has plagued classical philosophers like Plato and modern economists like Joseph Schumpeter: "Can we regulate democratically systems of enormous complexity—or must we settle for regulating through technocratic means?"[106] The default answer, absent a robust discussion of the present financial state of affairs, surely will be the latter.

The consequences of financialization not only complicate the ability to achieve a healthy debate over the structure, efficiency, and fairness of the financial industry, but also obscure conditions in which Hayek's theories on planning may be assessed. Planning in the financialized society—as witnessed in the recent financial crisis—is not so much the attempt by government to coordinate resources in the direction of some social goal. Rather, planning is often undertaken as much for rescue as for guidance. Planning in recent years has involved the construction of highly technical strategies to escape immediate, potentially disastrous problems posed by developments in markets that many Americans considered necessary. The loan of TARP funds and even government purchases of equity in insurance and banking companies generally were supported, although they led some bloggers to christen Federal Reserve Chairman Ben Bernanke the "finance dictator" even as others praised him as preventing collapse of the global economy.

Whatever the public impression of these "planning" actions, they involved the construction of recovery blueprints more so than development plans. Market disruptions have done more than simply encourage government encroachments into the financial sector, however. In some cases they convolute the determination of means and ends. Dembinski states that "when infinite multiplication of assets becomes an end in itself, an ultimate goal that predominates over others, finance becomes a tyrant."[107] He describes financialization as the "culminating phase" of what Karl Polanyi termed "the great transformation."[108] According to Dembinski, financialization is the manifestation of the loss of social and political control over economy in which, "in the absence of any countervailing forces, [economics and finance] have come to prevail over metaphysics, society, and politics."[109] Calls for political reforms are ineffectual—"pious hopes or idealistic incantations"—that have little if any possibility of success.[110] Dembinski is among those who speak of the increasingly deterministic quality of contemporary finance, which pulls assets into its domain, at an alarming rate, and deprives them of meaning.[111]

Hayek surmised that the elimination of subjective choice through the rising encroachments of government poses the greatest threat to both meaning and liberty in economic life, which remains a danger through the continual expansion of state power. Hayek may not have foreseen a more immediate concern: meaning can be lost even as choice seemingly is enabled. Choice inundates consumers and investors today, but the mask of a financialized economy obscures the lack of true options available. Complex investment products, financial illiteracy, and even misrepresentation of investment options by those who market them inhibit true choice. Investors swim in a sea of stocks, bonds, mutual funds, and other instruments of nominal diversity that often belies truth. Mutual funds, for example, often significantly "overlap" other funds in asset composition such that the *appearance* of diversity betrays the reality. Bill Chennault, the Executive Director of Instructional Technology and Information Systems at Kansas City Kansas Community College, found significant overlap in mutual funds and particularly within fund families. Investigating the popular Janus family of funds, he found an average 19 percent overlap among the asset holdings of 12 Janus funds, ranging as high as 66 percent overlap between the Janus Worldwide Fund and Janus Overseas Fund.[112] The likelihood that many "owners" of these mutual funds do not realize the extent of overlap (and, incidentally, pay different fund managers separate fees to "manage" the same assets)[113] furthers the illusion of choice in investment. Investor ignorance concerning the assets held in the funds they own, moreover, deprives those investments of meaning.

Dembinski agrees with those who suggest that the only force powerful enough to stem this deterministic system is "one based on the question of meaning."[114] Citing Jean-Baptiste de Foucauld, Dembinski states that the human spirit itself contains within it the "sole antidote to the implacable logic" of finance, technology, and efficiency in its insistence on a life of meaning—one that values preservation of relationships more than technical efficiency.[115] Alexis de Tocqueville, an astute commentator on American society, noted that civil society is an essential source of meaning in democracies like the United States. In addition to instilling purpose and meaning in American culture, the rich diversity of intermediate organizations in the United States provides a potentially critical resource for addressing "how" finance might be reformed that would seem to ameliorate concerns from constituencies across the ideological spectrum.

The greater involvement of civil society in the financial system would conform to Hayek's vision of minimal government and his preference for societal decisions deriving from spontaneous interactions in the private sphere. Such an approach to contemporary financial problems, especially concerning the need for greater transparency and industry oversight, should also appeal to those who are receptive to government involvement but "prefer" solutions that originate in the private sector. This group would seem to constitute a vast cross-section of Americans who recognize pitfalls to both government regulation and private-sector concentration. Most importantly, a regulatory system that draws from public-spirited, intermediate organizations for its values offers the possibility for breaking through the present technocratic regime. As will be seen, however, civil society is itself hamstrung by financial concerns and the involvement of vested interests that often encroach upon the mission, and even integrity, of these organizations.

Conclusion

The alternate road posed by financialization does not refute Hayek's theory of how free societies can devolve into serfdom. Rather, it supplements his views with some realistic assumptions concerning markets that have come to light in recent years. First, asset pricing in highly financial economies appears less stable than in traditional agricultural or industrial economies, limiting the ability of the pricing system to efficiently allocate resources and naturally curb market power. Second, distinctions between "public" and "private" become opaque as market economies grow in institutional and technological sophistication. Those market participants that *should* look out for the public interest will change as markets evolve and particular actors find themselves in powerful, privileged niche positions, often through good fortune as much as business acumen. Finally, the maxim revised here as "*planning* fills a void" seems more relevant than in the past because the financialized economy appears to accent volatility and uncertainty. In conditions of perceived disorder, institutions evolve and relationships form to plug the coordination gap, as parties seek greater certainty to their actions.

A major complication with Hayek's spontaneous order is that spontaneity occasionally works against order. Hayek offers a convincing argument that a democratic society that "embarks on planning" takes a significant step down the path to serfdom; yet it is also true that a society that ignores the need for some economic coordination may defer to forms of *coordinated competition* between specialized interests "over the heads" of citizens, leading to political instability. In criticizing the pretensions of planners who believe they can judiciously terminate processes where they wish, Hayek says, "there is such a thing as the inherent logic of events, which forces us forward on a given path whether we logically think it out beforehand or not."[116] Hayek certainly is correct. Yet his observation applies to *laissez faire* as much as command planning. The former also has an inherent logic that leads its advocates to counsel inaction even in the face of rising market concentration and makes them less observant of the possibility for producers to act in ways that effectively constitute planning.

These observations make a civil society solution an appealing alternative to the ideas of both those who see greater government oversight of the financial sector as the answer, as well as those who insist that unregulated markets will naturally correct any abuses or moral hazards that form. Addressing present problems through civil society also should appeal to all those who desire to re-inject meaning into economic life. The next chapter demonstrates, however, that the financialization of American civil society threatens the ability of its organizations to fulfill their critical mediating roles between citizens and large institutions, both public and private. The steady encroachment of financial values and interests erodes the "altruistic spirit" of religious, civic, and educational institutions needed to help form moral citizens for self-government and to preserve economic justice. Effectively countering the cultural impact of financialization requires first addressing its effects on the institutions critical to both individual and social development.

Notes

1 Friedrich August von Hayek, "Banquet Speech," Nobel Banquet, December 10, 1974; available at www.nobelprize.org/nobel_prizes/economic-sciences/laureates/1974/hayek-speech.html; cited in William Easterly, *The Tyranny of Experts: Economists, Dictators, and the Forgotten Rights of the Poor* (New York: Basic Books, 2013), 39. For a summary of the "debate that never happened" between Hayek and the more technocratically inclined Nobel laureate Gunnar Myrdal, see Easterly, *The Tyranny of Experts*, 39–42.

2 Milton Friedman, "Introduction" to F. A. Hayek, *The Road to Serfdom*, Fiftieth Anniversary Edition (Chicago: University of Chicago Press, 1994), xvii.

3 Quoted in Tamara Keith, "Austrian School Economist Hayek Finds New Fans," (November 11, 2011); available at www.npr.org/2011/11/15/142307737/austrian-school-economist-hayek-finds-new-fans.

4 "Friedrich August von Hayek—Facts"; available at www.nobelprize.org/nobel_prizes/economic-sciences/laureates/1974/hayek-facts.html.

5 Kayla Tausche and Amara Omeokwe, "Dodd–Frank Turns 3, but Slew of Rules are Still Unwritten"; available at www.cnbc.com/id/100906282.
6 The dramatic growth in power by the Federal Reserve in 2008 also led Congressman Barney Frank (D-MA) to remark that "it's been inappropriate in a democracy." See David Wessel, "Economics—Financial Crisis: Inside Dr. Bernanke's E.R.—As Obama Considers Reappointing the Fed Chairman, a Look at How He Took on More Power," *Wall Street Journal*, Eastern edition [New York, NY] July 18, 2009: W.3; available via ProQuest ABI Inform.
7 Hayek, *The Road to Serfdom*, 61.
8 Thomas I. Palley, "Financialization: What It Is and Why It Matters," Levy Economics Institute, Working Paper no. 525 (December 2007): 6; available at www.levyinstitute.org/pubs/wp_525.pdf.
9 Editorial Desk, "Tackling Student Loan Debt," *Los Angeles Times* (June 14, 2014) Part A, p. 14.
10 Karen Dynan, "Changing household financial opportunities and economic security," *Journal of Economic Perspectives* vol. 23, no. 4 (2009): 54.
11 The Federal Reserve Board, "Household Debt Service and Financial Obligations Ratios" [last updated on March 18, 2014]; available at www.federalreserve.gov/releases/housedebt/. See also the associated bulletin: Karen Dynan, Kathleen Johnson, and Karen Pence, "Recent Changes to a Measure of U.S. Household Debt Service"; available at www.federalreserve.gov/pubs/bulletin/2003/1003lead.pdf.
12 Liana Arnold, "2013 Credit Card Debt Study"; available at www.cardhub.com/edu/2013-credit-card-debt-study/.
13 Board of Governors of the Federal Reserve System, "Consumer – G19" (February 2014); available at www.federalreserve.gov/releases/G19/Current/.
14 Richard Carter, "Keeping Up With Innovation in Lending," *Global Banking & Finance Review* (September 11, 2013); available at www.globalbankingandfinance.com/keeping-up-with-innovation-in-lending/.
15 Jim Hawkins, "The CARD Act on Campus," *Washington and Lee Law Review* vol. 69, no. 3 (Summer 2012): 1512–31.
16 Annie Lowery, "Federal Budget Deficit Falls to Smallest Level Since 2008," *New York Times* Economy (February 27, 2014); available at www.nytimes.com/2014/02/28/business/economy/federal-deficit-falls-to-smallest-level-since-2008.html?_r=0.
17 *The Economist*, "Finance and Economics: The Sewers of Jefferson County; American Municipal Finances," *The Economist* 401.8762 (December 3, 2011): 89.
18 *The Economist*, "Finance and Economics."
19 Cited in *The Economist*, "Finance and Economics." European governments have fared even worse, and their collective seat of authority, the European Economic Community, has been unable to corral the forces of financialization that encouraged countries to incur enormous debt in the overleveraged decades since the inception of the Euro. Italy, Greece, Spain, and Ireland are the most widely reported of European countries struggling with public debt, which for the EU as a whole was estimated at $16.08 trillion as of June 2011. See Central Intelligence Agency, "Debt-External," *The World Factbook*; available at www.cia.gov/library/publications/the-world-factbook/fields/2079.html.
20 Thomas I. Palley, *The Economics of Finance Capital Domination* (New York: Palgrave Macmillan, 2013), 60–1.
21 Palley, *The Economics of Finance Capital Domination*, 61.
22 Hayek, *The Road to Serfdom*, 61. Hayek defended the minimal state against the persistent ideal of a planned society that "unites almost all single-minded idealists." He noted that "adoption of the social planning for which they clamor can only bring out the concealed conflict between their aims." See Hayek, *The Road to Serfdom*.
23 Robert Shiller, *The New Financial Order: Risk in the 21st Century* (Princeton, NJ: Princeton University Press, 2003), 1.

24 Hayek, *The Road to Serfdom*, 78.
25 Hayek, *The Road to Serfdom*, 78.
26 Hayek, *The Road to Serfdom*, 78–9. Hayek stated further that

> democratic control may prevent power from becoming arbitrary, but it does not do so by its mere existence. If democracy resolves on a task which necessarily involves the use of power which cannot be guided by fixed rules, it must become arbitrary power.
>
> See Hayek, *The Road to Serfdom*, 79.

27 There is some disagreement as to whether Hayek advocated a "minimal state." In his review of Hayek's *The Constitution of Liberty*, Francis Fukuyama insisted that "Hayek's warnings from the mid-20th century about society's slide toward despotism, and his principled defense of a minimal state, have found strong political resonance." "Friedrich A. Hayek: Big Government Skeptic," *New York Times* Sunday Book Review, May 6, 2011; available at www.nytimes.com/2011/05/08/books/review/f-a-hayek-big-government-skeptic.html?_r=1&ref=review. However, Ellen Frankel Paul insists that Hayek's allowance for government intervention in key social areas precludes his inclusion in the minimalist camp. Despite Paul's conclusion, the minimal state commonly has been used to describe Hayek's view of appropriate government and that practice is continued here. See Ellen Frankel Paul, "Hayek on Monopoly and Antitrust in the *Crucible of United States* v. *Microsoft*," *NYU Journal of Law & Liberty* 1 (2005): 168.
28 Hayek, *The Road to Serfdom*, 79.
29 See Ben Protess, "Merrill and Credit Suisse Fined for Subprime Deals," *New York Times* DealB%k (March 26, 2011); available at http://dealbook.nytimes.com/2011/05/26/merrill-and-credit-suisse-fined-for-subprime-deals/?_php=true&_type=blogs&_r=0.
30 Hayek, *The Road to Serfdom*, 64.
31 Hayek, *The Road to Serfdom*, 65.
32 H. J. Laski, "Labor and Constitution," *New Statesman and Nation*, No. 81 (new ser.), September 10, 1932, p. 277; quoted in Hayek, *The Road to Serfdom*, 70. Hayek offers an extended note to provide context for the quotation where he says that in elaborating these ideas, Laski's "determination that parliamentary democracy must not be allowed to form an obstacle to the realization of socialism is even more plainly expressed: See Hayek, *The Road to Serfdom*, 71 note 2.
33 Hayek, *The Road to Serfdom*, 70 (emphasis added).
34 Hayek, *The Road to Serfdom*, 72. Hayek says "to draw up an economic plan in this fashion is even less possible than, for example, successfully to plan a military campaign by democratic procedure." See Hayek, *The Road to Serfdom*.
35 Hayek, *The Road to Serfdom*, 74.
36 Hayek, *Law, Legislation and Liberty*, vol. 1, *Rules and Order* (Chicago: University of Chicago Press, 1973), 8, 13.
37 Hayek, *The Road to Serfdom*, 61.
38 Hayek, *The Road to Serfdom*, 75.
39 Hayek, *The Road to Serfdom*, 72–3.
40 See Aaron Blake, "Who is Grover Norquist?" *Washington Post* (November 26, 2012); available at www.washingtonpost.com/blogs/the-fix/wp/2012/11/26/who-is-grover-norquist/.
41 Jeffrey R. Blease and David T. Ralston, Jr., " 'Buy American' Provision in Stimulus Legislation Poses Serious Compliance Challenges for Public Works Contractors and DHS Suppliers," (February 17, 2009); available at www.foley.com/buy-american-provision-in-stimulus-legislation-poses-serious-compliance-challenges-for-public-works-contractors-and-dhs-suppliers-02–17–2009/.
42 Massachusetts Office of the Inspector General, "American Recovery and Reinvestment Act Oversight: October 1, 2009 – September 31, 2011," (November 2011).

43 Dan Eggen, "Public Interest Groups Decry Obama's Strict Lobbying Rules," *Washington Post* (April 1, 2009); available at www.washingtonpost.com/wp-dyn/content/article/2009/03/31/AR2009033104074.html.
44 Editorial Board, "A Dodd–Frank capitulation on mortgage down payments," *Washington Post* (September 5, 2013); available at www.washingtonpost.com/opinions/a-dodd-frank-capitulation-on-mortgage-down-payments/2013/09/05/76097130–162f-11e3–804b-d3a1a3a18f2c_story.html.
45 Hayek, *The Road to Serfdom*, 50–1.
46 Hayek, *The Road to Serfdom*, 49–50.
47 Hayek, *The Road to Serfdom*, 56.
48 Ben Jackson, "Freedom, the Common Good, and the Rule of Law: Lippman and Hayek on Economic Planning," *Journal of the History of Ideas* vol. 73: no. 1 (January 2012): 54.
49 See Hayek, "The Use of Knowledge in Society," *American Economic Review* 35, no. 4 (1945): 519–30.
50 Patric Hendershott, Robert Hendershott, and James Shilling, "The Mortgage Finance Bubble: Causes and Corrections," *Journal of Housing Research* 19, iss. 1 (2010): 1–6.
51 Hendershott, Hendershott, and Shilling, "The Mortgage Finance Bubble."
52 "Feds Announce $25B Settlement over Foreclosure Abuse," *Fox News.com* (February 9, 2012); available at www.foxnews.com/politics/2012/02/09/feds-announce-25b-settlement-over-foreclosure-abuse/.
53 Hayek, *Monetary Theory and the Trade Cycle*, trans. N, Kaldor and H. M. Croome (New York: Augustus M. Kelley, 1933), 21; quoted in Gerald P. O'Driscoll, "Keynes and Hayek: What Have We Learned?" *Journal of Private Enterprise* 27(1) (2011): 33.
54 Robert E. Prasch, "The Dodd–Frank Act: Financial Reform or Business as Usual?" *Journal of Economic Issues* vol. XLVI, no. 2 (June 2012): 552.
55 "Greenspan concedes error on regulation," *New York Times* (October 24, 2008), p. B1 of the New York edition; quoted in Michael Lounsbury and Paul M. Hirsch, "Markets on Trial: Toward a Policy-Oriented Economic Sociology," 5; in *Markets on Trial: The Economic Sociology of the U.S. Financial Crisis: Part A*, eds. Michael Lounsbury and Paul M. Hirsch (Bingley, UK: Emerald Group Publishing Limited, 2010).
56 See, for example, Robert P. Murphy, "Evidence that the Fed Caused the Housing Boom"; available at http://mises.org/daily/3252.
57 Michael Perelman, "The Economics of Crisis and the Crisis of Economics as Seen from the US Epicenter," *World Review of Political Economy* vol. 1, no. 1 (Spring 2010): 74–5.
58 Protess, "Merrill and Credit Suisse Fined for Subprime Deals."
59 Peter J. Boettke and Nicholas A. Snow, "The Servants of Obama's Machinery: F. A. Hayek's The Road to Serfdom Revisited?—A Reply," *Eastern Economic Journal*, vol. 38 (2012): 431.
60 Hayek, *The Road to Serfdom*, 117 (emphasis added).
61 Hayek consistently lobbied for such clear distinctions, even in his more policy-oriented writings. See, for example: Hayek, "Substitute for Foreign Aid," *The Freeman* (April 6, 1953): 482–4.
62 Hayek, *The Road to Serfdom*, 68.
63 Linette Lopez, "Elizabeth Warren Introducing a Bill that would be Wall Street's Worst Nightmare," *BusinessInsider* Finance (July 11, 2013); available at www.businessinsider.com/warren-bill-to-bring-back-glass-steagall-2013–7#ixzz35aPlFcmn.
64 Michael Lewis, *Flash Boys: A Wall Street Revolt* (New York: W. W. Norton & Company, 2014), 42–3 (emphasis Lewis's).
65 Lewis, *Flash Boys*, 43.

66 Adam Smith, *The Wealth of Nations*: Vol. 1, edited by R. H. Campbell, A. S. Skinner, and W. B. Todd (Oxford: Clarendon Press, 1976) Book 1, Chap. 10.
67 Paul Dembinski, "Financial Ethics Trapped by Financialization," *Ethikundgesellschaft* vol. 2 (2009): 2; available at www.ethik-und-gesellschaft.de/mm/EuG-2–2009_Dembinski.pdf.
68 Hayek, *The Road to Serfdom*, 57.
69 Hayek, *The Road to Serfdom*, 58.
70 Hayek, *The Road to Serfdom*, 59.
71 Hayek, *The Road to Serfdom*, 55 (emphasis added).
72 John Munkirs, "Centralized Private Sector Planning: An Institutionalist's Perspective on the Contemporary U.S. Economy," *Journal of Economic Issues* vol. 17, no. 4 (December 1983): 933–4, 948–53.
73 Munkirs, "Centralized Private Sector Planning," 951.
74 Munkirs, "Centralized Private Sector Planning," 938–9, 958.
75 Munkirs, "Centralized Private Sector Planning," 964 (emphasis Munkirs').
76 Munkirs, "Centralized Private Sector Planning," 961.
77 Munkirs, "Centralized Private Sector Planning," 961.
78 Munkirs, "Centralized Private Sector Planning," 680–1, 695–700.
79 Caroline Salas Gage, "What's Fed to Do as 15 of 18 Banks Fixing Libor Aren't American," *Bloomberg.com* (August 9, 2012); available at www.bloomberg.com/news/2012–08–09/what-s-fed-to-do-as-15-of-18-banks-fixing-libor-aren-t-american.html.
80 James O'Toole, "Banks accused of defrauding homeowners by rigging Libor," *CNNMoney* (October 16, 2012); available at http://money.cnn.com/2012/10/16/news/companies/libor-homeowners-mortgages/index.html.
81 Munkirs, "Centralized Private Sector Planning," 963.
82 For example, see Luiz Carlos Bresser-Pereira, "The Global Financial Crisis and a New Capitalism?" *Journal of Post Keynesian Economics* vol. 32, no. 4 (Summer 2010): 499–534 and Werner De Bondt, "The Crisis of 2008 and Financial Reform," *Qualitative Research in Financial Markets* vol. 2, no. 3 (2010): 137–56.
83 Paul, "Hayek on Monopoly and Antitrust," 168.
84 Hayek notes that this is an extension of the Marxist principle of the "concentration of industry" that had become prevalent in his time. See Hayek, *The Road to Serfdom*, 49.
85 Hayek, The Road to Serfdom, 52–3.
86 Hayek, The Road to Serfdom, 46.
87 Quoted in Cyrus Sanati, "10 Years Later, Looking at Repeal of Glass–Steagall," *New York Times* DealB%k (November 12, 2009); available at http://dealbook.nytimes.com/2009/11/12/10-years-later-looking-at-repeal-of-glass-steagall/.
88 Federal Reserve Bank of Dallas, "Issues: Bank Mergers: Creating Value or Destroying Competition," (Third Quarter, 1998); located at www.dallasfed.org/banking/fii/fii9803.pdf. See also Ben Steverman, 2008. "Small Banks: How Fragile Are They? Credit troubles at many smaller institutions are mounting—and plunging shares make it harder to raise capital to cover losses," *Bloomberg Businessweek* (June 25, 2008); available at www.bloomberg.com/bw/stories/2008-06-25/small-banks-how-fragile-are-they-businessweek-business-news-stock-market-and-financial-advice.
. 89 Hayek, *The Constitution of Liberty*, The Definitive Edition, ed. Ronald Hamowy (Chicago, University of Chicago Press, 1960), 203.
90 Paul, "Hayek on Monopoly," 175.
91 Hayek, *The Road to Serfdom*, 216–17.
92 Paul, "Hayek on Monopoly," 180.
93 Paul, "Hayek on Monopoly," 172.
94 Linda E. Fishman, "Just Feed Me the Sausage: One Congressional Staffer's View," *Milbank Quarterly* vol. 1, no. 1 (2003): 145.

95 Zachary R. Mider and Jesse Drucker, "The IRS Challenges a Hedge Fund Tax Trick," *Bloomberg Businessweek* (July 3, 2013); available at www.businessweek.com/articles/2013–07–03/the-irs-challenges-a-hedge-fund-tax-trick.
96 Quoted in Mider and Drucker, "The IRS Challenges a Hedge Fund Tax Trick."
97 Matthew Desmond, "Is Democratic Regulation of High Finance Possible?" *Annals of the American Academy of Political and Social Science* vol. 649: 1 (September 2013): 182.
98 Desmond, "Is Democratic Regulation of High Finance Possible?" 182.
99 Desmond, "Is Democratic Regulation of High Finance Possible?" 183.
100 Jonathan Stempel, "Lawsuit Claims CME Gave High-Frequency Traders Special Access," Reuters, U.S. Edition; available at www.reuters.com/article/2014/04/14/us-cme-highfrequencytrading-lawsuit-idUSBREA3D16Z20140414.
101 In response to this perceived unfairness, Katsuyama has established an alternative exchange, IEX, with a "governor" for HSTs that artificially lowers the speed of their access to bring them in line with other traders. Theoretically, this new exchange forces HSTs to "compete," trading based on estimations of risk and return rather than taking advantage of a system that enables virtually certain profits through privileged access. See Lewis, *Flash Boys*, 172–9.
102 Michael Crittenden and David Enrich, "TARP Cash Isn't Moving Forward: Treasury Says Lending Has Fallen Among Banks Getting Government Aid," *Wall Street Journal* Markets (April 16, 2009); available at http://online.wsj.com/news/articles/SB123981607918021761.
103 The 1956 Bank Holding Company Act required those firms owning or controlling significant shares in two or more banks to register with and agree to periodic examination by the Federal Reserve Board. A major thrust of the law was to enable the Fed to regulate the expansion of banks across state boundaries in order to prevent what some feared could be the destruction of the local banking industry. See Benjamin J. Klebaner, "The Bank Holding Company Act of 1956," *Southern Economic Journal* vol. 24, no. 3 (January 1958): 313–26.
104 Quoted in "Clinton Signs Legislation Overhauling Bank Laws," *New York Times.com* (November 13, 1999); available at www.nytimes.com/1999/11/13/business/clinton-signs-legislation-overhauling-banking-laws.html.
105 K. Sabeel Rahman, "Envisioning the Regulatory State: Technocracy, Democracy, and Institutional Experimentation in the 2010 Financial Reform and Oil Spill Statutes," *Harvard Law School Journal on Legislation* vol. 48 (2011): 567; quoted in Desmond, "Is Democratic Regulation of High Finance Possible?" 183.
106 Desmond, "Is Democratic Regulation of High Finance Possible?" 183.
107 Dembinski, "Financial Ethics."
108 Dembinski, "Financial Ethics," 16.
109 Dembinski, "Financial Ethics," 15.
110 Dembinski, "Financial Ethics," 15.
111 Dembinski, "Financial Ethics," 2.
112 Bill Barnhart, "Tracking Overlap As It Undermines Fund Diversity," *Chicago Tribune* (September 27, 1998); available at http://articles.chicagotribune.com/1998–09–27/business/9809270050_1_janus-worldwide-fund-overlap-growth-stock-fund.
113 Barnhart, "Tracking Overlap As It Undermines Fund Diversity."
114 Dembinski, "Financial Ethics," 16.
115 Dembinski, "Financial Ethics," 16. He calls the principal threat to the socioeconomic fabric "the expansion of transactions at the expense of relationships." See Dembinski, "Financial Ethics," 18.
116 Hayek, "Genius for Compromise," *Spectator* (January 26, 1945), 75.

Bibliography

Arnold, Liana. "2013 Credit Card Debt Study." *CardHub.com* (n.d.). www.cardhub.com/edu/2013-credit-card-debt-study/; accessed on June 23, 2014.

Barnhart, Bill. "Tracking Overlap as It Undermines Fund Diversity." *Chicago Tribune*, September 27, 1998. http://articles.chicagotribune.com/1998-09-27/business/9809270050_1_janus-worldwide-fund-overlap-growth-stock-fund; accessed on June 1, 2014.

Blake, Aaron. "Who Is Grover Norquist?" *Washington Post*, November 26, 2012. www.washingtonpost.com/blogs/the-fix/wp/2012/11/26/who-is-grover-norquist/; accessed on April 2, 2014.

Blease, Jeffrey R. and David T. Ralston, Jr. "'Buy American' Provision in Stimulus Legislation Poses Serious Compliance Challenges for Public Works Contractors and DHS Suppliers." *Foley.com*, February 17, 2009. www.foley.com/buy-american-provision-in-stimulus-legislation-poses-serious-compliance-challenges-for-public-works-contractors-and-dhs-suppliers-02-17-2009/; accessed on June 27, 2014.

Boettke, Peter J. and Nicholas A. Snow. "The Servants of Obama's Machinery: F. A. Hayek's The Road to Serfdom Revisited?—A Reply," *Eastern Economic Journal*, vol. 38 (2012): 428–33.

Bondt, Werner de. "The Crisis of 2008 and Financial Reform." *Qualitative Research in Financial Markets* 2, no. 3 (2010): 137–56.

Bresser-Pereira, Luiz Carlos. "The Global Financial Crisis and a New Capitalism?" *Journal of Post Keynesian Economics* 32, no. 4 (Summer 2010): 499–534.

Carter, Richard. "Keeping Up with Innovation in Lending." *Global Banking & Finance Review*, September 11, 2013. www.globalbankingandfinance.com/keeping-up-with-innovation-in-lending/; accessed on April 16, 2014.

Central Intelligence Agency. "Debt-External." *World Factbook*. CIA, (n.d.). www.cia.gov/library/publications/the-world-factbook/fields/2079.html; accessed on July 5, 2012.

Crittenden, Michael, and David Enrich. "TARP Cash Isn't Moving Forward: Treasury Says Lending Has Fallen among Banks Getting Government Aid." *Wall Street Journal Markets*, April 16, 2009. http://online.wsj.com/news/articles/SB123981607918021761; accessed on June 24, 2014.

Dembinski, Paul H. "Financial Ethics Trapped by Financialization." *Ethikundgesellschaft* 2, (2009): 1–23. www.ethik-und-gesellschaft.de/mm/EuG-2–2009_Dembinski.pdf; accessed on October 5, 2011.

Desmond, Matthew. "Is Democratic Regulation of High Finance Possible?" *Annals of the American Academy of Political and Social Science* 649, no. 1 (September 2013): 180–4.

Dynan, Karen. "Changing Household Financial Opportunities and Economic Security." *Journal of Economic Perspectives* 23, no. 4 (2009): 49–68.

Dynan, Karen, Kathleen Johnson, and Karen Pence. "Recent Changes to a Measure of U.S. Household Debt Service." *FederalReserve.gov*, March 18, 2014. www.federalreserve.gov/pubs/bulletin/2003/1003lead.pdf.

Easterly, William. *The Tyranny of Experts: Economists, Dictators, and the Forgotten Rights of the Poor*. New York: Basic Books, 2013.

The Economist. "Finance and Economics: The Sewers of Jefferson County; American Municipal Finances." *The Economist*, December 3, 2011, 401.8762 edition.

Eggen, Dan. "Public Interest Groups Decry Obama's Strict Lobbying Rules." *Washington Post*, April 1, 2009. www.washingtonpost.com/wp-dyn/content/article/2009/03/31/AR2009033104074.html; accessed on June 23, 2014.

Federal Reserve Bank of Dallas. "Issues: Bank Mergers: Creating Value or Destroying Competition." *DallasFed.org*, Third Quarter 1998. www.dallasfed.org/banking/fii/fii9803.pdf; accessed on November 23, 2011.

The Federal Reserve Board. "Household Debt Service and Financial Obligation Ratios." *FederalReserve.gov*, March 18, 2014. www.federalreserve.gov/releases/housedebt//; accessed on April 13, 2014.

Federal Reserve System, Board of Governors. "Consumer – G19." *FederalReserve.gov*, February 2014. www.federalreserve.gov/releases/G19/Current/; accessed on April 16, 2014.

Fishman, Linda E. "Just Feed Me the Sausage: One Congressional Staffer's View." *The Milbank Quarterly* 1, no. 1 (2003): 143–6.

FoxNews.com. "Feds Announce $25B Settlement over Foreclosure Abuse." *FoxNews.com*, February 9, 2012. www.foxnews.com/politics/2012/02/09/feds-announce-25b-settlement-over-foreclosure-abuse/; accessed on July 2, 2014.

Friedman, Milton. "Introduction." In Friedrich August von Hayek, *The Road to Serfdom*, Fiftieth Anniversary Edition, ix–xx. Chicago: University of Chicago Press, 1994.

Fukuyama, Francis. "Friedrich A. Hayek: Big Government Skeptic." *New York Times* Sunday Book Review, May 6, 2011. www.nytimes.com/2011/05/08/books/review/f-a-hayek-big-government-skeptic.html?_r=1&ref=review; accessed on December 2, 2011.

Gage, Caroline Salas. "What's Fed to Do as 15 of 18 Banks Fixing Libor Aren't American." *Bloomberg.com*, August 9, 2012. www.bloomberg.com/news/2012-08-09/what-s-fed-to-do-as-15-of-18-banks-fixing-libor-aren-t-american.html; accessed on June 24, 2014.

Hawkins, Jim. "The CARD Act on Campus." *Washington and Lee Law Review* 69, no. 3 (Summer 2012): 1471–534.

Hayek, Friedrich August von. "Banquet Speech." Speech presented at the Nobel Banquet, December 10, 1974. www.nobelprize.org/nobel_prizes/economic-sciences/laureates/1974/hayek-speech.html.

Hayek, Friedrich August von. *The Constitution of Liberty*. Edited by Ronald Hamowy. The Definitive Edition. Chicago: University of Chicago Press, 1960.

Hayek, Friedrich August von. "Genius for Compromise." *Spectator*, January 26, 1945.

Hayek, Friedrich August von. *Law, Legislation and Liberty*. Vol. 1. Rules and Order. Chicago: University of Chicago Press, 1973.

Hayek, Friedrich August von. *Monetary Theory and the Trade Cycle*. Translated by N. Kaldor and H. M. Croome. New York: Augustus M. Kelley, 1933.

Hayek, Friedrich August von. *The Road to Serfdom*. Fiftieth Anniversary Edition. Chicago: University of Chicago Press, 1994.

Hayek, Friedrich August von. "Substitute for Foreign Aid." *The Freeman* 8, no. 14 (April 6, 1953): 482–4.

Hayek, Friedrich August von. "The Use of Knowledge in Society." *American Economic Review* 35, no. 4 (September 1945): 519–30.

Hendershott, Patric, Robert Hendershott, and James Shilling. "The Mortgage Finance Bubble: Causes and Corrections." *Journal of Housing Research* 19, no. 1 (2010): 1–16.

Jackson, Ben. "Freedom, the Common Good, and the Rule of Law: Lippman and Hayek on Economic Planning." *Journal of the History of Ideas* 73, no. 1 (January 2012): 47–68.

Keith, Tamara. "Austrian School Economist Hayek Finds New Fans." *NPR.org*, November 11, 2011. www.npr.org/2011/11/15/142307737/austrian-school-economist-hayek-finds-new-fans; accessed on November 21, 2011.

Klebaner, Benjamin J. "The Bank Holding Company Act of 1956." *Southern Economic Journal* 24, no. 3 (January 1958): 313–26.

Laski, H. J. "Labor and Constitution." *New Statesman and Nation* 4, no. 81 (September 10, 1932): 276–8.

Lewis, Michael. *Flash Boys: A Wall Street Revolt*. New York: W. W. Norton & Company, Ltd., 2014.

Lopez, Linette. "Elizabeth Warren Introducing A Bill That Would Be Wall Street's Worst Nightmare." BusinessInsider Finance, July 11, 2013. www.businessinsider.com/warren-bill-to-bring-back-glass-steagall-2013-7#ixzz35aPlFcmn; accessed on June 24, 2014.

Los Angeles Times Editorial Desk. "Tackling Student Loan Debt." *Los Angeles Times*, June 14, 2014, sec. A14.

Lounsbury, Michael and Paul M. Hirsch. "Markets on Trial: Toward a Policy-Oriented Economic Sociology." In *Markets on Trial: The Economic Sociology of the U.S. Financial Crisis: Part A*, edited by Michael Lounsbury and Paul M. Hirsch, 5–26. Bingley, UK: Emerald Group Publishing Limited, 2010.

Lowery, Annie. "Federal Budget Deficit Falls to Smallest Level since 2008." *New York Times* Economy, February 27, 2014. www.nytimes.com/2014/02/28/business/economy/federal-deficit-falls-to-smallest-level-since-2008.html?_r=0; accessed on April 14, 2014.

Massachusetts Office of the Inspector General. "American Recovery and Reinvestment Act Oversight: October 1, 2009–September 31, 2011." November 2011. www.mass.gov/ig/publications/arra/arra-advisories-and-grant-reviews/arrasummaryupdate.pdf; accessed on March 22, 2015.

Mider, Zachary R. and Jesse Drucker. "The IRS Challenges a Hedge Fund Tax Trick." *Bloomberg Businessweek*, July 3, 2013. www.businessweek.com/articles/2013-07-03/the-irs-challenges-a-hedge-fund-tax-trick; accessed on May 14, 2013.

Munkirs, John. "Centralized Private Sector Planning: An Institutionalist's Perspective on the Contemporary U.S. Economy." *Journal of Economic Issues* 17, no. 4 (December 1983): 931–67.

Murphy, Robert P. "Evidence That the Fed Caused the Housing Boom." *Mises.org*, December 15, 2008. http://mises.org/daily/3252; accessed on July 10, 2014.

New York Times. "Clinton Signs Legislation Overhauling Bank Laws." November 13, 1999. www.nytimes.com/1999/11/13/business/clinton-signs-legislation-overhauling-banking-laws.html; accessed on May 6, 2014.

New York Times. "Greenspan Concedes Error on Regulation." *New York Times*, October 24, 2008, New York edition, sec. B1.

Nobel Media. "Friedrich August von Hayek—Facts." *NobelPrize.org*, www.nobelprize.org/nobel_prizes/economic-sciences/laureates/1974/hayek-facts.html; accessed on July 10, 2014.

O'Driscoll, Gerald P. "Keynes and Hayek: What Have We Learned?" *Journal of Private Enterprise* 27, no. 1 (2011): 29–38.

O'Toole, James. "Banks Accused of Defrauding Homeowners by Rigging Libor." *CNN Money*, October 16, 2012. http://money.cnn.com/2012/10/16/news/companies/libor-homeowners-mortgages/index.html; accessed on June 2, 2014.

Palley, Thomas I. *The Economics of Finance Capital Domination*. New York: Palgrave Macmillan, 2013.

Palley, Thomas I. "Financialization: What It Is and Why It Matters." Working Paper no. 525, Levy Economics Institute, 2007. www.levy.org; accessed on March 22, 2011.

Paul, Ellen Frankel. "Hayek on Monopoly and Antitrust in the Crucible of United States v. Microsoft." *NYU Journal of Law & Liberty* 1, no. 0 (2005): 167–204.

Perelman, Michael. "The Economics of Crisis and the Crisis of Economics as Seen from the US Epicenter." *World Review of Political Economy* 1, no. 1 (Spring 2010): 70–80.

Prasch, Robert E. "The Dodd–Frank Act: Financial Reform or Business as Usual?" *Journal of Economic Issues* XLVI, no. 2 (June 2012): 549–56.

Protess, Ben. "Merrill and Credit Suisse Fined for Subprime Deals." *New York Times* DealB%k, March 26, 2011. http://dealbook.nytimes.com/2011/05/26/merrill-and-credit-suisse-fined-for-subprime-deals/?_php=true&_type=blogs&_r=0; accessed on June 23, 2014.

Rahman, K. Sabeel. "Envisioning the Regulatory State: Technocracy, Democracy, and Institutional Experimentation in the 2010 Financial Reform and Oil Spill Statutes." *Harvard Law School Journal on Legislation* 48, no. 2 (Summer 2011): 555–90.

Sanati, Cyrus. "10 Years Later, Looking at Repeal of Glass–Steagall." *New York Times* DealB%k, November 12, 2009. http://dealbook.nytimes.com/2009/11/12/10-years-later-looking-at-repeal-of-glass-steagall/; accessed on November 22, 2011.

Shiller, Robert. *The New Financial Order: Risk in the 21st Century*. Princeton, NJ: Princeton University Press, 2003.

Smith, Adam. *An Inquiry into the Nature and Causes of the Wealth of Nations*. Edited by R. H. Campbell, A. S. Skinner, and W. B. Todd. Vol. 1. Oxford: Clarendon Press, 1976.

Stempel, Jonathan. "Lawsuit Claims CME Gave High-Frequency Traders Special Access." Reuters, April 14, 2014, U.S. edition. www.reuters.com/article/2014/04/14/us-cme-highfrequencytrading-lawsuit-idUSBREA3D16Z20140414; accessed on May 17, 2014.

Steverman, Ben. "Small Banks: How Fragile Are They? Credit Troubles at Many Smaller Institutions Are Mounting—and Plunging Shares Make It Harder to Raise Capital to Cover Losses." *Bloomberg Businessweek*, June 25, 2008. www.bloomberg.com/bw/stories/2008-06-25/small-banks-how-fragile-are-they-businessweek-business-news-stock-market-and-financial-advice; accessed on April 1, 2015.

Tausche, Kayla, and Amara Omeokwe. "Dodd–Frank Turns 3, but Slew of Rules Are Still Unwritten." *CNBC.com*, July 23, 2013. www.cnbc.com/id/100906282; accessed on September 16, 2013.

Washington Post Editorial Board. "A Dodd–Frank Capitulation on Mortgage Down Payments." *Washington Post*, September 5, 2013. www.washingtonpost.com/opinions/a-dodd-frank-capitulation-on-mortgage-down-payments/2013/09/05/76097130-162f-11e3-804b-d3a1a3a18f2c_story.html; accessed on July 2, 2014.

Wessel, David. "Economics—Financial Crisis: Inside Dr. Bernanke's E.R.—As Obama Considers Reappointing the Fed Chairman, a Look at How He Took on More Power." *Wall Street Journal*. July 18, 2009, sec. W3. Available via ProQuest ABI Inform; accessed on April 4, 2014.

4 The financialization of civil society

On November 10, 2014, the Cystic Fibrosis Foundation (CFF) announced that it was selling the royalty rights for the drug Kalydeco and other cystic fibrosis medicines to Royalty Pharma, a for-profit firm that acquires the intellectual property and other rights to medicines from private companies and research institutions that develop pharmaceuticals. The foundation provided over $100 million in funding to Vertex Pharmaceuticals to help produce Kalydeco, and has pledged at least $50 million more. What was astounding about the announcement was the amount paid to the CFF—$3.3 billion—over four times more than previous royalty purchases of this kind.[1] Media coverage of this transaction launched the CFF into the national spotlight as various groups debated the ethics of what has come to be called "venture philanthropy," in which charitable organizations often benefit handsomely from their investments in for-profit firms.

In addition to funding pharmaceutical development, the CFF provides capital to over 100 treatment centers throughout the U.S. that help combat this disabling genetic disorder, which causes the thickening of mucus and other body fluids in the lungs, pancreas, and other organs, greatly shortening the lifespan of those with the disease. Cystic fibrosis affects only around 30,000 Americans,[2] which means that products developed to treat it are categorized as "specialty drugs" and are often very expensive. The annual cost of Kalydeco for a single patient is more than $300,000. Annual sales for Kalydeco reached $371.3 million dollars in 2013 and are projected to hit the $460 million mark in 2014.[3]

News of CFF's royalty deal led to questions concerning its financial practices and concerns about priorities with respect to its primary constituent group—those who suffer from cystic fibrosis. While CEO Robert J. Beall justified the CFF's investments in pharmaceutical development by saying that the Foundation's windfall "will allow us to supercharge our efforts to help all people with cystic fibrosis live long, healthy, and fulfilling lives,"[4] others question whether this type of funding produces inherent conflicts of interest. In the case of CFF and Kalydeco, critics have suggested that, as a tax-exempt nonprofit, the CFF has a responsibility to help defray the cost of the drug to sufferers of the disease. Others maintain that the Foundation's money is better used as venture capital, facilitating the creation of other breakthrough drugs. Adding to the controversy is that some nonprofit foundations that also engage in venture philanthropy do not accept royalties on the products their funding supports as, for example, the Michael J. Fox Foundation and its funding of Parkinson's disease therapies.[5]

For philanthropic foundations and other organizations with charitable missions, royalty rights to financially lucrative property and products can make for ethically difficult decisions. In the case of those that receive royalties for drug sales, efforts to subsidize costs for treatment may often reduce the funding organization's royalty revenue. Sales of royalty rights can produce windfall gains as in the case of CFF and Kalydeco. Where should the line be drawn between maximizing a foundation's return on investment and providing financial relief to those who suffer from a disease that is the object of its investment? Is a "return-on-investment" approach to allocating resources appropriate for such organizations at all? In the case of CFF and Kalydeco, announcements concerning the drug's development have at times caused the stock price of Vertex to fluctuate, prompting executives in the company to trade shares. In 2012, Sen. Charles Grassley (R-Iowa) wrote a letter to the Securities and Exchange Commission (SEC) questioning whether Vertex executives "might have taken advantage of erroneous information to profit from stock sales."[6] Critics also have pointed to the salaries of executives in the CFF itself, described as "very high for those who are managing a supposed charity."[7] The CFF-Vertex case prompts the question whether the association of charitable organizations with high risk and potentially high-return for-profit firms encourages the escalation of executive salaries commonly associated with financialization.

This chapter addresses the increasing financial emphasis among nonprofit and voluntary organizations in the United States and how it is contributing to the financialization of American society. Virtually all institutions from houses of worship to schools and hospitals are becoming more financially interested in outcomes that can distract them from their basic missions. Some may find comfort in that observation, believing that the market is, in all cases, the best institution for the determination of social priorities and allocation of society's limited resources. However, even as venture philanthropy and various hybrid business-charity organizations have grown rapidly in recent decades, the network of financial interests also is becoming increasingly difficult to navigate for "investors" who may not consider themselves investors at all, but rather donors to charitable causes.

Innovations in the manipulation of capital that have accented financialization in the for-profit world are bleeding over into the nonprofit sector, diminishing the vibrant pluralism that is a major component of American "exceptionalism." Alexis de Tocqueville's famous characterization of the United States as a "nation of joiners" depends on, if not "disinterested," then at least less financially interested institutions for citizens to "join." Voluntary associations are critical in helping those less fortunate, serving as watchdogs over government agencies and major corporations, and keeping citizens informed and engaged on social issues, among other functions. These organizations also provide a critical moral foundation to offset those largely self-interested and relative values that develop in the marketplace. The ongoing transformation of the U.S. from a nation of joiners to a nation of investors detaches Americans from personal connections to those causes that give their lives meaning beyond the workplace. It also defies principles of notable social philosophers who have observed that moral economies require intermediate institutions sufficiently insulated from the contingencies of politics and economics.

The influence of money in the civil sphere

At least part of the reason for the increasing influence of funding and finance in the nonprofit world has to do with major changes in American society going back to the New Deal. That seismic shift in the approach to social welfare ushered in a major role for government in the establishment of a social safety net. However, around the 1970s—the period from which we have traced the rise of financialization—attitudes about welfare and social services began to change markedly. A growing realization of the infeasibility of the "Great Society" model along with persistent American antisocialist sentiments began to shift the provision of charity and welfare services in the direction of nonprofit organizations. These private groups, however, were highly dependent on public funds. A study by Lester Salamon in 1987 showed that by the early '80s, more than 40 percent of funding for social service nonprofits came from government sources.[8] Similarly, scholars have noted how a "new federalism" arrived during the Reagan years and began to significantly alter the government-nonprofit relationship, draining away public sources of revenues and making charities and other social service providers more dependent on their own resources. The rise of funding uncertainty in the period resulted in strategic moves within nonprofit organizations to gain greater financial security, including heightened political activity to "influence the flow" of resources.[9]

Principles of "resource dependency theory," which observes the impact of external resources on firm behavior, make this conclusion unsurprising. Chao Guo, for example, has observed studies of this period that show how the governing boards of nonprofit firms came to be seen as "co-optive devices in the quest for government funding" in an era of increasing competition for public funds.[10] Guo also observes that the greater focus on funding in these organizations "has serious implications for the variation in community representation on an organization's board," often shifting board composition in favor of professional and business "elites" who are generally more experienced in grant writing and other means of acquiring capital.[11] The bias of nonprofits toward the vision of elites likely results not so much from discrimination against particular classes as from the fact that members of the elite simply know better the workings of the funding system and nonprofits capitalize on that knowledge.

In certain ways, nonprofits emerged from this period with a keener competitive spirit much like their for-profit counterparts, which was necessitated by the scramble for scarcer sources of capital. The influence of business professionals in nonprofit boardrooms accented this change, yet, as will be seen, it also may have diminished the value pluralism of American society as motivations converge across the for-profit/nonprofit divide. This impact of commercial interests in the nonprofit world is of increasing importance because of the growth in the American nonprofit sector itself. It is estimated, for example, that around 13 percent of private-sector employees work for nonprofit firms in New England. Strikingly, however, "it is not necessarily the poorest communities that have the most social-welfare organizations but often the richest, because they are the ones with the resources and organizing capacity to create such organizations."[12] In their aptly titled "Golfing Alone? Corporations, Elites, and Nonprofit Growth in 100 American Communities," Christopher Marquis, Gerald F. Davis, and Mary Ann Glynn observe the complex interconnection between private corporations and civil society institutions, particularly in areas where there is significant concentration of for-profit firms.[13] Given this influence, it is unsurprising that the dominant values of the American corporation should bleed into the nation's charities and social service organizations.

More "innovative" financial attitudes have filtered into social sectors where the goal of monetary return traditionally has been subordinated to more altruistic motives. Fear of falling behind, financially speaking, has permeated the cultures of NGOs, religious organizations, educational institutions, nonprofit healthcare systems, and other groups in a way consistent with the financialization of the American economy more generally. Early signs of this transition were observed when social service and relief organizations began to use a growing technological infrastructure to improve their fundraising capabilities. World Vision U.S. launched its website in 1997, and one of its first fundraising campaigns that accepted online donations supported the southern Sudanese in their tragic civil war. In July 1997 alone, after only a few months with a Web presence, the agency took in $70,000 online from 170 donors. Similarly, the website for Food for the Hungry became the organization's second leading funding source after only four years of operation.[14]

But opening up additional funding sources does not necessarily mean increasing participation in those intermediate institutions that forge American civil society. In certain cases, it might mean reducing certain forms of participation as donors point-and-click their contributions rather than show up. Robert Putnam's seminal *Bowling Alone* addressed how technological change may have negatively influenced participation in civil society with a resultant loss of social capital. According to MIT urban studies professor Xavier de Souza Briggs, the term social capital "has taken on a circus-tent quality; all things positive and social can be piled underneath"—yet de Souza Briggs offers a succinct and quite helpful definition: social capital "refers to resources stored in human relationships, whether casual or close."[15] Social capital is the social benefits that derive from the interactions of human beings. Those benefits were called into question by the publication of Putnam's book in 2000 and its evidence showing that a kind of individual isolation facilitated by technology—television in particular—was diminishing civic engagement.[16]

While *Bowling Alone* received immediate popular acclaim, some of Putnam's social science colleagues quickly pounced, suggesting that he revealed biases regarding forms of civic participation that caused him to exaggerate the decline of social capital. Irene Taviss Thomson described Putnam's "romantic image of community" and "distaste for self-interested actions" that devalue the contributions to social capital of personal activities such as "letter-writing and petition-signing."[17] Thomson also perceived Putnam's emphasis on the negative effects of television as reflecting an attitude that civic participation must be local and personal. Putnam viewed the Internet "as a threat to 'bridging' social capital because it fosters communication among those with shared interests."[18] Thomson countered by suggesting that the relative absence of self-interested groups on the Internet and its ability to "cut across demographic categories" meant that the medium may well generate social capital rather than depleting it.[19] Furthermore, statistics seem to indicate that our newest generation definitely prefers technology-mediated forms of community; a Pew Research Center survey found that 81 percent of Millennials have a presence on Facebook with a "median friend count" of 250, far eclipsing statistics for the previous generation.[20] The major theme of the report summarizing the survey is that Millennials are "detached from institutions" even as they are "networked with friends."[21]

Irrespective of scholarly differences on what constitutes civic participation, Putnam's thesis that civil society is in decline struck a nerve with a wide audience, but it may be that more institutional and less technological reasons exist to explain the contemporary loss of social capital. Financial preoccupation, bottom-line thinking, and fiscal destabilization often associated with financialization can constitute forms of "institutional distraction" that negatively impact civil society as well. Intermediate organizations find themselves preoccupied with financial issues, often to the exclusion of the services they provide to clients, adherents, and the wider society. This theory is consistent with others' views that the intensity of financial interests, practices, and values is reshaping American organizations. In describing the "centrality of finance to American society," University of Michigan management professor Gerald F. Davis goes so far as to suggest that its ascendance "effectively ended the reign of the society of organizations":

> The "society of organizations" is no longer the enveloping force it was when [Peter] Drucker and [Carl] Kaysen wrote. Instead, the cognitive model that holds sway for many is that of the *investor*. Students attending college are "investing in their human capital," while people who join a bowling league or the PTA are thereby "investing in their social capital." In a portfolio society, the organization man has been replaced by the daytrader, buying and selling various species of capital, from homes reconceived as options on future price increases, to a college education whose estimated net present value informs the choice of school and course of study, to children whose Little League games might be an apt context to cultivate potential clients.[22]

Davis notes that we "cannot go back to a system of corporate-sponsored welfare capitalism any more than we can return to feudalism."[23] Neither can we remain where we are in our present cultural configuration, however, given the social and economic problems that have emerged. The widening distribution of income, racial and political polarization, and the decay of traditional social institutions insist on the need for reform. We still need "personalized" forms of communal organization for security, deliberation, and expression, and it is debatable whether technologically dependent forms of community alone can suffice to generate adequate social capital and inspire a virtuous citizenry.

Religious groups and civic organizations are common models when illustrating the mediating forms of community between individuals and the state that are based on something beyond self-interest. And there is more than a romantic attachment to these organization types as exemplars. Putnam and the other authors of *Making Democracy Work: Civic Traditions in Modern Italy* show how the civic involvement of citizens is positively related to good governance, economic function, and even the extent to which a society is able to democratize.[24] They conclude that tangible benefits exist for the development of civil society institutions that go beyond the aesthetics of a more communalized society.

A major problem in reviving this key cultural layer is the pervasive emphases on "efficiency" and "return" in the financialized American culture of today. These dominant goals reorient organizations whose traditional missions have been other-regarding to focus on internal performance measures and they foster increasingly financial competition among civil society groups. Some of these changes are implied in alterations to the organizational structures of nonprofit firms. For example, the 2013 Nonprofit Employment Practices Survey showed that 31 percent of nonprofits expected to see job growth in the fundraising/development area in 2013, compared with only 16 percent that expected growth in that area in 2011. Moreover, job growth was expected in finance/administration/operations by 17 percent of firms in 2013, compared with only 6 percent of companies in 2011. These figures contrast with a mere 1 percent increase in the number of nonprofits that anticipated job growth in "direct services" (35 to 36 percent) during those same years, suggesting that finance, administration, and fundraising are experiencing disproportionately greater resource gains than direct services in nonprofit firms.[25]

These statistics complement a trend going back to the 1990s in which nonprofits increasingly measured their performance according to their *fundraising effectiveness*. The influence of these firms was often simplistically associated with their size, so that the amount of funds raised came to be a principal performance measure, inspiring those smaller fish in the eleemosynary pond to get big.[26] Nonprofits measuring performance in terms of size, fundraising effectiveness, and income conforms to a similar trend among for-profit corporations, whose exaggerated emphases on financial performance and share price are considered evidence of financialization. Financial measures for firms generally are appealing because they are relatively easy to acquire and use and also are considered more "objective" than social indicators.[27] What is not considered, however, is whether this "objectivity" in measurement may lead to preoccupation with resources *at the expense of* organizational mission.

Certain nonprofit organizations may have difficulty incorporating more instrumental measures of performance (including financial results) with those measures that tie more directly to mission. Robert D. Herman and David O. Rentz contend, for example, that determination of successful outcomes for women's shelters or centers that aid victims of child abuse is a highly complicated exercise. Moreover, they note the difficulty of arriving at standards of performance capable of pleasing everyone: "stakeholders often differ markedly in their judgments of the effectiveness of the same NPO [nonprofit organization]."[28] This inclination toward objective measurement of often highly subjective institutional goals can also lead to an exaggerated emphasis on revenue as evidence of NPO success.[29] The low-hanging fruit approach to performance measurement typically means that expenses also become a key objective. Research from 2007 revealed that while around 60 percent of NPOs collect data "on outcomes and results," some 97 percent collect data "on program expenditures and other expenditures."[30] Thus, the most complex social service organizations with respect to outcome measurement may have internal incentives to emphasize more objective measures of performance located on income statements and balance sheets; this practice arises because of difficulties assessing more subjective performance measures associated with their services.

James Madison University management professors William Ritchie and Robert Kolodinsky observe one negative consequence that seems to have resulted from the pragmatic turn to financial and other objective measures of nonprofit performance. They contend that emphasis on investment performance "may be inadvertently providing an incentive for managers to invest NPO assets in financial instruments that exceed established risk thresholds."[31] Published in 2003, the authors' article is remarkably prescient with respect to the risky investments undertaken by religious groups, educational institutions, and various nonprofits revealed in recent years.

In the aftermath of high-profile scandals, the United States government has attempted to enforce greater transparency and accountability on all corporate entities; those value changes likely result from the scandals themselves. Subsequent to the Sarbanes–Oxley Act of 2002 that applied primarily to for-profit companies, regulations have gone into effect at both state and local levels that require certification and audit of nonprofit financial statements as well as independent audit of nonprofit boards. Financial improprieties by executives at prominent national nonprofits such as the United Way, Red Cross, and The Nature Conservancy prompted a strong public outcry and many state-level initiatives for enhanced regulation.[32] In New York, for example, the state's Nonprofit Revitalization Act of 2013 went into effect, designed to strengthen financial reporting and accountability, prevent conflicts of interest, and require an independent audit/oversight function on firms that reach a certain size.[33] These increasingly popular laws have some obvious benefits, but scholars have observed potential problems, such as dampening incentives for participation by demanding greater audit responsibilities from board members who "volunteer" with limited time to participate. Thomas E. Hartman provides support for this argument by noting that, in the for-profit world, implementation of Sarbanes–Oxley led firms to increase director pay to compensate for the increased demands.[34]

Steven Rathgeb Smith observes other potentially negative consequences for nonprofits resulting from law and policy changes. He notes how not only more stringent audit functions increasingly are applied to nonprofits but also that "performance contracts" with particular state agencies ratchet up the competition on groups that in the past have had relatively stable business relationships and income sources. These new arrangements often involve transition from a cost reimbursement to a fee-for-service structure, and they can apply pressure on nonprofit firms to add management information systems and " 'professionalize' the administrative infrastructure," which can have significant implications for both the mission and focus of organizations. In effect, altering the resource structure of these organizations "may be at variance with the previous programmatic focus of the organization."[35]

Smith's principal concern is also a major concern of this book. Small nonprofits "are also very value driven, so many community nonprofits have little interest in expanding their earned income."[36] Large nonprofits will have advantages over their smaller brethren in their ability to hire development staff.[37] These competitive advantages may well "rescale" the nonprofit sector. All organizations will be forced to focus more intently on income and administration in order to acquire the necessary tools to meet state compliance rules. Viewed from another angle, the values of firms across the board likely will change as increased government oversight requires them to adjust their practices to accommodate state requirements. And these accommodations must take place within a mounting "stockholder paradigm" that is more consistent with Sarbanes–Oxley. Yet, as Lumen Mulligan observes, this "is completely inapposite in the nonprofit sector." Mulligan posits the stakeholder model as the appropriate "normative premise" in the nonprofit realm.[38] The need to balance interests of often diverse constituencies makes the stakeholder model clearly a better fit for nonprofit firms than the stockholder model that philosophically underpins the Sarbanes–Oxley reforms.

Despite questions regarding appropriateness, however, the shareholder model and its profit maximizing mentality continue their incursions into organizations that theoretically exist for charitable purposes. Nowhere is evidence more readily available to support that statement than in the healthcare industry.

The doctor as CFO

Healthcare may not be perceived as critical to the *moral* formation of Americans so as to teach them to become good citizens or instill foundational values. In another sense, however, the relationships formed within the healthcare system with its model of professionalism undoubtedly have been formative. The "care ethic" is more regularly practiced in the traditional relationship between individuals and their family doctors than perhaps any other social connection.

Similarly, the Hippocratic Oath, often reduced to "do no harm" is, in fact, much richer in content, describing the sanctity of relationships and the obligation of the physician to maintain purity in "life and art." Financial concerns, however, are reshaping relationships in the healthcare industry that potentially undermine the purity Hippocrates envisioned.

The documentary *Primary Concern* by Renée McKay and Joani Livingston described the growing difficulty of attracting new physicians into family practice. Pay differentials between specialists and primary care doctors continue to widen with rather dire prospects for the future of family physicians. A report in the *New York Times* revealed that, from 1995 to 2012, the inflation-adjusted income for dermatologists, gastroenterologists, and oncologists grew by over 50 percent while that for primary care doctors increased by approximately 10 percent, a gap attributed largely to insurance compensation rates for medical services.[39] Observing the consequences of this growing differential prompted a physician interviewed for the documentary to describe primary care doctors as an "endangered species."[40] The physician shortage is predicted to hit American inner cities and rural areas particularly hard as primary care doctors retire or leave the practice for more lucrative opportunities.

Interestingly, this primary care crisis is unfolding even as joint MD/MBA programs offered by American medical schools are exploding. Tufts University School of Medicine proudly cites its combined MD/MBA degree program as the first among the illustrious institutions of higher education in the Boston area. Tufts began offering this degree option in 1994 at a time when only eight such programs existed in the United States.[41] According to the American College of Physician Executives, today there are over 130 MD/MBA programs as well as two national organizations, the Association of MD/MBA Programs and National Association of MD/MBA Students, which aid graduates of these programs with placement and provide networking opportunities with other graduates.[42] The growth of these programs over the past two decades corresponds to the rising number of physicians who assume executive positions in the nation's hospitals, clinics, and healthcare systems.

"Physician executives" have not been immune from the wider debate in the United States concerning the growing divide between executive compensation and that of other workers, which has been cited as evidence of financialization. A controversy over pay levels at nonprofit hospitals began in 2014 when the *New York Times* revealed that Dr. Herbert Pardes, who had retired from the New York-Presbyterian Hospital as its president and CEO three years earlier, was still on the hospital payroll, largely in a development role, with total annual compensation of $5.6 million. Dr. Pardes earned some $2 million more than Dr. Steven Corwin, who succeeded him. The chairman of the hospital, Frank A. Bennack, Jr., stated that the hospital retained Dr. Pardes for "urgent fund-raising activities and a range of other institutional needs with which he could assist his superb successor."[43]

The revelation that a nonprofit institution was paying a "former" executive such a lavish sum was startling, and its reverberations were felt in the nation's capital. Senator Charles Grassley (R-Iowa), who has been particularly vocal on the issue of excessive executive compensation in nonprofit firms, stated that Dr. Pardes' compensation package illustrates how "major nonprofit hospitals often are indistinguishable from for-profit hospitals in their operations."[44] Adding to this perception was a statement included in New York-Presbyterian's tax return (public because it is nonprofit) that in determining compensation, the hospital relies on pay patterns in both for-profit and nonprofit health care systems, a practice acceptable under IRS regulations.[45]

The case involving Dr. Pardes and New York-Presbyterian only heightened the buzz that began in the academic world a year earlier. A study conducted through the Harvard University School of Public Health concluded that CEO compensation at nonprofit hospitals was more associated with levels of technology, hospital location, and patient satisfaction than with actual measures of patient care or benefits to the community. Statistics on readmission and hospital deaths showed little to no correlation to CEO pay, despite their frequent use in grading institutional quality.[46]

In 2013, a study by the Hay Group, a management consulting company with expertise in human resources, confirmed that the pay differential between executives and other employees was growing in the healthcare industry as a whole. A *Business Wire* article reporting on the study noted that while there was some "temperance in executive pay," CEO compensation continues on an upward trend while "nursing salary increases trend downward."[47] A Hay Group vice president and executive compensation practice leader for the company's Healthcare Practice division, Ron Seifert, observed changes in the industry that would seem to be driven primarily by financial considerations:

> It's more critical now than ever that hospitals and health systems properly incentivize and retain their executive talent. The environment has never been more complex: systems are becoming insurers, insurers are partnering with health systems, and CEOs are being charged with pushing the organization toward pay-for-performance and population health management.[48]

The frenzy of healthcare industry reorganization compounded by implementation of a national healthcare system has been called a "perfect storm" by several industry analysts, who see financial concerns at the core of the emerging crisis.

Financial demands press even physicians who are not in executive positions to make tough choices. Dr. Sandeep Jauhar's book *Doctored: The Disillusionment of an American Physician* reveals how the financial pressures of being a young doctor at a teaching hospital led him to take supplemental work at a private practice.[49] A primary motivating factor in Jauhar's writing the book was the demand for unnecessary testing of patients to bring in additional revenue, which led him to an ethical crisis. He observes how financial incentives along with "defensive medicine" practiced through an uncoordinated system of specialists not only wastes resources but also damages the quality of care in the American medical system.[50]

Financial conditions are impacting the nation's healthcare system in other ways. Expenses associated with professional liability may be a major factor endangering the very existence of private practice. The American Hospital Association Hospital Statistics report in 2012 showed a 32 percent increase in the "hospital employed physicians" since the year 2000.[51] *Becker's Hospital Review* issued a report showing that the percentage of physicians "intent on staying independent" dropped by 7 points between 2013 and 2014 alone, from 60 percent to 53 percent.[52] Professional liability issues undoubtedly are influencing this trend, yet they also have implications for hospitals that may influence the quality and availability of care. Some states have begun to adopt "corporate liability" or "corporate negligence" laws that make hospitals liable even for malpractice by physicians who are independent contractors and over whom hospitals have less control than "employee physicians."[53] This development risks making "hospital employee physicians" the dominant model in American healthcare, regardless of whether the traditional "independent" family physician model is preferred by patients or whether it has certain cultural benefits that extend beyond the immediate doctor-patient relationship.[54]

Researchers have shown how emphasis on financial measures of performance, even in nonprofit healthcare institutions, at times conflicts with the missions of those organizations. Jeffrey Kramer and Rexford E. Santerre conducted a study on 29 nonprofit hospitals in Connecticut from 1998 to 2006 and determined that pay incentives for CEOs often put them at odds with the community services they are intended to provide. They note that "not-for-profit hospital CEOs, at least in Connecticut, are motivated by pay incentives to increase the occupancy of privately insured patients at the expense of uncompensated care and public-pay patients."[55] Financial incentives of nonprofit hospitals (not just their CEOs) increasingly conflict with their missions of service to the community and raise controversies across the country. Hospital relocations that appear revenue motivated, for example, have led to public protests and even charges of racism. In Round Lake, Illinois, representatives of the Coalition to Save Community Hospitals (CSCH), drawn from different neighborhood and religious groups, attended a public hearing by the Illinois Health Facilities Planning Board and asserted that Advocate Health Care's move to construct a new hospital in Round Lake would be racially divisive. One reporter called the move an example of "medical white flight."[56]

Even in my own hometown, the Baptist hospital located in a low-income area moved to a more affluent corridor right off the interstate and only a couple of miles from the area's Catholic hospital (the only other large hospital in the community), raising some eyebrows. The Baptist hospital cited antiquated facilities as the primary motivation, but some residents saw the move as a means to escape becoming the "indigent-care" facility. Financial incentives, even for nonprofit healthcare providers, are fueling charges of discriminatory practices and leading to cultural divisions that parallel the nation's growing racial divide and income gap.

Some even question whether the term "nonprofit" should apply any longer to hospitals given that their compensation, debt, and administrative structures conform so closely to for-profits. At least from the standpoint of the "charitable hospital" that once was a major provider of healthcare to the poor, those organizations seem to be abandoning the nonprofit model and perhaps the more general class of civil society institutions altogether. The reason for this transition is financial. Monetary incentives and economic conditions have generally reshaped the industry to make it increasingly difficult to distinguish between institutions based on their profit motivations (or lack thereof). Studies have shown, for example, that, in addition to the convergence of compensation practices previously noted, there is also little difference in the capital structures of for-profit and nonprofit healthcare organizations.[57]

Guy David has shown how changes in the economic environment have encouraged "ownership switches"—from for-profit to nonprofit types and vice versa—and caused convergence across the industry in characteristics such as hospital size. According to David, his "model and empirical evidence both suggest that the differential ability to benefit from a given ownership status, and not some underlying difference in objectives, accounts for discrepancies in behavior across hospitals."[58] Again, the beginnings of this leveling of characteristics among hospital ownership types are traceable to roughly the same period to which we have traced the onset of American culture's financialization. David locates the beginning of this phenomenon in the mid-1960s and posits factors he believes shaped this transition such as the introduction of Medicare/Medicaid.[59] He also notes how differences in regulation, rules governing tax-exempt bonds, and other considerations shape the "ownership choices" of hospitals. Moreover, flexibility in the regulatory structure is such "that nonprofits' community-oriented behavior need not be altruistic or unselfish. The regulatory environment provides enough sticks and carrots to produce variation in behavior between for-profit and nonprofit hospitals."[60] One of David's major arguments is that nonprofit hospitals "choose" that status "despite the fact that they will be more likely to face outside pressure to provide free or unprofitable services. The cost of free care is a 'tax' paid by nonprofit hospitals to the communities in which they operate,"[61] in exchange for which they receive tax exemption and other benefits.

There is evidence, however, that some nonprofit hospitals are no longer willing to pay the "tax." Heartland Regional Medical Center in St. Joseph, Missouri, received national attention when it was revealed that as many as 6,000 of Heartland's patients had their wages garnished between 2009 and 2013 to pay bills owed to the hospital, despite Heartland receiving a tax exemption as a charitable institution.[62] The hospital teams with Northwest Financial Services and frequently has sued both adults in a two-wage-earner household, garnishing as much as 25 percent of the wages from one and 10 percent from the other as well as charging 9 percent interest on unpaid balances.[63] Heartland is quite "profitable" by nonprofit standards, collecting $605 million in revenues in 2013, which exceeded expenses by some $45 million.[64]

Changes in economic, legal and political conditions over time have caused a convergence between nonprofit and for-profit hospitals that calls into question whether differences between them justify tax exemption for the former. But the more salient question here is whether this financially driven change, along with economic conditions that are transforming traditional bonds like that between doctor and patient, is altering critical "social" relationships that undergird a culturally healthy as well as physically healthy society. Similar to the transition in the mortgage market from local providers to national and often online lenders, the changes taking place in healthcare go beyond the mere provision and acquisition of services.

If healthcare is a "commodity," then it would seem, at the least, to be a highly personal one. The financial influences that today depersonalize health services and cause for-profit and nonprofit institutions to converge structurally and operationally are subtly but significantly restructuring an element of civil society. Not the least of these is the status of professionals in the industry and its impact on those entering medical professions. A survey of 1,527 physicians by Jackson Healthcare in Georgia demonstrated that less than two-thirds of physicians would recommend a career in medicine to young people due to falling income, a rise in billing and collection problems, and the impact of these changes on the lifestyles of professionals.[65] For those who ignore such cautions, a heavily indebted existence (at least early in their careers) likely awaits, with a median cost of $278,455 to attend private medical school and a cost of $207,868 for their public school counterparts in 2013. This expense led to 36 percent of residents being more than $200,000 in debt and another 22 percent having debts ranging from $100,000 to $200,000.[66] Such indebtedness among physicians likely will continue to reshape the relationship between doctors and patients in the U.S.

Education and the bottom line

The growth of educational entrepreneurialism is fast changing both the institutional structure and cultural ethos of the American academy. An article titled "The Future of College?" appeared in *The Atlantic* in the summer of 2014 and questioned whether bold ventures like the Minerva Project, founded by Ben Nelson, a former executive at the online photo company Snapfish, are revolutionizing the concept of undergraduate liberal arts education. The Minerva idea follows on a legion of primarily online and often for-profit educational institutions that have formed in the Internet era, but it also differs in several key ways. First, the pedagogical architecture behind Minerva was developed by Stephen M. Kosslyn, formerly dean of Social Science at Harvard University and a distinguished cognitive neuroscientist.[67] The school has a dorm located in San Francisco but no lecture-styled classrooms; almost all courses are offered online, conducted by some distinguished academics, and are considered rigorous. Minerva hopes to compete with major Ivy League schools and other premier institutions by offering quality education at half the price. The Minerva alternative is leaner, cheaper, and thoroughly international. Because there are no libraries, gymnasiums, or lecture halls, future "campuses," perhaps more aptly described as "dorm locations," include Berlin and Buenos Aires, with Mumbai,

Hong Kong, New York, and London being possible future choices as well.[68] This market niche has been spawned primarily by the out-of-control cost of American higher education; elite private schools, in particular, continue to push the price of their educational services beyond the financial reach of a dwindling middle class.[69]

Nelson believes American higher education is both overpriced and stagnant. Predicting that the "lecture model will be obliterated," Nelson contends he is raising the status of for-profit education above the level of "evil" where it has been positioned by the many diploma mills that have exploded with the advent of the Internet. He is similarly critical of nonprofit college education, however.[70] In describing cost escalation in higher education generally, Nelson puts much of the blame on federal government subsidies that encourage the admission of high-risk students, and on tuition hikes to which federal money is often tied.[71] Minerva seeks to break the grip of high-priced traditional institutions by providing quality college education and flexible campus arrangements at reasonable prices.

The Minerva experiment and other novel forms of competition are drawing responses from the nation's private colleges and universities. Even storied institutions such as Stanford, Harvard, and Yale are offering online courses and degree programs.[72] These efforts in educational innovation, however, should take us "back to first principles," according to the onetime dean of Harvard University's undergraduate college, Harry R. Lewis. The former computer science professor admits "there's a market for people who want to be more efficiently educated," but Lewis asks, "How do you improve the efficiency of growing up?"[73] Financial burdens largely are prompting this question, as well as an even larger one: can efficiency be the driver to educational excellence? Extreme emphasis on cost efficiency tends to whittle down the purpose of education to fit an investment/return model that may clash with broader views of the purpose of education. Financialization of this vital sector has another, more demonstrable impact: it desensitizes both suppliers and consumers of education services, both for-profit and traditional, to the "price tags," often demonstrating institutions' questionable priorities and enticing students into extreme debt through "flexible" financing and the promise of future returns on the investment.

The radical escalation in higher education costs—up a staggering 1,225 percent between 1978 and 2014[74]—requires a similarly massive influx of money, especially for those private institutions that receive little or no state funds. That requirement is altering the nature of key positions within college administration. College presidents in many cases have been forced to "go to school" themselves to learn the fine art of development for institutions where fundraising can comprise the bulk of the job. It has not always been that way. D. A. Whetten and K. S. Cameron observe a "Golden Age" of university funding in the immediate post-World War period when enrollments were on the rise along with revenues, and the prestige of college administrators and professors was at an all-time high.[75] Subsequently, there was a significant change in the funding of higher education that forced institutions to more actively compete for education dollars.

Federal funds for colleges were greatly reduced beginning in the 1970s and grew more pronounced in the next decade, even as the prestige of degrees along with those of their institutions and faculties plummeted, and corporations engaged in competition with traditional colleges by training their own employees.[76]

Being thrown into vigorous competition for private donations as state money evaporated prompted many private schools to create or expand development departments and hone their fundraising techniques. David W. Breneman observes that "many small [private] colleges did not have a history of sophisticated fund-raising activities before the 1980s, but most advanced far along the learning curve during that decade."[77] In reality, they had no choice. Whetten and Cameron describe an era of financial insecurity in higher education, particularly during the 1970s.[78] Funds were scarce and public colleges and universities accounted for few fundraising campaigns, but that has all changed as state schools have narrowed the gap with their private counterparts. The 1990s came to be called the "billion-dollar decade" because it marked the beginning of a period when the threshold for significant fundraising levels reached $1 billion dollars among major institutions. However, Frank Rhodes, former president of Cornell University, also notes that the billion-dollar campaign reflects "the magnitude of the financial challenges facing many institutions as they seek to attract and retain high-quality faculty and staff, maintain their libraries, computing centers, dormitories, and other facilities." Rhodes says that private donations have transitioned from being a "welcome add-on that can provide a margin of excellence" to a form of support that "is essential to institutional survival."[79] By 1990, there were 141 colleges and universities in the "Philanthropy 400"—those 400 organizations receiving the most donated funds—which made these schools the largest single group in terms of donations.[80]

In this area, as in many others, evidence exists that financial practices and values are homogenizing institutions, as public and private universities now compete intensely for gifts. According to Brad Choate, who formerly worked as a development officer at The Ohio State University, "The difference between a public and a private university is in how you run it—with elected officials or not—rather than in how you fund it."[81] But the intensity of competition for funding sources among universities has also taken a toll on university officials. Former vice chancellor for development and university relations at the University of North Carolina at Chapel Hill, Gary Evans, commented, "Woe to be the fund raiser who wants to set a goal that is less than the competition's," implying the job-related risk of such under-ambition.[82] One disillusioned, unidentified first-year college president stated, "finances drive everything—I found that out in the first few months on the job. It dawned on me that I had over-romanticized what it was going to be like to be a president."[83] Fundraising today has expanded to affect not only presidents and development officers, but also deans, department chairs, athletic directors and coaches, and professors who seek funds for research and other projects.

Emphasis on the finances of institutions is altering liberal arts education generally. Private liberal arts colleges that have traditionally focused on broad-based curricula and the teaching of undergraduates rather than on faculty research play a unique role in American civil society. According to D. W. Breneman,

> the "privateness" means that certain values—religious and otherwise—can inform their mission in ways not possible at state institutions, while their small size makes possible a sense of community among students, faculty, and staff that can rarely be achieved in larger settings.[84]

Ozan Jaquette has provided statistical evidence, however, to show that mission drift is occurring among these schools as they respond to changes in the "enrollment economy." Jaquette argues that beginning around the 1970s, many "colleges became universities to grow and diversify enrollments (e.g., add graduate education) so that organizational stability would no longer be dependent on the traditional customer base of full-time, undergraduate students."[85]

Just as changes in consumer tastes were stimulated by the mass-produced goods associated with the era of Fordism described in previous chapters, so too were the tastes of American consumers of educational services changing for more specialized, often professional programs and curricula.[86] Breneman used data from the 1986 Higher Education General Information Survey (HEGIS) to show that a once-robust count of 600 liberal arts colleges had declined to 212. His conclusion "was as simple as it was disturbing: the liberal arts college as we know it is disappearing … and another type of institution—the professional college—is taking its place."[87]

Changes in student preferences for education arguably have been stimulated by the wider and increasingly financialized American culture. Competitive pressures made traditional liberal arts education seem more of a luxury in an environment where efficiency and "return on educational investment" were becoming important measures of academic success. But institutions themselves were also becoming more cognizant of the employment possibilities for students emerging from their programs. With unemployment in the U.S. rising to nearly 10 percent in the early 1980s, baccalaureate schools offering general humanities education began to rethink their educational models. According to Jaquette, three principal factors—"changing student preferences toward professional majors, a declining college-age population, and growth in competition from public universities"—caused a major shift among these schools "to the comprehensive university template, which encouraged curriculum and enrollment strategies that would increase organizational stability."[88] Administrative changes thought necessary to adapt to changing market conditions and contribute to the viability of both educational institutions and the students they graduate appear to have had other impacts as well.

A study by Matthew Kraatz, Marc Ventresca, and Lina Deng, specifically focusing on liberal arts schools, shows how institutions adopting "ostensibly innocuous innovations" can often lead to the subversion of critical organizational values. Building on the institutional theory of UC Berkeley professor Philip Selznick, they show how in the area of enrollment management and, specifically, through the "'strategic' use of financial aid," liberal arts colleges may be undermining the missions and values of their institutions. Their theory, which they describe with the term "precarious values and mundane innovations," was tested using a sample of 515 private colleges with a liberal arts focus and spans the years 1987 through 2006.[89]

In the case of liberal arts colleges, the rise of enrollment management as a critical function has been dramatic: only 3 percent of the 515 institutions surveyed by Kraatz and his colleagues had implemented enrollment management in 1987, but that figure jumped to 46 percent by 2006.[90] The authors note how colleges combining their admissions and financial aid units/functions establish a serious threat to those elites—especially longtime faculty and administrators—who are responsible for preserving essential values that, in many cases, define the institution. The internal dynamic that works to subvert institutional values combines these functions that presumably enhance efficiency and effectiveness. For example, the authors observe that, in most schools, financial aid was formerly defined by a largely charitable mission that, through changes in the enrollment management structure, has been transformed into one seeking higher return on investment. Likewise, the admissions function has lost the autonomy necessary to protect those values with which it is charged. Under the new structure, admissions personnel "heavily weight financial considerations (such as the student's ability to pay full tuition) as they evaluate applications."[91] The authors believe these changes result from liberal arts colleges empowering their "operative systems" often at the expense of their academic missions.[92]

Institutions of higher education also have become more sophisticated in their use of financial tools. In the 1990s, schools like American University, Vanderbilt University, and the University of Michigan began to participate in the swaps market in order to lower their cost of capital incurred through bond issues. Interest-rate swaps enable bond issuers like universities, municipal governments, and corporations to exchange the interest rate structures of the bonds they issue for other bond rate structures in order to lower their interest payment obligations as market conditions change. They do this as a hedge against exposure to interest-rate changes. An issuing institution, for example, may decide to swap some of its fixed-rate bond obligations for lower-rate variable interest bonds, pegged to a market index rate or some other standard rate, if the market conditions look favorable for the continuation of low interest rates. Of course, such a transaction takes on the risk that interest rates might actually rise and increase the debt burden of the institution.[93]

The enormous endowments of some of the nation's most prestigious universities make engaging in the swaps market to lower the cost of capital an alluring but also risky business. This was seen in dramatic fashion in 2009, when Harvard University had to pay $497.6 million dollars to "exit" interest-rate swap contracts totaling $1.1 billion associated with bonds issued to fund additional graduate student housing, a medical research building, and a new Center for Government and International Studies.[94] Harvard entered into swaps to reduce its exposure to the variable-rate debt it issued for these development projects, fearing that interest rates would rise. Because of the financial crisis and subsequent recession, central banks instead began cutting benchmark rates to historically low levels, causing Harvard's swap transactions to lose value and requiring the University to post substantial collateral to cover its obligations under those contracts. In 2009, Harvard sold additional bonds worth $2.5 billion, some of the proceeds of which were used to get out of the swap contracts. Making matters worse, Harvard reported in the same year that its endowment dropped from $36.9 billion to $26 billion, which led to employee layoffs, hiring and salary freezes, and early retirement offerings.[95]

Harvard is not alone in experiencing financial losses resulting from participation in interest-rate swaps. Georgetown, Yale, the University of Connecticut and other schools have lost substantial funds in trying to guess the direction and magnitude of interest-rate changes. Specifically referencing Harvard's losses, Robert Doty, who works for American Governmental Services in Sacramento as a municipal finance adviser, stated it shows "people don't understand the complexity of the products they are buying and selling and that doesn't begin and end with mortgage securities."[96] The Harvard example also shows that, even in the predominantly nonprofit and traditionally conservative realm of higher education, financial techniques can entice administrators to take major risks without understanding the potential consequences of their actions.[97]

Debt in higher education today, however, is more commonly associated with students than with the institutions they attend. The Indybay news organization in California asked 300 students at Sonoma State to take a survey on their student loans, anticipating that many respondents would reveal that they are thousands of dollars in debt. The astonishing result, however, was that around 80 percent did not know how much debt they had incurred or the interest rates they were paying.[98] The survey also disclosed the thin margin at which students were operating with respect to college expenses. When students were asked if they could remain in school if an additional $500 fee increase were applied to their bills, 55 percent responded either that they would not be able to continue or were unsure whether they could continue.[99]

The continued escalation of student debt in the U.S. is beginning to inspire activism among civil society groups. At the beginning of the fall 2014 semester, students at Everest College learned that the Rolling Jubilee Fund, a group that emerged from Occupy Wall Street, had acquired and abolished their student loans, the total amount of which was over $3.8 million. Everest is a subsidiary institution of the for-profit Corinthian Colleges, which is being sued by the Consumer Financial Protection Bureau of the federal government for alleged predatory lending practices.[100] Other goals of Rolling Jubilee's debt abolition were to encourage students to unionize and take collective action against a college financing system that makes students the most indebted class in America and to show how "consumer debt can be purchased for cents on the dollar."[101] The Everest College student debt cancellation follows Rolling Jubilee's 2013 purchase and abolishment of $1.2 million in personal debt and medical debt totaling $13.5 million for some 2,693 people that the organization acquired for only

$400,000. Rolling Jubilee primarily uses crowd sourcing to fund its debt relief campaigns in a way that involves the wider society in helping alleviate fellow citizens' debt problems.[102]

Other cases illustrate that the financing of college education is particularly prone to abuse. A major student loan "charity," EduCap, Inc., became embroiled in controversy when the IRS alleged that it operated inappropriately for a company receiving tax exemption. EduCap was said to be charging exorbitant interest on its loans to students even as its CEO and her husband were receiving millions in monetary compensation and cashing in on other benefits such as allowing EduCap's private jet to be used by family and friends.[103] Ethical transgressions at for-profit firms is troubling enough; extension of similar problems into the sector that ostensibly has adopted a "society first" commitment has a far more degrading impact on social ethics. One expects the Wall Street financier to be obsessed with money making, but the leaders of charities and public service organizations are held to a higher standard.

Still, civil society mobilization has great potential not only to expose abuses but also to help reestablish distinctions between for-profit and nonprofit groups. As in Rolling Jubilee's assistance to Everest College students, civil society groups can educate both consumers and investors in financial decision making and serve to remind the broader society why nonprofits and their tax exemptions exist.

Capital innovation and organizational confusion

Eric Thurman, the CEO of the consulting firm Geneva Global that provides research, grant management, and other services to philanthropists throughout the world, observed a statistic, the likes of which has become all too common in the aftermath of natural disasters. The World Bank reported that total contributions to victims of the December 26, 2004, tsunami in Indonesia averaged around $36,000 for every displaced person, ten times the country's per capita GDP; yet more than a year after the tsunami, only a small fraction of the money donated had reached victims.[104] Relief efforts for disasters in Thailand, Sri Lanka, Haiti, and elsewhere have experienced similar results. Massive amounts of capital designed to relieve human suffering either never reaches its intended recipients or does so only after considerable delay.

The Cystic Fibrosis Foundation example in the introduction to this chapter presents a similar question: Will the new drug developed with the aid of the foundation's resources be affordable for the CFF's primary constituents, those who suffer with the disease? Decisions concerning the appropriate uses of capital seem increasingly complex. Moreover, continual reconstitution of capital in this age of financialization is impacting American civil society and complicating the distinction between for-profit and nonprofit firms. A bevy of new buzz terms surrounding charitable groups—social entrepreneurship, strategic philanthropy, and venture philanthropy to name a few—create confusion among donors or investors, who are left to decide how to best employ their resources.

The ease with which capital can be manipulated may also encourage nonprofits to emphasize more efficient acquisition and mobilization of financial capital at the expense of doing the hard work of organizing volunteers and engaging clients directly. Certain benefits to the deployment of financial capital in philanthropy can *potentially* be enormous, as the CFF example illustrates; yet risks are often higher not only to capital itself but also to organizational mission and values. Seemingly endless varieties of capital manipulation that have attended financialization and filtered into civil society are today prompting serious identity questions among civic, philanthropic, and other groups founded to provide social benefits.

The search for revenue sources over the past couple of decades has encouraged nonprofits to experiment with organizational forms and new "lines of business." A study of hospitals, universities, and museums from the early 1990s revealed that unrelated business income jumped by almost 35 percent between 1990 and 1993.[105] Changing resource demographics in the nonprofit world commanded the quest for revenues. Private contributions dropped dramatically from 53 percent of total operating expenditures in 1964 to around 24 percent in 1993, which was followed by a sharp reduction in volunteer hours going to nonprofits in the late 1980s and early 1990s.[106] These changes in funding and volunteering trends have prompted some firms to capitalize on certain tax benefits, to commercialize operations in order to bring in new revenue streams, or both. Joseph T. Cordes and Burton A. Weisbrod concluded that "differential taxation encourages nonprofits to pursue commercial ventures that they would otherwise avoid by providing excess financial returns that nonprofits can exploit because of their tax-exempt status."[107] In another report, Weisbrod also pointed to considerable anecdotal evidence of a "dramatic change in nonprofit sector finance" in the liberal application of user fees, including the rise of tuition costs, hospital room rates, admission fees to museums and zoos, and the expansion of user fees in other industries designed to charge "the very people whom they were established to help."[108] These observations led Weisbrod to conclude, "Nonprofit organizations confront a dilemma, as does public policy toward them: How to balance pursuit of their social missions with financial constraints, when additional resources may be available from sources that would distort those social missions."[109] The dilemma Weisbrod observed in the 1990s has not been resolved; in fact, it has expanded as more imaginative forms of capital have proliferated. As traditional revenue sources dissipate, nonprofits are more tempted to ignore the potential consequences for their missions that may be associated with new or expanded sources.

Social entrepreneurship is one innovative means to bring additional capital to the nonprofit sector. It attempts to bridge best practices from the commercial and nonprofit worlds, and it has paved the way for the contributions of successful entrepreneurs who may be turned off by traditional forms of philanthropic giving. Roger Martin and Sally Osberg attempt to dissect the term, taking the term "entrepreneurship" back to its roots in the work of French economist Jean-Baptiste Say, who defined the entrepreneur as "one who 'shifts economic resources out of an area of lower and into an area of higher productivity and greater yield.' "[110] Entrepreneurship also has long been associated with Austrian economist Joseph Schumpeter's notion of "creative destruction."[111] But Schumpeter's construct has a markedly different connotation in the nonprofit as opposed to the for-profit world. Even in the market exchange context, creative destruction suggests that economic progress often necessitates product obsolescence, the deskilling of workers, and forms of economic dislocation. In the social context where relationships and social capital are commonly the goals, destruction of existing forms in order to further progress is likely to have unintended consequences. What may be lost in the focus on social entrepreneurship and other novel methods of "giving back" to society is the continuing need for grassroots social service organizations to meet the human need for relationships as much as material goods.

There are similarities between business and social entrepreneurs. Neither is primarily motivated by money but rather by zealous pursuit of a vision, "deriving considerable psychic reward from the process of realizing their ideas."[112] But the business entrepreneur is accountable to investors who require financial return. By contrast, the social entrepreneur "aims for value in the form of large-scale, transformational benefit that accrues either to a significant segment of society or to society at large."[113] That is one interpretation of "aim," but the term is so malleable that methods are virtually unlimited and, therefore, subject to the whims of the entrepreneur. Ian Eppler, a student at Brown University, observes the problem, writing that social entrepreneurship "is the epitome of a buzzword; it is a term that means something slightly different to everyone and ultimately nothing to anyone, facilitating obfuscation and equivocation."[114] Roger Martin and Sally Osberg note how such definitional problems can confuse roles in social service provision. They insist that "equilibrium" should be preserved among different roles in the provision of social benefits; yet they observe how new models of philanthropy and social ventures have confused roles played by different actors that today require clarification:

> In the pure form, the successful social entrepreneur takes direct action and generates a new and sustained equilibrium; the social activist influences others to generate a new and sustained equilibrium; and the social service provider takes direct action to improve the outcomes of the current equilibrium.[115]

In the same way that equilibrium among roles must be preserved, so there must also be equilibrium between labor and capital in the sector so as to preserve the humanity of services provided. Moreover, achieving equilibrium does not mean simply that appropriate proportions of labor and capital are maintained but also that the "type" of capital employed is appropriate to the recipients of its benefits as well as to those responsible for working with financial capital in achieving those benefits. Financialization's incursions into civil society threaten to disrupt that equilibrium, generally favoring innovative new forms of capital to more compassionate provisions of social service.

The challenge today is recognizing that our remarkable ability to manipulate capital tends to promote disequilibrium by favoring capital over labor. Despite the dogged insistence of neoclassical economists to the contrary, the level of money in almost any social enterprise changes things. Financialization in general has promoted novelty in capital manipulation often at the expense of human relationships. It can also obfuscate the actions of those who would cheat to advance their own interests. Those new forms today are entering religious organizations, voluntary associations, and other charitable groups in ways that can potentially change their cultures. The question is how to maintain the appropriate balance in those organizations because it is not only the services they provide but *how* those services are funded and provisioned that impacts the broader culture within which they operate.

Another popular source of capital for nonprofits in recent decades is cooperative funding arrangements between for-profits and nonprofits. Licensing agreements, for example, where a nonprofit allows a for-profit firm to use its name in the sale of products, can offer substantial returns. Those agreements can also lead to conflicts of interests and clashes concerning the respective "reputations" of partners and other issues. In one case, the American Medical Association (AMA) entered into an agreement with Sunbeam, a major supplier of health products, in which the AMA would receive royalties for the sale of Sunbeam products it endorsed.[116] Responses to the deal, not only among members of the 150-year-old medical association but also concerned observers, were overwhelmingly negative, believing that the AMA's credibility would be compromised. The reaction was so strong that the board of trustees for the AMA cancelled key provisions that would enable the AMA to profit from the deal with Sunbeam, and the board was compelled to adopt a policy that the AMA would not enter into future endorsement or royalty deals or engage in "exclusive" corporate partnerships.[117]

The venture philanthropy model, as described in the CFF example, continues to reshape the philanthropic landscape. However, some question whether venture philanthropy's days are numbered, and the reason lies in its own ethos: the incessant quest for novelty in funding methods. Joanna Jacobson observes that "finding the 'new' new thing is the primary occupation of several well-intentioned philanthropies"; yet, this obsession led "to a dramatic shift in philanthropic dollars to high-risk startups, diverting money away from traditional nonprofit organizations."[118] The downside to venture philanthropy, as Jacobson sees it, is that it feeds "a beast that is already well sated": venture philanthropy's hunger for constantly seeking out the "new thing," which results in a proliferation of startup nonprofits with ideas, funding, and often inexperienced leaderships that "are not ready for prime time."[119] The major problem is the opportunity cost of funding such efforts: often well-established social service providers that have long track records and stable administrations are passed over for gambles on new ventures with "possibilities."

In the case of the CFF, the Foundation today stands at a critical moment in its history. A massive infusion of capital has forced a decision: the organization must decide whether to emphasize greater return on investment in potential new medicines or continue its traditional methods of providing broad-based benefits in serving its constituents. These decisions writ large have the potential to alter fundamentally the very ethos of the American nonprofit sector and the provision of social services.

Perhaps the increased emphasis on finance among nonprofits is not only culturally inspired by financialization but also results from a related attitude among, perhaps many, that there is a natural affinity between objective measures of performance in both the financial and nonprofit sectors. Eric Thurman suggests as much by commenting that "measuring life change can be remarkably easy."[120] Thurman goes on to list examples such as "income growth, improved nutrition, access to healthcare" and others, but, while objective measures of material life change can be relatively easy to acquire, the cultural benefits are more complex. It is the appropriate "composition" of capital—human, financial, and other forms—and not simply requiring more of these resources, that is important. Just as shortages of capital can hamstring firms, so too major influxes of "high-maintenance" capital can overwhelm organizations; moreover, they can reshape organizational cultures and missions. Even large inflows of simple donations can unbalance the provision of services, as in the case of the Indonesia tsunami, resulting in inadequate or "untimely" aid going to intended recipients. Balance must be achieved among human, financial, and other forms of capital in those organizations formed to provide social benefits so they can succeed.

Conclusion

In a presentation on "effective philanthropy" at a meeting of the American Philosophical Society in April, 2004, Stanley Katz told the audience that despite problems in public/private partnerships in philanthropy, "I hope we can rethink it rather than discard it. I am not worried about the 'heart' in philanthropy. I am worried about its mind."[121] Continuing with Katz's analogy, one should recognize that the mind has considerable control over the functioning of the heart. In the case of philanthropy, if our minds become too enamored with financial novelty and efficient resource allocation at the expense of the humane provision of benefits, then the heart is likely to follow the mind's lead.

The financial mind has been much at work in other areas of American civil society with questionable results. One aspect of higher education that was not discussed previously and may not come immediately to mind with regard to civil society is that of collegiate athletics. Inclusion of college sports programs in this chapter on civil society may seem misplaced, but on Saturday afternoons in the fall, there is probably no stronger communal bond rallying around a singular "cause" anywhere in the country. If a measure of the strength of civil society is loyalty to an institution and the transmission of values (some good, some bad), then college football ranks highly indeed. The fans who participate in those rituals do not profit from them; rather, they often spend thousands of dollars per year following their favorite teams around the country, tailgating in the RVs customized with their teams' colors and logos, plopping down major outlays for plane fare, meals, fuel, and lodging.

In college athletics, monetary measures of success are becoming valued above all others. Even with departments spanning the arts and sciences, medicine, business, law, education, and other disciplines that produce copious research and talented graduates who go on to major accomplishments, success in institutions of higher education as a whole is often reduced to wins and losses on the football field. Wins translate into television contracts, which mean big bucks not only from the value of those contracts but also ticket revenue, increased donations from alumni, and income universities receive from the sale of sports paraphernalia.

In October 2011, *The Atlantic* created shockwaves by featuring an exposé on what might be described as the financialization of college athletics. Taylor Branch's "The Shame of College Sports" described a presentation by Sonny Vaccaro, the "sneaker pimp," who had secured lucrative sponsorship contracts over the years between Nike, Adidas, and Reebok and big-time university conferences and programs. In a meeting with the Knight Commission on Intercollegiate Athletics, Vaccaro was asked by the president emeritus of Penn State University, Bryce Jordan, why a university should serve "as an advertising medium for your industry?" Branch describes Vaccaro's reply:

> Vaccaro did not blink. "They shouldn't, sir," he replied. "You sold your souls, and you're going to continue selling them. You can be very moral and righteous in asking me that question, sir," Vaccaro added with irrepressible good cheer, "but there's not one of you in this room that's going to turn down any of our money. You're going to take it. I can only offer it."[122]

Vaccaro's confidence was boosted by the reality of money's influence even in ostensibly "amateur" athletics. The Southeastern Conference (SEC) was the first to eclipse $1 billion in revenues from its athletic programs in 2010. Its millions of fans across the American Southeast have contributed to the drive for "profits," whatever the tax-status of these athletic programs' home institutions. Big-time programs at state universities in Michigan, Florida, and Texas can bring in $40 to $80 million per year after compensating coaches with seven- or even eight-figure contracts. A *Washington Post* story citing the *Chronicle of Higher Education* reported that head football coaches' pay in the NCAA now averages around four times the pay of college presidents.[123] While big-time revenue is made by big-time schools, smaller institutions struggle just to keep their athletic programs alive. Many of those that struggle are traditional liberal arts schools that have "done things right," but market conditions have changed such that those schools wishing to preserve the ethical and social benefits of collegiate sports may be forced to eliminate them if they cannot produce the financial results.

Perhaps the desire of many to hold the present college athletic system together, however unfair or duplicitous it may seem at times, stems from a deep-seated, if almost inarticulable belief that when cultural institutions founded for purposes of achievement without monetary gain completely disappear, the society as a whole will suffer. The financialization of American civil society portends similar consequences unless we learn to tame financial capital and once again make it an important means to *other* ends rather than an end in itself.

Notes

1 Joseph Walker and Jonathan D. Rockoff, "Cystic Fibrosis Foundation Sells Drug's Rights for $3.3 Billion," *Wall Street Journal* (Updated November 19, 2014); available at http://online.wsj.com/articles/cystic-fibrosis-foundation-sells-drugs-rights-for-3–3-billion-1416414300?tesla=y&mg=reno64-wsj&url=http://online.wsj.com/article/SB11401573521024413408604580286760275011550.html.
2 Cystic Fibrosis Foundation website, "Frequently Asked Questions"; available at www.cff.org/AboutCF/Faqs/.
3 Walker and Rockoff, "Cystic Fibrosis Foundation Sells Drug's Rights for $3.3 Billion."
4 Quoted in Marc S. Reisch, "Cystic Fibrosis Foundation Gets $3.3 Billion For Royalties," *Chemical & Engineering News* vol. 92, no. 47 (November 24, 2014): 7.
5 Reisch cites the Leukemia & Lymphoma Society and JDRF, a "diabetes research foundation," as examples of other nonprofit organizations that invest in pharmaceutical development and do accept royalties from the drug sales of companies with which they partner. See Reisch, "Cystic Fibrosis Foundation," 7.
6 See "Grassley Seeks Update on Any SEC Review of Vertex Pharmaceuticals' Stock Spike"; available at www.grassley.senate.gov/news/news-releases/grassley-seeks-update-any-sec-review-vertex-pharmaceuticals%E2%80%99-stock-spike.
7 Health Care Renewal, "Is the Cystic Fibrosis Foundation a Charity or a Venture Capital Firm?"; available at http://hcrenewal.blogspot.com/2013/06/is-cystic-fibrosis-foundation-charity.html. The article states that "total compensation and stock holdings" for Vertex CEO Jeffrey M. Leiden in 2012 was more than $5.65 million in 2012 while Cystic Fibrosis Foundation CEO Robert J. Beall reportedly made more than $1 million in 2011 according to the Foundation's Form 990.
8 L. Salamon, "Partners in Public Service: The Scope and Theory of Government–Nonprofit Relations," in *The Nonprofit Sector: A Research Handbook*, W. W. Powell, ed. (New Haven, CN: Yale University Press, 1987), 99–117; cited in Richard D. Heimovics, Robert D. Herman, and Carole L. Jurkiewicz Coughlin, "Executive Leadership and Resource Dependence in Nonprofit Organizations: A Frame Analysis," *Public Administration Review* 53, no. 5 (September–October, 1993): 420.
9 Heimovics, *et al.*, cite W. Bielefeld, "Funding Uncertainties and Nonprofit Strategies in the 1980s," *Nonprofit Management and Leadership* 2, no. 4 (1992): 381–401; in Heimovics, Herman, and Jurkiewicz Coughlin, "Executive Leadership and Resource Dependence," 421.
10 Kirsten A. Grønbjerg, *Understanding Nonprofit Funding: Managing Revenues in Social Services and Community Development Organizations* (San Francisco: Jossey-Bass, 1993); and Ralph M. Kramer and B. Grossman, "Contracting for Social Services," *Social Service Review* 61: 32–55; cited in Chao Guo, "When Government Becomes the Principal Philanthropist: The Effects of Public Funding on Patterns of Nonprofit Governance," *Public Administration Review* vol. 67, no. 3 (May–June 2007): 461.
11 Guo, "When Government Becomes the Principal Philanthropist," 461.
12 Christopher Marquis, Gerald F. Davis, and Mary Ann Glynn, "Golfing Alone? Corporations, Elites, and Nonprofit Growth in 100 American Communities," *Organization Science* 24, no. 1 (2013): 41.

13 The authors define elite-oriented nonprofits as those "organizations that focus on the enrichment of the local cultural environment or the preservation of elite-oriented values and traditions" whereas social-welfare nonprofits are those "organizations that address the amelioration of local social problems or human needs in the community." Marquis, Davis, and Glynn, "Golfing Alone?" 42 (emphasis authors').
14 Christine J. Gardner, "Nonprofits Tap New Donors with Internet Fundraising," *Christianity Today* 24, 14 (December 7, 1998): 26–7.
15 Xavier de Souza Briggs, "Social Capital and the Cities: Advice to Change Agents," *National Civic Review* vol. 86, no. 2 (Summer 1997): 111, 112.
16 Many of Putnam's ideas were put forth in an earlier article that appeared in *Political Science and Politics*. In that article he noted a downward trend in "trusting and joining" among citizens that spans various demographics and impacts both urban and rural areas in the United States. See Robert D. Putnam, "Tuning In, Tuning Out: The Strange Disappearance of Social Capital in America," *Political Science and Politics*, vol. 28, no. 4 (December 1995): 670.
17 Irene Taviss Thomson, "The Theory That Won't Die: From Mass Society to the Decline of Social Capital," *Sociological Forum* 20, no. 3 (September 2005): 441.
18 Thomson cites Putnam, *Bowling Alone: The Collapse and Revival of Community* (New York: Simon & Schuster, 2000), 178; in Thomson, "The Theory That Won't Die," 441.
19 Thomson, "The Theory That Won't Die," 441.
20 "Millennials in Adulthood: Detached from Institutions, Networked with Friends," Pew Research Social & Demographic Trends (March 7, 2014); available at www.pewsocialtrends.org/2014/03/07/millennials-in-adulthood/.
21 "Millennials in Adulthood."
22 Gerald F. Davis, "The Rise and Fall of Finance and the End of the Society of Organizations," *Academy of Management Perspectives*, vol. 23, no. 3 (August 2009): 39. Davis states that the rise of finance means that

> corporations are no longer the organizing principle of U.S. society. As a result, we are left to pick up the pieces of an economic crisis saddled with institutions and a conceptual model of society suited for an era that has passed.

He also notes how the transition to a portfolio society meant that "household welfare was increasingly tied to the vagaries of financial markets." See Davis, "The Rise and Fall of Finance," 27, 28, 40.
23 Davis, "The Rise and Fall of Finance," 41.
24 Robert D. Putnam, Robert Leonardi, and Raffaella Y. Nanetti, *Making Democracy Work: Civic Traditions in Modern Italy* (Princeton, NJ: Princeton University Press, 1994).
25 See "2013 Nonprofit Employment Practices Survey"; available at www.nonprofithr.com/wp-content/uploads/2013/03/2013-Employment-Trends-Survey-Report.pdf. The survey/report is prepared by the firm NonprofitHR with the assistance of The Improve Group.
26 Robert D. Herman and David O. Renz, "Nonprofit Organizational Effectiveness: Contrasts Between Especially Effective and Less Effective Organizations," *Nonprofit Management & Leadership* vol. 9, no. 1 (Fall 1998): 24, 32.
27 William J. Ritchie and Robert W. Kolodinsky, "Nonprofit Organization Financial Performance Measurement: An Evaluation of New and Existing Financial Performance Measures," *Nonprofit Management and Leadership* 13, no. 4 (Summer 2003): 378.
28 Herman and Renz, "Nonprofit Organizational Effectiveness," 24.
29 Herman and Renz, "Nonprofit Organizational Effectiveness," 33.
30 J. G. Carman, "Evaluation Practice among Community-Based Organizations: Research into the Reality," *American Journal of Evaluation* 28(1) (2007): 60–75;

cited in Kelly LeRoux and Nathaniel S. Wright, "Does Performance Measurement Improve Strategic Decision Making? Findings From a National Survey of Nonprofit Social Service Agencies," *Nonprofit and Voluntary Sector Quarterly* XX(x); available at http://nvs.sagepub.com/content/early/2010/04/02/0899764009359942.

31 Ritchie and Kolodinsky, "Nonprofit Organization Financial Performance Measurement," 379.

32 Joseph Mead, "Confidence in the Nonprofit Sector through Sarbanes–Oxley-Style Reforms," *Michigan Law Review* 106, no. 5 (March 2008): 883–4.

33 The New York law mandates nonprofits with at least 20 employees and revenues of $1 million or more to implement a whistleblower policy and all nonprofit firms with at least $100,000 in revenue to obtain an independent audit of their financials. Joshua S. Rubenstein, Ronni G. Davidowitz, and Mal L. Barasch, "The New York Non-Profit Revitalization Act of 2013 – Important Changes Affecting New York Nonprofit Entities and Charitable Trusts," *The National Law Review* (February 24, 2014); available at www.natlawreview.com/article/new-york-non-profit-revitalization-act-2013-important-changes-affecting-new-york-non.

34 Thomas E. Hartman, "The Cost of Being Public in the Era of Sarbanes–Oxley," June 15, 2006; cited in Mead, "Confidence in the Nonprofit Sector," 893.

35 Steven Rathgeb Smith, "The Challenge of Strengthening Nonprofits and Civil Society," *Public Administration Review* 68, Supplement to Volume 68: The Winter Commission Report Revisited: 21st Century Challenges Confronting State and Local Governance and How Performance Can Be Improved (December 2008): S136.

36 Smith, "The Challenge of Strengthening Nonprofits and Civil Society," S138.

37 Smith, "The Challenge of Strengthening Nonprofits and Civil Society," S138.

38 Lumen N. Mulligan, "What's Good for the Goose Is Not Good for the Gander: Sarbanes–Oxley-Style Nonprofit Reforms," *Michigan Law Review* 105, no. 8, The Louis & Myrtle Moskowitz Conference on the Impact of Sarbanes–Oxley on Doing Business (June 2007): 2005.

39 Elizabeth Rosenthal, "Patients' Costs Skyrocket; Specialists' Incomes Soar," *New York Times* (January 18, 2014); available at www.nytimes.com/2014/01/19/health/patients-costs-skyrocket-specialists-incomes-soar.html?_r=0.

40 See http://primaryconcernmovie.com/ for information on accessing the documentary.

41 See http://medicine.tufts.edu/Education/MD-Programs/Combined-Degree-Programs/MDMBA.

42 For information on growth in MD/MBA programs see www.med.upenn.edu/educ_combdeg/documents/ACPEDualMDMBAProgramsOnTheRiseSept2010.pdf. For information on the Association of MD/MBA Programs see http://mdmbaprograms.com/4.html.

43 Anemona Hartocollis, "At New York-Presbyterian Hospital, Its Ex-C.E.O Finds Lucrative Work," *New York Times* (July 15, 2014); available at www.nytimes.com/2014/07/16/nyregion/at-newyork-presbyterian-hospital-its-ex-ceo-finds-lucrative-work-.html?_r=0. Perhaps hinting at similarity between the insular nature of executive compensation in nonprofit hospitals and that of Wall Street firms, Hartocollis observed that "executive compensation continued to rise at major New York hospitals even after the stock market crash of 2008." See Hartocollis, "At New York-Presbyterian Hospital."

44 Hartocollis, "At New York-Presbyterian Hospital."

45 Hartocollis, "At New York-Presbyterian Hospital."

46 Karen E. Joynt, Sidney T. Le, E. John Orav, and Ashish K. Jha, "Compensation of Chief Executive Officers at Nonprofit U.S. Hospitals," *Journal of the American Medical Association Internal Medicine* 174, no. 1 (2014): 61–7 [originally published online in 2013].

47 "Hay Group's Annual Healthcare Compensation Study Shows More Executives

Being Paid Based on Long-Term Incentive Plans," *Business Wire* [New York], November 12, 2013; available via ProQuest ABI Inform.

48 Quoted in "Hay Group's Annual Healthcare Compensation Study."

49 Sandeep Jauhar, *Doctored: The Disillusionment of an American Physician* (New York: Farrar, Straus and Giroux, 2014).

50 See "Cardiologist Speaks from the Heart about America's Medical System," transcript from Jauhar's August 19, 2014 interview with Terry Gross on National Public Radio's "Fresh Air"; available at www.wbur.org/npr/341632184/cardiologist-speaks-from-the-heart-about-americas-medical-system.

51 American Hospital Association, AHA Hospital Statistics, vii (5th edn 2012); cited in Starlett M. Miller, "From Private Practice to Hospital Employment: How Employing Physicians Impacts Hospital Liability for Physician Malpractice," *Healthcare Liability & Litigation* 14, no. 2 (May 2012): 1.

52 Anuja Vaidya, "The Decline of the Independent Physician: 8 Statistics," *Becker's Hospital Review* (June 27, 2014); available at www.beckershospitalreview.com/hospital-physician-relationships/the-decline-of-the-independent-physician-8-statistics.html.

53 Miller, "From Private Practice to Hospital Employment," 3.

54 Another powerful piece of evidence showing that financial and monetary concerns are influencing the healthcare industry and those relationships it supports is evidence that billing issues have become a major component in quality of care measures. In 2013, TransUnion Healthcare conducted a survey that showed patients whose billing experience is positive provide higher overall marks for quality of care. According to *Becker's Hospital Review*, "the patient's financial experience is often a provider's final touch point with them following a care encounter and can wield a disproportionate influence on patient satisfaction results." See "Defining Value: The Case for including Financial Experience as a Measure on Hospital Surveys," *Becker's Hospital Review*, August 14, 2014; available at www.beckershospitalreview.com/finance/defining-value-the-case-for-including-financial-experience-as-a-measure-on-hospital-surveys.html.

55 Jeffrey Kramer and Rexford E. Santerre, "Not-for-Profit CEO Performance and Pay: Some Evidence from Connecticut," *Inquiry* 47, no. 3 (Fall 2010): 249.

56 *PR Newswire*, "Proposed Round Lake Hospital Draws Protestors from City, as Groups Charge Advocate with 'Medical White Flight,'" (June 5, 2007); available at www.prnewswire.com/news-releases/proposed-round-lake-hospital-draws-protestors-from-city-as-groups-charge-advocate-with-medical-white-flight-57846222.html.

57 John Trussel, "A Comparison of the Capital Structures of Nonprofit and Proprietary Health Care Organizations," *Journal of Health Care Finance* 39, no. 1 (2012): 1–11.

58 Guy David, "The Convergence between For-Profit and Nonprofit Hospitals in the United States," *International Journal of Health Care Finance and Economics* 9, no. 4 (2009): 404.

59 David, "The Convergence," 404–8.

60 David, "The Convergence," 422.

61 David, "The Convergence," 423.

62 Chris Arnold and Paul Kiel, "When Nonprofit Hospitals Sue Their Patients"; available at www.npr.org/2014/12/19/371202059/when-a-hospital-bill-becomes-a-decade-long-pay-cut.

63 Arnold and Kiel, "When Nonprofit Hospitals Sue Their Patients."

64 A major employer in St. Joseph, the Triumph Foods pig slaughterhouse with 2,800 employees, had 255 workers whose wages were garnished by Heartland in 2013, a startling 91 percent of total employees at the facility. Other nonprofit hospitals in the area have been less financially aggressive, such as the much larger Barnes Jewish Hospital chain that filed only 26 suits for nonpayment in 2013 (compared to 2,200

filed by Heartland) and which automatically cuts its standard rates by 25 percent for the uninsured and does not charge interest on their payment plans. See Arnold and Kiel, "When Nonprofit Hospitals Sue Their Patients."

65 Dani Gordon, "Physicians Unlikely to Encourage Young People to Enter the Field, Survey Finds," *Becker's Hospital Review* (June 24, 2014); available at www.beckershospitalreview.com/hospital-physician-relationships/physicians-unlikely-to-encourage-young-people-to-enter-the-field-survey-finds.html.

66 Helen Adamopoulos, "Medical school debt on the rise: 5 key statistics," *Becker's Hospital Review* (August 11, 2014); available at www.beckershospitalreview.com/hospital-physician-relationships/medical-school-debt-on-the-rise-5-key-statistics.html.

67 Graeme Wood, "The Future of College?" *The Atlantic*, vol. 314, no. 2 (August 13, 2014): 55.

68 Wood, "The Future of College?" 53.

69 To provide an idea of the relative price increase of higher education versus consumer products, *Bloomberg* reported that tuition costs at American universities have risen an astounding 1,225 percent since 1978. In that same time period, the consumer price index (CPI) rose only 279 percent. See Michelle Jamrisko and Ilan Kolet, "College Tuition Costs Soar: Chart of the Day," *Bloomberg.com* (August 15, 2014); available at www.bloomberg.com/news/2014–08–18/college-tuition-costs-soar-chart-of-the-day.html.

70 "As if nonprofits aren't money-driven!" Nelson exclaimed to Wood. "They're just corporations that dodge their taxes." See Wood, "The Future of College?" 55. Wood also cites Paul Campos, "The Law-School Scam," *The Atlantic* (September 2014); available at www.theatlantic.com/features/archive/2014/08/the-law-school-scam/375069/; in Wood, "The Future of College?"

71 Wood, "The Future of College?" 54–5.

72 See http://academicearth.org/.

73 Quoted in Wood, "The Future of College?" 59.

74 To offer some perspective, that figure compares with only a 279 percent increase in the consumer price index in the same period. See Jamrisko and Kolet, "College Tuition Costs Soar."

75 D. A. Whetten and K. S. Cameron, "Administrative Effectiveness in Higher Education," *Review of Higher Education* 9(1) (1985): 35; cited in W. Bruce Cook, "Fund Raising and the College Presidency in an Era of Uncertainty," *Journal of Higher Education* 68, no. 1 (January/February 1997): 55.

76 Cook, "Fund Raising and the College Presidency," 55.

77 D. W. Breneman, *Liberal Arts Colleges: Thriving, Surviving, or Endangered?* (Washington, DC: The Brookings Institution, 1994), 33–4; quoted in Cook, "Fund Raising and the College Presidency," 58.

78 Whetten and Cameron, "Administrative Effectiveness in Higher Education," 35; quoted in Cook, "Fund Raising and the College Presidency in an Era of Uncertainty," 55.

79 F. H. T. Rhodes, "The Importance of Fundraising," in G. A. Budig, ed., *A Higher Education Map for the 1990s* (New York: American Council on Education/Macmillan, 1992), 65; quoted in Cook, "Fund Raising and the College Presidency," 62.

80 "The Philanthropy 400," *Chronicle of Philanthropy* (November 13, 1991): 1, 19–20.

81 Quoted in K. Grassmuck, "'History-making' Drive Expected to Raise $500 million in Private Funds for Ohio State, Inspire Other Colleges," *Chronicle of Higher Education* (January 10, 1990): A30; in Cook, "Fund Raising and the College Presidency," 63.

82 Quoted in A. L. Bailey, "Fund Drives Get Bigger, Broader: 65 College Goals Top $100 Million," *Chronicle of Higher Education* (September 2, 1987): A75; in Cook, "Fund Raising and the College Presidency," 65.

83 Quoted in R. H. Woodroof, "Internal Conflict and the First-time President: An

Administrative Succession Model for Private Colleges Seeking "First-time" Presidential Candidates." Unpublished doctoral dissertation, University of California, Los Angeles, CA, 1993; quoted in Cook, "Fund Raising and the College Presidency," 70.

84 D. W. Breneman, "Are We Losing Our Liberal Arts Colleges"? *American Association of Higher Education Bulletin* 43, 3–6; quoted in Ozan Jaquette, "Why Do Colleges Become Universities? Mission Drift and the Enrollment Economy," *Research in Higher Education* 54, 5 (August 2013): 516.

85 Jaquette, "Why Do Colleges Become Universities?" 515.

86 Jaquette, "Why Do Colleges Become Universities?" 516.

87 Jaquette includes a note: "[Breneman's] initial sample of 600 liberal arts colleges was based on the 1987 Carnegie Classification." Breneman used the classification of liberal arts colleges as institutions awarding 40 percent or more of their Bachelor of Arts degrees in the liberal arts and not having substantial programs in graduate education. See Breneman, 3; quoted in Jaquette, "Why Do Colleges Become Universities?" 516.

88 Jaquette, "Why Do Colleges Become Universities?" 520.

89 Matthew S. Kraatz, Marc J. Ventresca, and Lina Deng, "Precarious Values and Mundane Innovations: Enrollment Management in American Liberal Arts Colleges," *Academy of Management Journal* 53, no. 6 (December 2010): 1523.

90 Kraatz, *et al.*, "Precarious Values and Mundane Innovations," 1525.

91 Kraatz, *et al.*, "Precarious Values and Mundane Innovations," 1526.

92 Kraatz, *et al.*, "Precarious Values and Mundane Innovations," 1526.

93 Katherine Reynolds, "Universities Entering Swaps Market to Take Control of Debt," *The Bond Buyer* (May 4, 1998): 30.

94 John Lauerman and Michael McDonald, "Harvard's Bet on Interest Rate Rise Cost $500 Million to Exit," *Bloomberg.com* (October 17, 2009); available at www.bloomberg.com/apps/news?pid=newsarchive&sid=aHou7iMlBMN8. Moody's Investors Service was cited as the source identifying the goals of Harvard's fundraising efforts through these bonds. A Harvard spokesperson stated that many of the swaps transactions were initiated in 2004 when Lawrence Summers, who would become President Obama's director of the National Economic Council, was president of the University. See Lauerman and McDonald, "Harvard's Bet on Interest Rate Rise."

95 Lauerman and McDonald, "Harvard's Bet on Interest Rate Rise."

96 Quoted in Lauerman and McDonald, "Harvard's Bet on Interest Rate Rise."

97 The State of California's college and university system has come under considerable budget pressure due to the state's broader financial problems and significant cuts to its education budgets. Debt has grown throughout the system, with the Cal Poly San Luis Obispo campus reaching $433 million in indebtedness by 2012. Garnering even more attention, however, Sonoma State University (SSU) saw its debt burden rise to $233 million in same period. While that figure is less than that of five other schools, it is 6.75 percent of the California state university system's $3.3 billion revenue bond debt while SSU's undergraduate student population is only 7,381 students, roughly 2 percent of 347,000 undergraduates in the system overall. Adding to the controversy has been an aggressive capital expansion campaign under the leadership of SSU President Ruben Armiñana to transition the former commuter campus to a largely residential facility housing around 3,100 students. Fears that the administration's aggressive expansion campaign will ultimately be reflected in housing costs, student fees, and cuts in other areas has led to protests by both students and faculty. See Jeremy Hay, "Sonoma State's Debt Burden Rises," *The Press Democrat* (March 4, 2012); available at www.watchsonomacounty.com/2012/03/education/sonoma-states-debt-burden-rises/.

98 Jennifer Johnstone, "Sonoma State Student Unaware of Crazy Debt after College,"

Indybay Newsitem, North Bay/Marin, Education & Student Activism (December 8, 2013); available at www.indybay.org/newsitems/2013/12/08/18747483.php?printable=true.

99 Johnstone, "Sonoma State."

100 Jana Kasperkevic, "Occupy Activists Abolish $3.85m in Corinthian Colleges Students' Loan Debt," *Guardian* (September 17, 2014); available at www.theguardian.com/money/2014/sep/17/occupy-activists-student-debt-corinthian-colleges.

101 Kasperkevic, "Occupy Activists."

102 Kasperkevic, "Occupy Activists." "Crowd sourcing" is the process of securing capital for ventures by appealing to large groups of people, often using social media.

103 Deborah L. Rhode and Amanda K. Packel, "Ethics and Nonprofits," *Stanford Social Innovation Review* 11 (Summer 2009); available at www.ssireview.org/articles/entry/ethics_and_nonprofits. The authors cite Sharyl Attkisson, "Student Loan Charity Under Fire: Is One Educational Charity Abusing Their Status with Lavish Travel and Huge Salaries?" CBS News, March 2, 2009; Sharyl Attkisson, "Loan Charity's High-Flying Guests Exposed: Educational Nonprofit under Fire for Transporting Politicians with Money That Could Have Gone to Students," CBS News, March 3, 2009.

104 Eric Thurman, "Performance Philanthropy: Bringing Accountability to Charitable Giving," *Harvard International Review*, vol. 28, no. 1 (Spring 2006): 18.

105 Joseph T. Cordes and Burton A. Weisbrod, "Differential Taxation of Nonprofits and the Commercialization of Nonprofit Revenues," *Journal of Policy Analysis and Management*, vol. 17, no. 2, Special Issue: The Commercialism Dilemma of the Nonprofit Sector (Spring 1998): 211.

106 Virginia Ann Hodgkinson and Murray S. Weitzman, *Nonprofit Almanac* (San Francisco: Jossey-Bass, 1996), table 2.13; cited in Burton A. Weisbrod, "Guest Editor's Introduction: The Nonprofit Mission and Its Financing," *Journal of Policy Analysis and Management* 17, no. 2 (Spring 1998): 169.

107 Cordes and Weisbrod, "Differential Taxation," 213.

108 Weisbrod, "Guest Editor's Introduction," 166.

109 Weisbrod, "Guest Editor's Introduction," 167.

110 Jean-Baptiste Say, quoted in J. Gregory Dees, "The Meaning of 'Social Entrepreneurship,'" reformatted and revised, May 30, 2001. http://csi.gsb.stanford.edu/sites/csi.gsb.stanford.edu/files/TheMeaningofsocialEntrepreneurship.pdf; in Roger L. Martin and Sally Osberg, "Social Entrepreneurship: The Case for Definition," *Stanford Social Innovation Review* (Spring 2007); available at www.ssireview.org/articles/entry/social_entrepreneurship_the_case_for_definition.

111 The authors reference Schumpeter's *Capitalism, Socialism, and Democracy* (New York: Harper, 1975), 82–5; in Martin and Osberg, "Social Entrepreneurship."

112 Martin and Osberg, "Social Entrepreneurship."

113 Martin and Osberg, "Social Entrepreneurship."

114 Ian Eppler, "The Problem with 'Social Entrepreneurship': A Student's Perspective," *Stanford Social Innovation Review* (April 13, 2012); available at www.ssireview.org/blog/entry/the_problem_with_social_entrepreneurship_a_students_perspective.

115 Martin and Osberg, "Social Entrepreneurship."

116 J. Gregory Dees, "Enterprising Nonprofits," *Harvard Business Review*, vol. 67, no. 1 (January/February 1998): 55–6.

117 Dees, "Enterprising Nonprofits," 55.

118 Joanna Jacobson, "Has Venture Philanthropy Passed Its Peak?" *Stanford Social Innovation Review* (February 26, 2013); available at www.ssireview.org/blog/entry/has_venture_philanthropy_passed_its_peak.

119 Jacobson, "Has Venture Philanthropy Passed Its Peak?"

120 Eric Thurman, "Performance Philanthropy," 19.

121 Stanley N. Katz, "What Does It Mean to Say That Philanthropy is 'Effective'? The

Philanthropists' New Clothes," *Proceedings of the American Philosophical Society*, vol. 149, no. 2 (June 2005): 131.

122 Taylor Branch, "The Shame of College Sports," *The Atlantic* (September 7, 2011); www.theatlantic.com/magazine/archive/2011/10/the-shame-of-college-sports/308643/.

123 Jena McGregor, "Tackling College Football Coaches' High Pay," *Washington Post* (November 7, 2013); available at www.washingtonpost.com/blogs/on-leadership/wp/2013/11/07/tackling-college-football-coaches-high-pay/.

Bibliography

Adamopoulos, Helen. "Medical School Debt on the Rise: 5 Key Statistics." *Becker's Hospital Review*, August 11, 2014. www.beckershospitalreview.com/hospital-physician-relationships/medical-school-debt-on-the-rise-5-key-statistics.html; accessed on August 18, 2014.

Arnold, Chris, and Paul Kiel. "When Nonprofit Hospitals Sue Their Poorest Patients." *NPR.org*, December 19, 2014. www.npr.org/2014/12/19/371202059/when-a-hospital-bill-becomes-a-decade-long-pay-cut; accessed on December 19, 2014.

Attkisson, Sharyl. "Loan Charity's High-Flying Guests Exposed: Educational Nonprofit under Fire for Transporting Politicians with Money That Could Have Gone to Students." CBS News, March 3, 2009.

Attkisson, Sharyl. "Student Loan Charity under Fire: Is One Educational Charity Abusing Their Status with Lavish Travel and Huge Salaries?" CBS News, March 2, 2009.

Bailey, A. L. "Fund Drives Get Bigger, Broader: 65 College Goals Top $100 Million." *Chronicle of Higher Education*, September 2, 1987, sec. A72–A73.

Bielefeld, Wolfgang. "Funding Uncertainties and Nonprofit Strategies in the 1980s." *Nonprofit Management and Leadership* 2, no. 4 (Summer 1992): 381–401.

Blitch, Bird. "Defining Value: The Case for Including Financial Experience as a Measure on Hospital Surveys." *Becker's Hospital Review*, August 14, 2014. www.beckershospitalreview.com/finance/defining-value-the-case-for-including-financial-experience-as-a-measure-on-hospital-surveys.html; accessed on August 18, 2014.

Branch, Taylor. "The Shame of College Sports." *The Atlantic*, September 7, 2011; www.theatlantic.com/magazine/archive/2011/10/the-shame-of-college-sports/308643/; accessed on July 14, 2014.

Breneman, David W. "Are We Losing Our Liberal Arts Colleges?" *American Association of Higher Education Bulletin* 43, no. 2 (October 1990): 3–6.

Breneman, D. W. *Liberal Arts Colleges: Thriving, Surviving, or Endangered*? Washington, DC: The Brookings Institution, 1994.

Briggs, Xavier de Souza. "Social Capital and the Cities: Advice to Change Agents." *National Civic Review* 86, no. 2 (Summer 1997): 111–17.

Business Wire. "Hay Group's Annual Healthcare Compensation Study Shows More Executives Being Paid Based on Long-Term Incentive Plans, Especially at Larger Hospital Systems." *Business Wire [New York]*, November 12, 2013. www.businesswire.com/news/home/20131112005512/en/Hay-Group%E2%80%99s-Annual-Healthcare-Compensation-Study-Shows#.VRrCMfnF-6M; accessed on July 17, 2014.

Campos, Paul. "The Law-School Scam." *The Atlantic*, September 2014. www.theatlantic.com/features/archive/2014/08/the-law-school-scam/375069/.

Carman, Joanne G. "Evaluation Practice among Community-Based Organizations: Research into the Reality." *American Journal of Evaluation* 28, no. 1 (March 2007): 60–75.

Cook, W. Bruce. "Fund Raising and the College Presidency in an Era of Uncertainty." *Journal of Higher Education* 68, no. 1 (February 1997): 53–86.

Cordes, Joseph T., and Burton A. Weisbrod. "Differential Taxation of Nonprofits and the Commercialization of Nonprofit Revenues." *Journal of Policy Analysis and Management*, Special Issue: The Commercialism Dilemma of the Nonprofit Sector, 17, no. 2 (Spring 1998): 195–214.

Cystic Fibrosis Foundation Website. "Frequently Asked Questions." *CFF.org*, March 12, 2014. www.cff.org/AboutCF/Faqs/; accessed on November 26, 2014.

David, Guy. "The Convergence between For-Profit and Nonprofit Hospitals in the United States." *International Journal of Health Care Finance and Economics* 9, no. 4 (December 2009): 403–28.

Davis, Gerald F. "The Rise and Fall of Finance and the End of the Society of Organizations." *Academy of Management Perspectives* 23, no. 3 (August 2009): 27–44.

Dees, J. Gregory. "Enterprising Nonprofits." *Harvard Business Review* 67, no. 1 (February 1998): 55–67.

Dees, J. Gregory. "The Meaning of 'Social Entrepreneurship.'" reformatted and revised, May 30, 2001 http://csi.gsb.stanford.edu/sites/csi.gsb.stanford.edu/files/TheMeaningofsocialEntrepreneurship.pdf.

Eppler, Ian. "The Problem with 'Social Entrepreneurship': A Student's Perspective." *Stanford Social Innovation Review*, April 13, 2012. www.ssireview.org/blog/entry/the_problem_with_social_entrepreneurship_a_students_perspective; accessed on December 27, 2014.

Gardner, Christine J. "Nonprofits Tap New Donors with Internet Fundraising." *Christianity Today* 42, no. 14 (December 7, 1998): 26–7.

Gordon, Dani. "Physicians Unlikely to Encourage Young People to Enter the Field, Survey Finds." *Becker's Hospital Review*, June 24, 2014. www.beckershospitalreview.com/hospital-physician-relationships/physicians-unlikely-to-encourage-young-people-to-enter-the-field-survey-finds.html; accessed on August 18, 2014.

Grassley, Chuck. "Grassley Seeks Update on Any SEC Review of Vertex Pharmaceuticals' Stock Spike." June 11, 2012. www.grassley.senate.gov/news/news-releases/grassley-seeks-update-any-sec-review-vertex-pharmaceuticals%E2%80%99-stock-spike; accessed on November 26, 2014.

Grassmuck, K. "'History-Making' Drive Expected to Raise $500 Million in Private Funds for Ohio State, Inspire Other Colleges." *Chronicle of Higher Education*, January 10, 1990, sec. A29–A31.

Grǿnbjerg, Kirsten A. *Understanding Nonprofit Funding: Managing Revenues in Social Services and Community Development Organizations*. San Francisco: Jossey-Bass, 1993.

Gross, Terry. Cardiologist Speaks from the Heart about America's Medical System. Interview by Sandeep Jauhar. Transcript, August 19, 2014. www.wbur.org/npr/ 341632184/cardiologist-speaks-from-the-heart-about-americas-medical-system; accessed on October 1, 2014.

Guo, Chao. "When Government Becomes the Principal Philanthropist: The Effects of Public Funding on Patterns of Nonprofit Governance." *Public Administration Review* 67, no. 3 (May–June 2007): 458–73.

Hartman, Thomas E. "The Cost of Being Public in the Era of Sarbanes–Oxley" August 2, 2007. www.foley.com/files/Publication/6202688d-eebc-42bc-8169-5dfb14ef3ced/Presentation/PublicationAttachment/666c1479-ea9c-4359-bb07-5f71a18166f6/Foley-2007SOXstudy.pdf; accessed on April 1, 2015

Hartocollis, Anemona. "At New York-Presbyterian Hospital, Its Ex-C.E.O Finds Lucrative Work." *New York Times*, July 15, 2014. www.nytimes.com/2014/07/16/nyregion/at-newyork-presbyterian-hospital-its-ex-ceo-finds-lucrative-work-.html?_r=0; accessed on July 17, 2014.

Hay, Jeremy. "Sonoma State's Debt Burden Rises." *The Press Democrat*, March 4, 2012. www.watchsonomacounty.com/2012/03/education/sonoma-states-debt-burden-rises/; accessed on June 6, 2014.

Health Care Renewal. "Is the Cystic Fibrosis Foundation a Charity or a Venture Capital Firm?" *HCRenewal.blogspot.com*, June 10, 2013. http://hcrenewal.blogspot.com/2013/06/is-cystic-fibrosis-foundation-charity.html; accessed on November 26, 2014.

Heimovics, Richard D., Robert D. Herman, and Carole L. Jurkiewicz Coughlin. "Executive Leadership and Resource Dependence in Nonprofit Organizations: A Frame Analysis." *Public Administration Review* 53, no. 5 (September–October 1993): 419–27.

Herman, Robert D. and David O. Renz. "Nonprofit Organizational Effectiveness: Contrasts between Especially Effective and Less Effective Organizations." *Nonprofit Management and Leadership* 9, no. 1 (Fall 1998): 23–38.

Hodgkinson, Virginia Ann and Murray S. Weitzman. *Nonprofit Almanac*. San Francisco: Jossey-Bass, 1996.

Jacobson, Joanna. "Has Venture Philanthropy Passed Its Peak?" *Stanford Social Innovation Review*, February 26, 2013. www.ssireview.org/blog/entry /has_venture_philanthropy_passed_its_peak; accessed on October 18, 2014.

Jacquette, Ozan. "Why Do Colleges Become Universities? Mission Drift and the Enrollment Economy." *Research in Higher Education* 54, no. 5 (August 2013): 514–43.

Jamrisko, Michelle, and Ilan Kolet. "College Tuition Costs Soar: Chart of the Day." *Bloomberg.com*, August 18, 2014. www.bloomberg.com/news/2014-08-18/college-tuition-costs-soar-chart-of-the-day.html; accessed on January 8, 2015.

Jauhar, Sandeep. *Doctored: The Disillusionment of an American Physician*. New York: Straus and Giroux, 2014.

Johnstone, Jennifer. "Sonoma State Student Unaware of Crazy Debt after College." *Indybay Newsitem*, December 8, 2013. www.indybay.org/newsitems/2013/12/08/18747483.php?printable=true; accessed on June 2, 2014.

Joynt, Karen E., Sidney T. Le, E. John Orav, and Ashish K. Jha. "Compensation of Chief Executive Officers at Nonprofit U.S. Hospitals." *Journal of the American Medical Association Internal Medicine* 174, no. 1 (January 2014): 61–7.

Kasperkevic, Jana. "Occupy Activists Abolish $3.85m in Corinthian Colleges Students' Loan Debt." *Guardian*, September 17, 2014. www.theguardian.com/money/2014/sep/17/occupy-activists-student-debt-corinthian-colleges; accessed on December 21, 2014.

Katz, Stanley N. "What Does It Mean to Say That Philanthropy Is 'Effective'? The Philanthropists' New Clothes." *Proceedings of the American Philosophical Society* 149, no. 2 (June 2005): 123–31.

Kraatz, Matthew S., Marc J. Ventresca, and Lina Deng. "Precarious Values and Mundane Innovations: Enrollment Management in American Liberal Arts Colleges." *Academy of Management Journal* 53, no. 6 (December 2010): 1521–45.

Kramer, Jeffrey, and Rexford E. Santerre. "Not-for-Profit CEO Performance and Pay: Some Evidence from Connecticut." *Inquiry* 47, no. 3 (Fall 2010): 242–51.

Kramer, Ralph M., and Bart Grossman. "Contracting for Social Services." *Social Service Review* 61, no. 1 (March 1987): 32–55.

Lauerman, John, and Michael McDonald. "Harvard's Bet on Interest Rate Rise Cost $500

Million to Exit." *Bloomberg.com*, October 17, 2009. www.bloomberg.com/apps/news?pid=newsarchive&sid =aHou7iMlBMN8; accessed on June 6, 2014.
LeRoux, Kelly, and Nathaniel S. Wright. "Does Performance Measurement Improve Strategic Decision Making? Findings From a National Survey of Nonprofit Social Service Agencies." *Nonprofit and Voluntary Sector Quarterly* 39, no. 4 (August 2010): 571–87; http://nvs.sagepub.com/content/early/2010/04/02/0899764009359942; accessed on August 14, 2014.
Marquis, Christopher, Gerald F. Davis, and Mary Ann Glynn. "Golfing Alone? Corporations, Elites, and Nonprofit Growth in 100 American Communities." *Organization Science* 24, no. 1 (2013): 39–57.
Martin, Roger L. and Sally Osberg. "Social Entrepreneurship: The Case for Definition." *Stanford Social Innovation Review* 5, no. 2 (Spring 2007): 28–39. www.ssireview.org/articles/entry/social_entrepreneurship_the_case_for definition; accessed on July 16, 2014.
McGregor, Jena. "Tackling College Football Coaches' High Pay." *Washington Post*, November 7, 2013. www.washingtonpost.com/blogs/on-leadership/wp/2013/11/07/tackling-college-football-coaches-high-pay/; accessed on July 30, 2014.
McKay, Renée and Joani Livingston. "Primary Concern." *PrimaryConcernMovie.com*, April 2013. http://primaryconcernmovie.com/.
Mead, Joseph. "Confidence in the Nonprofit Sector through Sarbanes–Oxley-Style Reforms." *Michigan Law Review* 106, no. 5 (March 2008): 881–900.
Miller, Starlett M. "From Private Practice to Hospital Employment: How Employing Physicians Impacts Hospital Liability for Physician Malpractice." *Healthcare Liability & Litigation* 14, no. 2 (May 2012): 1–4.
Mulligan, Lumen N. "What's Good for the Goose Is Not Good for the Gander: Sarbanes–Oxley-Style Nonprofit Reforms." *Michigan Law Review* 105, no. 8 (June 2007): 1981–2009.
NonprofitHR Solutions, and the Improve Group. "2013 Nonprofit Employment Practices Survey." NonprofitHR Solutions LLC, 2013. www.nonprofithr.com/wp-content/uploads/2013/03/2013-Employment-Trends-Survey-Report.pdf; accessed on November 7, 2014.
Pew Research Center. "Millennials in Adulthood: Detached from Institutions, Networked with Friends." *Pew Research Social & Demographic Trends*, March 7, 2014. www.pewsocialtrends.org/2014/03/07/millennials-in-adulthood/; accessed on June 1, 2014.
"The Philanthropy 400." In *Chronicle of Philanthropy*, November 13, 1991, 1, 19–20. *PR Newswire*. "Proposed Round Lake Hospital Draws Protestors from City, as Groups Charge Advocate with 'Medical White Flight.'" *PR Newswire*, June 5, 2007. www.prnewswire.com/news-releases/proposed-round-lake-hospital-draws-protestors-from-city-as-groups-charge-advocate-with-medical-white-flight-57846222.html; accessed on September 10, 2014.
Putnam, Robert D. *Bowling Alone: The Collapse and Revival of American Community*. New York: Simon & Schuster, 2000.
Putnam, Robert D. "Tuning In, Tuning Out: The Strange Disappearance of Social Capital in America." *Political Science and Politics* 28, no. 4 (December 1995): 664–83.
Putnam, Robert D., Robert Leonardi, and Raffaella Y. Nanetti. *Making Democracy Work: Civic Traditions in Modern Italy*. Princeton, NJ: Princeton University Press, 1994.
Reisch, Marc S. "Cystic Fibrosis Foundation Gets $3.3 Billion for Royalties." *Chemical & Engineering News* 92, no. 47 (November 24, 2014): 7.
Reynolds, Katherine M. "Deals: Universities Entering Swaps Market to Take Control of Debt." *The Bond Buyer* 324, no. 89 (May 5, 1998): 30.

Rhode, Deborah L., and Amanda K. Packel. "Ethics and Nonprofits." *Stanford Social Innovation Review* 7, no. 3 (Summer 2009): 29–35.

Rhodes, F. H. T. "The Importance of Fundraising." In *A Higher Education Map for the 1990s*, edited by G. A. Budig, 64–70. New York: American Council on Education/ Macmillan, 1992.

Ritchie, William J., and Robert W. Kolodinsky. "Nonprofit Organization Financial Performance Measurement: An Evaluation of New and Existing Financial Performance Measures." *Nonprofit Management and Leadership* 13, no. 4 (Summer 2003): 367–81.

Rosenthal, Elizabeth. "Patients' Costs Skyrocket; Specialists' Incomes Soar." *New York Times*, January 18, 2014. www.nytimes.com/2014/01/19/health/patients-costs-skyrocket-specialists-incomes-soar.html?_r=0; accessed on August 15, 2014.

Rubenstein, Joshua S., Ronni G. Davidowitz, and Mal L. Barasch. "The New York Non-Profit Revitalization Act of 2013 – Important Changes Affecting New York Nonprofit Entities and Charitable Trusts." *National Law Review*, February 24, 2014. www.natlawreview.com/article/new-york-non-profit-revitalization-act-2013-important-changes-affecting-new-york-non; accessed on August 13, 2014.

Salamon, L. "Partners in Public Service: The Scope and Theory of Government-Nonprofit Relations." In *The Nonprofit Sector: A Research Handbook*, edited by W. W. Powell, 99–117. New Haven, CN: Yale University Press, 1987.

Schumpeter, Joseph A. *Capitalism, Socialism, and Democracy*. New York: Harper, 1975.

Smith, Steven Rathgeb. "The Challenge of Strengthening Nonprofits and Civil Society." *Public Administration Review* 68, no. 1 (December 2008): 132–45.

Thomson, Irene Taviss. "The Theory That Won't Die: From Mass Society to the Decline of Social Capital." *Sociological Forum* 20, no. 3 (September 2005): 421–48.

Thurman, Eric. "Performance Philanthropy: Bringing Accountability to Charitable Giving." *Harvard International Review* 28, no. 1 (Spring 2006): 18–20.

Trussel, John. "A Comparison of the Capital Structures of Nonprofit and Proprietary Health Care Organizations." *Journal of Health Care Finance* 39, no. 1 (January 2012): 1–11.

Vaidya, Anuja. "The Decline of the Independent Physician: 8 Statistics." *Becker's Hospital Review*, June 27, 2014. www.beckershospitalreview.com/hospital-physician-relationships/the-decline-of-the-independent-physician-8-statistics.html; accessed on August 18, 2014.

Walker, Joseph, and Jonathan D. Rockoff. "Cystic Fibrosis Foundation Sells Drug's Rights for $3.3 Billion." *Wall Street Journal*, November 19, 2014. http://online.wsj.com/articles/cystic-fibrosis-foundation-sells-drugs-rights-for-3-3-billion-1416414300?tesla=y&mg=reno64-wsj&url=http://online.wsj.com/ article/SB11401573521024413408604580286760275011550.html; accessed on November 26, 2014.

Weisbrod, Burton A. "Guest Editor's Introduction: The Nonprofit Mission and Its Financing." *Journal of Policy Analysis and Management* 17, no. 2 (Spring 1998): 165–74.

Whetten, D. A., and K. S. Cameron. "Administrative Effectiveness in Higher Education." *Review of Higher Education* 9, no. 1 (1985): 35–49.

Wood, Graeme. "The Future of College?" *The Atlantic* 314, no. 2 (August 13, 2014): 51–60.

Woodroof, R. H. "Internal Conflict and the First-Time President: An Administrative Succession Model for Private Colleges Seeking 'First-Time' Presidential Candidates." Unpublished doctoral dissertation, University of California, Los Angeles, 1993.

5 The religious allure of finance

French philosopher and sociologist Pierre Bourdieu once wrote that the "truth of the religious enterprise" is actually "two truths: an economic one and a religious one, which denies the first."[1] The financialization of American Christianity that is explored in this chapter reinforces Bourdieu's observation, demonstrating how financial influence has gained hold over churches and other religious organizations largely through *denial of their duality*. Economics and finance have come to wield significant influence over American Christian organizations as leaders often are unable to bring appropriately theological understandings of money and other forms capital into conversation with their memberships. Just as often, individual Christians seem unable to reconcile their spiritual beliefs with their financial needs, and both groups find it difficult to apply religious principles to the economic issues surrounding their churches as worldly institutions. Religious establishments must also exist as economic ones—denial of this reality avoids a tension at the core of Christian faith that is essential to its moral authority and prophetic voice.

This chapter examines the financialization of American Christianity within the broader context of a society in which financial influence has risen to new heights. Emphasis here on American Christian churches is not to suggest that other religious groups have been immune to financial forces but rather that the demographically dominant Christian faith traditions are all that a single chapter can reasonable accommodate. Importantly, the development of a Dow Jones Islamic Market Index and the expansion of Jewish, Islamic, and other investment alternatives within the increasingly broad category of "faith-based investment" insist that non-Christian religious groups and their adherents also are influenced by the continual expansion of the financial economy. All institutions in American civil society must engage finance in ways that expose them to its potential to reshape their values. Unfortunately, Christian churches and their affiliated organizations have been caught up in the same financial exuberance that has afflicted much of secular society: failed derivative investments, "too good to be true" mortgage deals, and even Ponzi schemes that bilk congregants of their savings. These problems attenuate the distinct prophetic voices of institutions needed to balance the growing financial preoccupation of American culture and help promote a more virtuous economy.

The financialization of the American Church

Finance has had a powerful though largely unrecognized influence on American religious culture. Perhaps the most intense period of secularization in the nation's history was financially inspired, as chronicled in George Marsden's *The Soul of the American University.* A major influence shaping what are today secular but were once religiously affiliated institutions like Dartmouth College and the University of Chicago was the role played by philanthropic organizations such as the Carnegie Pension Fund. Established in 1906, the Carnegie Pension Fund endowed retirement funds for university teachers but only for those schools not controlled by a denomination.[2] Such enticements from philanthropists in the period financially incentivized religiously affiliated colleges and universities to drop their denominational identities in exchange for financial gifts. Many succumbed in the age when some prominent American philanthropists considered "sectarian religion" socially divisive and intellectually backward.

This financial influence on American religion has tended to vary with general economic conditions. In the 1920s, the progressivist spirit of investment infused Christian culture, typified in weekly financial columns in Christian media and the planning of ostentatious "skyscraper churches" as fusions of spiritual functionality and financial pragmatism, which rivaled today's most city-like megachurches.[3] The proposed Broadway Temple of Dr. Christian F. Reisner—designed to span a city block, include 24 stories of apartment space, cover 26 million square feet, and be topped by a 34-foot rotating cross—was the most ambitious of these efforts.[4]

While the intensely commercial Christianity symbolized by the skyscraper church abated with the coming of depression and world war, a growing business attitude resurfaced, especially among Protestant denominations, and accelerated dramatically in the 1970s and 1980s. Money once again became more important in the operation not only of churches but also, as discussed in previous chapters, with religiously affiliated educational institutions and social service organizations. Beginning in this period that corresponds to the wider financialization of American society, churches increasingly have become "finance dependent" in ways that, while often fueling growth, have also exposed them to mission drift in some cases and mismanagement or fraud in others. Moreover, this dependency has contributed to divisions within churches, often between clergy and laity, and even to a perception in the broader culture that financial interestedness limits the ability of churches to fulfill their spiritual responsibilities.

Princeton sociologist Robert Wuthnow has written extensively about the crisis in American churches for some time, recognizing that the crisis commonly portrayed in the media as political in nature can also be attributed to financial causes. Wuthnow offers a comment that, at first glance, might seem to undermine the financialization thesis presented in this book:

> Many of us may think the churches are already paying too much attention to [financial] issues. But the reality is just the opposite. Clergy are reluctant to

> talk about finances because they know this topic makes people uncomfortable. So they tiptoe around the issues rather than addressing them directly.[5]

Wuthnow does not mean, however, that finance is not a major change agent in American religious culture. Far from it. Rather, he insists that ministers do a poor job relating to their congregations' money concerns, and this inability to communicate is a powerful influence that shapes the nature and relationships of American Christianity. The inability to talk effectively with congregants about finance means that the money issues fester to the point that the mission and values of religious institutions can be compromised. The common tiptoeing around money concerns that Wuthnow describes takes time and energy; it also means exacerbating divisions between clergy and laity because the two groups cannot discuss challenges that will not go away. The principal difficulty is locating the appropriate theological and ethical positions from which religious leaders can speak to financial issues.

Surveys show that money pressures preoccupy leadership and laity alike. Moreover, they reveal how pastors can be remarkably out of touch with parishioners' financial problems, even those pastors who attempt to incorporate teachings on debt and stewardship in their sermons. Despite the astronomical growth of household indebtedness in the first decade of this century, a LifeWay Research study conducted between November 2007 and February 2008 showed that only 25 percent of pastors in Southern Baptist Convention (SBC) churches agreed that their members have "a significant amount of personal debt" even as 65 percent of them had offered sermons on stewardship and tithing in the past 12 months.[6] By the same token, church members seem remarkably unwilling to approach their ministers concerning work or financial matters, even those ethical in nature. In one survey, only 4 percent of respondents expressed willingness to speak with their pastors concerning job-related stress; and, only 13 percent reported that they would seek spiritual counseling about a "major ethical dilemma" at work whereas 54 percent revealed that they would speak with their boss about such an issue.[7]

Religious leaders and laity are both financially fixated in ways that cause divisions between them. Ministers report being "overwhelmed" with financial issues, more from an institutional than individual standpoint, yet in ways that make them seemingly as "self-interested" as the laity. Wuthnow notes that church leaders are often more than willing to discuss church finances—capital campaigns, tithing innovations, and other aspects of finance—unrelated to their members' personal finances.[8] On the other hand, laypersons find it difficult to escape financial pressures and their identities as workers even as they desire spiritual "relief" from those concerns. That they find little respite from financial issues in their church lives and generally are unwilling to seek counsel from ministers on such issues leads to continual frustration that is little relaxed on Sunday mornings. These factors combined illustrate a strange preoccupation by both groups that, despite their inability to speak effectively with each other on financial issues, arguably contributes to the financialization of American culture.

Inability to communicate on money matters also increases the likelihood that churches will find themselves in financial problems, which only exacerbates these concerns.

This divide within the American Christian community reinforces two forms of financial preoccupation, both of which are problematic for the church. Wuthnow describes the Grace Church in the Midwestern U.S. as representing the "'new wave' in American religion."[9] The 7,000-member church, which became nondenominational because it believed its tie to the Assembly of God churches a "disadvantage," has grown rapidly. Described as "the church of tomorrow, the church of the new middle class at the end of the twentieth century," Grace Church has an operating budget equivalent to the aggregate budgets of around 50 average-size churches. But while it appears to be sound financially, Wuthnow believes this image is deceiving. The $3 million construction project the church has undertaken is expected to be paid for in three years, yet, because per capita giving is relatively low, Grace Church relies on attracting new members any time it needs to fund a major program.[10] Furthermore, as "more than a quarter of its annual income is directly tied to fees paid for specific services such as schooling, counseling, babysitting, book sales, and video rentals," it has also "inadvertently cultivated a fee-for-service mentality rather than a spirit of sacrificial giving," which Wuthnow describes as serving well those who desire the services but not necessarily the community at large. He notes as well that less than 1 percent of Grace Church's budget is allocated to giving for benevolence, less than annual church spending on "printing supplies and postage."[11]

The inconsistency of giving among their memberships is a problem that binds both financially strapped churches and others like Grace Church that have significant income but also large operating budgets and more investment exposure. Rather than fiscal stability promoted through tithing, churches have turned in recent years toward need-based, targeted giving reflective of the dynamic nature of money management often characteristic of members' business and family lives.[12] Wuthnow notes that this giving style corresponds to the increasingly corporate structure of American churches with specialized departments and functions, inspiring forms of internal competition over scarce resources. He also observes that, in some churches where members "had given to special appeals needed to meet mortgage payments" those efforts hurt the ability of churches to cover basic expenses such as staff salaries. Parishioners commonly shift money away from general offerings to specific causes rather than give to those causes *in addition* to regular tithes.[13]

This business-like approach to church finance that focuses on targeted giving and meeting the goals of capital campaigns has fueled an entire industry designed to help churches secure the resources they need.[14] Middle-class megachurches like Grace Church use professional fundraisers to mount generally effective, high-publicity fundraising campaigns; sometimes their campaigns return tens of millions of dollars. But churches of this size are particularly vulnerable to the harsh economic realities that face other large American establishments. Like corporate giants, megachurches fly high, providing consultants and employees with substantial incomes when business is good. When business falters, they are forced to lay off staff and to cut programs severely.[15] And on the other end of the financial spectrum, smaller churches with limited budgets and few to no paid staff may find church revenues inadequate even to pay the bills.

This internal financial emphasis on the part of American churches means less money available for the needy. Even expanding, well-funded institutions often give more the "appearance" of benevolence rather than making significant contributions to their communities. Stephen Edward McMillin observes a "stark" transformation among American churches that provide social services from "a communitarian view of human nature to a market-based, individualistic view," which undoubtedly influences this outcome. He sees contemporary churches as contributing to a "privatized, economic, and individualistic 'Civil Society' " as opposed to the more communal form of previous eras.[16] Wuthnow perhaps reinforces this idea by quoting one church leader as saying that for all seeming good his church does for others, "I don't think our efforts could be considered more than token. We just don't really have that overriding focus … what we're talking about is only a few hundred dollars and a few people."[17] The reason for such window dressing in community service is that the major emphasis of most middle-class churches is on internal programs, "often shaped by another prevailing middle-class value: the idea that one's activities should be *results oriented*."[18] The results orientation of American churches likely is shaped by a similar focus of the nation's business culture that has been driven by financialization, leading both churches and businesses to target programs with "immediate payoffs" rather than funding longer-term programs with perhaps riskier and less immediate impact.

Other Christian institutions and even individuals are similarly affected by money issues, even when they may not realize it. Wealth often subtly gets in the way of mission. Kenyan scholar and theologian Zablon Nthamburi describes how "missionaries have been stunned and astonished to discover that their resources, job security, and Western lifestyle elevate them to the ranks of the rich in most communities," where "lifestyle contradicts the biblical message" and "the effectiveness of the Gospel is hindered by insensitive affluence that makes social relationships not only difficult but embarrassing."[19] Jonathan Bonk similarly notes how the relative wealth of North American missionaries, in particular, that is unfathomable by the people they serve results in a kind of "insular prosperity" that enables the "Western Church to engage in numerous expensive, efficient, and even useful activities overseas," and yet isolates missionaries, "rendering much of their effort either unproductive or counterproductive."[20]

The financial peril of American church leadership is found in its common inability to speak from appropriately spiritual and ethical perspectives on money matters, which is not always associated with embarrassment resulting from too much wealth. In some cases, it results from financial negligence, illiteracy, debt problems, or "investments gone bad." Whatever the reason, churches must find the moral authority to speak out on financial problems. As Wuthnow observes,

> the churches can save themselves by focusing more attention on the meanings of stewardship, by preaching more actively about stewardship, by helping their members connect their faith to their work, by responding to the pressures and anxieties that grow out of contemporary jobs and careers, and by rediscovering the churches' prophetic voice on matters of money and materialism.[21]

The failure of congregational leaders to accomplish those purposes only amplifies the stubborn financial problems of churches and their members.

The spiritual significance of finance

Diverse approaches to money issues in American churches—some painstakingly avoid discussion while others attempt to be full-service financial counseling and investment organizations—actually contribute to the financialization of American Christianity. Even in churches that avoid financial issues, those problems commonly distract from the ability of churches to minister to the faithful because financial concerns remain highly important, and members carry their concerns and the expectations surrounding them right into the sanctuary. On the other hand, for the type of church that vigorously accommodates the financial needs of the membership, the deficiency is often failure to appropriately position money concerns within a theological framework that allows religious leaders to engage financial topics prophetically. Either way, financial issues can distract churches from their central mission of providing spiritual and moral guidance to the faithful.

The frequent inability or unwillingness of pastors to spiritually counsel members on financial concerns is complemented in a rather strange way by their pragmatic discussions of their churches' finances. In a study of endowed Presbyterian congregations, Dean R. Hoge and Loren B. Mead note an inattention to theological principles with respect to congregational leaders' perspectives on their churches' endowments that is "striking":

> The [congregational leaders] who talked to us about endowments were very articulate in speaking about the funds, the management, and the priority systems, but there was a lack of any theological language or ideas in the mix. Participants did not use biblical or theological ideas or language other than "stewardship" and "mission." Instead, the operative language was of "responsibility," "accountability," and "careful management." The guiding principle of handling endowments seemed to be what the courts describe as the "prudent man" rule.[22]

It is evident that American churches face more complex issues concerning finances than the simple inability to engage financial concerns. Some churches, in fact, may address the financial needs of members *too* well. Many modern churches preach an amazing variety of "prosperity Gospels," frequently offering sessions in financial planning and budgeting, bankruptcy counseling, investment advice, and other services. Megachurches providing these services commonly assume the configuration of retail malls and attempt to provide one-stop shopping for members' financial as well as religious lives. They generally have higher average giving by their memberships but also higher costs, and they seem more willing to engage in innovative financial techniques to improve the bottom line, especially when they are experiencing monetary problems.[23] While they are financially strong in good times because of their size, they can also be more financially vulnerable in downturns, as seen during the recent financial crisis. A "State of the Plate" report showed that among categories of churches based on congregation size, the largest percent of declines in giving in 2010 was reported by megachurches (47 percent), as compared, for example, to churches with 1,000–1,999 attendees, where only 26 percent of churches reported declines.[24] In short, changes in general economic conditions appear to influence giving in large churches more so than in small ones.

Distinctive religious attitudes toward money may be contributing to the financialization of American Christianity as well. Peter Mundey, Hilary Davidson, and Patricia Snell Herzog have observed significantly dissimilar views toward money between evangelical and mainline Protestant groups. Both cultures "sacralize" aspects of money, but they do so in different ways. The authors show how the evangelical Lakeside Community Church in Indiana adheres to a "*comprehensive sacralized frame* conceptualizing giving as an act of worship in which God is given back that which is rightfully His."[25] They also described the mainline Hillside Church, also of Indiana, as responding to a "bounded sacralized frame that conceptualizes money as profane, but the outcomes of giving as sacred—viewing giving primarily as a way to support aspects of church-life that individuals deem sacred."[26]

While there are differences between these forms of sacralization, both views may be problematic. From an investment standpoint, viewing money as itself "sacred," as emphasized in the practices of Lakeside Church, may entice congregations to withhold funds out of reverence from purposes necessary for the church to carry out its mission. Or, in extreme cases, churches may take chances they would not with "profane funds" in order to express their appreciation of this "holy capital." On the other hand, viewing church money as purely instrumental, as does Lakeside Community Church, may encourage churches with this attitude to follow the herd in investment, engaging in whatever new instruments and practices are fashionable, regardless of whether expertise exists within the church to do so responsibly. A healthier view would seem to be somewhere in the middle, regarding "church money" as less profane than corporate cash but not sacred in itself. This moderate view of money might lead to a more temperate investment approach and encourage conservative appropriation of church funds in ways that lessen the potential for churches to get in financial trouble. It might also level the expectations of churches generally with respect to money, refocusing attention on the spiritual lives of their congregations.

Even the handling of money in churches can impart attitudes that have potential value consequences. Impersonal forms of giving and the outsourcing of fundraising campaigns may not help the overall image of churches with respect to money; still, they are becoming increasingly popular. Churches today take advantage of electronic collection services for both weekly tithes and targeted giving to specific causes. The Shrine of the Most Blessed Sacrament Church in Washington, for example, realized an increase in members who give through electronic means from around 20 percent in 2007 to approximately 50 percent by 2011.[27]

Large churches often provide for "direct deposit," and the 9,000-plus-member Cross Church of Springdale, Arkansas, has installed "giving kiosks" that allow gifts to the church to be made by debit or credit card. The church's senior pastor, Ronnie Floyd, predicts that electronic giving will one day be the dominant method of making gifts to houses of worship: "It is secure and convenient. Many churches are beginning to use giving kiosks in their church lobbies for people to take advantage of while they are attending worship. This is all a cultural reality." Floyd sees no choice in the matter, stating, "Either the church can adjust or get left behind."[28] Most findings show online giving to churches is "catching up" with the general trends of online giving and electronic payment in the American economy.[29] Brian Kluth, who analyzes religious giving and contributes to the annual "State of the Plate" survey, estimates that more than 40 percent of American churches now accept online donations.[30]

Growth in this form of religious giving has spawned a new industry. Companies such as Easy Tithe in Dallas, Texas, and Faith Direct of Alexandria, Virginia, have formed, specializing in processing electronic payments for churches, charging either a flat fee or taking a "cut" of receipts, and displacing early attempts by "pioneer" churches in electronic donations that used PayPal or similar services.[31] According to Kluth, the advantage of electronic giving is the consistency of receipts for churches since members need not be present to give. Father O'Leary of the Boston Cathedral even believes that "e-donors" are more liberal with their gifts than those who prefer to contribute cash. "I think people feel freer to use their credit card," O'Leary stated. "If you have to go into your wallet and say, should I give $2 or $5, and nobody knows my name, you might give the $2, but who knows."[32]

Emphasis on fundraising absent the ability to address finance from a theological perspective can intensify the idea that American churches have become more money focused at the expense of their spiritual missions. It can also heighten the perception of an unhealthy division between a church's revenue activities and its religious practices. Wuthnow quotes a female member of an American Methodist church who stated that regarding money matters, the church "talks the talk but does not walk the walk." She notes her church's stress on raising capital for a new building, but that it does not minister to the real-life financial experiences of church members. When asked if the church "help[s] her understand money in a more godly way," she replied, "No, they just want more of it!"[33] Wuthnow pointed out that this was no young malcontent but a longtime church member who serves on multiple conference-wide committees.[34]

My family can relate. In support of a capital campaign at the Catholic Church my wife and I attend, a husband-and-wife team representing the building committee called on us, to solicit our support. We were among those selected because we were part of a core constituency of regular contributors to the Church as identified by the Steier Group, a company that bills itself as "a national fundraising and development firm which specializes in feasibility studies, capital campaigns and public relations for nonprofit organizations,"[35] which the church contracted to spearhead the campaign. The organization produced highly professional literature, and the couple who called on us was gracious and answered most of our questions about the $2.3 million expansion. They also provided a donation figure, much like the "Fair Share" method of United Way that my wife and I have become accustomed to over the years, which was based on our pattern of regular church giving. We expressed concern that the website, which was well designed with respect to the fundraising program details, provided little information about what the money was actually intended for. We also expressed concerns about the general "internal" focus of our Church with regard to its expenditures and our hope that the parish would begin to look externally for more opportunities to use its resources. The wife of the team that visited our home said she would investigate the website issue; indeed, later that evening she telephoned to voice agreement that the website contained little information about what the money would be used for. She told me that she would contact the member of the Steier Group who was helping to coordinate our church's campaign to let them know our concerns.

In retrospect, what bothered us most about the experience was the same attitude that bothered the Methodist woman Wuthnow described. Despite our voicing concerns about the church's intention in using its capital and the couple's willingness to follow up on one of those concerns, they really just wanted money. That is not unusual, of course. Americans are called on to give to any number of groups on a regular basis. But being solicited by one's church should be different. Parishioners should have more opportunities to discuss congregational priorities and how best to direct resources. And, while some churches undoubtedly enable such discussions to a greater degree than others, all should be able to provide theological perspectives on financial issues. Religious perspectives on capital and its uses, both within churches and in the wider community, can help offset the narrow focus of the financialized society, which measures all tasks by the same yardstick, emphasizing bottom-line results with their implied value implications. Unfortunately, American churches have come to accept—just as have other American institutions—a primary maxim of financialization: the most efficient way forward is always best, irrespective of its consequences for community.

The financing of religion and the loss of focus

Church bond financing is a traditional link between church finances of yesteryear and those of today. Financing for the aforementioned Broadway Temple skyscraper church was to be accomplished by a mix of loans and the sale of some $2 million worth of bonds, advertised with the slogan "Buy These Bonds and Let God Come to Broadway."[36] Debt problems, cost overruns, and a sagging economy led to the project's demise.[37] The point is that churches have issued bonds for years to fund construction and other projects requiring large infusions of capital; yet the church's unique place in American society makes financing and investment surrounding it susceptible to forms of manipulation. For example, possibilities for "affinity fraud" in American churches are high given the level of trust by adherents in these institutions and in their fellow congregants. Affinity fraud is the type that takes advantage of a common attachment among members in organizations that form around some mutual interest (typically spiritual or social) rather than a common financial stake or political worldview.[38]

The combination of financial problems in American churches, many of which are attributable to the recent crisis, and the willingness of some persons to exploit religious devotion for monetary gain, contributed to "church bonds" securing an undesirable place in the category of "examination and enforcement priorities" issued by the Financial Industry Regulatory Authority (FINRA) in 2012.[39] Attorney Robert W. Pearce, P.A., observes how

> church bond salespersons have been able to capitalize on the low interest rate environment and the desire for a relatively secure source of income, primarily by retirees—the impact of an increasing number of church bond defaults on retirees' investment portfolio[s] has been devastating.[40]

Growth in affinity fraud spans denominational lines and impacts many religious investors as unethical investment "advisers" hawk products they tout as supporting church capital campaigns, religious missions, etc., and often solicit members within churches to offer testimonials as to the "soundness" and even "sacredness" of these investments.

Kevin Phillips suggests that along with the degree of loyalty adherents have to their faith, the degree to which financial success is held in esteem by a particular religious group seems to influence the vulnerability of its members to affinity fraud. He references a report from the *Ogden Standard-Examiner* in 1989 that stated that

> the cultural emphasis in the Mormon Church that equates financial success with spiritual success, and an unquestioning allegiance to authority figures, may partly explain why 10,000 Utah investors have been swindled out of more than $200 million during the last decade.[41]

Swindling of the faithful hardly has been unique to Mormonism, however. As mentioned briefly in the introduction, the Baptist Foundation of Arizona (BFA) created a Ponzi scheme based on Arizona real estate that cost many loyal Baptists substantial sums of money. For example, Forest and Lee Bomar, an elderly couple caught up in the scam, rolled over their entire $235,000 retirement nest egg from an IRA into what were supposed to be secure fixed-rate investments through the BFA that "would be used for Christian things."[42] Instead, their investment was lost and the Bomars were forced to live on a minimal pension, income from Social Security, and any money that lawyers were able to extract from what remained of the BFA.[43] There has even been a case of Amish affinity fraud where a 77-year-old Ohio man was indicted for allegedly scamming some $17 million from 2,700 other Amish congregants. An estimate in *The Economist* has affinity fraud in the U.S. amounting to tens of billions of dollars over the past decade, with religious affinity fraud making up the majority of cases.[44]

Perhaps even more challenging to the church bond industry than fraud, however, has been the financially precarious existence of many houses of worship that resulted from risky financing and investment practices associated with the recent crisis. As has been seen, churches have not fared much differently from other American institutions with respect to debt and investment problems. In some cases, churches have taken out multimillion-dollar balloon loans to finance expansion projects and experienced the same problems as other American institutions that took advantage of flexible financing.

Church construction in the U.S. rose dramatically in the 1990s and reached the $9 billion mark in 2003 thanks in part to innovative forms of financing that have developed in recent years. New methods deviate from the traditional model in which a loan was obtained through a community bank at a fixed rate and for a set duration. Often a "congregant banker" served as a liaison between the church and financial institution in such deals.[45] Today, churches acquire a variable rate, "interest only" balloon, and other riskier loan products from credit lenders across the country and even beyond. While more flexible financing arrangements led to the boom in church construction, they also led to major increases in church debt and bankruptcy. Church bankruptcies skyrocketed from 2008 when only 24 churches were sold at foreclosure into the hundreds only two years later. The CoStar Group produced statistics showing that between 2010 and March of 2012, some 270 churches were sold because of loan default, with approximately 90 percent of those sales stemming from "lender-triggered foreclosure," disproportionately impacting churches in states like Florida, California, Georgia, and Michigan—those also hardest hit by residential foreclosures.[46]

A record for annual church foreclosures was realized in 2011 as banks sold off 138 churches.[47] Even worse, Scott Rolfs, who serves the Ziegler investment bank as its managing director of Religious and Education Finance, suggests that church foreclosure numbers may understate the problem of what, sadly, might be called "church delinquency": "Churches are among the final institutions to get foreclosed upon because banks have not wanted to look like they are being heavy handed with the churches."[48] But it is not only banks and other "secular" lenders that have pressured churches into foreclosure. Reuters' Tim Reid observed that the Evangelical Christian Credit Union (ECCU) was "particularly aggressive in lending to religious institutions" and, in cases of default, has initiated foreclosure on churches such as the Solid Rock Christian Church in Memphis, Tennessee. In 2008, Solid Rock acquired a $2.9 million loan from the ECCU to fund a major building project to house its expanding congregation but, after exhausting its savings, wound up in default. The ECCU not only foreclosed on the church but has also attempted to auction it off—a move the church is fighting legally as it attempts to restructure its debt.[49]

Not only expansive, young megachurches have got into financial trouble; in some cases, smaller conservative churches or even centuries-old institutions have wound up in foreclosure. The Saint Andrew Anglican Church of Easton, Maryland, borrowed $850,000 to buy a Gothic revival-styled building, once home to a Roman Catholic parish. The idea was inspired by its bishop Joel Marcus Johnson, who believed his theologically conservative appeal that rejects "Episcopal innovations, such as ordaining female priests," would lead to rapidly expanding his 50 or so congregants. The plan did not work out and the Church was foreclosed in August of 2008 by Talbot Bank of Easton.[50]

Before one comes down too hard on mortgage companies that lend to churches, however, it should be recognized that, in many cases, they themselves have been pressed to the limits of solvency. The credit overextensions of American churches also have jeopardized those organizations willing to lend them money. The *Wall Street Journal* reported that "financial problems are crimping a church building boom that began in the 1990s, when megachurches multiplied, turning many houses of worship into suburban social centers complete with bookstores, gyms and coffee bars."[51] Florida's real estate bust of recent years impacted one lender, Church Mortgage and Loan Corporation of Maitland, Florida, which was unable to sell the ten church properties on which it foreclosed as real estate values went south. Unable to pay its own bondholders the $18 million it owed them, Church Mortgage and Loan was forced to file for Chapter 11 bankruptcy.[52]

These debt problems facing American churches are increasingly common. Yet, according to Rolfs, "the church foreclosure market isn't anything extraordinary." Rather, "it's simply another byproduct of the credit bubble."[53] From another perspective, however, the rapid growth in church foreclosures is extraordinary if one considers that houses of worship, perhaps more so than other institutions of civil society, should operate by a higher standard regarding debt.

It is not only religious "institutions" that have been hammered with credit problems over the past decade. Individual Christians have taken advantage of innovations in debt financing just as other Americans. And the response to the insolvency of many Christian families has had a significant economic impact of its own. Nashville-based Christian financial adviser Dave Ramsey advertises that he turned his once debt-ridden life around, established a 13-week course through his "Financial Peace University," which helped approximately 200,000 indebted individuals in 2006 to address their debt problems. Ramsey claims that the "average family" that completes his course wipes out around $5,300 worth of debt while saving $2,700 in only 91 days.[54] And Ramsey's success is not unique; as one journalist observed, "peddling biblically based financial advice has turned into a cottage industry," with radio programs providing Christian financial advice reaching as many as a million listeners a week.[55]

Some of that advice centers on faith-based investment, which has grown significantly over the past couple of decades. The growth in diversity and sophistication of religious investment is illustrated well by the Everence Company, a ministry of the Mennonite Church and parent organization of the Praxis funds.[56] Everence provides a full suite of services for both individual and corporate clients, providing loans and various depository instruments, financial planning, retirement plans, health insurance, and annuities, among other offerings. Its webpage even advertised a "Money Talks video contest" for youth with the description: "Get creative, share a story, express your ideas in the newest Money Talks contest – open to young people, ages 15 to 25 – featuring cash rewards for your winning work!"[57] One of the principal purposes of Everence, however, is to enable faith-based investment on the part of the Mennonite community through its mutual funds and money market accounts. Its website lists 31 different denominational groups within the general "Anabaptist faith community."[58]

Faith-based mutual funds (FBFs) invest in assets consistent with the beliefs and values of particular faith traditions, the primary categories being Protestant, Catholic, and Islamic funds with total assets under management of around $30 billion in October 2012.[59] The funds apply asset "screens" to ensure consistency with the values of faith groups with which they are affiliated. Some studies have shown significantly higher loads (fees) on faith-based funds as well as overall lower asset turnover. Scholars have suggested that low asset turnover relative to non-FBFs may result from "the restricted universe of investment choices FBFs have that result from a plethora of exclusive screens."[60] Relative to other socially responsible funds, FBFs are shown to have lower fees and expense ratios.[61] From their beginnings in 1986 to 2013, FBFs grew to number 79 as reported by Morningstar, from the The Timothy Plan, an evangelically oriented fund billed as "America's first pro-life, pro-family, Biblically-based mutual fund group," to the Aquinas group of funds whose investment guidelines are established by the U.S. Conference of Catholic Bishops, and countless other funds.[62] These funds offer not only Christian investors but also those of other faith traditions, and even those who adhere to no faith tradition, distinct investment alternatives that are based on religious values.

With respect to the investments of churches and their affiliated organizations, the range of investment options has broadened significantly in recent years. Emerging relationships between hedge funds and religious organizations are reshaping the dynamic between faith traditions and investment and bringing together two groups that have been perhaps least transparent with respect to their assets. Hedge funds are highly secretive concerning their investment holdings and strategies, seeing them as their principal assets that provide competitive advantage and distinguish a particular fund from the rest of the crowd. Religious groups have been hesitant to reveal the overall size and composition of their investments as well.[63] First Amendment protections help shield the assets of faith-based institutions from public scrutiny.

The greater volatility of hedge funds and certain investment practices like short-selling, the practice of selling a security not actually owned (typically it is "borrowed") for purposes of buying it later in anticipation that the price will go down—has made hedge funds controversial investment alternatives for religious groups, as described in Chapter 1 in the case of the Anglican Church. Yet churches and other religious organizations, by and large, have the same objectives as most other investors. The same holds true for those who manage faith-based investments. Laura Berry, who heads the Interfaith Center on Corporate Responsibility in New York, has stated,

> I don't know a single faith-based chief investment officer who does not want to produce alpha for his or her fund. The question really is how to be sure hedge funds are producing alpha in ways that are consistent with the organization's mission.[64]

The questions are whether staying true to mission and "producing alpha" are compatible objectives and what kinds of shortcuts might be alluring to groups attempting to accomplish both.

Hedge funds traditionally have been reluctant to apply costly screens to their portfolios to attract religious investors; however, that now appears to be changing. Just as the Anglican Church and its clerical pension fund have overcome opposition to hedge-fund investing, it appears that the funds themselves increasingly are willing to meet religious investors somewhere in the middle by offering screened investment alternatives. The screens typically include restricting investment in pornography, tobacco, gambling, alcohol, abortion products and services, weapons manufacturers, and other industries deemed to go against the teachings of particular religious groups.[65] Those screens can be tailored according to particular beliefs, but at additional cost.

Hedge fund investing by faith-based groups is in its early stages. A few institutions have taken the plunge and are pioneering this form of investment among religiously affiliated organizations. In the case of Dignity Health of San Francisco, both institutional and investment complexity can come together to complicate the true meaning of "faith based." Dignity Health has invested some $800 million in SRI-screened hedge funds diversified through 20 different (unnamed) hedge fund managers.[66] In 2012, Catholic Healthcare West (CHW) became Dignity Health and the new organization left the auspices of the Roman Catholic Church, although it has stated its intention to continue abiding by the values and mission of the former Catholic institution, including a commitment not to provide abortion services. However, Dignity Health is a parent organization of both Catholic and secular hospitals, which leads some to question whether preventing secularization of the entire "system" is possible.[67]

Adding to the speculation was a ruling by federal district court Judge Thelton Henderson in 2014 that Dignity Health's pension fund is not a "church plan" and thus falls under federal pension rules. The company maintained that its plan should fall under the looser guidelines governing church plans because "its pension plan is maintained by a tax-exempt entity controlled by or associated with a church or association of churches."[68] Further complicating the situation is that this ruling occurred in the hearing of a class-action suit brought by 60,000 employees of the company, who claim that Dignity Health's pension plan is underfunded to the tune of $1.2 billion.[69] The intersection of religion and healthcare makes for particularly sticky situations, complicated further by ownership structures and financial practices, with respect to the ability of religiously affiliated organizations to abide by their missions and values.

It appears that the hedge fund industry gradually is making a commitment to provide products screened according to religious values; that change is likely to make achievement of faith-based investment through these instruments easier, but religious groups must decide whether common practices of hedge funds are consistent with their values and theological principles. Short-selling of securities and various forms of derivative instruments should be evaluated from the distinct theological positions of faith groups before they invest. The general lack of transparency in the industry is another consideration that may have theological relevance. While the coming together of these disparate groups—hedge funds and religious institutions—may potentially bring values into a form of investment with an unsavory reputation, it also has potential pitfalls. Not the least of these is that religious organizations investing with hedge funds may become complacent with those companies' screens and practices and lack the diligence to continually monitor their investments.

One hopeful sign is the apparent recognition by faith groups, and perhaps even some hedge fund organizations, that investment practices can have real social impact. The *will* of religious groups to invest according to their values is not as much a concern as is their *ability* to do so. The nascent attempts of hedge funds to meet religious groups half way by providing investment screens consistent with their values is encouraging, but the complexity of these products and intensity of competition for returns still create challenges for religiously affiliated organizations as they attempt to navigate the dynamic environment of contemporary investment.

Financial scandals in the American Catholic Church

The allure of finance and accounting methods for religious organizations can be observed not only in attempts to maximize returns on their investments or better distribute their resources in providing social benefits. Sadly, church finances have become a key part of the Catholic Church sex abuse scandal in the U.S., as evidenced by the bankruptcies of parishes sued by victims and, in some cases, the use of "stealth accounts" to cover up abuses. In the Archdiocese of St. Paul and Minneapolis, a "secret financial system" enabled Church leaders to move funds among specially coded accounts that allowed for the processing of payments to mask clergy misconduct. In the case of Rev. Stanley F. Kozlak, the Archdiocese provided a "disability retirement payment" of $1,900 per month and another $970 per month until the priest reaches the age of 67 and is able to draw full Social Security benefits in order to get the priest, who fathered a child, to leave the Church "quietly."[70] Minnesota Public Radio cited "internal financial reports" showing that the Archdiocese had paid almost $11 million through stealth accounts in a nine-year span to cover up priest abuse scandals. The account for "disability pay" actually became code for payments covering "improper behavior," and the "don't-ask culture kept archdiocese employees from probing deeper."[71] These examples show how money today directs church practice and has reshaped its values.

Using stealth accounts to cover up abuse exposed the Church to financial improprieties. The former accounting director for the Archdiocese of St. Paul and Minneapolis, Scott Domeier, is serving jail time for embezzlement and submitting improper tax returns after it was revealed that he had stolen over $650,000 from the Archdiocese. The secret accounting system even supported different account numbers for particular types of abuse. The account 1–515 was used to pay costs related to priests who allegedly abused children while account 1–516 was used for costs connected to adult abuse.[72] In his trial, Domeier's attorney, Terry Duggins, attempted to produce evidence that Domeier was required to process payments for the priests who allegedly committed the abuses, although the judge in the case would not allow the evidence to be introduced. Duggins took the claims to the news media and told reporters that his client considered the payments to be "morally wrong, unethical and possibly illegal." Domeier has related to media groups that the Church was making payments to nine priests against whom there were strong allegations of sexual misconduct. His statements were supported by an Archdiocese canon lawyer, Jennifer Haselberger, who told Minnesota Public Radio that she discovered the payments and reported the irregularities to Archbishop John Nienstedt. Haselberger ultimately resigned her post with the Church in April of 2013.[73]

Settlements of sexual abuse cases across the nation are jeopardizing Catholic institutions and, tragically, making them more financially focused. As of 2012, the Church had settled some $3.3 billion worth of claims ($1.3 billion in California alone) that have caused eight dioceses to go bankrupt.[74] These settlements are occurring even as giving to churches by American Catholics is decreasing and the number of parishioners entering Catholic ministries as priests and nuns is in sharp decline. The sex abuse scandal has greatly damaged the Church's reputation, but its rather callous monetary response to the tragedy is having a similarly negative impact. *The Economist* reported that "some dioceses have, in effect, raided priests' pension funds to cover settlements and other losses." And while for a publicly traded American company, regulatory restrictions help prevent such acts, "in the church, retirement is still largely in the gift of the bishop. Retirement plans for priests are typically set up as diocesan trusts rather than proper pension funds with structured benefits."[75] The financial retrenchment of the American Catholic Church puts it at odds with the faithful, not only in legal battles stemming from abuse, but also with respect to the Church's secrecy concerning financial settlements and the source of funds used to accomplish them. Catholics are left wondering whether their gifts are being used to silence pedophile priests or their victims.[76] That doubt, and the value changes it is inspiring within the Church, may be as significant in driving a wedge between the Church leadership and its membership as the abuse itself. The question remains: even if the Catholic Church can save itself from financial ruin, can it resuscitate itself spiritually and reassume its moral voice in American society?

Almost as disconcerting as the individual acts of abuse have been the use of accounting and financial means to cover up those acts. Bad people exist in organizations of any size; however, when the badness works its way into an organization's chart of accounts, the problems effectively become institutionalized. Financial liability associated with the sex abuse scandal is fast making the American Catholic Church the most "financially interested" institution in the country. Its assets are under siege by thousands of claimants whose lawsuits threaten to wipe out the Church's vast network not only of churches but also hospitals, colleges, and charitable organizations (Catholic Charities, for example, is the nation's largest such organization, employing 65,000 workers who attempt to meet the needs of ten million people).[77]

These revelations within the American Catholic Church were followed by what hopefully is good news concerning the "business" of Catholicism: Pope Francis's efforts to reform the Institute for the Works of Religion—the so-called "Vatican Bank." The Pope has decided to replace much of the Bank's top management, many of them clergy with little expertise in finance, with an international cast of professional laypersons with far more experience, breaking up what has been referred to as the "Italian monopoly."[78] For years, the Vatican Bank has been accused of money laundering, corruption, and poor management practices that have allowed money to flow through the institution with grossly inadequate paper trails. Australian Cardinal George Pell, who is the Church's new "finance czar," has voiced the goal of making the Institute for the Works of Religion "boringly successful."

Perhaps the wider goal of the Christian, not just Catholic, church in the United States should be to make its financial operations "boringly successful." Simply avoiding the scandals, bankruptcies and investment losses of recent years is inadequate; the church should serve as an example for the nation that shows clearly that its role is a higher one that must appropriately balance the demands of revenue generation with Christian theological and social values. Statements from religious leaders that their churches can maximize their ministries' services by maximizing their investment portfolios have a callousing effect. In a culture as intensely competitive and money driven as that of the United States, some institutions are needed to offset such influences, not reinforce them. Given the extent to which money concerns guide the operations of voluntary associations, educational institutions, and other intermediate organizations observed in the last chapter, houses of worship might be seen as the last vestiges of "disinterestedness," which certain of the nation's Founders thought essential to the preservation of the American ethos.

Conclusion

In spite of the stealth accounts to pay for clerical abuse, religious investments in hedge funds, church bankruptcies, and other headline grabbing issues, perhaps the most damning evidence of American Christianity's financialization is found in a comment by John W. Kennedy in an article for *Christianity Today*: "There is little difference between the amounts that Christians and non-Christians earn, spend, save, charge, or donate to charities."[79] While some scholars might challenge the last point on charitable donations, much of Kennedy's comment rings true. Blatant abuses—sexual, financial, and otherwise—are and sadly will forever be part of the human condition. Perhaps more concerning, however, is that religious belief seems to mean so little with respect to more mundane human behavior. American "religious" culture is increasingly a mirror image of the broader, politically and financially charged culture that it often criticizes. Part of the reason may well have to do with normalizing processes that make us all accountable primarily to one common motivation—achieving our objectives by maximizing results. Every institution in the financialized society, first and foremost, must meet basic financial needs to ensure its survival. No higher purpose eclipses that singular objective.

Seeming absence of higher purpose can even lead religious organizations to behavior that jeopardizes their very identities. Recent activities that not only further financialize American churches but politicize them as well are discouraging. Religious groups increasingly are using their resources to further their political interests by forming PACs and collecting money for political candidates. The intensely contested Mississippi GOP senatorial contest between incumbent Thad Cochran and Tea Party challenger Chris McDaniel featured an interesting twist that may portend even greater erosion of the church's moral voice due to financial influence. Many political commentators charged that Cochran won the runoff by soliciting the votes of non-Republicans to vote against McDaniel. Questions arose subsequently concerning an advertisement that ran in the *Mississippi Link* imploring its readers to turn out to vote for Senator Cochran. The controversy stemmed from the ad's being paid for by a political action committee called "All Citizens for Mississippi" that "shares an address and leadership" with the New Horizon Church International in Jackson. Making matters worse, the PAC appears not even to have existed at the time the advertisement ran, suggesting that New Horizon may have been the source of this political contribution.[80] "All Citizens for Mississippi" was founded by Bishop Ronnie Crudup, Sr., Senior Pastor of the New Horizon Church, and it reportedly raised $144,685 in the last two weeks of June alone.[81] Several political pundits have suggested that Cochran would not have won the election without the late appeal to the state's Democrats and, more generally, to its African-American citizens.

The case raises some obvious First Amendment questions concerning government subsidy of politically active religious groups benefiting from tax exemption. More concerning here, however, is the possibility for even greater financial influence to find its way into churches. Other religious groups around the country are forming "affiliated" PACs to support candidates and legislative agendas, creating their own political units and soliciting contributions, thereby extending the influence of money (and politics) even more directly into American houses of worship.

In an editorial for *Newsweek*, Rabbi Marc Gellman offers another reason why the United States and other liberal democracies need religious, educational, and civic organizations that are not vested in financial outcomes to the degree of others. "Bad times for the economy, means bad times for the places where we go to flee the predations of the economy," Gellman writes. "Without places of faith and hope, our financial losses will pale before our loss of charity, community and the bundling that keeps us all from breaking when we are alone and afraid."[82] Gellman recognizes there is no refuge in a nation where *every institution has a financial stake that supersedes all other commitments*. Such a scenario implies a constant flux among traditions that is highly unstable ground on which to construct a society.

Gellman's words reflect old wisdom. For more than a century, a variety of social and religious thinkers have recognized the importance of civil society institutions, which must be more resistant than other groups to both financial exuberance and financial disturbance, among other of life's contingencies. They are not only places of sanctuary in hard times but places that form character for hard times—and they are able to do so because there has been something of a consensus for most of American history that some groups should remain beyond the fray of political and economic contingency to provide a solid moral foundation for both democratic governance and the market economy. As that foundation decays, then arguably so, too, does the American experiment.

Notes

1 Pierre Bourdieu, *Practical Reason: On the Theory of Action* (Stanford, CA: Stanford University Press, 1998), 114.

2 George M. Marsden, *The Soul of the American University: From Protestant Establishment to Established Nonbelief* (New York: Oxford University Press, 1996), 281–2.

3 *The Christian Herald* 48 (December 5, 1925); quoted in Rolf Lundén, *Business and Religion in the American 1920s*, Contributions in American Studies Series, no. 91 (New York: Greenwood Press, 1988), 39 & 81. A Protestant magazine called *The Christian Herald*, for example, ran a weekly investment column for subscribers that covered topics like budget planning and it allowed advertising by banks, investment firms, and trust companies that encouraged believers to invest with them. An advertisement by the Trust Company of Florida titled "What Shall it Profit a Man?" read "What profit is there in keeping money safely invested, but without an adequate interest return? The only value in having money is in making it earn more, and all it is capable of earning." *The Christian Herald* 48 (December 5, 1925); quoted in Lundén, *Business and Religion in the American 1920s*, 39.

4 Financing for the massive construction project, which ultimately failed, was to be financed through "a two-million-dollar loan and through the sale of second mortgage, 5 percent, cumulative interest bonds, which raised another $2,000,000." See Lundén, *Business and Religion in the American 1920s*, 80.

5 Robert Wuthnow, *The Crisis in the Churches: Spiritual Malaise, Fiscal Woe* (New York: Oxford University Press, 1997), vi.

6 LifeWay Research is the research division of the nonprofit LifeWay Resources, founded in 1891 and headquartered in Nashville, Tennessee, which has almost 200 stores throughout the United States and provides Christian literature, audio/visual materials, and other resources to churches. For information on the LifeWay Research report, see *The Courier*, "LifeWay Research: Pastors Unaware of Church Member Debt," (January 21, 2009); available at http://baptistcourier.com/2009/01/lifeway-research-pastors-unaware-of-church-member-debt/.

7 Wuthnow, "The Crisis in the Churches," in *Financing American Religion*, eds. Mark Chaves and Sharon L. Miller (Walnut Creek, CA: AltaMira Press, 1999), 70.
8 Wuthnow, "The Crisis in the Churches," in *Financing American Religion*, 72–3.
9 Wuthnow, *The Crisis in the Churches*, 51.
10 Wuthnow, *The Crisis in the Churches*, 51.
11 Wuthnow, *The Crisis in the Churches*, 51.
12 In counseling pastors on church funding, Joseph R. Miller writes that "you need to elicit more participants of obedience-based (not need-based) giving people. Train your people in Biblical principles of stewardship that are part of our primary occupation … encourage them to begin by practicing the tithe principle as first fruits giving to Christ … then encourage sacrificial gifts beyond the tithe," in "Funding the Local Church," quoted in James Hudnut-Beumler, *In Pursuit of the Almighty's Dollar: A History of Money and American Protestantism* (Chapel Hill, NC: The University of North Carolina Press, 2007), 217.
13 Wuthnow, *The Crisis in the Churches*, 175.
14 Some firms bill themselves as full-service consulting firms for churches while others are more specialized, such as Church Development Services, the website of which states that the two services they typically provide "involve planning and capital fundraising." They also have "expertise in church finances, financial feasibility, and how to organize finances so the church is vibrant and remains a viable during and after the expansion campaign is completed." See www.churchdevelopment.com/services/consulting/.
15 Wuthnow, *The Crisis in the Churches*, 52.
16 Stephen Edward McMillin, "Faith-Based Social Services: From Communitarian to Individualistic Values," *Zygon*, vol. 46, no. 2 (June 2011): 482, 489.
17 Quoted in Wuthnow, *The Crisis in the Churches*, 194.
18 Wuthnow, *The Crisis in the Churches*, 199 (emphasis Wuthnow's). Wuthnow includes a footnote describing one pastor as saying:

> I think the hardest thing for people to do is to become excited about giving if you never see the connection between the beneficiary and the one who gives it, where you actually feel that you've really benefited somebody. You just kind of throw money into a pool, and you're never quite sure what happens. People are more results oriented.

See Wuthnow, *The Crisis in the Churches*, 270, n. 17.
19 Zablon Nthamburi, "An African Viewpoint on Wealthy Missionaries," in Jonathan J. Bonk, *Missions and Money: Affluence as a Missionary Problem Revisited*, Revised and Expanded Edition (Maryknoll, NY: Orbis Books, 2006), xviii.
20 Bonk, "Introduction to the First Edition," in *Missions and Money*, xxviii–xxix.
21 Wuthnow, *The Crisis in the Churches*, 12.
22 Dean R. Hoge and Loren B. Mead, "Endowed Congregations," in *Financing American Religion*, eds. Mark Chaves and Sharon L. Miller (Walnut Creek, CA: AltaMira Press, 1999), 92–3.
23 Wuthnow, *The Crisis in the Churches*, 237. Interestingly, and somewhat at odds with other research, a 2013 survey by Leadership Network of Dallas, Texas, revealed that churches with more than 2,000 average attendees were "thriving" despite the tough economic conditions of recent years. Only 3 percent of those surveyed reported that they had been "very negatively" impacted by the economy while around 33 percent said "they had not been affected at all." See Adelle M. Banks, "Megachurches are Thriving in Hard Times, Survey Says," *Christian Century*, vol. 130, no. 7 (April 3, 2013): 15.
24 Lillian Kwon, "Survey: Financial Strain Worsens for More Churches," *The Christian Post* (March 24, 2010); available at www.christianpost.com/news/survey-financial-strain-worsens-for-more-churches-44439/. Kwon, citing "The State of the Plate"

report, stated that even the 20,000-attendee Saddleback Church of Rev. Rick Warren was behind on its budget projections for donations until Warren's year-end appeal brought in $2.4 million in gifts. See Kwon, "Survey."

25 Peter Mundey, Hilary Davidson, and Patricia Snell Herzog, "Making Money Sacred: How Two Church Cultures Translate Mundane Money into Distinct Sacralized Frames of Giving," *Sociology of Religion* 72, no. 3 (2011): 322 (emphasis authors').

26 Mundey, Davidson, and Herzog, "Making Money Sacred," 323 (emphasis authors'). The authors argue "that understanding the processes and rituals of giving in these two churches helps to illuminate different conceptualizations of the sacred and the ways in which they compel self-sacrificial behaviors." See Mundey, Davidson, and Herzog, "Making Money Sacred."

27 Susan Schept, "Church Collection Plates may go Empty as Electronic Giving Rises," Reuters (January 23, 2011); available at www.reuters.com/article/2011/01/23/us-churches-donations-idUSTRE70M10C20110123.

28 Chris Bahn, "Churches Introduce Electronic Tithing," *Arkansas Business News* (May 6, 2013); available at www.arkansasbusiness.com/article/92329/churches-introduce-electronic-tithing.

29 Online giving is now said to average around 33 percent of total giving. See Marcia Frellick, "Churches Embrace Online Credit, Debit Card Donations," *Fox Business* (February 21, 2011); available at www.creditcards.com/credit-card-news/churches-embrace-online-credit-debit-card-donations-1273.php.

30 Cited in Shannon Mullen, "No Cash when the Collection Plate Arrives? No Problem," *Marketplace* (January 25, 2013); available at www.marketplace.org/topics/your-money/no-cash-when-collection-plate-arrives-no-problem.

31 See Schept, "Church Collection Plates may go Empty as Electronic Giving Rises," and Bahn, "Churches Introduce Electronic Tithing."

32 Quoted in Mullen, "No Cash when the Collection Plate Arrives? No Problem."

33 Wuthnow, *The Crisis in the Churches*, 25.

34 Wuthnow, *The Crisis in the Churches*, 25.

35 See http://steiergroup.com/.

36 W. Livingston Larned, excerpts from "Editorial" in *The Daily Reporter*, White Plains, N.Y.; in *Popular Science Monthly*, vol. 107, no. 2 (August 1925): 4.

37 Catherine Ku, "NYC That Never Was: A Methodist Skyscraper Church on Broadway," (August 15, 2013); available at http://untappedcities.com/2013/08/15/nyc-that-never-was-methodist-skyscraper-church-on-broadway/.

38 See U.S. Securities and Exchange Commission, "Affinity Fraud: How To Avoid Investment Scams That Target Groups"; available at www.sec.gov/investor/pubs/affinity.htm.

39 Robert W. Pearce, "Investors Nationwide Beware—Church Bonds are Risky and Illiquid Investments"; available at http://seekingalpha.com/instablog/5396101-robert-w-pearce/1622201-investors-nationwide-beware-church-bonds-are-risky-and-illiquid-investments.

40 Pearce, "Investors Nationwide Beware." Pearce notes that a primary source of church bond illiquidity results from the relative small size of church bond issuances (often $10 million or less),

> which translates into a lack of any secondary market for the bonds to trade in. In addition, the true financial condition and creditworthiness of church bond issuers are difficulty to determine because their underlying source of revenue is never really clear.

See Pearce, "Investors Nationwide Beware."

41 *Ogden (Utah) Standard-Examiner*, August 26, 1989; quoted in Kevin Phillips, *Bad Money: Reckless Finance, Failed Politics, and the Global Crisis of American Capitalism* (New York: Viking, 2008), 94.

42 Laura Bruce, "Affinity Scammers Bilk the Faithful in the Name of Greed," *Bankrate.com* (August 8, 2001); available at www.bankrate.com/finance/investing/affinity-scammers-bilk-the-faithful-in-the-name-of-greed-1.aspx.
43 Bruce, "Affinity Scammers."
44 "Fleecing the Flock: The Big Business of Fleecing People Who Trust You," *The Economist* (January 28, 2012); available at www.economist.com/node/21543526.
45 Tom Hals, "Special Report: Holy Bubble! Churches Struck Down by Foreclosures," Reuters (April 1, 2010); available at www.reuters.com/article/2010/04/01/us-church-financing-idUSTRE63020J20100401.
46 Tim Reid, "Banks Foreclosing on Churches in Record Numbers," Reuters (March 9, 2012); available at www.reuters.com/assets/print?aid=USBRE82803120120309.
47 Reid, "Banks Foreclosing on Churches in Record Numbers."
48 Reid, "Banks Foreclosing on Churches in Record Numbers."
49 Reid, "Banks Foreclosing on Churches in Record Numbers."
50 Suzanne Sataline, "In Hard Times, Houses of God Turn to Chapter 11 in Book of Bankruptcy—Strapped Churches Can't Pay the Mortgage After Borrowing Binge; St. Andrew at Auction," *Wall Street Journal* (December 23, 2008): A.1.
51 Sataline, "In Hard Times," A.1.
52 Sataline, "In Hard Times."
53 Quoted in Reid, "Banks Foreclosing on Churches in Record Numbers."
54 John W. Kennedy, "The Debt Slayers: There's a Reason There Are More Christian Financial Advisers than Ever," *Christianity Today* (May 2006): 41.
55 Kennedy, "The Debt Slayers," 42. The chairman of Crown Financial Ministries, Ron Blue, has observed that in the period from 1990 to 2006, in which household wealth increased by almost four times to around $50 trillion, financial service advisers grew in number by around ten times. He estimated that there were 1 million advisers in 2006, around 1,000 of those having been trained through his Christian Financial Professionals Network.
56 The Praxis Value Index A fund earned its investors a return of 32.13 percent in 2012. See Tim Grant, "Investing in Your Values: Socially Conscious Mutual Funds are Quickly Growing," *Pittsburg Post-Gazette*, Sooner Edition (June 6, 2013), section C, p. 1.
57 Awards are given to the winning young people's designated charities. See www.everence.com/moneytalks/#sthash.BU1nJj0i.dpuf.
58 See www.everence.com/who-we-serve/.
59 David Kathman, "Getting Religion With Faith-Based Mutual Funds," *Morningstar Advisor* (November 5, 2012); available at www.morningstar.com/advisor/t/65920341/getting-religion-with-faith-based-mutual-funds.htm.
60 W. Ghoul and P. Karam. "MRI and SRI Mutual Funds: A Comparison of Christian, Islamic (Morally Responsible Investing), and Socially Responsible Investing (SRI) Mutual Funds." *Journal of Investing*, vol. 16, no. 2 (2007): 96–102; cited in John C. Adams and Parvez Ahmed, "The Performance of Faith-Based Funds," *Journal of Investing* 22, no. 4 (Winter 2013): 84.
61 Adams and Ahmed, "The Performance of Faith-Based Funds," 89.
62 See Grant, "Investing in Your Values," Section C, p. 1; and Kathman, "Getting Religion With Faith-Based Mutual Funds."
63 Christine Williamson, "Hedge Fund Firms Accepting Screens to get Faith-Based Business," *Pensions&Investments Online* (August 23, 2012); available at www.pionline.com/article/20120823/ONLINE/120829945/hedge-fund-firms-accepting-screens-to-get-faith-based-business.
64 Quoted in Williamson, "Hedge Fund Firms Accepting Screens." Producing "alpha" is a measure of how a particular investor's portfolio performs on a risk-adjusted basis relative to an industry benchmark for that asset class. If the benchmark is the S&P500 and that index achieves a 7 percent annual return while a particular portfolio achieves

a 10 percent return (after adjusting for risk), then it has produced an alpha of 3 percent.

65 Williamson, "Hedge Fund Firms Accepting Screens."

66 Williamson, "Hedge Fund Firms Accepting Screens."

67 "Catholic Healthcare West becomes Dignity Health, Will They Provide Abortions?" *Catholic Online* (January 25, 2012); available at www.catholic.org/news/health/story.php?id=44532.

68 Kathy Robertson, "Dignity Health Pension Plan is not a Church Plan, Court Rules—Again," *Sacramento Business Journal* (July 24, 2014); available at www.bizjournals.com/sacramento/news/2014/07/24/dignity-health-pension-plan-is-not-a-church-plan.html.

69 Robertson, "Dignity Health Pension Plan."

70 Tom Scheck, "Secret Accounts Paid for Clergy Misconduct but left Church open to Financial Abuse," Minnesota Public Radio (January 23, 2014); available at http://minnesota.publicradio.org/collections/catholic-church/2014/01/23/secret-accounts-kept-clergy-misconduct-quiet-but-left-archdiocese-finances-exposed/.

71 Scheck, "Secret Accounts Paid for Clergy Misconduct."

72 Scheck, "Secret Accounts Paid for Clergy Misconduct."

73 Emily Gurnon, "Archdiocese Will Review Priest Misconduct Cases, Archbishop Says," *Pioneer Press* (October 1, 2013); available at www.twincities.com/crime/ci_24216078/archdiocese-will-review-priest-misconduct-cases-archbishop-says. See also Madeleine Baran and Tom Scheck, "Former Archdiocesan Accountant: Church Paid Priests Despite Sexual Misconduct," Minnesota Public Radio (September 20, 2013); available at www.mprnews.org/story/2013/09/30/catholic-church/former-archdiocesan-accountant-church-paid-priests-despite-sexual-miscond.

74 *The Economist*, "Earthly Concerns: The Catholic Church Is as Big as Any Company in America. Bankruptcy Cases Have Shed Some Light on Its Finances and Their Mismanagement," (August 18, 2012); available at www.economist.com/node/21560536/print.

75 *The Economist*, "Earthly Concerns."

76 *The Economist*, "Earthly Concerns."

77 *The Economist*, "Earthly Concerns."

78 "Pope Francis reforms scandal-ridden Vatican Bank in hopes of making it 'boringly successful,'" *NPR NewsHour* (July 9, 2014); transcript available at www.pbs.org/newshour/bb/pope-francis-reforms-scandal-ridden-vatican-bank-hopes-making-boringly-successful/.

79 Kennedy, "The Debt Slayers," 41.

80 Derek Willis, "A Church-PAC Link Raises Questions in Mississippi," *New York Times* (June 16, 2014); available at www.nytimes.com/2014/06/17/upshot/ a-church-pac-link-raises-questions-in-mississippi.html.

81 Fredreka Schouten, "Report Shows Close Ties between 2 Pro-Cochran Super PACS," *USA Today* (July 16, 2014); available at www.usatoday.com/story/news/politics/2014/07/16/pro-cochran-super-pac-fundraising-jackson-church/12718397/.

82 Marc Gellman, "How the Financial Crisis Affects U.S. Churches," *Newsweek* (March 13, 2010); available at www.newsweek.com/how-financial-crisis-affects-us-churches-92083.

Bibliography

Adams, John C., and Parvez Ahmed. "The Performance of Faith-Based Funds." *Journal of Investing* 22, no. 4 (Winter 2013): 83–92.

Bahn, Chris. "Churches Introduce Electronic Tithing." *Arkansas Business News*, May 6, 2013. www.arkansasbusiness.com/article/92329/churches-introduce-electronic-tithing; accessed on August 4, 2014.

Banks, Adelle M. "Megachurches Are Thriving in Hard Times, Survey Says." *Christian Century* 130, no. 7 (April 3, 2013): 14.

Baran, Madeleine, and Tom Scheck. "Former Archdiocesan Accountant: Church Paid Priests Despite Sexual Misconduct." Minnesota Public Radio. *MPRNews.org*, September 20, 2013. www.mprnews.org/story/2013/09/30/catholic-church/former-archdiocesan-accountant-church-paid-priests-despite-sexual-miscond; accessed on August 1, 2014.

Bonk, Jonathan. "Introduction to the First Edition." in *Missions and Money: Affluence as a Missionary Problem Revisited.* Revised and Expanded Edition., by Jonathan J. Bonk, xxvii–xxx. Maryknoll, NY: Orbis Books, 2006.

Bourdieu, Pierre. *Practical Reason: On the Theory of Action.* Stanford, CA: Stanford University Press, 1998.

Bruce, Laura. "Affinity Scammers Bilk the Faithful in the Name of Greed." *Bankrate.com*, August 8, 2001. www.bankrate.com/finance/investing/affinity-scammers-bilk-the-faithful-in-the-name-of-greed-1.aspx; accessed on August 19, 2014.

Catholic Online (NEWS CONSORTIUM). "Catholic Healthcare West Becomes Dignity Health, Will They Provide Abortions?" *Catholic.org*, January 25, 2012. www.catholic.org/news/health/story.php?id=44532; accessed on July 28, 2014.

The Courier. "LifeWay Research: Pastors Unaware of Church Member Debt." *The Courier*, January 21, 2009. http://baptistcourier.com/2009/01/lifeway-research-pastors-unaware-of-church-member-debt/; accessed on July 21, 2014.

The Economist. "Earthly Concerns: The Catholic Church Is as Big as Any Company in America. Bankruptcy Cases Have Shed Some Light on Its Finances and Their Mismanagement." *The Economist* August 18, 2012. www.economist.com/node/21560536/print; accessed on August 20, 2014.

The Economist. "Fleecing the Flock: The Big Business of Fleecing People Who Trust You." *The Economist* January 28, 2012. www.economist.com/node/21543526; accessed on August 19, 2014.

Frellick, Marcia. "Churches Embrace Online Credit, Debit Card Donations." *Fox Business*, February 21, 2011. www.creditcards.com/credit-card-news/churches-embrace-online-credit-debit-card-donations-1273.php; accessed on August 4, 2014.

Gellman, Marc. "How the Financial Crisis Affects U.S. Churches." *Newsweek*, March 13, 2010. www.newsweek.com/how-financial-crisis-affects-us-churches-92083; accessed on July 28, 2014.

Ghoul, Wafica, and Paul Karam. "MRI and SRI Mutual Funds: A Comparison of Christian, Islamic (Morally Responsible Investing), and Socially Responsible Investing (SRI) Mutual Funds." *Journal of Investing* 16, no. 2 (Summer 2007): 96–102.

Grant, Tim. "Investing in Your Values: Socially Conscious Mutual Funds Are Quickly Growing." *Pittsburg Post-Gazette*, June 6, 2013, Sooner Edition edition, sec. C1.

Gurnon, Emily. "Archdiocese Will Review Priest Misconduct Cases, Archbishop Says." *Pioneer Press*, October 1, 2013. www.twincities.com/crime/ci_24216078/archdiocese-will-review-priest-misconduct-cases-archbishop-says; accessed on August 1, 2014.

Hals, Tom "Special Report: Holy Bubble! Churches Struck Down by Foreclosures." Reuters, April 1, 2010. www.reuters.com/article/2010/04/01/us-church-financing-idUSTRE63020J20100401; accessed on March 31, 2015.

Hoge, Dean R. and Loren B. Mead. "Endowed Congregations." In *Financing American Religion*, edited by Mark Chaves and Sharon L. Miller, 87–94. Walnut Creek, CA: AltaMira Press, 1999.

Hudnut-Beumler, James. *In Pursuit of the Almighty's Dollar: A History of Money and American Protestantism.* Chapel Hill, NC: The University of North Carolina Press, 2007.

Kathman, David. "Getting Religion with Faith-Based Mutual Funds." *Morningstar Advisor*, November 5, 2012. www.morningstar.com/advisor/t/65920341/getting-religion-with-faith-based-mutual-funds.htm; accessed on October 12, 2014.

Kennedy, John W. "The Debt Slayers: There's a Reason There Are More Christian Financial Advisers than Ever." *Christianity Today* 50, no. 5 (May 2006): 40–3.

Ku, Catherine. "NYC That Never Was: A Methodist Skyscraper Church on Broadway." *UntappedCities.com*, August 15, 2013. http://untappedcities.com/2013/08/15/nyc-that-never-was-methodist-skyscraper-church-on-broadway/; accessed on October 14, 2014.

Kwon, Lillian. "Survey: Financial Strain Worsens for More Churches." *The Christian Post*, March 24, 2010. www.christianpost.com/news/survey-financial-strain-worsens-for-more-churches-44439/; accessed on August 5, 2014.

Larned, W. Livingston. "Excerpts from 'Editorial' in The Daily Reporter." *Popular Science Monthly* 107, no. 2 (August 1925): 4.

Lundén, Rolf. *Business and Religion in the American 1920s*. Contributions in American Studies Series, No. 91. New York: Greenwood Press, 1988.

Marsden, George M. *The Soul of the American University: From Protestant Establishment to Established Nonbelief*. New York: Oxford University Press, 1996.

McMillin, Stephen Edward. "Faith-Based Social Services: From Communitarian to Individualistic Values." *Zygon* 46, no. 2 (June 2011): 482–90.

Mullen, Shannon. "No Cash When the Collection Plate Arrives? No Problem." *Marketplace.org*, January 25, 2013. www.marketplace.org/topics/your-money/no-cash-when-collection-plate-arrives-no-problem; accessed on July 30, 2014.

Mundey, Peter, Hilary Davidson, and Patricia Snell Herzog. "Making Money Sacred: How Two Church Cultures Translate Mundane Money into Distinct Sacralized Frames of Giving." *Sociology of Religion* 72, no. 3 (2011): 303–26.

Nthamburi, Zablon. "An African Viewpoint on Wealthy Missionaries." In *Missions and Money: Affluence as a Missionary Problem Revisited*, Revised and Expanded Edition., by Jonathan J. Bonk, xviii–xix. Maryknoll, NY: Orbis Books, 2006.

PBS NewsHour. "Pope Francis Reforms Scandal-Ridden Vatican Bank in Hopes of Making It 'Boringly Successful.'" PBS NewsHour, July 9, 2014. www.pbs.org/newshour/bb/pope-francis-reforms-scandal-ridden-vatican-bank-hopes-making-boringly-successful//; accessed on August 1, 2014.

Pearce, Robert W. "Investors Nationwide Beware—Church Bonds Are Risky and Illiquid Investments." *Seekingalpha.com*, March 6, 2013. http://seekingalpha.com/instablog/5396101-robert-w-pearce/1622201-investors-nationwide-beware-church-bonds-are-risky-and-illiquid-investments; accessed on July 27, 2014.

Philips, Kevin. *Bad Money: Reckless Finance, Failed Politics, and the Global Crisis of American Capitalism*. New York: Viking, 2008.

Reid, Tim. "Banks Foreclosing on Churches in Record Numbers." Reuters, March 9, 2012. www.reuters.com/assets/print?aid=USBRE82803120120309; accessed on July 27, 2014.

Robertson, Kathy. "Dignity Health Pension Plan Is Not a Church Plan, Court Rules—Again." *Sacramento Business Journal*, July 24, 2014. www.bizjournals.com/sacramento/news/2014/07/24/dignity-health-pension-plan-is-not-a-church-plan.html; accessed on July 28, 2014.

Sataline, Suzanne. "In Hard Times, Houses of God Turn to Chapter 11 in Book of Bankruptcy—Strapped Churches Can't Pay the Mortgage after Borrowing Binge; St. Andrew at Auction." *Wall Street Journal*, December 23, 2008, sec. A1.

Scheck, Tom. "Secret Accounts Paid for Clergy Misconduct but left Church open to Financial Abuse," Minnesota Public Radio. January 23, 2014; available at http://minnesota.

publicradio.org/collections/catholic-church/2014/01/23/secret-accounts-kept-clergy-misconduct-quiet-but-left-archdiocese-finances-exposed/; accessed on August 1, 2014.

Schept, Susan. "Church Collection Plates May Go Empty as Electronic Giving Rises." Reuters, January 23, 2011. www.reuters.com/article/2011/01/23/us-churches-donations-idUSTRE70M10C20110123; accessed on August 4, 2014.

Schouten, Fredreka. "Report Shows Close Ties between 2 Pro-Cochran Super PACS." *USA Today*, July 16, 2014. www.usatoday.com/story/news/politics/2014/07/16/pro-cochran-super-pac-fundraising-jackson-church/12718397/; accessed on August 8, 2014.

U.S. Securities and Exchange Commission. "Affinity Fraud: How to Avoid Investment Scams That Target Groups." *Sec.gov*, (n.d.). www.sec.gov/investor/pubs/affinity.htm; accessed on December 30, 2014.

Williamson, Christine. "Hedge Fund Firms Accepting Screens to Get Faith-Based Business." *Pensions&Investments Online*, August 23, 2012. www.pionline.com/article/20120823/ONLINE/120829945/hedge-fund-firms-accepting-screens-to-get-faith-based-business; accessed on September 12, 2014.

Willis, Derek. "A Church-PAC Link Raises Questions in Mississippi." *New York Times*, June 16, 2014. www.nytimes.com/2014/06/17/upshot/a-church-pac-link-raises-questions-in-mississippi.html; accessed on August 8, 2014.

Wuthnow, Robert. "The Crisis in the Churches." In *Financing American Religion*, edited by Mark Chaves and Sharon L. Miller, 67–78. Walnut Creek, CA: AltaMira Press, 1999.

Wuthnow, Robert. *The Crisis in the Churches: Spiritual Malaise, Fiscal Woe*. New York: Oxford University Press, 1997.

6 *Ad Fontes*

Returning to the sources of American economic exceptionalism

Americans commonly forget that financial problems were at the core of a destabilizing factionalism that threatened, in the nation's early years, to tear it apart. While debts associated with the Revolutionary War jeopardized the solvency of both national and state governments, on wobbly legs to begin with, Shay's Rebellion in Western Massachusetts illustrated that American "patriots," believing that they were being sold out to foreign interests and eastern bankers, would resort to violence to bring about what they considered economic justice. Other events surrounding the formation of a national bank and the development of a national currency were equally divisive. In their disunity, however, they both engendered popular activism and helped solidify an American spirit of voluntarism that, until recently, has been one of the nation's defining characteristics.

Historians have disagreed vigorously as to the philosophical sources of the American ethos, one that has contributed to unparalleled economic growth yet also witnessed periods of selflessness by American citizens in committing their time, treasure, and energy to the greater good. Some scholars cite the prevalence of republican ideals in the founding period while others contend that the principles of classical liberalism were most formative to the early Republic. Founding documents reveal that no consensus existed either on the structure or the types of moral supports needed for a fledgling American economy that would make it competitive with the established powers of Europe. Alexander Hamilton's nationalist financial vision conflicted with Thomas Jefferson's early agrarianism, and both philosophies were complemented by those of John Adams and Benjamin Rush, whose lingering commitments to republicanism led them to believe that to endure, self-government and a market economy require a virtuous citizenry.

The philosophical continuum of early American economic thought was diverse. Latent in the thought of many was a nagging question of how American industrialization, the expansion of a market economy, and the nation's continued extension into a vast frontier would impact the ethics of contributors to its material development. For Adams and Rush, religion and education should both actively promote virtue; on the other hand, both Jefferson and Madison shared with the English liberal philosopher Adam Smith a "preference for good institutional design over direct attempts to foster virtue in the citizenry."[1] The challenge for all was to devise a legal and institutional structure that inspired moral behavior from citizens who simultaneously followed their economic interests.

Rather than attempt to determine the winners and losers of these early debates, this chapter looks to the dialogue itself and historical accounts of it, demonstrating that a richer economic discourse existed in the early decades of the American Republic than at present. Loss of depth to that discourse shapes not only the nation's economic fortunes but also the character of its people and the values of its institutions. Despite generating considerable entrepreneurial energy for those seeking to improve their material lots, the victory of Hayek's subjectivist ethic and its coexistence with the neoliberal theory of markets has zapped the American social imagination with the idea that any constructive attempt to better order ourselves will infringe upon liberty.[2] Neoliberals commonly point out how political correctness has narrowly framed public discourse so as to characterize the only legitimate solutions to social problems as those stemming from government. Yet a general neoliberal consensus is equally reductionist, particularly on matters of economic policy. It stifles what could be a rich conversation that draws on a rich history: as the early nation embraced its vast frontier, the spontaneous emergence of voluntary associations and other intermediate organizations provided a necessary structure for social order amid diverse communities as well as a moral and institutional framework for the development of citizens for both self-government and participation in a market economy.

These associations were not universally welcomed. Both Hamilton and George Washington, remaining inherently skeptical of voluntary groups that might undermine the achievement of "commercial" unity, placed more confidence in the creation of national markets supported by a national bank. In their visions, a national bank would serve as "the 'cement of interest' that would bind Americans across space."[3] In reality, however, the spontaneous development of private organizations of many stripes became essential to social and moral development, particularly on the frontier. Even as many feared its potential divisiveness, the rise of civil society as a dynamic institutional response to innumerable challenges in the emerging American social order answered many of the Founders' questions regarding how to achieve stability and moral development.

Returning to these early debates and the social changes that took place around them should provide an idea of how the American financial system has gone astray in recent years and taken much of society with it. Much wealth today has come from mercurial financial change that offers far less opportunity to synthesize its attendant social and ethical consequences. Financialization's detachment of wealth from social contribution fosters a kind of self-imposed social isolation among many, forged by a radical liberalism. History may provide clues regarding how to tame those culturally deteriorative forces.

The role of virtue in the early American economy

In an address given at the American Museum on the eleventh anniversary of the signing of the Declaration of Independence, Revolutionary-era poet and political thinker Joel Barlow stated that

> whenever democratic states degenerate from those noble republican virtues which constitute the chief excellency, spring, and even basis of their government, and instead of industry, frugality, and economy, encourage luxury, dissipation and extravagance, we may justly conclude that ruin is near at hand.[4]

Barlow's sentiments were hardly rare. A common refrain in the period declared, "No virtue, no commonwealth."[5] For early Americans, religion was the most important check on public corruption and immorality. Gordon Wood observes how "Christianity fostered benevolence, a love of one's fellow man and of the community. Religion was the strongest promoter of virtue, the most important ally of a well-constituted republic."[6] Yet not only churches were charged with nurturing a virtuous citizenry; selfless statesmen and, eventually, secular, socially minded organizations also would prove necessary for providing the moral foundation for progress.

In the individualistic context of American society, virtue was liberalized. The liberalization, even mechanization, of virtue is nowhere more evident than in Benjamin Franklin's *Autobiography*. Franklin's list of virtues emphasized "Order," so as to "Let each part of your Business have its time"; "Frugality" in that one should "Make no Expense but to do good to others or yourself: i.e., Waste nothing"; and "Industry," accompanied by Franklin's instruction that one "lose no time. Be always employ'd in something useful. Cut off all unnecessary actions."[7] The uniquely *American virtue* that emerged to fill the moral void in the new Republic was utilitarian in a way that fueled commerce, yet to describe it also as "Christian" is likely an overstatement. Some of its elements had deistic roots; even observers such as D. H. Lawrence noted that Franklin's system for the cultivation of virtue, developed not only in his *Autobiography* but even more so in his *Dissertation on Liberty*, sought to create from the human person a "moral machine … work[ed] with a little set of handles or levers."[8] Importantly, however, this framework focused on the individual; republican, or civic, virtue was thought to be something else.

Franklin's ideas on voluntarism also were formative. In a review of Kathleen McCarthy's *American Creed: Philanthropy and the Rise of Civil Society*, Oliver Zunz relates McCarthy's view of Franklin as

> the spokesman for the many when he related his own experiences in volunteering, giving, and governing.… His variety of associational ventures, the ways in which he managed to secure public support for them, his attempts to turn both the government and the market to the service of educational institutions and good works, and his eventual support of abolitionism, make his writings and biography the embodiment of the [American] creed.[9]

Franklin's penchant for reason insisted that even virtuous behavior must be calibrated with precision.

While others such as Benjamin Rush saw the source of virtue as emotional rather than intellectual and mechanical, few disagreed on the importance of fostering it in the citizenry.[10] Emphasis on industry as a virtue rose in popularity during the colonial period in distancing American culture from the idler notion of virtuous living in the Old Country. Michel-Guillame-Jean de Crévecoeur, a product of the French aristocracy and a naturalized American citizen, was of like mind with Franklin concerning the importance of industriousness to the formation of virtue. For Crévecoeur, different kinds of labor were structured in a natural hierarchy as to their formative value in the production of virtue at which farming stood at the head.[11] According to Lynn A. Parks, Crévecoeur was the "first notable American writer" to reveal the abuses of a "monied class" that received disproportionate rewards for its contribution of what in reality was unproductive labor.[12]

This identification of "monied interests" as less virtuous than agricultural laborers and craftsmen prevailed even among "American aristocrats" such as John Adams. Often accompanied by wariness that the growth of bankers and lawyers was undermining a developing American economic ethos, many Americans in the founding period made a critical distinction not unlike Crévecoeur's between "productive" work in agriculture and crafts and those more parasitic forms of money making practiced by bankers and lawyers that served to deprive more industrious Americans of hard-earned rewards. Adams expressed these fears in a letter to Jefferson, in 1813, in which he wrote of "foreign Aristocracies.... Sowing their seeds in this country.... Not from Virtues and Talents so much as from Banks and Land Jobbing."[13] For his own part, Jefferson was so fearful of the changing nature of property and its growing concentration that he briefly entertained ideas for its redistribution, which he considered "a politic measure, and a practicable one." Rising inequality led him to advocate what he described as its "silent lessening" through a system of progressive taxation that would exempt from taxes those below a certain level of income.[14]

Virtue and luxury existed at odds in the minds of many early Americans. While some European societies accepted virtue as concentrated among an elite cohort of aristocrats, American advocates of republicanism believed a major emphasis of the American experiment was to promote political, economic, and legal institutions capable of disbursing virtue broadly. Because the nature of any free, affluent society is such that liberties can quickly devolve into the *libertinism* that attends luxury, wide distribution of virtue was believed by some to be essential.

Americans were always suspicious of "classical" republican virtue if that meant giving over one's personal ambitions for the sake of the state or engaging in Ciceronian-like oration. Paul Gilje notes how republican ideals often had political and commercial inspiration, appealing to Americans as a form of resistance against the English, particularly through the refusal to import certain goods. The claim that "Americans were too virtuous to need the imported luxury items" became a popular justification for their actions.[15] Accordingly, virtue could be a tool for subtle forms of rebellion as well one to curb materialism. With respect to more ambitious goals, in *Federalist No. 10*, Madison observes a significant limitation to republican statesmanship: "It is in vain to say that enlightened statesmen will be able to adjust these clashing interests, and render them all subservient to the public good. Enlightened statesmen will not always be at the helm."[16] Realizing this limitation, Madison turned toward the more "liberal" notion of balancing factions against each other in hopes that the common good might be determined through the interplay of largely self-interested individuals and institutions.

Madison's *Federalist No. 39* clearly articulates the unique form of American republicanism that developed toward the end of the eighteenth century. In addressing the question of whether "the general form and aspect of the government be strictly republican," Madison asserts its necessity on which "to rest all our political experiments on the capacity of mankind for self-government." Yet he follows by observing the many (often despotic) governmental forms that go by the name "republican" in Europe, from the "absolute" rule of hereditary nobility in Venice to the government of Holland, "in which no particle of the supreme authority is derived from the people."[17] For Madison, a true form of republican, "representative" government must combine the best of nationalist and Federalist ideals. Madison reveals the compromise needed to form the new government in *Federalist No. 38*, where he addresses the Constitution's detractors, writing,

> It is a matter both of wonder and regret, that those who raise so many objections against the new Constitution should never call to mind the defects of that which is to be exchanged for it. It is not necessary that the former should be perfect; it is sufficient that the latter is more imperfect.[18]

The emerging synthesis in Madison's conception of the American social order came to be rather broadly accepted. How influential Madison was in its acceptance remains a matter of debate. Regardless, historian Jean Yarbrough contends the Founders "did not choose liberal democracy over republicanism. Their plan was far more ambitious: they sought to combine the advantages of liberal freedom and republican virtue, without the disadvantages of either."[19] For Madison, achievement of this end meant institutionally balancing factions such that no single group could gain control over the whole. Yet Madison's plan also necessitated some measure of virtue in the people, for no government was capable of of protecting the people's liberty unless it facilitated the free association of individuals with the hope that their interactions would reinforce virtuous conduct. Madison writes, "No theoretical checks, no form of government, can render us secure. To suppose that any form of government will secure liberty or happiness without any virtue in the people is a chimerical idea."[20] As in all his designs for the American government, Madison perceived the need to balance those best practices of governments in history by conceiving institutional forms that distributed power with the aim that such a structure might also preserve, if not a virtuous, then at least a moral, citizenry. A nation of vast resources, diverse social groups, and boundless ambitions required not the enforcement of a common ideology but a centralized constitutional system to facilitate the dynamic interaction of citizens, while preventing the dominance of any one group.[21]

The virtue synthesis of John Locke

The liberalization of the United States in the early nineteenth century convinces many scholars that a thoroughly "republican view" of the American founding is vastly overblown. In reality, virtue had to compete with other influences in the period that shaped American behavior in ways too complex to credit any single source. Contending that historians such as Gordon Wood and J. G. A. Pocock too easily dismiss Enlightenment and other influences that shaped the nation, some scholars assert true republicans in the classical sense were likely few in number, often pointing toward a Lockean liberal influence on the Founders. Scholars such as Joyce Appleby, John Diggins, Steven Dworetz, Jerome Huyler, Isaac Kramnick, and Barry Alan Shain are convinced that the "republican" emphasis of Wood, Pocock, and Bernard Bailyn is overdone.[22]

In Joshua Foa Dienstag's estimation, however, the arguments of both sides are problematic. Focusing on the pervasive use of terms such as "virtue," "corruption," and "slavery," the republican faction emphasizes too much the rhetoric of the age.[23] Similarly, those who advocate the importance of Lockean influence in the founding period seem taken with Founder references to "the incomparable Locke," convinced of his influence by the frequency with which the Founders cited his works.[24] According to Dienstag, the major hurdle faced by the Lockean contingent is their inability to overcome a dualistic interpretation of Locke's influence on American founding values represented principally in the views of C. B. Macpherson and Leo Strauss. The majority of those who have hoped for a Lockean consensus as the primary philosophical influence on the early American political ethic cannot accept "that a devout Puritan could, at the same time as he defended a radical spiritual egalitarianism, defend also an unfettered property right and the rank inequalities of wealth that would result from that right."[25] Dienstag himself contends that while the concept of self-sacrifice was prevalent, it stemmed not from "polis-centered public-mindedness (as in republican thought) but from an inward-looking ideal of self-denial"—what he terms a "worldly asceticism" articulated in the distinctly Christian philosophy of Locke.[26] He points out that advocates of Locke's influence deny the very "frame of mind" that Max Weber attributed to European society in *The Protestant Ethic and the Spirit of Capitalism*.[27] Christian altruism and a spirit of acquisitiveness can exist side by side in ways that are highly productive.

There is reason for some confusion among scholars concerning how Locke's notion of "Christian" virtue differed from principles of contemporary political liberalism, however. In certain writings, Locke's thought leaned more republican than liberal in ways that may have influenced the American Founders. In *Some Thoughts Concerning Education*, for example, Locke writes,

> It seems plain to me, that the principle of all virtue and excellency lies in a power of denying ourselves the satisfaction of our own desires, where reason does not authorize them. This power is to be got and improv'd by custom, made easy and familiar by an early practice.[28]

Locke's republican leanings seem preoccupied with taming the passions and achieving the kind of self-discipline that inevitably will be strained in a more liberal society of the kind he proposes. "Virtue is harder to be got than a knowledge of the world," Locke said, "and if lost in a young man, is seldom recover'd."[29]

In advocating for Lockean asceticism, Dienstag observes that the virtue language of the American founding period has a "perfectly plain Lockean provenance," also quoting Locke from *Some Thoughts Concerning Education*:

> As the strength of the body lies chiefly in being able to endure hardships, so also does that of the mind. And the great principle and foundation of all virtue and worth is placed in this, that a man is able to deny himself his own desires, cross his own inclinations, and purely follow what reason directs as best, though the appetite lean the other way.[30]

Through articulating a unique form of virtue ethics that drew from Christian and republican sources, Locke thus blended together Christian and republican forms of virtue in common subordination to human reason. According to Locke, in the early stages of an individual's development, human beings needed a more traditional republican form of virtue to be able to deny themselves and serve community. Locke understood that, as human beings develop, they "liberalize" around more self-interested notions of personal gain; absent the continuation of Christian and other moral influences, they may lose self-control. Dienstag observes that Locke emphasizes not so much the republican virtues of "courage, virility, or devotion to the polis" but rather the "self-regarding Christian virtues of prudence, frugality, and industriousness."[31] These virtues are stressed in the writings of both Jefferson and Adams, and they united the two Founders on the virtue of labor and the danger of man's unlimited passions.[32] This synthesis of traditions helped to reconcile the ideologies of American leaders who often found themselves locked in contentious political battles.

Colin Kidd has also observed how the idea of "self-rule" blended virtue and liberty in ways that combine the best of both republicanism and Lockean liberalism. The Scottish Enlightenment was a natural ally in this process, "dedicated to discovering methods by which a provincial culture could create forms of social virtue without having to rely on republican political institutions unavailable to a province that was, like America, uncomfortable with its status."[33] The question was how to retain virtue in the rapidly liberalizing American culture and on a frontier expanding beyond the ability of religious and moral institutions to keep pace:

> Religion retained a nagging presence in American republican anxieties. Republican ideology was no sunny celebration of freedom and self-government. Its predominant characteristic was a dark pessimism prompted by the entropy law of republics: so onerous were the burdens of self-rule that most republics tended to degenerate into anarchy and eventual despotism.

> The nascent American republic was wracked by worry about the dangers which might befall its experiment in government. Financial speculation, standing armies, and luxurious consumption all threatened to undermine the moral supports of republican society.[34]

Although these debates did not directly contribute to the formation of American civil society, they were important to creating a moral and intellectual climate favorable to its development. As Jack Rakove writes,

> To suggest the constitutional disputants of the 1780s said relatively little about the nature of American civil society is not to say that ideas about civil society formed no part of their general intellectual inheritance. If John Locke and Adam Smith can both be described as founding theorists of a modern concept of civil society, their American readers must have absorbed critical elements of their theories.[35]

The importance of the Lockean liberalism-classical republicanism argument is that both traditions differ dramatically from the dominant, present-day neoliberalism. Even if we acknowledge an emphasis on individual rights and private property that existed in what Dienstag sees as the Lockean asceticism of the day, "the Founders' Lockeanism cannot be abruptly equated with twentieth-century liberalism."[36] The autonomy of the individual has grown beyond either Lockean or Smithian conceptualizations of the individual as the age of consumerism displaces the practice of Christian aestheticism. Although both self-interest and selflessness are evident in times of social crisis, the triumph of finacialization largely has eliminated virtue as a goal of the American economy.

The moral challenges of a modern American financial system

The standard view of the American economy's development has been one of an evolution from agriculture to manufacturing to finance; others think that "finance-led" economic growth beginning in the late nineteenth century greatly influenced the development of the nation's early economy. Peter Rousseau and Richard Sylla note a remarkable evolution from the 1780s, when financial system resources were virtually nonexistent, to the 1820s, at which time the U.S. "had a financial system that was innovative, large, and perhaps the equal of any in the world."[37] Scholars consider Alexander Hamilton, whose efforts in convincing Congress to charter a national bank in 1791 both stabilized U.S. currency and elevated its credit status, the unquestioned leader in the development of a modern American financial system that helped fuel the nation's fast growth. Hamilton's efforts also inspired the rapid rise of state-chartered banks from only three in 1789 to 31 by the end of the 1790s.[38]

Perhaps the least appreciated of American founding documents is Hamilton's "First Report on Public Credit." A work of "political economy" in the truest sense, the report was more "than a bit of brilliant financiering." Hamilton's larger intent was to "create a powerful public opinion bulwarked in favor of the central government" by discussing the central issue of paper currency.[39] The concern was that as paper money could be produced so readily, it was inherently valueless, liable to manipulation, forgery, inflation, and other maladies. As Madison wrote in *Federalist No. 44*,

> The loss which America has sustained since the peace from the pestilent effects of paper money on the necessary confidence between man and man; on the necessary confidence in the public councils; on the industry and morals of the people, and on the character of republican government, constitutes an enormous debt against the states.[40]

Madison's comments demonstrate obvious concern over the social and moral effects of paper currency, not simply its economic consequences.

Contemporary Americans knowledgeable of the Founders' views on banking and finance may view their fear of paper currency as naïve, yet the Founders expressed legitimate concerns over the dangers of abstraction, and concentration of wealth. In his report "National Bank," issued to Congress on December 14, 1790, Hamilton articulated the purpose of the bank and crafted a vision of its future role in providing for the liquidity of capital, allowing large sums to be "lent and paid, frequently through a variety of hands, without the intervention of a single piece of coin."[41] The restriction of currency printing to the federal government, given in the Constitution, addressed concerns that the ease of producing paper money made it so liable to abuse.[42]

The architect of the national bank was a social theorist as well as economist; Hamilton recognized both the advantages and the potential cultural damage that could accrue to the more fluid system of capital he proposed. Although paper currency was designed to permit freer capital flows, some of Hamilton's accompanying ideas have been described as "unusual." Consider, for example, the Bank Act, in which Hamilton proposed to cap at 6 percent the interest rate the bank could receive on its loans; this limitation could also be construed as an attempt to account for the potential abuse of paper currency. Like both Jefferson and Madison, Hamilton also feared the corruptive potential of bank directors' power. Regarding stockholders, Hamilton also thought it unwise to allow their votes to be in direct proportion to the stocks they held. He proposed that while those with a larger number of shares should have a greater number of votes, the maximum number of votes in the national bank by any shareholder should be capped at 30.[43] In more general terms, these cautions may be seen as Hamilton's wise counsel for the American economy today: where financial power is concentrated, capital becomes easier to manipulate, and the system is subject to human corruption. That perhaps the most zealous advocate for a centralized banking system in the founding period had concerns about its power and potential to influence political and civil society speaks volumes about the corruptive potential of free-flowing capital.

The Founders, notably both Jefferson and Madison, held a common attitude of skepticism toward banks. Jefferson's view was particularly hostile: in Hamilton's financial system, Jefferson perceived the potential not only for economic turmoil but also political dissolution. In a letter to President Washington on September 9, 1792, Jefferson admitted "this was not merely a speculative difference," claiming that Hamilton's "system flowed from principles averse to liberty, and was calculated to undermine and demolish the Republic, by creating an influence of his department over the members of the Legislature...."[44] Convinced that replacing metal-backed with paper currency led to destabilizing fluctuations and caused withdrawal of capital "from useful improvements and employments to nourish idleness," Jefferson wished to ensure American independence while preserving a moral foundation to its modernizing economic machinery, which he thought should remain rooted in agriculture.[45] More than any other single interest, banking in the United States concentrated wealth and power among a few elites, which he viewed as contrary to the egalitarianism he considered foundational to liberty in the new nation.[46]

Jefferson's observations of the social consequences of Shay's Rebellion—the Massachusetts uprising caused by aggressive debt collection and taxation in the economic aftermath of the Revolutionary War—led to his realization that at least a minimum of financial knowledge in the population was necessary to avoid such calamities. Debt could lead to social instability, especially if the indebted were uneducated on the nature of their predicament. A broad education with specific training in the workings of the "modern" economy was necessary to prevent similar occurrences in the future.[47] Even James Madison, whose youthful economic idealism leaned libertarian, was led by a growing pragmatism that, as it matured, also viewed negatively the social implications of modern banking. In an 1827 letter to J. K. Paulding, he wrote:

> With regard to the Banks, they have taken too deep and wide a root in social transactions to be got rid of altogether, if that were desirable. In providing a convenient substitute, to a certain extent, for the metallic currency, and a fund of credit which prudence may turn to good account, they have a hold on public opinion.... As now generally constituted their advantages whatever they may be, are outweighed by the excesses of their paper emissions, and by the partialities and corruption with which they are administered.[48]

Madison's opposition to the national bank has been cited variously as based on constitutional grounds, the danger of bank runs, and fear of the loss of metal backing for currency. But evidence exists of other, more relevant concerns here. In particular, Madison considered that a national bank along with rising national debt would foster a "spirit of speculation within and without the government."[49] His objection to the construction of a national bank because of the possibility of its fueling a more speculative culture suggests his concern for the bank's moral as well as fiscal impact.

Hamilton had no such fears but expressed concern, on occasion, about the concentration of power among bank directors. In theorizing about the kind of virtue needed in the American system of political economy, Hamilton draws on his knowledge of history. Countless historical examples of leaders who forced their nations into war over "bigotry," "petulance," and "cabals" are joined by the American rebel Daniel Shays: "If Shays had not been a DESPERATE DEBTOR, it is much to be doubted whether Massachusetts would have been plunged into a civil war."[50] Hamilton's point in his recollections is that "commercial republics, like ours, will never be disposed to waste themselves in ruinous contentions with each other. They will be governed by mutual interest, and will cultivate a spirit of mutual amity and concord."[51] Echoing the "enlightened self-interest" of Adam Smith, Hamilton believed a commercial system that freed each to pursue his interests could temper the passions that led to the great tragedies of history. A natural system of liberal virtue would prevent any modern-day Pericles from whimsical war making.

Skepticism regarding the greater volatility of a paper-based American financial system continued to concern the Founders in their discussions of the American political economy. Some politicians drew connections between the nation's banking and credit system and the persistence of its political rivalries. Cathy Matson notes how "skeptics spoke from statehouses and pulpits attacking banks as reservoirs of aristocratic privilege."[52] Whereas, Federalists such as Hamilton feared majority rule; Democratic-Republicans such as Jefferson feared an aristocracy of the elite. Madison proposed to allay fears by balancing institutions so that no particular faction could deny others their liberty. Yet, despite Madison's institutional solution, Johann Neem observes that both Federalists and Jeffersonian Republicans "did not imagine, much less desire, a civil society composed of self-created associations and private nonprofit institutions."[53] Their deliberations and compromises, however, helped to energize the American social imagination, propelling groups toward the resolution of social problems since the founding era. Discussion of the dangers likely encouraged many Americans to recognize their responsibilities for the novel experiment in social order in which they were involved.

Enter the common man

The research of Michael Merrill and Sean Wilentz has revealed that early American "elites" were not the only participants in the discourse that helped shape the nation's unique system of political economy. "Plebian writers" such as Walter Brewster, Abraham Clark, and Simon Hough contributed a significant body of political and economic writings that represented the sentiments of the common man.[54] Of particular note was the Massachusetts farmer William Manning, whose insightful examinations of American society in the founding era offer a fascinating glimpse into popular sentiments. Manning adopted the common class distinction between "the Few and the Many" that provided the trope for much political radicalism in the period. According to Merrill and Wilentz, "the Few" in that paradigm

> consisted of a minority of wealthy, learned, polished, and moneyed men—Manning included rentiers, professionals, stock jobbers, speculators, merchants, and government officers—who did not live by their labor, and whose incomes vastly exceeded their contributions to society. On the other side was the great majority, those who lived by the labor of their own hands—artisans, laborers, and ordinary farmers like himself.[55]

Though Manning suffered from the educational limitations of his class, he possessed an extraordinary ability to discern the cultural forces shaping American society in his day. A significant exploration in *The Key of Liberty* concerns the informal credit system that developed among common folk in America, eventually coming to serve as much more than a means of capital distribution. Debts among trading partners in the local economies of the early American Republic

> were social obligations, to be honored, not sold—part of a dense web of interlocking local commitments, including (not incidentally in William Manning's case) the web of inheritance that bound together the different generations of a single family.[56]

Debt entailed more than a monetary obligation; it served as a marker and bond among citizens that established trust between transacting parties and, perhaps ironically, even served as a sign of security in a period of American history before the coming of the welfare state.[57]

Manning was no radical leveler. Echoing Jefferson's notion of a "natural aristocracy of talent and virtue," he recognized that "from the great varieties of capacities, strength, and abilities of men, there always was and always will be a very unequal distribution of property in the world."[58] Nevertheless, he astutely observed that while business and government have an obligation to keep both private and public credit in good standing, when it serves their purposes, they often use their power to the opposite end. Interestingly, what Manning calls "the great scuffle between the Few and the Many" is primarily financial, not political:

> as the interests of the Few—and their incomes—lie chiefly in money at interest, rents, salaries, and fees that are fixed on the nominal value of money, they are interested to have the money scarce and the prices of labor and produce as low as possible.[59]

The combination of low wages and the scarcity of money "bring the Many into distress and compel them into a state of dependence on the Few for favors and assistance in a thousand ways."[60] He observed a "moral hazard" of the capitalist economy early on—in an economy of financial concentration, bad credit can be a lucrative business. Business and legal interests often combine forces to pass legislation that advances their interests at the expense of the people and, in Manning's view, that of the nation.[61]

William Manning's populist prescience, though it lacks the contemporary terminology, articulates well some of the afflictions of modern finance. Events of the past decade have borne out Manning's observations that certain incentives weaken the system, advantaging the few at the expense of the many. His writing distinguished clearly between real workers, which he saw embodied in the American farmer and laborer, and those "money-interests" that often combine with political power in ways contemporary economists describe as "rent seeking" behavior. Importantly, he also identified those professionals such as ministers, schoolmasters, and physicians who, while gaining wealth without bodily labor, live honestly and "for the benefit of the community," earning professional credentials "so they all naturally unite to make these professions as honorable and lucrative as possible."[62] It is the laborer, however, who "supports the whole" and lays the groundwork for those classes that earn their livings with their minds to exist at all. In this way, Manning articulates a definite hierarchy of occupations based on social contribution that is wildly out of vogue today; yet his criticism suggests a constant need to reflect on the real contributions by all members in society not only as a means to discern just reward but, more fundamentally, to help develop the character of American workers, maintain some connection to economic justice, and preserve stability between social classes.

Manning's populist views had an even more radical and eloquent expression in the voice of Thomas Paine. Joseph Stromberg, libertarian research fellow at the Independent Institute, believes that

> Paine's political ideology was part and parcel of what has been called the 'American synthesis'—that particular combination of ideas and themes from republican theory, early liberalism, English law, and Protestantism, which Americans fielded in their war of national liberation.[63]

Stromberg's assertion is perhaps something of a stretch, yet there is little doubt that Paine's take on political economy occupies the leftmost part of a synthetic continuum of early American thought. As such, he offered a distinct prophetic voice concerning the evils of government and concentrations of power so inflammatory at times that some labeled him an anarchist.[64]

Similar to both Manning and even many of the Founding elite, Paine expresses distrust of paper currency and notes the unequal distribution of resources to which Manning refers in *The Key to Liberty*. In his essay "Death and Taxes," Paine offers an interesting description of money that resonates with modern sensibilities: "The natural effect of increasing and continuing to increase paper currency is that of banishing the real money. The shadow takes place of the substance till the country is left with only shadows in its hands."[65] Paper symbolized the ephemeral, destructible, ultimately vapid store of value inappropriate for a robust American economy in the context of liberty. Yet Paine's economic philosophy, much like his life, was highly enigmatic. William Hogeland has noted a fascinating turn in Paine's career when he took employment with the person often cited as the founder of the first national bank in the U.S., Robert Morris:

> Skeptical of knee-jerk populism, [Paine] had high hopes for national finance. The strangest of bedfellows, Paine and Morris were working together at weird cross purposes. Paine's vision, diametrically opposed to Morris's, was like Morris's in being a national one. Along with "the madman of the Alleghenies" Herman Husband, who also saw through state-focused elites' pandering to populism and thought an egalitarian national government might be better empowered to hold greed in check, Paine's radical democracy made him an offbeat kind of federalist.[66]

Despite his libertarian leanings, Paine saw nationalism as consistent with human liberty in a way most Anti-Federalists did not. He deviated from many of his ideological allies by placing much trust in a strong national government, whose institutions should enforce the blessings of liberty. According to Hogeland, "For Thomas Paine, American finance policy must dedicate itself to economic equality."[67] Though Paine is consonant with Manning in observing the "natural" inequality of resources, his own writings express the view that this very ontological reality makes greed and avarice even more detestable.[68] The natural conditions of life "will ever produce that effect [inequality], without having recourse to the harsh, ill-sounding names of avarice and oppression."[69] Paine's "nationalist libertarianism" makes him one of the most unique political thinkers in American history; his death as a pauper, having worked with Morris on the first national bank, only amplifies that uniqueness.

The remarkable energy surrounding banking and finance in American history has inspired ample social imagination and many social movements. In the nineteenth century, a Frenchmen observed perhaps most keenly the malleability of American culture and distinctive relationships among politics, religion, and economy that made the nation unique if not exceptional.

Reclaiming those "habits of the heart"

Perhaps no nineteenth-century philosopher better understood the novelty of the American experiment, not only in its social but also its spiritual and moral manifestations, better than Alexis de Tocqueville. The French savant, whose travels through the United States in the 1830s inspired his own social imagination, identified both the perils and the promise of a new nation committed to liberty. But while his *Democracy in America* was his work most famously associated with American culture, Tocqueville offers perhaps an even more prescient insight into contemporary American society in his exploration of pre-revolutionary France in *The Old Regime and the Revolution*:

> People today, no longer attached to one another by any ties of caste, class, guild or family, are all too inclined to be preoccupied with their own private

> interests, too given to looking out for themselves alone and withdrawing into a narrow individualism where all public virtues are smothered. Despotism, rather than struggling against this tendency, makes it irresistible, because it takes away from citizens all common feeling, all common needs, all need for communication, all occasion for common action. It walls them up inside their private lives.[70]

In Tocqueville's time, despotic forces in French society were largely political. The classic examples in Tocqueville's text were products of European aristocracies; in the context of an *Ancien Régime*, despotism flourished under the weight of the nobility, tradition, and limits on opportunity for the masses, dividing the people and taking away the sense that they shared "common needs." But other forces can accomplish these ends with equal facility. In the present, development of a financial system that encourages dependency on obtuse methods and instruments can dash that "common feeling" necessary for well-functioning democracy. In the early days of the American Republic, however, such divisions were often the product of clashing cultural forces on the frontier.

Frederick Jackson Turner famously observed, "The peculiarity of American institutions is, the fact that they have been compelled to adapt themselves to the changes of an expanding people."[71] He describes how frontier values tended to center on the family; likewise, frontiersmen were not as politically invested as the Atlantic elite and tended to value land over institutions. On the one hand, that encouraged despotism in the form of lawlessness and corruption. On the other, it fostered tolerance and cooperation between settlers. According to Turner,

> Democracy born of free land, strong in selfishness and individualism, intolerant of administrative experience and education, and pressing individual liberty beyond its proper bounds, has its dangers as well as its benefits. Individualism in America has allowed a laxity in regard to governmental affairs which has rendered possible the spoils system and all the manifest evils that follow from the lack of a highly developed civic spirit.[72]

The frontier naturally engendered a spirit of equality. While divisions existed among different ethnic and religious groups, great difficulties and dangers met settlers who journeyed into unpopulated regions; those dangers inspired associations among Americans, who overcame their religious and ethnic differences, in seeking security. People on the frontier also resented East Coast luxury and those who benefited from it. Gradually, however, attitudes changed from desiring benefits from the government to offset the hardships of the frontier to a simpler claim, as Marco Sioli observes:

> The discrepancies clearly visible between the hard frontier life and the comfort they imagined coastal Eastern inhabitants enjoyed, provoked the request for "equal sacrifices." This frontiersman credo acted as part of a

> "moral economy" undergoing change from below no less fundamental than that proceeding among the middle and upper groups. Increasingly the whole concept of an organic reciprocity in society at best limited to certain groups, times and places, was giving way. Frontiersmen, from their own experience, set aside the idea of an obligation of the governing classes to protect the poor and industrious part of mankind in favor of a demand for equality.[73]

At the same time that Madison and other Founders championed balanced institutions and at least some disinterestedness in public servants, civil society institutions emerged to provide the cultural infrastructure unattainable in a relatively weak system of government. Tocqueville was its most clear sighted observer:

> Americans of all ages, all stations in life, and all types of dispositions are forever forming associations. There are not only commercial and industrial associations in which all take part, but other [*sic*] of a thousand different types—religious, moral, serious, futile, very general and very limited, immensely large and very minute. Americans combine to give fêtes, found seminaries, build churches, distribute books, and send missionaries to the antipodes.... Finally, if they want to proclaim a truth or propagate some feeling by the encouragement of a great example, they form an association. In every case, at the head of any new undertaking, where in France you would find the government or in England some territorial magnate, in the United States you are sure to find an association.[74]

The American spirit of voluntarism brings citizens out of their parochial interests and forces them to think of the whole society.[75] Dislocations brought about by rapid migration in the absence of political and social infrastructure could be severe. Voluntary associations on the frontier provided these, as well as other benefits such as the amelioration of "the destructive side of entrepreneurship."[76] As Charles Sellers put it in *The Market Revolution: Jacksonian America, 1815–1846*, "rapidly spreading channels of trade were replacing an unpressured security of rude comfort with an insecurity.... In every new area the market invaded, competition undermined neighborly competition."[77] Yet voluntary associations mitigated not only the consequences but also the social conditions that led to forms of unneighborly competition.

Using the town of Jacksonville, Illinois, as a model, Don Harrison Doyle offers three critical functions provided by voluntary associations in nineteenth-century America. First, they "helped to define status and leadership roles in a young community," establishing "transportable" identities that helped stabilize the social order. Second, organizations such as reform societies and fraternal lodges "provided important training for local entrepreneurs and politicians." Finally, "voluntary associations were powerful tools for the integration of various factions, at least within a broad middle-class, Protestant portion of the community."[78] This last benefit that Doyle observes had particularly ubiquitous application on the frontier. The diversity of groups that invaded such immense, disordered territory had real potential to degenerate into conflict and prevent community formation. But Doyle notes how spontaneous organization among Americans prevented this from happening:

> Most voluntary associations encouraged mixing across otherwise divisive social boundaries because they deliberately stood for nothing that anyone could seriously disagree with: brotherhood, self-improvement, family security, voluntary temperance. Churches and political parties, explained one ardent Odd Fellow, cannot by "the very nature and being of these organizations [provide] a platform broad enough and wide enough upon which all men can stand. . . ." But the principles of Odd Fellowship, he went on, "are as high as the heavens, as broad as the world and as vast as eternity."[79]

Tocqueville observed that one of the conditions at the heart of free associations, the assumption of equality, was much more than a political concept.[80] The notion of equality was shaped by the interaction of "material life conditions and immaterial factors (patterns of thought, behavior, and moral values) that generates mores: different notions, various opinions, and ideas that shape mental habits ('*moeurs*')".[81] These *moeurs* were the glue, the common frame of mind and habits of the heart that bound citizens who did not profess allegiance to a sovereign in the way of European aristocratic societies. Material equality was not the principal form that bound the citizens together, though it played a role. Tocqueville's belief that material conditions impact those patterns of thought and habits of the heart that bind free citizens together in a democratic order differed from the neoliberal attitude that politics should not limit wealth distribution; in the neoliberal paradigm, material equality has little to do with social solidarity, and the source or kind of wealth attained is not viewed as socially or politically significant.

These associations that have bound American society together for much of its history were no one's design. Jean Bethke Elshtain notes how the Constitution's framers "paid little explicit attention" to civil society institutions, counting instead on "a social deposit of intergenerational trust, neighborliness, and civic responsibility" that can no longer be assumed today.[82] Tocqueville recognized the potential for such cultural devolution in both American and French societies. The power of equality and freedom to provide retreat into a thoroughly self-interested *Gesellschaft* was the greatest danger in the emerging, enlightened theories of social order. In his native country, the transformation from "*citoyen* to *bourgeois*" proceeded with little resistance.[83] In the United States, minus the baggage of "permanent associations" that divided the individual from the general interest too rigidly, the "art of association" became the hallmark of American society, providing a dynamic mediating function between the good of the individual and that of the greater community. In this regard, Tocqueville makes an observation that would appear to need qualification were it applied to contemporary American society:

> if an American were condemned to confine his activity to his own affairs, he would be robbed of one half of his existence; he would feel an immense void in the life which he is accustomed to lead, and his wretchedness would be unbearable.[84]

As a Pew Forum survey revealed, American Millennials today are less involved with social groups they attend in person even as they are heavily "networked."[85]

Tocqueville was less concerned with strictly governmental despotism than he was fearful of administrative centralization that threatened the "differentiated" civil society of free associations at the heart of democracy.[86] A vibrant core of civil institutions protects society from development of more oppressive *governmental* despotisms that directly endanger human liberty.[87] Administrative centralization forges dependency of the people and is thus a forerunner to the state despotism that so often preoccupies political thinkers. But free associations do more than simply buffer citizens against potential government intrusion. They also reinforce "common feelings" and the "equality of conditions" Tocqueville observed in the United States, conditioning patterns of habit and thought and binding a diverse culture.

Creating a "nation of joiners"

Francis Fukuyama contends that the U.S. has never been the intensively individualistic nation many Americans have assumed. Rather, he echoes Tocqueville, asserting, "It has always possessed a rich network of voluntary associations and community structures to which individuals have subordinated their narrow interests."[88] "Subordinated" may be too strong, but it is true that America traditionally has been a "nation of joiners." The irony is that this nation of joiners arose over the objections of elites who sought to exert their status through state authority and established religion in newly settled territories. Often, their political ambitions and confrontations with other elites actually called forth a spirit of voluntarism that developed in ways no one group could control.[89]

Sociologist Robert Nisbet observes the uniqueness of American culture as it has evolved in direct response to what the Founders feared and were unable to resolve ideologically: "it is the continued existence of this array of intermediate powers in society, of this plurality of 'private sovereignties,' that constitutes, above anything else, the greatest single barrier to the conversion of democracy from its liberal form to its totalitarian form."[90] The development Nisbet observes was not by design, though the extensive debates among the Founders regarding the need for a virtuous citizenry and how American society might engender it undoubtedly played a role. More important were the changing dynamics of the culture and demands of growing populations in regions with little political or religious infrastructure. Civil society developed in these regions out of necessity. Government has helped to shape civil society through processes such as chartering that led to property rights and various legal privileges, granting associations "public legitimacy."[91] Yet the formation of a nation of volunteers resulted from a cultural value that arose in response to demands for social order and a base for social morality that government alone could not satisfy.

As the nation expanded westward, the fringes of New England witnessed the development of what Francis Fukuyama calls "spontaneous sociability," a subset of social capital that forms as organizations emerge in those institutional layers between family and government. Spontaneous sociability in the American context was forged out of necessity as populations formed in regions with inadequate material and social infrastructure, and with little political guidance to chart the way forward.[92] Civil society organizations arose naturally to fill the void, providing what Robert Putnam calls social "lubricant."[93]

Voluntary organizations were more than just "social lubricant," however; they were essential to survival. As communities formed in undeveloped territories, settlers organized around voluntary groups to survive. Social imaginations were energized toward the formation of associations that depended on neither legislative initiatives nor state sponsorship. For example, competition among Connecticut, Massachusetts, and New York missionary societies in serving an Ohio population that expanded some five-and-a-half times between 1800 and 1810 led to more than missionizing; it also contributed to the westward expansion of "social, cultural, and financial capital."[94] That competition also indirectly prevented established churches from arising in Vermont, Ohio, and other newly forming western states, as the pluralism of their immigrant populations offered no clear-cut ecclesial choice. But this break with the established order in religion toward more voluntarist expression on the frontier encouraged development of new associations of many kinds.[95] Large groups such as the American Bible Society, the American Tract Society, and American Temperance Society had thousands of members; perhaps more importantly, beyond the major institutions were smaller, local organizations that themselves numbered in the thousands, as Clifford Griffin estimated there were 3,000 tract societies, 1,000 antislavery societies, and 900 Bible societies by 1839.[96]

As the nation spread westward, the spontaneous formation of institutions had unintended, but arguably positive, consequences for American democracy. What was realized in this dynamic process as missionary societies and other groups tried their hands at community formation was that "social capital could develop from below through the voluntary actions of ordinary people in horizontal relationships rather than the vertical hierarchical ties that had long defined the ideal social order."[97] Dynamic development of social capital was among the novel forms of American economic development that led to a remarkably orderly pattern of expansion, especially given the lack of infrastructure in the hinterland. Ironically, however, many of those who pioneered these social constructions desired a "consensual public sphere"[98] rather than the seeming institutional free-for-all that was forming dynamically. Neem notes that "elite politicians and ministers" initially sought conformity in supporting the formation of communities, fearing the dissolution of social order in the booming populations of western New England and the Ohio River Valley. Conservative groups such as New England's Standing Order encountered pushback from Jeffersonian Republicans hypersensitive to any organizing activities as possible threats to liberty.[99] Thus, institutionally, as the nation settled its frontier, conversations in newly developing lands mirrored the founding debates concerning how to balance order and freedom.

Allen Bogue is among historians who have recorded incidences of social fragmentation and contention, especially in regions where migrant agricultural communities were constructed with inadequate supports of institutional religion and social norms. Bogue sees evidence of such structural and normative deficiencies in "high crime rates, resort to emotional religion, heavy incidence of mental disease, and continued mobility."[100] But while Bogue emphasizes that disorder on the frontier provided opportunities for some who had little motivation for building anything beyond their own fortunes, it also offered those less civilized regions of America a fresh pallet for painting something grander than what could be found in the cities. "Inhabitants of the backcountry," writes Gregory Nobles, "cannot be seen simply as political escapists who fled to the frontier to avoid all authority; they wanted not so much less government as better government, closer to the people and more responsive to local control."[101]

Events like Shay's Rebellion in Massachusetts and the Whiskey Rebellion in Pennsylvania, and the existence of Maine's "timber pirates" and Vermont's Green Mountain Boys demonstrated divisive class distinctions on the frontier.[102] Collectivist strains in Christian social thought that formed in particular along the Ohio River led by religious visionaries like George Rapp, Joseph Bimeler, and Jemima Wilkinson sought to return to the communal sharing they perceived to be consistent with the ethic of Jesus.[103]

Still, this cultural differentiation and mix of settlement motivations was more formative than conflictual. It inspired the human imagination and led to dynamic and innovative methods of social integration far superior to what government bureaucracies could have designed or the eastern establishment promoted. The idea that civil society institutions are necessary for the preservation of both liberty and morality in the dynamism of a liberal market order is an implicit, evolved first principle of the American Republic. The frontier merely offered an organic, variegated environment in which to practice this principle.

Conclusion: wealth and virtue in contemporary America

Joyce Appleby has observed the formative contradictions of capitalism in the American experience. It was cultural glue in the early stages, enfranchising those who traditionally toiled on the margins of European societies, and its productive potential was everywhere on display, allowing an upstart "new world" to eclipse the wealth of its parentage. Yet the sheer rapidity with which it conquered had social effects: "Capitalism caused a crisis of meaning wherever it acquired sufficient momentum to push aside the obstacles to innovation."[104] The enfranchisement of various classes that Appleby detects at various points in American history can be morally affirming. Yet, capitalism also can disenfranchise and become morally denigrating even, or perhaps particularly, in periods of monumental growth.

Americans are strongly inclined to assume that growth, of whatever form, also contributes to the ethics of those who experience it, without considering the structure of markets and nature of human interactions that leads to growth. There has been greater recognition in previous eras of American history of the possible cultural consequences of concentration in banking and finance, primarily in how dependency arises from a centralized system that multiplies moral hazards and disconnects wealth from real contribution. Citing Cathy Matson's work on the economics of the early American Republic, Gilje offers a simple statement that neatly characterizes the difference between Americans then and today: "Americans thought hard about what direction their economy should take."[105] Our chronological distance from the revolution and the individualistic influences of neoliberalism inhibits reflection on the social and moral consequences of the economic system. We do not reflect on its workings; we simply demand that it *work*. Yet, the recent financial crisis exposed the kind of moral problems that caused previous generations of Americans to think hard about their social order.

American social criticism has made a healthy habit of questioning the sources of wealth and, in turn, the legitimacy of inequality. Americans have exhibited respect for "wealth well won" but also skepticism of riches that cannot be attached to some identifiable social good; the great deference exhibited toward financial wealth today is a relatively new phenomenon benefiting greatly from modern economic ideologies.[106] Despite a financial event that should have taken us to our knees and prompted fundamental explorations of the highly financialized American economy, little "thinking" about the direction of the American economy has occurred. The good news is that many of the resources that inspired early Americans to think hard are still available. Yet the transition to a more contractual society over time undoubtedly has shifted much of the burden that once fell on Christian and "liberal" virtue to an already overstressed legal and regulatory system. The broad boundaries of law are the parameters *within which* individuals are formed constructively for civic duties and market participation by myriad institutions; the law itself is not a moral guide.

Putnam's work showing decline in civic engagement due to individual distraction by television and other entertainments has cast doubt on the nation as constituted by "joiners." Daniel Elazar sees a broader cultural change that took place during the 1960s and the "shift to egoism, namely to individualism strictly as self-concern, with a concomitant erosion of American institutions."[107] The rising financial interestedness of those religious and civic groups Americans traditionally have *joined* in subordinating their private desires to the public good creates further doubt concerning the proposition that America is a nation of joiners. Moreover, financialization appears to have become an enabler of the kind of administrative centralization that can lead to the despotism Tocqueville feared. Public spirit and the common feeling are being lost as religious, educational, and civic groups increasingly are financially interested in ways that may or may not benefit their memberships and the wider society. Just as investors are increasingly unsure of the uses their financial capital is directed to, so are "joiners" also increasingly unsure of the motives of those organizations they join. Revisiting the founding period helps to reestablish the importance of private, collective action by Americans in taking back responsibility for both their material and moral direction.

One could suggest, as does Thomas Pangle, that virtue in the early Republic centered on liberty. "If the Federalist Papers do not look to virtue as the end of free government," Pangle writes, "they do tend to treat liberty as an end and as a kind of virtue."[108] Yet the *Federalist Papers* and other founding documents also imply that the distance from revolutionary ideals has determined this waning dependence on virtue. War against Great Britain demanded great measures of self-sacrifice and devotion to country. The formation of a modern economy has required something distinctly different: the industriousness of each in pursuing his own rewards in a land of unlimited opportunity.[109] The tension this cultural transformation entailed required turning to law for resolution. According to Pangle, "Publius, following Locke, tries to find the surest ground of human dignity in a natural, competitive self-assertion that is susceptible to regulation not so much by 'sentiment' and custom as by 'reason' embodied in *law*."[110]

Pangle's observation may help explain why our recent attempts to tame capital focus almost exclusively on law and regulation rather than the development of social capital or individual virtue. Yet these other sources are still available to us. Americans can rationally conclude that the country largely has exhausted the capabilities of law in keeping financial capital focused on the range of human ends for which it is responsible. Despite having moved away from Christian and republican values in favoring economic growth over moral development, the American tradition can return to those sources. Similarly, Americans once conceived voluntarism and association as the keys to preservation not only of the American social order but also of its moral foundation and even the identities of its citizens. This ethic did not bother to label itself. It simply existed and helped to inspire a political, social, and economic miracle threatened today, ironically, by the affluence of the society it created.

Notes

1 Samuel Fleischacker, "Adam Smith's Reception among the American Founders, 1776–1790," *The William and Mary Quarterly*, Third Series, vol. 59, no. 4 (October 2002), 923.

2 For example, see Daniel Stedman Jones, *Masters of the Universe: Hayek, Friedman, and the Birth of Neoliberal Politics* (Princeton, NJ: Princeton University Press, 2012).

3 Johann N. Neem, *Creating a Nation of Joiners: Democracy and Civil Society in Early National Massachusetts* (Cambridge, MA: Harvard University Press, 2008), 11. Neem notes, in particular, how Washington pointed to the Whiskey Rebellion as evidence of the destabilizing characteristics of voluntary associations, condemning them for this reason. See Neem, *Creating a Nation of Joiners*.

4 Joel Barlow, "An Oration Delivered … in Hartford … July the Fourth, 1787 …," "Oration Delivered at Petersburg," American Museum, 2 (1787), 138, 420; quoted in Gordon S. Wood, *The Creation of the American Republic, 1776–1787* (Chapel Hill, NC: The University of North Carolina Press, 1969 [Published for the Institute of Early American History and Culture at Williamsburg, VA]), 418.

5 Wood, *The Creation of the American Republic*, 418.
6 Wood, *The Creation of the American Republic*, 427.
7 Benjamin Franklin, *The Autobiography and Other Writings*, ed. Kenneth Silverman (New York: Penguin Books, 1986), 83.
8 D. H. Lawrence, *Studies in Classic American Literature* (1924; reprint, New York: Penguin, 1977), 22; quoted in Colleen E. Terrell, " 'Republican Machines': Franklin, Rush, and the Manufacture of Civil Virtue in the Early Republic," *Early American Studies*, vol. 1, no. 2 (Fall 2003): 112–13. Reinforcing Lawrence's observations, Terrell contends that

> Franklin portrays the acquisition of virtue as a manufacturing process in all its stages: a mechanic craft whose methods exploit the mechanism of the human mind, producing a citizen whose behavior, as Lawrence long ago lamented, bears remarkably automatic features.

See Terrell, "Republican Machines," 113.
9 Oliver Zunz, "Philanthropy as Creed: The Encounter between Past and Present," *Reviews in American History*, vol. 32, no. 4 (December 2004): 510.
10 Terrell, "Republican Machines," 123.
11 Hector St. John Crévecoeur [Michel-Guillame-Jean de Crévecoeur], *Letters from an American Farmer* (London: J. M. Dent, 1945), 12; quoted in Lynn A. Parks, *Capitalism in Early American Literature*: *Texts and Contexts*, Studies on Themes and Motifs in Literature Series, vol. 27, ed. Horst S. Daemmrich (New York: Peter Lang, 1996), 35.
12 Other prominent themes in Crévecoeur's letters are his admiration for the absence of luxury in America and the fact that "rich and poor are not so far removed from each other as they are in Europe." For more, see Crévecoeur, *Letters from an American Farmer*, 40; quoted in Parks, *Capitalism in Early American Literature*, 36.
13 Lester J. Cappon, ed., *The Adams-Jefferson Letters*, 2 vols. (Williamsburg, VA: Institute of Early American History and Culture, 1959), 1: 409; quoted in Parks, *Capitalism in Early American Literature*, 50. "Land-jobbing" would best be described today as land speculation, where property is purchased not for "productive use" but rather for purposes of profiting from its appreciation in price.
14 Thomas Jefferson, *The Papers of Thomas Jefferson*, ed. Julian P. Boyd, 24 vols. (Princeton, NJ: Princeton University Press, 1953), 8: 681–2; cited in Parks, *Capitalism in Early American Literature*, 48.
15 Paul A. Gilje, "The Rise of Capitalism in the Early Republic," in *Wages of Independence: Capitalism in the Early American Republic* (Lanham, MD: Rowman & Littlefield, 2006), 8–9.
16 James Madison, *The Federalist No. 10*; available at www.constitution.org/fed/federa10.htm.
17 Madison, *Federalist No. 39* ["The Conformity of the Plan to Republican Principles," *Independent Journal* (January 16, 1788)]; available at www.constitution.org/fed/federa39.htm.
18 Madison, *Federalist No. 38*; available at http://thomas.loc.gov/home/histdox/fed_38.html.
19 Jean Yarbrough, "Republicanism Reconsidered: Some Thoughts on the Foundation and Preservation of the American Republic," *The Review of Politics*, vol. 41, no. 1 (January 1979): 63.
20 James Madison, "Speech at the Virginia Ratifying Convention," June 20, 1788; quoted in Jonathon Eliot, ed., *Debates on the Adoption of the Federal Constitution*, 5 vols. (Philadelphia, 1901), III: 536–7; cited in Yarbrough, "Republicanism Reconsidered," 71.
21 Madison distances himself from the classical republican vision. With regard to commercial competition, Madison, unlike colleagues such as Jefferson, perceived no

need to employ virtue in limiting "avarice," seeing instead that competition "serves to vivify and invigorate all the channels of industry and to make them flow with greater activity and copiousness." Thomas Pangle quotes Publius from *The Federalist No. 12* in making this point. See Thomas L. Pangle, "The *Federalist Papers*' Vision of Civic Health and the Tradition Out of Which That Vision Emerges," *Western Political Quarterly*, vol. 39, no. 4 (1986): 595–6.

22 Joshua Foa Dienstag, "Serving God and Mammon: The Lockean Sympathy in Early American Political Thought," *The American Political Science Review*, vol. 90, no. 3 (September 1996), 498. Dienstag contends,

> In arguing that the founders were Lockean, it is not necessary to deem them simply proto-capitalists. It is instead a matter of understanding the sources of the founders' often self-sacrificing theory in Locke's Christian liberalism. Modern historians have been too eager to find in every antipossessive individualist utterance of the founders clear evidence of republican political theory.

Dienstag cites Wood's *The Creation of the American Republic*, 53ff. See Dienstag, "Serving God and Mammon."

23 In *The Creation of the American Republic, 1776–1787*, Wood's argument places considerable weight on speech as representative of values. See Dienstag, "Serving God and Mammon," 501.

24 Dienstag, "Serving God and Mammon," 500.

25 Dienstag, "Serving God and Mammon," 500.

26 Dienstag, "Serving God and Mammon," 498, 501.

27 Dienstag, "Serving God and Mammon," 500.

28 John Locke, "Some Thoughts Concerning Education, 1692," section 38; available at the Modern History Sourcebook website; www.fordham.edu/halsall/mod/1692locke-education.asp.

29 John Locke, "Some Thoughts Concerning Education, 1692," section 70.

30 John Locke, "Some Thoughts Concerning Education," vol. 8 (London: Thomas Tegg; reprinted in Germany: Scientia Verlag Aalen, 1963 [1823]), 33; quoted in Dienstag, 502.

31 Dienstag, "Serving God and Mammon," 507. Like Madison and Hamilton, Jefferson had doubts that maintaining a virtuous citizenry in such a vast, pluralistic, and rapidly expanding republic was a realistic possibility. Jefferson took comfort, however, in a bountiful natural resource that the other two found less compelling: the agricultural economy was that continuously developing on the American frontier. In 1787, Jefferson wrote to Madison that the font of virtue would remain adequate "as long as agriculture is our principal object, which will be the case, while there remains vacant lands in any part of America." See Thomas Jefferson to James Madison, December 20, 1787, in *The Papers of Thomas Jefferson*, vol. 8, p. 426; quoted in Daniel Kemmis, *Community and the Politics of Place* (Norman, OK: University of Oklahoma Press, 1990), 19.

32 Dienstag, "Serving God and Mammon," 507.

33 James T. Kloppenberg, "The Virtues of Liberalism: Christianity, Republicanism, and Ethics in Early American Political Discourse," *Journal of American History*, vol. 74, no. 1 (June 1987): 17.

34 Colin Kidd, "Civil Theology and Church Establishments in Revolutionary America," *The Historical Journal*, vol. 42, no. 4 (December 1999): 1018.

35 Jack N. Rakove, "Once More into the Breach: Reflections on Jefferson, Madison, and the Religion Problem," in *Making Good Citizens: Education and Civil Society*, eds. Diane Ravitch and Joseph P. Viteritti (New Haven, CN: Yale University Press, 2001), 236–7.

36 Dienstag, "Serving God and Mammon," 497.

37 Peter L. Rousseau and Richard Sylla, "Emerging Financial Markets and Early US Growth," *Explorations in Economic History* 42 (2005): 3.

38 J. van Fenstermaker, *The Development of American Commercial Banking: 1782–1837* (Kent, OH: Kent State University Press, 1965), 13; in Rousseau and Sylla, "Emerging Financial Markets and Early US Growth," 4–5.

39 Edward C. Lunt, "Hamilton as a Political Economist," *Journal of Political Economy*, vol. 3, no. 3 (June 1895): 293.

40 Madison, *Federalist No. 44*; available at http://thomas.loc.gov/home/histdox/fed_44.html.

41 Alexander Hamilton, "National Bank," *The Works of Alexander Hamilton; Comprising His Correspondence, and His Political and Official Writings, Exclusive of the Federalist, Civil and Military*, Volume III, ed. John C. Hamilton (New York: John F. Trow, Printer, 1850), 109. Interestingly, in light of what has happened with public subsidy of home ownership and its contribution to financial crisis, Hamilton had recommended in a letter to Robert Morris, who became the U.S. Superintendent of Finance from 1781 to 1784, that government might become involved in land deals, even suggesting that "the bank might in this way acquire vast property." That recommendation was subsequently eliminated from Hamilton's plans for the National Bank. See Lunt, "Hamilton as a Political Economist," 296.

42 Hamilton, "National Bank," 124.

43 For more, see Lunt, "Hamilton as a Political Economist," 299.

44 Jefferson, "Letter to President George Washington," in *The Complete Jefferson*, ed. Saul K. Padover (New York: Tudor Publishing, 1943), 271.

45 Roland Baumann is among those historians who perceive a "pro-Jeffersonian bias" in this long-running debate over Hamilton's Federalist finance versus Jefferson's agrarian vision. Baumann notes how scholars have used the "Protest and Remonstrance" resolution issued by the Virginia House of Delegates in 1790 and George Logan's Letters Addressed to the Yeomanry of the United States, which, among other things, "accused Hamilton of trying to create a 'moneyed aristocracy' that would promote commerce at the expense of agriculture." Baumann references Charles A. Beard, *Economic Origins of Jeffersonian Democracy* (New York, Macmillan, 1915), especially chapters 5–7, Richard R. Beeman, *The Old Dominion and the New Nation, 1788–1801* (Lexington, Ky., 1972), 78–82, and Frederick B. Tolles, "George Logan, Agrarian Democrat: A Survey of His Writings," *PMHB*, 75 (July 1951): 260–78; in "'Heads I Win, Tails You Lose': The Public Creditors and the Assumption Issue in Pennsylvania, 1790–1802," *Pennsylvania History* vol. 44, no. 3 (July 1977): 231.

46 Jefferson letter to Abbé Salimankis (March 14, 1810), in *The Writings of Thomas Jefferson*, Library Edition, vol. VII, ed. Andrew A. Lipscomb (Washington, DC: The Thomas Jefferson Memorial Association, 1904), 379;. See also Jefferson, *The Papers of Thomas Jefferson*, 8: 681–2, cited in Parks, *Capitalism in Early American Literature*, 48.

47 Dorfman references Jefferson's letters to David Hartley, July 2, 1787, in *The Writings of Thomas Jefferson*, edited by Paul Leicester Ford (New York and London, 1895), vol. 6, 150; and to Colonel William Smith, November 13, 1787, in Ford, ed., *The Writings of Thomas Jefferson*, 372–3, in Joseph Dorfman, "The Economic Philosophy of Thomas Jefferson," *Political Science Quarterly*, vol. 55, no. 1 (March 1940): 104.

48 Madison, "Letter to J. K. Paulding," March 10, 1827; in Gaillard Hunt, ed., *The Writings of James Madison* (New York: Putnam, 1900), vol. 9, 23.

49 Madison, *The Papers of James Madison*, 17 vols., eds. William T. Hutchison, *et al.* (Chicago: University of Chicago Press (Vols. 1–10)); (Charlottesville: University Press of Virginia (Vols. 11–17; 1962–1991, vol. 14)), 274; quoted in Colleen A. Sheehan, "*Madison* v. *Hamilton*: The Battle over Republicanism and the Role of Public Opinion," *The American Political Science Review*, vol. 98, no. 3 (August

2004): 408. On Madison's opposition to a national bank, see Sheehan, "*Madison* v. *Hamilton*," 407–409.

50 Hamilton, *The Federalist No. 6*, Letter to the People of the State of New York "Concerning Dangers from Dissensions between the States," *Independent Journal* (November 14, 1787); available at www.constitution.org/fed/federa06.htm.

51 Hamilton, *The Federalist No. 6*. Regarding the illusions of classical civilization, Hamilton asks:

> Is it not time to awake from the deceitful dream of a golden age, and to adopt as a practical maxim for the direction of our political conduct that we, as well as the other inhabitants of the globe, are yet remote from the happy empire of perfect wisdom and perfect virtue?

See Hamilton, The Federalist No. 6.

52 Cathy D. Matson, "Capitalizing Hope: Economic Thought and the Early National Economy," *Journal of the Early Republic*, vol. 16, no. 2 Special Issue on Capitalism in the Early Republic (Summer 1996): 283.

53 Neem, *Creating a Nation of Joiners*, 172.

54 William Manning, *The Key of Liberty: The Life and Democratic Writings of William Manning, "A Laborer," 1747–1814*, eds. Michael Merrill and Sean Wilentz (Cambridge, MA: Harvard University Press, 1993), xii.

55 Merrill and Wilentz, "Introduction" to *The Key of Liberty*, 4.

56 Merrill and Wilentz, "Introduction" to *The Key of Liberty*, 12.

57 There is little doubt that Shay's Rebellion radicalized Manning to the view that manipulations of credit, in combination with unequal systems of taxation, can be as oppressive as any government army. Often, these could compound oppression as creditors sought government protection in exploiting the masses. Manning directs specific criticism at the Society of the Cincinnati, composed largely of former Continental Army officers and their French allies, and its membership being strongly represented among those "speculators, stock jobbers, and land jobbers" Manning detested. These classes were parasitic in Manning's eyes, depleting wealth without offering services that contributed to the nation in any meaningful way. For more, see Manning, *The Key of Liberty*, 144–5.

58 Manning, *The Key of Liberty*, 136.

59 Manning, *The Key of Liberty*, 137.

60 Manning, *The Key of Liberty*, 137.

61 Manning, *The Key of Liberty*, 141–2, 145–6.

62 Manning, *The Key of Liberty*, 136.

63 Joseph R. Stromberg, "The Economic Thought of Thomas Paine"; available via the Ludwig Mises Institute website at https://mises.org/pdf/asc/Paine6.PDF.

64 His unconventional religious views reinforced his social radicalism and engendered even more labeling. Teddy Roosevelt was said to have called Paine "a filthy little atheist." Quoted in Stromberg, "The Economic Thought of Thomas Paine."

65 Paine, "Death and Taxes," in *Selected Writings of Thomas Paine*, ed. Richard Emery Roberts (New York: Everybody's Vacation Publishing Co., 1945), 229; quoted in Stromberg, "The Economic Thought of Thomas Paine."

66 William Hogeland, "How John Adams and Thomas Paine Clashed Over Economic Equality," Huffington Post (March 28, 2011 [updated May 28, 2011]); available at www.huffingtonpost.com/william-hogeland/how-john-adams-and-thomas_b_841563.html.

67 Hogeland, "How John Adams and Thomas Paine Clashed Over Economic Equality."

68 Merrill and Wilentz observe that while still an open question, "it is almost inconceivable that [William Manning] was not well acquainted with Paine's ideas." See "Introduction" to *The Key of Liberty*, 57.

69 *Selected Writings of Thomas Paine*, 248; quoted in Stromberg, "The Economic Thought of Thomas Paine."

70 Alexis de Tocqueville, Preface to *The Old Regime and the Revolution*, vol. 1, The Complete Text, eds. Francois Furet and Francoise Melonio, trans. Alan S. Kahan (Chicago: University of Chicago Press, 1998), 87.

71 Frederick Jackson Turner, "The Significance of the Frontier in American History (1893)," in *Rereading Frederick Jackson Turner "The Significance of the Frontier in American History" and Other Essays* (New Haven, CN: Yale University Press, 1998), 31–2.

72 Turner, "The Significance of the Frontier," 55.

73 Marco M. Sioli, "The Democratic Republican Societies at the End of the Eighteenth Century: The Western Pennsylvania Experience," *Pennsylvania History*, vol. 60, no. 3 (July 1993): 293.

74 Alexis de Tocqueville, *Democracy in America* (New York: 1969), 513.

75 Conservative groups such as New England's Standing Order encountered pushback from Jeffersonian Republicans who were hypersensitive to any organizing activities as possible threats to liberty. In many ways, the institutional development that took place in newly developing lands mirrored the founding debates concerning the balancing of order and freedom. For more, see Johann Neem, "Creating Social Capital in the Early American Republic: The View from Connecticut." *Journal of Interdisciplinary History* 39, no. 4 (Spring 2009): 476–7.

76 Bradley J. Birzer, "Expanding Creative Destruction: Entrepreneurship in the American Wests," *The Western Historical Quarterly*, vol. 30, no. 1 (Spring 1999), 62.

77 Charles Sellers, *The Market Revolution*: *Jacksonian America, 1815–1846* (New York: Oxford University Press, 1991), 153; quoted in Birzer, "Expanding Creative Destruction," 367.

78 Don Harrison Doyle, "Social Theory and New Communities in Nineteenth Century America," *The Western Historical Quarterly* 8, no. 2 (April 1977): 161–2.

79 Internal quotations taken from an untitled speech by B. F. Bristow before the IOOF Illini Lodge, No. 4, reprinted in *Jacksonville Journal*, February 23, 1865; quoted in Doyle, "Social Theory and New Communities in Nineteenth Century America," 163–4. The Odd Fellows to which Doyle refers is an altruistic fraternal lodge, still alive today, that developed in seventeenth-century Britain and saw its first American order organized in Baltimore in 1817. Hundreds of such organizations provided moral enrichment and institutional structure as the United States expanded westward; see www.ioof.org/IOOF/About_Us/About_US/IOOF/About.aspx?hkey=98dab621-cf44–4b0d-b4f1–5a1b5e8326d6.

80 By Tocqueville's observations, this equality

> gives a particular turn to public opinion and a particular twist to the laws, new maxims to those who govern and particular habits to the governed. I soon realized that the influence of this fact extends far beyond political norms and laws, exercising dominion over civil society as much as over the government; it creates opinions, gives birth to feelings, suggests customs, and modifies whatever it does not create.

For more, see Tocqueville, *Democracy in America*, vol. I, 9; quoted in Henk E. S. Woldring, "State and Civil Society in the Political Philosophy of Alexis de Tocqueville," *Voluntas*: *International Journal of Voluntary and Nonprofit Organizations*, vol. 9, no. 4 (December 1998): 369.

81 Woldring, "State and Civil Society," 370–1.

82 Jean Bethke Elshtain, "Democracy on Trial: The Role of Civil Society in Sustaining Democratic Values," in *The Essential Civil Society Reader*: *The Classic Essays*, ed. Don E. Eberly (Lanham, MD: Rowman & Littlefield Publishers, Inc., 2000), 104.

83 According to Dana Villa, "the French bourgeoisie succumbed entirely to this

tendency, withdrawing into private affairs while viewing self-interest as the driving force of society." See Dana Villa, "Hegel, Tocqueville, and 'Individualism,'" *The Review of Politics* vol. 67, no. 4 (Autumn 2005): 663–4.

84 Alexis de Tocqueville, *Democracy in America*, vol. 1, trans. Reeve (New York: Vintage, 1990), 250 [Villa also offers Alexis de Tocqueville, *De la Démocratie en Amérique* in *Oeuvres II*, *Bibliothéque de la Plétiade* (Paris: Éditions Gallimard, 1992), 279]; quoted in Villa, "Hegel, Tocqueville, and 'Individualism,'" 667.

85 Pew Forum, "Millennials in Adulthood Detached from Institutions, Networked with Friends," March 7, 2014; available at www.pewsocialtrends.org/2014/03/07/millennials-in-adulthood/.

86 Woldring, "State and Civil Society," 364.

87 Woldring cites Tocqueville, *Democracy in America*, vol. I, ed. J. P. Mayer (New York: Harper and Row, 1988), 89. "If the individualistic attitude of citizens is strong, and their social and political engagement is weak, then, according to Tocqueville, the temptation of government is great to usurp administrative power." See Woldring, 366.

88 Francis Fukuyama, "Social Virtues and the Creation of Prosperity," in *The Essential Civil Society Reader*, 262.

89 The evolution of Harvard College's governance structure serves as an excellent example. Chapter 5 of the Massachusetts Constitution of 1780 described Harvard College's rights and privileges even as it outlined those "responsibilities" accruing to Harvard and other educational institutions in the commonwealth, encouraging "private societies and public institutions" to promote "agriculture, arts, sciences, commerce, trades, manufactures, and a natural history of the country; to countenance and inculcate the principles of humanity and general benevolence, public and private charity, industry and frugality, honesty and punctuality in their dealings...." Such republican visions began to fade not only as government authority spread across broad geographical regions but also as various groups struggled for control of the institution. For more, see Massachusetts Constitution of 1780; available at www.nhinet.org/ccs/docs/ma-1780.htm; accessed on October 20, 2014.

90 Robert A. Nisbet, *The Quest for Community: A Study in the Ethics of Order and Freedom* (New York: Oxford University Press, 1953), 232, 235; cited in Neem, *Creating a Nation of Joiners*, 3.

91 Neem, *Creating a Nation of Joiners*, 4.

92 Neem cites the Masonic lodge as "the one voluntary association that seemed to meet the universal approbation among American leaders"; lodges promoted fraternity, but they also fostered development of republican virtues, civic and moral education, and the arts and sciences in ways that "transcended political and social divisions." Some Masons claimed that the organization overcame the limitations of denominational churches in that regard. See Neem, *Creating a Nation of Joiners*, 30–1.

93 Quoted in Francis Fukuyama, "Social Virtues and the Creation of Prosperity," in *The Essential Civil Society Reader*, 260.

94 Neem cites Charles Taylor, *Modern Social Imaginaries* (Durham, 2004); in "Creating Social Capital in the Early American Republic," 478.

95 Neem observes a fascinating aspect of this dynamic in the fact that Congregationalists of the Connecticut Missionary Society, including the president of Yale, Reverend Timothy Dwight and his colleague the Reverend Lyman Beecher, were so concerned about establishing institutional checks on the morals of frontiersmen, that they authored a statement encouraging settlers "by all means [to] unite, form churches and societies, as early as possible." According to Neem, this passionate appeal suggested that "perhaps voluntary religious and moral societies could act in lieu of the established church and the corporate Standing Order." General Association of Connecticut, An Address to the Emigrants from Connecticut, and from New England Generally, in the New Settlements in the United States (Hartford, 1817); quoted in Neem, "Creating Social Capital in the Early American Republic," 484.

96 Clifford S. Griffin, *Their Brothers' Keepers: Moral Stewardship in the United States, 1800-1865* (New Brunswick, N.J., 1960); cited in Neem, "Creating Social Capital," 489–90. Neem summarizes the uniquely American contribution to social order liberalization in the early nineteenth century:

> If the social order was not divinely ordained, citizens could turn to voluntary associations to transform it even further. Americans undertook their new responsibilities with earnest seriousness—hence the myriad outreach efforts by middle-class Americans to the poor and immigrant populations. They recognized that the social order could be changed by their own actions, whether for such conservative purposes as sabbatarianism and temperance, or for such radical ones as abolition and female suffrage. The moral order, Americans discovered, was their own creation, not just something inherited and eternal.

See Neem, "Creating Social Capital in the Early American Republic," 491–2.

97 Neem, "Creating Social Capital in the Early American Republic," 477.

98 Quoted in Neem, "Creating Social Capital in the Early American Republic," 476.

99 Neem, "Creating Social Capital in the Early American Republic," 476–7.

100 Allen G. Bogue, "Social Theory and the Pioneer," *Agricultural History*, vol. 34 (1960): 33; quoted in Don Harrison Doyle, "Social Theory and New Communities," 153.

101 Gregory H. Nobles, "Breaking into the Backcountry: New Approaches to the Early American Frontier, 1750–1890," *The William and Mary Quarterly*, Third Series, vol. 46, no. 4 (October 1989): 666.

102 Charles Post, *The American Road to Capitalism: Studies in Class Structure, Economic Development and Political Conflict, 1620–1877* (Leiden, The Netherlands: Koninklijke Brill NV, 2011), 73–87.

103 See "Chapter Two" in Charles McDaniel, *God and Money: The Moral Challenge of Capitalism* (Lanham, MD: Rowman & Littlefield, 2007).

104 Joyce Appleby, "The Vexed Story of Capitalism Told by American Historians," *Journal of the Early Republic*, vol. 21, no. 1 (Spring 2001): 16. Appleby observes that

> in these situations, human agency is most salient, for particular persons made the choices and weakened the precepts, rules of thumb, and inhibitions that regulated behavior. No one path could have been predicted. Nor could any specific set of ideas explain outcomes, for change invariably carried contradictions within it.

See Appleby, "The Vexed Story of Capitalism," 16–17.

105 Gilje, "The Rise of Capitalism in the Early Republic," 180.

106 Even Hamilton voiced such concerns. In a letter to James Duane in 1780 concerning the appropriate offices to guide the nation's economy, Hamilton recognized the need to separate powers between the nation's "Financier" and whoever would preside over the country's commercial trade. "The Financier should not direct the affairs of trade," Hamilton wrote, "because for the sake of acquiring reputation by increasing revenues, he might adopt measures that would depress trade." Similarly, in touting the invaluable benefits of a central bank to both government and proprietors, Hamilton notes how it might help stem the depreciation of "our new money" since "the monied men have not an immediate interest to uphold its credit. They may even in many ways find it their interest to undermine it." Hamilton to James Duane [Liberty Pole, New Jersey, September 3, 1780]; available at http://founders.archives.gov/documents/Hamilton/01–02–02–0838; accessed on September 29, 2014.

107 Daniel J. Elazar, "Tocqueville and the Cultural Basis of American Democracy," *Political Science and Politics*, vol. 32, no. 2 (June 1999): 208.

108 Pangle elaborates in the text:

while it is true that Publius is reluctant to make republican government into a mere means to safety or material well-being; it is equally true that he speaks as if the longing for republican government were, in the final analysis, neither as pressing nor as deeply rooted as the need for protection of life, private property, and individual independence.

For more, see Pangle, "The *Federalist Papers*' Vision," 597, 597–8.

109 These tensions are obvious in the *Federalist Papers*, in which the influence of liberal philosophy encouraged "humanity's natural quest for security, material prosperity, and diverse personal tastes and enjoyments. Yet the authors of the *Papers* cannot part with their conviction as to the nobility of republican self-government." See Pangle, "The *Federalist Papers*' Vision," 599.

110 Pangle, "The *Federalist Papers*' Vision," 600 (emphasis Pangle's).

Bibliography

Appleby, Joyce. "The Vexed Story of Capitalism Told by American Historians." *Journal of the Early Republic* 21, no. 1 (Spring 2001): 1–18.

Baumann, Roland. "'Heads I Win, Tails You Lose': The Public Creditors and the Assumption Issue in Pennsylvania, 1790–1802." *Pennsylvania History* 44, no. 3 (July 1977): 195–232.

Beard, Charles A. *Economic Origins of Jeffersonian Democracy*. New York: Macmillan, 1915.

Beeman, Richard R. *The Old Dominion and the New Nation, 1788–1801*. Lexington: University Press of Kentucky, 1972.

Birzer, Bradley J. "Expanding Creative Destruction: Entrepreneurship in the American Wests." *The Western Historical Quarterly* 30, no. 1 (Spring 1999): 45–63.

Bogue, Allan G. "Social Theory and the Pioneer." *Agricultural History* 34, no. 1 (January 1960): 21–34.

Cappon, Lester J., ed. *The Adams-Jefferson Letters*. 2 vols. Williamsburg, VA: Institute of Early American History and Culture, 1959.

Crévecoeur, Hector St. John. *Letters from an American Farmer*. London: J. M. Dent, 1945.

Dienstag, Joshua Foa. "Serving God and Mammon: The Lockean Sympathy in Early American Political Thought." *The American Political Science Review* 90, no. 3 (September 1996): 497–511.

Dorfman, Joseph. "The Economic Philosophy of Thomas Jefferson." *Political Science Quarterly* 55, no. 1 (March 1940): 98–121.

Doyle, Don Harrison. "Social Theory and New Communities in Nineteenth Century America." *The Western Historical Quarterly* 8, no. 2 (April 1977): 151–65.

Elazar, Daniel J. "Tocqueville and the Cultural Basis of American Democracy." *Political Science and Politics* 32, no. 2 (June 1999): 207–10.

Elshtain, Jean Bethke. "Democracy on Trial: The Role of Civil Society in Sustaining Democratic Values." In *The Essential Civil Society Reader: The Classic Essays*, edited by Don E. Eberly, 101–22. Lanham, MD: Rowman & Littlefield Publishers, Inc., 2000.

Fleischacker, Samuel. "Adam Smith's Reception among the American Founders, 1776–1790." *The William and Mary Quarterly* 59, no. 4 (October 2002): 897–924.

Franklin, Benjamin. *The Autobiography and Other Writings*. Edited by Kenneth Silverman. New York: Penguin Books, 1986.

Fukuyama, Francis. "Social Virtues and the Creation of Prosperity." In *The Essential*

Civil Society Reader: The Classic Essays, edited by Don E. Eberly, 257–66. Lanham, MD: Rowman & Littlefield Publishers, Inc., 2000.
Gilje, Paul A. "The Rise of Capitalism in the Early Republic." In *Wages of Independence: Capitalism in the Early American Republic* (Lanham, MD: Rowman & Littlefield, 2006), 1–22.
Hamilton, Alexander. *The Federalist No. 6* "Letter to the People of the State of New York Concerning Dangers from Dissensions between the States," *Independent Journal* (November 14, 1787). *Constitution.org*, November 14, 1787. www.constitution.org/fed/federa06.htm; accessed on September 29, 2014.
Hamilton, Alexander. "National Bank." In *The Works of Alexander Hamilton*; *Comprising His Correspondence, and His Political and Official Writings, Exclusive of the Federalist, Civil and Military*, edited by John C. Hamilton, III: 106–46. New York: John F. Trow, Printer, 1850.
Hamilton, Alexander. Letter to James Duane [Liberty Pole, New Jersey, September 3, 1780] http://founders.archives.gov/documents/Hamilton/01-02-02-0838.
Hogeland, William. "How John Adams and Thomas Paine Clashed over Economic Equality." *Huffington Post*, March 28, 2011. www.huffingtonpost.com/william-hogeland/how-john-adams-and-thomas_b_841563.html; accessed on September 24, 2014.
Jefferson, Thomas. *The Papers of Thomas Jefferson*. Edited by Julian P. Boyd. 24 vols. Princeton, NJ: Princeton University Press, 1953.
Jefferson, Thomas. *The Writings of Thomas Jefferson*. Edited by Andrew A. Lipscomb. Library Edition. Vol. VII. Washington, DC: The Thomas Jefferson Memorial Association, 1904.
Jones, Daniel Stedman. *Masters of the Universe*: *Hayek, Friedman, and the Birth of Neoliberal Politics*. Princeton, NJ: Princeton University Press, 2012.
Kemmis, Daniel. *Community and the Politics of Place*. Norman, OK: University of Oklahoma Press, 1990.
Kidd, Colin. "Civil Theology and Church Establishments in Revolutionary America." *The Historical Journal* 42, no. 4 (December 1999): 1007–26.
Kloppenberg, James T. "The Virtues of Liberalism: Christianity, Republicanism, and Ethics in Early American Political Discourse." *Journal of American History* 74, no. 1 (June 1987): 9–33.
Lawrence, D. H. *Studies in Classic American Literature*. New York: Penguin, 1977.
Locke, John. *Some Thoughts Concerning Education*. Vol. 8. Germany: Scientia Verlag, 1963.
Locke, John. "Some Thoughts Concerning Education, 1692." *Fordham.edu*, (n.d.). Modern History Sourcebook. www.fordham.edu/halsall/mod/1692locke-education.asp; accessed on October 6, 2014.
Lunt, Edward C. "Hamilton as a Political Economist." *Journal of Political Economy* 3, no. 3 (June 1895): 289–310.
Madison, James. *The Federalist No. 10*. *Daily Advertiser*, November 22, 1787. www.constitution.org/fed/federa10.htm; accessed on September 26, 2014.
Madison, James. *The Federalist No. 38*. *New York Packet*, January 15, 1788. http://thomas.loc.gov/home/histdox/fed_38.html; accessed on October 20, 2014.
Madison, James. *The Federalist No. 39* "The Conformity of the Plan to Republican Principles." *Independent Journal*, January 16, 1788. www.constitution.org/fed/federa39.htm; accessed on September 29, 2014.
Madison, James. *The Federalist No. 44*. *New York Packet*, January 25, 1788. http://thomas.loc.gov/home/histdox/fed_44.html; accessed on November 3, 2014.

Madison, James. "Speech at the Virginia Ratifying Convention." Presented at the Virginia Ratifying Convention, Virginia, June 20, 1788.
Madison, James. *The Writings of James Madison*. Edited by Gaillard Hunt. Vol. 9. New York: Putnam, 1900.
Manning, William. *The Key of Liberty: The Life and Democratic Writings of William Manning, "A Laborer," 1747–1814*. Edited by Michael Merrill and Sean Wilentz. Cambridge, MA: Harvard University Press, 1993.
Matson, Cathy D. "Capitalizing Hope: Economic Thought and the Early National Economy." *Journal of the Early Republic* 16, no. 2 (Summer 1996): 273–91.
McDaniel, Charles. "Chapter Two." In *God and Money: The Moral Challenge of Capitalism*. Lanham, MD: Rowman & Littlefield, 2007.
Neem, Johann N. *Creating a Nation of Joiners: Democracy and Civil Society in Early National Massachusetts*. Cambridge, MA: Harvard University Press, 2008.
Neem, Johann N. "Creating Social Capital in the Early American Republic: The View from Connecticut." *Journal of Interdisciplinary History* 39, no. 4 (Spring 2009): 471–95.
Nisbet, Robert A. *The Quest for Community: A Study in the Ethics of Order and Freedom*. New York: Oxford University Press, 1953.
Nobles, Gregory H. "Breaking into the Backcountry: New Approaches to the Early American Frontier, 1750–1890." *The William and Mary Quarterly*, Third Series, 46, no. 4 (October 1989): 641–70.
Padover, Saul K. ed. *The Complete Jefferson*. New York: Tudor Publishing, 1943.
Paine, Thomas. "Death and Taxes." In *Selected Writings of Thomas Paine*, edited by Richard Emery Roberts. New York: Everybody's Vacation Publishing Co., 1945.
Pangle, Thomas L. "The *Federalist Papers*' Vision of Civic Health and the Tradition Out of Which That Vision Emerges." *The Western Political Quarterly* 39, no. 4 (December 1986): 577–602.
Parks, Lynn A. *Capitalism in Early American Literature*. Edited by Horst S. Daemmrich. Vol. 27. Studies on Themes and Motifs in Literature Series. New York: Peter Lang, 1996.
Pew Forum, "Millennials in Adulthood Detached from Institutions, Networked with Friends," March 7, 2014; available at www.pewsocialtrends.org/2014/03/07/millennials-in-adulthood/; accessed on October 7, 2014.
Post, Charles. *The American Road to Capitalism: Studies in Class Structure, Economic Development and Political Conflict, 1620–1877*. Leiden, The Netherlands: Koninklijke Brill NV, 2011.
Rakove, Jack N. "Once More into the Breach: Reflections on Jefferson, Madison, and the Religion Problem." In *Making Good Citizens: Education and Civil Society*, edited by Diane Ravitch and Joseph P. Viteritti, 233–62. New Haven, CN: Yale University Press, 2001.
Rousseau, Peter L., and Richard Sylla. "Emerging Financial Markets and Early US Growth." *Explorations in Economic History* 42, no. 1 (January 2005): 1–26.
Sellers, Charles. *The Market Revolution: Jacksonian America, 1815–1846*. New York: Oxford University Press, 1991.
Sheehan, Colleen A. "Madison v. Hamilton: The Battle over Republicanism and the Role of Public Opinion." *The American Political Science Review* 98, no. 3 (August 2004): 405–24.
Sioli, Marco M. "The Democratic Republican Societies at the End of the Eighteenth

Century: The Western Pennsylvania Experience." *Pennsylvania History* 60, no. 3 (July 1993): 288–304.

Stromberg, Joseph R. "The Economic Thought of Thomas Paine." *Mises.org*, (n.d.). http://mises.org/pdf/asc/Paine6.PDF; accessed on September 24, 2014.

Taylor, Charles. *Modern Social Imaginaries*. Durham: Duke University Press, 2004.

Terrell, Colleen E. " 'Republican Machines': Franklin, Rush, and the Manufacture of Civil Virtue in the Early Republic." *Early American Studies* 1, no. 2 (Fall 2003): 100–32.

Tocqueville, Alexis de. *De la Démocratie en Amérique*. Oeuvres II, Bibliothéque de La Plétiade. Paris: Éditions Gallimard, 1992.

Tocqueville, Alexis de. *Democracy in America*. Translated by George Lawrence. Vol. 1. New York: Doubleday Anchor, 1969.

Tocqueville, Alexis de. *Democracy in America*. Edited by J. P. Mayer. Vol. I. New York: Harper and Row, 1988.

Tocqueville, Alexis de. *Democracy in America*. Translated by Henry Reeve. Vol. 1. New York: Vintage, 1990.

Tocqueville, Alexis de. Preface to *The Old Regime and the Revolution*. Vol. 1, The Complete Text. Edited by Francois Furet and Francoise Melonio, trans. Alan S. Kahan. Chicago: University of Chicago Press, 1998, 87.

Tolles, Frederick B. "George Logan, Agrarian Democrat: A Survey of His Writings." *Pennsylvania Magazine of History and Biography* 75, no. 3 (July 1951): 260–78.

Turner, Frederick Jackson. "The Significance of the Frontier in American History (1893)." In *Rereading Frederick Jackson Turner "The Significance of the Frontier in American History" and Other Essays*, 31–60. New Haven, CN: Yale University Press, 1998.

Van Fenstermaker, J. *The Development of American Commercial Banking: 1782–1837*. Kent, Ohio: Kent State University Press, 1965.

Villa, Dana. "Hegel, Tocqueville, and 'Individualism.' " *The Review of Politics* 67, no. 4 (Autumn 2005): 659–86.

Woldring, Henk S. "State and Civil Society in the Political Philosophy of Alexis de Tocqueville." *Voluntas: International Journal of Voluntary and Nonprofit Organizations* 9, no. 4 (December 1998): 363–73.

Wood, Gordon S. *The Creation of the American Republic, 1776–1787*. Chapel Hill, NC: The University of North Carolina Press, 1969.

Yarbrough, Jean. "Republicanism Reconsidered: Some Thoughts on the Foundation and Preservation of the American Republic." *The Review of Politics* 41, no. 1 (January 1979): 61–95.

Zunz, Oliver. "Philanthropy as Creed: The Encounter between Past and Present." *Reviews in American History* 32, no. 4 (December 2004): 506–11.

7 Recovering ethics and virtue in financial discourse

The global financial crisis that began in 2008 revealed an extensive vocabulary unknown to many Americans that, for a period, dominated the national conversation. As the crisis deepened, new terms emerged to describe those ideas, instruments, and processes that presaged financial collapse. Media reports were filled with expressions such as "fiscal cliff," "systemic risk," and "casino finance" that implied peril and commanded attention, though many hearing these words failed to comprehend their meaning. Association with an economic period consistently described by economists and government officials as "the worst since the Great Depression" amplified the negative impact of this vocabulary on American public discourse.

While the unsettling influence of such language wanes with recent signs of economic recovery, ongoing financialization infuses a general financial way of thinking and speaking that, as shown previously, impacts not only the business culture but also institutions of American civil society. Financialization has been accompanied by a dominant discourse that erodes all others, carving away at the diversity of American culture. It also has the invidious effect of accenting the financial literacy gap that divides the nation between those with the knowledge and capital to compete and those without. Financialization stipulates that finance must be the driver, the standard to which all must adapt, regardless of whether its rhetoric and rationality have a dehumanizing effect, or whether its techniques evolve so as to destabilize the global economy. In this regard, finance appears to have reached theological status as an "object of ultimate concern," leveraging Paul Tillich's famous phrase.

The irony, however, is that while finance has taken on near religious significance as the lifeblood of global society, its status as a fitting object of ethical and theological inquiry fades with each wave of innovation. This unfortunate distancing of moral perspectives from a sector with weighty cultural consequences is reinforced by the encroachments of finance's disenchanting rhetoric. Financial language grows increasingly proprietary in articulating standards by which to measure progress not only for businesses but also for institutions that exist for more than profit. Its conceptual and linguistic challenges, however, often intimidate ethicists and theologians into silence, creating an insular discourse that deprives important actors of the ability to contribute to more *fully human* development, heightening potential for the kinds of abuses recently witnessed.

Absent the inclusion of religious and other voices, financial logic and rhetoric will continue to displace others, undermining the pluralist ethic that supports self-government and the market economy while realizing unsustainable distributions of wealth and power. Theologians are challenged with returning to their distinct resources in order to develop constructive doctrine that can help reestablish what is "real" in economic life, reorienting the financial system toward truly human ends.[1] Ethicists must do more than highlight the system's injustices. Elaboration of normative perspectives on economic issues, particularly with regard to finance, is necessary to prevent further drift toward a system where the principal object has become profit maximization often with little regard for ethical, and in some cases legal, boundaries.

This chapter demonstrates that despite finance's encroachments into American civil society, resources still exist to help restore integrity and reestablish "virtue" not only as a critical input to a moral economy but also as a legitimate derivative of economic action. For all its recent problems, finance and the civil society that supports it have a unique opportunity not simply to restore industry ethics but also potentially to establish finance as a beachhead for the development of a more virtuous economy. In finance, the first step is to recover an appropriate discourse capable of bringing discussions of ethics and virtue into legitimacy, pointing beyond technical issues that are the obsession of industry insiders to the core problems that have detached financial capital from the individuals and institutions it exists to support.

The monopolization of public discourse

Financialization's invidious effects are reinforced by rhetoric that subtly reshapes not only financial norms but those of the wider society. Marieke De Goede describes finance itself as a "discursive domain made possible through performative practices, which have to be articulated and rearticulated on a daily basis."[2] De Goede builds on Michel Foucault's discourse theory in showing how "knowledge, ideas, and ideology no longer follow material production and institutions, but are *a requirement for* material and institutional possibilities."[3] The ideas and ideology that enable the production of wealth, however, require a dynamic language for expression. That language itself is shaped by cultural changes that can redefine the meaning of established terms, in some cases even legitimizing former vices by ascribing to them "higher" purposes.

For decades viewed as a type of "gambling," lotteries have been transformed into legitimate means of revenue generation in the United States, even appropriate for funding public education, as is common today. Their legitimacy has arrived, as with forms of speculative trading in financial markets, through the reinforcement of "economic necessity"[4] language that lauds their benefits to schoolchildren as much as state budgets. The legitimation of gambling is part of a more general, highly utilitarian discursive transformation that continually extends its reach. The financialized society imparts a strong inclination that whatever makes money for a legitimate cause itself necessarily becomes legitimate.

In the early 1970s, a similar rhetorical transformation removed the stigma of gambling from the options market and contributed, arguably, to the financialization of American culture. Robert Merton, Fischer Black, and Myron Scholes pioneered development of a financial model that was to become the definitive theory of option pricing and led to the latter two receiving the Nobel Prize in Economics.[5] Presentation of their findings coincided with the opening of the Chicago Board Options Exchange (CBOE) in 1973. Donald MacKenzie and Yuval Millo have demonstrated the significance of the Black-Scholes model in determining how the options market functions. Interestingly, at its inception, the model "did not accurately predict option prices in the CBOE, with deviations of 30 to 40 percent common in the first months of option trading."[6] Rubenstein later showed how deviations of actual option pricing from the Black-Scholes model were reduced dramatically to approximately 2 percent for the period between August 1976 and August 1978.[7] MacKenzie and Millo showed that this gap narrowed significantly because traders began using "theoretical value sheets" to generate bid prices that incorporated the language and logic of the Black-Scholes model. Importantly, the Black-Scholes model added "implied volatility" to the mix in valuing options; traders began to speak of buying or selling volatility in ways that changed both the vernacular and behavior of the exchange, providing evidence of performativity.[8] The power of Black-Scholes made it the standard model for the option market regulatory mechanism and the "autoquote" software created by the CBOE itself.[9]

The former legal counsel to the CBOE, Burton Rissman, observed how the Black-Scholes model elevated the status of option trading from the level of gambling with which it was associated in the late 1960s and early 1970s: "That issue fell away, and I think Black-Scholes made it fall away. It wasn't speculation or gambling, it was efficient pricing.... [Soon] I never heard the word 'gambling' again in relation to options."[10] Now entrenched in the economic system, options and other forms of derivative trading have seen their legitimacy enhanced once again from tools for hedging against economic contingencies to legitimate devices for money making that, as noted in the introduction, are employed by institutions across the religious-secular divide.

Other examples illustrate how seemingly descriptive models and forms of discourse can become prescriptive. MacKenzie builds on the work of Michael Callon and J. L. Austin in "performativity theory" to argue that the field of economics is not merely descriptive in explaining existing phenomena but rather performative in that it helps "bring that world into being."[11] He observes how theories can affect reality as in the case of "chartism," where prices are often shown to follow patterns that differ from what would be expected given market conditions in the absence of such price charting practices:

> In principle, any belief about pricing, if widely enough shared, could be performative. "Chartism," or "technical analysis," is replete with beliefs about the patterns that can be seen in price charts and their implications for future price movements. In the eyes of orthodox financial economics, these patterns

> are simply read by undisciplined observers into what are actually random walks. Note, however, that if there are enough chartists perceiving the same patterns and seeing in them the same implications, chartist beliefs may be self-fulfilling.[12]

Other changing articulations of finance significantly influence market reality. The widely heard assumption during the run-up to the crisis that past "fundamentals"—those financial ratios and other standards of measurement that help determine a company's valuation and the wider economy's overall health—were no longer relevant in the "new economy," shaped the financialization of discourse and allowed innovative but often unstable financial practices to gain legitimacy. Klaus Schaeck observes that the transactions of financial intermediaries, believed to have "better information than other agents," are often perceived in markets as lead signals and "can cause herding effects and hence instill [market] over- or underreaction."[13] Recognition of this phenomenon leads Schaeck to recommend that banks develop investment products that "reap excess returns in equity markets" while meeting "investors' emotional needs."[14]

Pronouncements by prominent economists that at a national level "debt doesn't matter"[15] may well have influenced the wider culture given the escalation of corporate and consumer indebtedness. The fact that liberal economists such as Paul Krugman have suggested that the nation's debt problems are wildly exaggerated,[16] along with the significant deficit spending by the ostensibly conservative administrations of Ronald Reagan and George W. Bush, led to the "immateriality of debt" assuming a place in that rarefied realm of issues on which some conservatives and liberals apparently agree. While many analysts predicted the system would return to more traditional measures of stock valuation and financial health after the "tech bust" of the 1990s, they were forced to issue quite similar predictions during the financial crisis. Pundits ignored the persistence of new standards and the mark they made in the public consciousness. According to Nigel Thrift, vice chancellor of the University of Warwick, "elements of the new economy will live on. To write it off simply as a discourse is to misunderstand discourse's materiality."[17] In other words, how we talk about—or fail to talk about—economics has real implications for economic behavior and outcomes.

Language has significant implications for the ways societies both come to see themselves and function; yet the language that helps to forge values and shape attitudes may or may not be grounded in an objective reality or moral truth. As Murray Davis explains, the primary reason theories of social science rise to importance has to do more with their ability to attract attention and cause a stir among those in the field than to describe the real world.[18] Language is crucial to the attention grabbing potential of ideas capable of reshaping the global economy. Principles of neoclassical economics influence the institutions within which they circulate. Emphasis on rational actors, "perfect" information, and profit maximization in the neoclassical vernacular creates a rhetorical framework within which processes of financialization can flourish.

The "rational choice" theory of the Chicago School, with its emphasis on the extension of market logic and terminology to education, religion, marriage and family, crime and punishment and virtually all other realms, has helped extend efficiency and maximization language even to the most sacred, intimate areas of life.[19] But "maximizing behavior" involves risk; and, as we have seen with the Anglican Church, nonprofit hospitals, private colleges, and other institutions, such language appears to shape values and behaviors even in entities that, at least theoretically, do not exist primarily for profit. Thus, Milton Friedman did not simply present a theory in his 1970 *New York Times Magazine* article insisting that the sole responsibility of the corporation is to earn a profit.[20] He articulated an idea of immense rhetorical force that influenced not only businesses but also the broader culture, including even institutions with presumably "higher" callings that feel competitive pressure like all others. When a theory reaches a discursive critical mass—as, for example, when it infuses American business schools and convinces students trained in these institutions that its veracity is beyond question—it achieves materiality.[21]

Ironically, just as Friedman stated that the value of an economic model is not measured by the reality of its assumptions but rather the accuracy of its predictions, so an analogous principle may be derived for higher level economic assumptions—normalization can occur even when theories seem to defy reality. Fabrizio Ferraro, Jeffrey Pfeffer, and Robert Sutton note how theories "become self-fulfilling when, regardless of their initial ability to predict and explain behavior, they become accepted truths and norms that govern behavior."[22] A principal means of this self-fulfillment is rhetoric. We become what we speak to a large extent, irrespective of whether that speech conforms to any objective reality; and language "affects what people see, how they see it, and the social categories and descriptors they use to interpret their reality."[23] The ideas and assumptions of economics are particularly powerful because "through their effect on actions and decisions, they produce a world that corresponds to the assumptions and ideas themselves."[24] In other words, the economic rhetoric through which many ideas are articulated in contemporary society has tremendous power to shape the social order. Economic rhetoric is particularly potent because it appeals to our survival instincts.

James Arnt Aune's book *Selling the Free Market: The Rhetoric of Economic Correctness* shows the progression of a libertarian-tinged "rhetoric of economic correctness" and its broad penetration of American public discourse. Aune cites the influences of Friedman, Ayn Rand, Robert Nozick, Charles Murray, and other zealous defenders of free market principles who have advocated an ethic of efficiency and its application even to morally challenging issues. For example, Aune cites the rhetorical force of Isaac Ehrlich's empirical model that demonstrates the "deterrent effect" of capital punishment, and how Ehrlich's "'seven lives saved for every execution' argument" was important to the reinstitution of the death penalty in many states in the 1970s.[25] Aune shows the reach of intense anti-government/promarket logic even beyond academia in books like Murray's *What It Means to be Libertarian* (1997) and Nozick's *Anarchy, State, and*

Utopia (1974) that have enjoyed popular success. Evangelical religion also absorbed the market ethic into its literature with the enormous popularity of books such as Pat Robertson's *The New World Order* (1992).[26] Catholic authors too have lauded both the material and moral benefits of the free market in Michael Novak's *The Catholic Ethic and the Spirit of Capitalism* (1993) and countless other works by staunchly promarket Catholics such as George Weigel, Richard John Neuhaus, and Father Robert Sirico.

This literature praises the contributions to human liberty and efficient resource allocation of a market order built on individual choice and an unconstrained pricing system. As we have seen, however, neoclassical price theory has taken a significant "hit" with the coming of financialization. And American society's growing dependence on price as a measure of what is valuable and "good" means that price distorting financial methods are capable of doing cultural, not merely economic, damage. As Aune states: "*The problem arises when the neoclassical theory of price takes over the entire social and political world, displacing all alternative accounts of human motivation.*"[27] Lacking alternative accounts of what motivates human action, price becomes imbedded as *the* motivating force, narrowing a culture's conception of the person and excluding other voices from the economic conversation. The intensity of these forces insists that whatever disrupts the pricing mechanism distorts more than relative valuations; it also affects a society's relationships and moral foundations.

The discursive harm of financialization

As discourse has become financialized, the financial system has evolved from one in which capital is created and deployed for human ends to one having its own logic, language, and *telos*. The term "financialization" suggests an ultimate end for capital in itself that can conflict with human purposes. A purely efficient financial system achieves the maximum use of resources without respect to the social and moral implications of those uses. In observing that "financial practices do not exist prior to, or independently from, ideas and beliefs about them," De Goede notes that "the social and discursive nature of money and credit" is one where "discourses of financial rectitude and economic necessity have taken shape at the expense of other possible financial representations."[28] The discursive domain is restricted from engaging other possible discourses, in some cases, by the technical nature of financial language and, in others, by the public's relative inattention to financial matters beyond those issues that impact them directly. Thus, broad but shallow discussions of finance's role in society lean toward the more pressing issues of "financial rectitude and economic necessity," at the expense of substantive dialogue.

Financialization's discursive harm, then, is seen in its ability to shortcut deliberation about the financial sector's potential impact on those first principles that every society must revisit and reaffirm from time to time to preserve its foundational values. Modern finance insists that we trust its machinations, however obscure or amoral they may seem, with the confidence that some greater good will result. The financial industry insists we "trust the math"—the abstract value represented in a derivative contract is sound because the calculations "make sense" for the parties involved, irrespective of any consequences beyond those parties.

Economics, more generally, makes claims to objectivity as a positive science and attempts to prove its truth through reason. Its "daughter discipline" finance[29] is even more grounded in mechanistic operation and mathematical calculation that appeal to rational instincts. As Julie Nelson observes, the problem is that the intensity of appeals to "rational" truth inspires a dualism with other truth claims that dare to challenge the hegemony of economic reason:

> As a result of sharing the belief in that capitalist systems are fundamentally mechanical, much of the "critical" literature tends to fall into a pattern of simple reactivity in prescribing solutions. If economists and capitalists are pro-growth, then critics must be diametrically anti-growth; if the conventional approach is pro-globalization and large-scale, then critics must be diametrically pro-local and small-scale; if current elites are pro-technology, then critics must be diametrically Luddite and anti-technology; if policy debates focus on humans in industrialized societies; critics must diametrically venerate the wilderness, indigenous and non-human species; if those in control praise profits and private property, those who want change must advocate a complete disavowal of both.[30]

Seemingly obvious constructs shaped by discursive norms can sustain inaccurate or inadequate understandings of reality. Nelson notes, for example, Jürgen Habermas's false conception of money as a "neutral, a-social medium," which is bolstered by a traditional view of money as backed by either metals or the legitimacy and solvency of state authority.[31] Nelson notes that such notions continue despite the absence of an international gold standard since the 1930s; thus, "money has long been a quintessential social construction: It has value precisely and only because (or when) people believe it has value."[32] Similarly, many claim the neutrality of markets in supporting exchange between parties without influencing their transactions. Yet markets have their own logic and values that impress upon participants and are grounded in assumptions that virtually everything is commodifiable and that relative value can be determined even among widely disparate objects of exchange.

The temporality of nation-states seen in the context of seemingly "immortal" finance[33] played out repeatedly in the crisis years. The very existence of Ireland, Greece, Spain, Portugal and other nations came into question because of fiscal problems that resulted from financial overextensions by their institutions and populations. If the Greeks cannot pay their bills then collectively they must be treated like any other creditor who fails to make good on commitments—"renegotiation of terms" may be possible, but, failing that, countries are subject to default and possibly dissolution. Greece as the cradle of Western Civilization is not under consideration; it is Greece the delinquent country that must be dealt with, and bailouts are considered not from the standpoint of rescuing Greece as a cherished cultural contribution but rather because of fears that it may undermine the European Union. This financialization of international discourse has occurred over decades and created a situation where financial capital must be appeased at great social and political cost.

Randy Martin has observed financialization's penetration beyond the business world and even the public square to gain a foothold in the American household. He observes various methodologies for introducing children to the benefits of financial life, such as Willard Stawski II's "Cash University" and his drill-sergeant approach of "tough love" that seeks to ingrain in children a kind of cost-benefit understanding of their relationship to the family.[34] Public institutions assist with "financial socialization" as well, such as a program at the University of Missouri (which Martin describes as parenting with an "invisible hand") and the University of Minnesota Extension's "Children and Money Series" where "every transaction is a learning opportunity" and "concepts of earning, spending, and saving comprise the terrible twos."[35]

Financial literacy is being promoted among young Americans in ways that some economists and financial specialists believe can lead to "financial democratization." The question is whether financial ethics will accompany and support these changes. Programs of financial education are critical to addressing the financial literacy gap in the U.S., but they should be balanced by religious instruction and education across disciplines that instill values needed to address the social and ethical challenges of financial markets. As the recent crisis has proven, technical training alone is insufficient. Other perspectives are needed to see beyond mere system mechanics to the underlying moral hazards and structural flaws that inevitably reveal human failings.

Linguistic obscurity, black boxes, and financial ethics

The wider rhetoric of mainstream economics primed the pump for more technical and opaque financial terms to penetrate public discourse. Clift observes the period when "complex financial concepts such as that of moral hazard" were suddenly "on everyone's lips" as the world was realizing the depth of economic crisis; yet this was also a time in which economic concerns became less focused on more accessible concepts like "efficient production and distribution of goods" than with the "early discovery of the next asset or credit bubble."[36] This displacement effect is a component of the financialization of discourse and has ethical implications. Clift's observation demonstrates more than a problem of priority—it signals that fundamental principles that give the market economy its ennobling qualities are being shaped and, in some cases, displaced by a form of rhetoric not only detached from the realities of most market participants but also, in many cases, inaccessible to them. Yet, as Denise Baden and Ian Harwood put it, "What we call things has attitudinal, affective and behavioral consequences."[37] It is not simply what we call things, however, that gives a market economy coherency. Some reasonably understandable, shared definitions must exist for those “things” so consumers and investors can interact in ways that yield efficient, ethical, and socially desirable outcomes.

Problems have emerged in contemporary finance with the proliferation of “black boxes,” which, according to MacKenzie, are those “devices, practices, or organizations that are opaque to outsiders, often because their contents are regarded as ‘technical.’ ”[38] Black-box finance is problematic both from technical and ethical perspectives. The technical challenges they present have been observed in the governance problems of financial firms where executives, in some cases, were unaware of their companies’ risk levels or general market positions, which often were determined by lower-level and more technical traders with questionable ethics or inadequate knowledge. Ethically, the challenges of black-box finance are even greater. Blind to what goes on in key pockets of the organization, management has difficulty discerning whether behavior is ethical (or even legal) while regulators and investors are levels yet removed. While the black-box metaphor is useful for comprehending the challenges of modernity, MacKenzie nonetheless notes that modern acquiescence to the black-box paradigm is “unsatisfactory intellectually.” Worse, “not to examine the contents of black boxes is to miss a critical part of how societies are constructed.”[39] Missing the “how” of social construction, we become more dependent on experts and those boxes they construct for the “what” and the “why.”

A few ethicists and theologians have attempted to open these black boxes in the postcrisis period.[40] Yet the divide between financial language and that of ethics and theology has grown so great that it limits possibilities for dialogue concerning critical issues that have been revealed. It is not only the technical nature of financial language that contributes to this impasse, however. There is also a general “lack of normative terminology in academic discourse relating to business” as well as “the lack of a moral language which people feel comfortable with”[41] that creates a block between ethics-theology and business disciplines, especially regarding finance. Lack of normative terminology in business makes religious and moral perspectives on commercial and financial values and practices more imperative; and it insists that ethicists, theologians, and philosophers must engage finance from their distinct *normative* positions, avoiding the temptation to adopt the language of the discipline to gain credibility. The credibility of religious and moral voices comes from their grounding in traditions that offer alternative, vitally needed ways of thinking about the financial world.

If performativity theory is accurate, then how we talk about economics and finance helps determine the kind of culture in which we live. In the case of finance, the barrage of technical terminology acts as shrink-wrap, protecting both the contents and the content-experts that manage financial black boxes from those who might question either the ethics or rationality of what happens in them. Absent a balanced rhetoric for assessing financial processes, discourse tends to be divided between the technical language of financial professionals and the negative rhetoric of many critics who emphasize finance’s inaccessibility and “abstractness.”[42] This immense discursive gap poses unique problems for financial ethics.

Alan Perlman, who as a forensic expert and "academically trained linguist" is well suited to observe the financialization of public discourse, notes that

> linguistic obscurity is a growth stock, especially today, when the very abstractness of electronic wealth allows infinite machinations and manipulations. The language that describes all of this can become so complex that the true workings of financial activities and investment instruments will elude people who lack the patience to read—and sophistication to understand—all the fine print (i.e., 99.9% of us).[43]

However financially educated the general population becomes, those financial professionals who spend their lives trying to outperform their rivals will stay ahead of the game and, of greater concern, often ahead of regulators charged with enforcing the rules. Rhetorical control of the industry and its influence on public discourse and policy are major components of an increasingly noncompetitive structure that coerces compliance.

Specialized language adds to the complexity endemic to the mass, modern economy, engendering feelings of helplessness that financialization exploits. Complexity and the numbing effect of bureaucracy in "a system that thrives on abstraction and boredom" become the greatest challenges to individual ethics. As Nelson asserts, "to the extent ... that people associate economics with calculation and impersonality, the bodily responses we generally rely on to alert ourselves to ethical concerns may become even more suppressed." Finance is perhaps the most impersonal and calculative element of the modern global economy—one that anesthetizes ethical senses to developments that make economic life less humane; finance uses language to deaden our ethical responses to its excesses. And that language need not be highly technical or obfuscatory to have negative social and ethical consequences. Jennifer Szalai observes how the system does not require falsification or overt deceit; between lawyers and financial specialists, the ability to obscure the actual obligations of parties or the risks involved in financial contracts "could be buried in the footnotes and, with some clever wording, made sufficiently dull to ensure that they would barely be seen as red flags."[44] Szalai's observation suggests that not only esoteric financial language but, in some cases, rhetorical banality *in droves* overwhelms parties, expanding the divide in financial knowledge and, thus, power.

Psychologists and linguists offer a reason for the insular nature of financial language with respect to religious and moral traditions. They have shown how the "language of business," in general, is founded on theoretically neutral and often "sanitized" terms that dissuade people from making ethical judgments about commercial activities, contributing to a kind of "moral muteness."[45] But muteness does not imply moral stasis. Anthony Giddens observes a "double hermeneutic" reinforced by language that both shapes and is shaped by the reality with which it interacts.[46] Miller expounds something like this double hermeneutic with respect to self-interest in Western culture. The "norm" as it has evolved "specifies self-interest both is and ought to be a powerful determinant of behavior.... In particular, it leads people to act and speak as though they care more about their material self-interest than they do."[47] The hermeneutic shapes our assumptions about reality; periodically, however, individuals awaken to distortions that belie our true nature. Occasionally, this awakening prompts forms of rebellion. Hence, the Occupy Movement tried to break the grip of an oppressive corporate discourse in finance by using hand signals and simple terminology in intergroup communication, famously (and comically) revealed in comedian Stephen Colbert's interview of the "leaders" of this leaderless movement.[48]

The grip of rhetoric over values extends beyond the financial realm and can be equally obscure and behavior influencing in other fields. Heggen and Wellard observe the "impact of neo-classical economic discourses on healthcare practices," which can be seen "in the adoption of the new language ... of the market place in the clinical environment."[49] They note the effectiveness of economic rhetoric in "subordinating other discourses" and how "this subordination has increased the distance nurses create between themselves and patients."[50]

Similarly, University of Massachusetts Boston scholar Carol Cohn relates how the specialized language used in the defense industry limited her ability to voice ethical concerns: "The better I became at this (insider) discourse, the more difficult it became for me to express my own ideas and values. While the language included things I had never been able to speak about before, it radically excluded others."[51]

These observations from the healthcare and defense industries have significant implications for the financialized society. That specialized language may suppress articulation of certain values implies that financial rhetoric analogously may limit the "value expression" function of financial markets. If true, it would restrict investors' ability to channel their capital to desired uses and limit their expression of religious and moral values through economic action.

Financial language erects a wall around the sector that makes it inaccessible, causing many theologians and ethicists to stay away; yet that wall is not fixed but growing. As the domain of finance expands and financial language becomes increasingly insular, the functional areas of life available to those who would offer religious or moral criticism are restricted; finance gradually becomes a law unto itself. The challenge is to unlock financial rhetoric and enrich it with religious and moral traditions capable of giving it greater meaning while illuminating the ethical shortcomings of the present financial system. Several guides, including virtue ethicists and Christian social thinkers, have offered constructs and terminology to aid such a process. The ones that follow were chosen because their thought presciently observes the challenges of a financialized society, even if unacquainted with its rhetoric, and offers constructive ideas for engaging those challenges.

Wilhelm Röpke: opposing "enmassment" and financialization

Austrian economics might seem an unlikely tradition in which to seek resources for better understanding how to re-embed the financial system in American cultural traditions and return it to the service of society. Principles of Austrian economics, in fact, might be seen as reinforcing the financialization of contemporary society because of the tradition's intense emphasis on the subjective choices of individuals in free markets and its perception of the "evolutionary" moral structure that supports markets. Friedrich Hayek's influence in twentieth-century economic thought and the political expression of his ideas in the Reagan and Thatcher administrations placed a heavy premium on individual liberty at the expense of all else, a subjectivism that left little room for traditional notions of morality and virtue. Hayek's morally fluid account of human progress has come to be associated with the Austrian School more generally; Ludwig Mises and other contributors to this so-called heterodox branch of economics held similar views that discounted actions deemed moral or virtuous unless they had proven value to group persistence in cultural evolution.[52] However, one member of the Austrian School stood out from his colleagues for recognizing the inadequacy of market forces alone in sustaining traditions essential to social and moral development. Wilhelm Röpke understood the necessity for "extra-economic" institutions, existing beyond the fray of political and economic contingency, to preserve social order and a moral economy. "Proof" of these traditions' cultural value is to come not only from their benefits to material progress but also through their contributions to a holistic vision of human flourishing. To Röpke, market determinations of their worthiness are less important than is their advancement of a "humane economy."[53]

Röpke refused to relinquish social vision to the determination of Hayek's spontaneous order, understanding that measures of human progress necessitate some ultimate end consistent not merely with an aggregation of individual goods but of a truly communal good. Believing that "ultimate values" demonstrate universal qualities, Röpke remained confident that narratives supporting a definite vision of the good society could have widespread benefits. Values such as justice, peace, and truth, which commonly bind social orders, exhibit uniformity to the extent they "assume a virtually objective character"; thus, the environmental conditions that engender such values might be observed and even replicated in different cultural contexts.[54] This mildly "constructivist" mindset is one element of Röpke's thought that distinguishes him within the Austrian tradition. Röpke implicitly argues for a narrative framework capable of directing production to a sustainable good but equally capable of promoting virtue among participants in the productive process.

Two critical components of Röpke's social thought demonstrate the relevance of his ideas to contemporary financialization. First, he recognized the tendency of powerful interests (particularly corporations), seeking surety amid insecurity, to pursue the "decoupling" of profit from social contribution (and loss from failure) in a way reflective of recent problems.[55] He showed decades in advance of the financial crisis how the "socialization of losses" weakens cultural bonds and demands a strong state, both "impartial and powerful," to "defend 'capitalism' against the 'capitalists'" who seek easy, risk-free returns at the expense of the community.[56] Röpke was adamant that market societies remain vigilant against this threat and resist the temptation to bail out large institutions for their failures.

Second, Röpke recognized a critical problem in developing an appropriate narrative configuration in modernity capable of sustaining virtue alongside material development. He considered *Vermassung*, commonly translated "enmassment," to be the dominant narrative account of an overly concentrated and quantitative capitalist system that poses an inherent threat to both traditional values and individual virtue. Röpke defines *Vermassung* as the explosion of population and "massification" of culture that, however sobering, emerges in his thought as an overwhelming force that inhibits liberty and the development of human personality.[57] Changes to the global financial system reveal many of the characteristics Röpke observed in enmassment generally: expansion of bureaucratic organizations, intense specialization of labor, immersion in numbers and technical jargon, and a general feeling of insecurity even among "experts" in finance and those made wealthy by it. Those are just some of the prescient observations that make Röpke's thought relevant today.

Röpke observed "cultural" problems resulting from the intense rationalization of economics. The mistake of many in his profession was in believing that the moral development of society could be left to the determination of a liberal or collectivist order, depending on whichever system of political economy they championed. The ethical blind spots in economics often result from the "restricted vision" of economists who generally tend "to neglect the market economy's characteristic of being merely a part of the spiritual and social total order" and try to define the whole of life by the rational outcomes of market decisions.[58] Röpke's distinctive social philosophy is built on the notion of consumer sovereignty in Mises' ideas for "market democracy"; Röpke also believed, however, that measured and responsible collective action is necessary to preserve traditional institutions, scale personalized markets for human flourishing, and enforce the rules of the game to direct economic actors toward virtue. Röpke believed any sustainable economic order must be morally regenerative and that a framework of not only legal but also proven civic institutions is indispensable to preserving ethics in economic relations.[59]

In Röpke's view, virtues necessary for the preservation of social morality, such as charity and hospitality, are formed within an ordered narrative structure that provides more than just integrating accounts of the settings in which ethical issues arise and may be resolved; they also provide positive visions of human flourishing.[60] Financialization today limits social vision to a narrow view of human possibilities, achieved largely through more efficient transfers of capital. The narrative structure for human development is similarly reduced by finance's encroachments into institutions that should provide alternative views and values to balance cultural development.

Röpke insisted that capitalist societies must adhere to the coupling principle, maintaining a clear connection between risk and reward in economic action, as much a moral as material imperative. Financialized society has strayed considerably from the coupling principle in recent years. A perception holds that incompetence and even duplicity have been rewarded as the linkage between executive pay and firm performance has eroded and as both corporations and individuals have been bailed out of imprudent decisions.[61] Röpke believed that disconnection of actions and outcomes in mass society has consequences not only for market results but also for the moral character of participants in those markets. He describes damage to that linkage as "one of the most disturbing disfigurements of the modern economic system."[62] Röpke understood that the "decoupling" of risk and reward and the willingness of those in charge to manipulate the system is directly related to ethical decline in business. The ideas and language Röpke employed in describing how market actions and their consequences must maintain close connection is potentially invaluable to a contemporary culture that has witnessed numerous bailouts and "renegotiations" to the point such action may be "anticipated." This is perhaps the most intransigent of all "moral hazards" emerging from the recent crisis.

In Röpke's social vision, civil society exists as a critical barrier to enmassment and enables the possibility of virtue. Given the similarities between enmassment and financialization, he likely would see civil society as equally important to address contemporary problems; for the present culture is experiencing both phenomena. For civil society to carry out its crucial responsibilities, however, at least some of its institutions must remain beyond the maelstrom of politics and markets so virtue can be cultivated. Röpke reiterates that, for the moral and spiritual care of society, "it is invaluable to have independent institutions beyond the arena of conflicts of interests—institutions possessing the authority of guardians of universal and lasting values which cannot be bought."[63] He offers specific examples from the areas of education, law, religion, philanthropy, and media as the types of institutions that should remain fortified from the encroachments of government and interest groups.[64] Even those institutions are subject to enmassment, however, which led Röpke to break from his Austrian colleagues to articulate a role for government in fostering environments for the development of virtue. The state should remain minimal, as Mises and Hayek advocated, but it must also remain strong enough to promote the development of the kind of citizen/consumer sovereignty necessary for self-government. In general, Röpke advocated balance achieved through what he termed "good corporativism" as necessary for a well-ordered and morally sound society.[65]

Röpke's vision of government's role should not be overemphasized. He warns that the potential "dangers of the welfare state are the more serious because there is nothing in its nature to limit it from within. On the contrary, it has the opposite and very vigorous tendency to go on expanding."[66] The propensity of governments (whether democratic or socialist) to implement ever-larger solutions to problems for which smaller solutions are called for yields a steady accumulation of policies and programs that crowd out private initiative, foster dependency, and "proletarianize" the population. Yet Röpke was more receptive to a positive role for the state in shaping society than either Mises or Hayek because he recognized that *both* public and private institutions tended to grow beyond control: while it is true there is a danger to the state's involvement in attempts to appropriately size industries and configure markets in an attempt to achieve justice and virtue, there is an even greater peril in taking a hands-off approach and allowing private producers to collude and combine with no oversight whatsoever. Moreover, Röpke's observation that proletarianism can arise even within ostensibly free societies has considerable relevance today, especially in light of contemporary's finance's technocratic tendencies that were observed in Chapter 2.

The remedy Röpke offered to what he called the "cult of the colossal," was conscious movement toward decentralization. In concert with the subsidiarity principle of Catholic Social Thought, Röpke conceived of "a shifting of the social center of gravity from above downwards; to the organic building up of society from natural and neighborly communities in a closed gradation starting with the family through parish and county to the nation. . . ."[67] Maintenance of honest competition is necessary because

> it cannot function unless it is based on certain definite ethical norms: general honesty and loyalty in business, adherence to the rules of the game, making excellence of workmanship a point of honor and instilling a certain professional pride which deems it humiliating to defraud, to bribe, or to misuse political power for one's own selfish purposes.[68]

He outlines policies of trust-busting and city planning, even extending his reform program to the "resurrection of a cultural hierarchy" to "give each rung of the ladder its appropriate place."[69]

Despite the positive role Röpke envisions for the state and his insistence that moral order requires traditional establishments, the market is the most essential component to Röpke's vision, specifically its function in coordinating and mediating values and individual aspirations for the society. Under the influence of *Vermassung*, however, with its specialization of duties and disproportions of power, the ability of markets to reconcile the "autonomy of the economic will" with that of state and society is made more difficult.[70] Additionally, specialization as a requirement of mass society is a technical configuration of production that has significant consequences for ethics. It can be an oppressive force resulting in a deprivation of experience that limits intellectual, spiritual, and moral development: "the highly specialized man is robbed of the chance to experience the fullness [sic] of his own personality; he becomes stunted."[71] Just as important, specialization limits possibilities for our *collective* development because, in the presence of powerful interest groups, individuals become convinced of their marginality to social guidance, a disincentive to participation. The role of voters, for example, becomes eviscerated for a proletarianized electorate operating in a climate of rising complexity and special interests positioned to master it. Markets are essential, therefore, not only in allocating goods but also in enabling the free expression that, ultimately, gives direction to society and secures liberty.

Röpke draws a sharp distinction between the moral potential of the truly "free market" economy and the more virtue-denying aspects of "capitalism."[72] This terminological distinction was for Röpke hugely important. The former implies an ennobling form of competition where participants succeed by their creativity and industriousness and make decisions with the good of the community in mind. The latter, then, is the historical form of economy developed in the nineteenth and twentieth centuries and too often characterized by collusion among vested interests and rent-seeking behavior that tend not only to misallocate resources but also to erode the human spirit.[73] Under this structure, civil society becomes critical to the preservation of virtue such that its composition cannot be left to the spontaneous order alone.

Civil society not only helps to forge a responsible citizenry; it also serves to check corporate power in situations where government can or will not. Importantly, the institutions that form civil society—houses of worship, civic organizations, educational institutions and others—also help define the particular narratives that facilitate ethical distinctiveness within the mass. Teleological vision, boundary definition, and rules for practical action all are cultivated to help guide the formation of individual virtue. Common characteristics between the mass society Röpke decried and the financialized society of today suggest his constructs and terminology might be equally important for articulating how to corral a financial system that increasingly dominates the people and institutions it should serve.

The "Jesuit economist" Bernard Dempsey: financialization as "institutional usury"

One of the most uniquely credentialed economists in American history was the Jesuit priest and theologian Bernard Dempsey, who received a doctorate in economics from Harvard and studied under Joseph Schumpeter. Dempsey was a disciple of Catholic Social Thought who expounded the economic wisdom of papal encyclicals and their contemporary relevance. His uniqueness lay in the grounding of his thought on interest and usury in Scholastic teaching. Dempsey's explorations of Scholastic economics led Joseph Schumpeter to cite him as a distinctive authority, combining a theologian's perspective with "professional training as an economist [that] put the methods and results of modern professional analysis at his command."[74] Dempsey's notable book, *The Functional Economy*, called attention to fiduciary devices that create wealth without concern for products produced or the workers involved in their production.[75] He recognized capital as a concept continually needing examination as organizational and technological change unfolds, an important insight into understanding the increasingly opaque financial techniques that "manufacture" wealth today.

Financial capital has significant moral and even theological implications. D. Stephen Long believes Dempsey may have been inspired by papal encyclicals such as Leo XIII's *Rerum Novarum* that warn of "voracious usury" to investigate the role of interest in the modern economy.[76] Although Dempsey's regard for Scholastic economic thought is obvious, it is in no way exclusive. He drew ideas from institutional economists like Schumpeter and honed his academic skills by learnedly critiquing the thought of Sir John Wicksell, J. M. Keynes, Ludwig Mises, and other theorists.[77] Still, he has admittedly limited influence in the academy. The Christian university at which I teach has no copy of *The Functional Economy* in its libraries. Perhaps scholars neglect Dempsey's contribution because the historical approach he took to advance economic ideas has been overwhelmed by the development of economics as a science. Another reason for Dempsey's relative obscurity likely has to do with his distinctly religious approach to economics. Yet that approach offers a timeless moral perspective that is needed today. Dempsey seamlessly traced the development of the modern economy from its classical origins through a period of profound Christian influence to show how old debates may inform contemporary issues.

In discussing religious contributions to the understanding of property rights, notions of just price, what will be called here "just credit," and the development of his idea of "institutional usury," Dempsey composes a model highly germane to the financialized economy of today. His primary point throughout *The Functional Economy* is to observe, in concert with Röpke, that, despite civilization's growth in economic sophistication, one must never lose sight of the fact that all economic processes and the capital they marshal must be oriented toward a central goal: the perfection of human persons.

As a starting point for understanding the true meaning of property, Dempsey returns to the term used by the Scholastics, *divisio rerum*, the "division of goods or resources."[78] The term was coined to illuminate the proportional division of labor and resources that occurred as the modern economy formed. According to Dempsey, "modern writing on economics and ethics does not sufficiently stress the correlative character of the two processes."[79] In a just economy, an appropriate understanding of property is key to connecting capital resources with labor in ways that contribute to the common good. Dempsey believes that the dissociation of capital from humanity is an unnatural condition that adversely affects social development.

Stressing the importance of maintaining appropriate proportionality in the division of private property and of labor, Dempsey notes that this balance promotes efficiency not only through specialization in production but also "by social economy arising from the resulting interdependence and cooperation."[80] However, he also believes that both "divisions"—of labor and of capital resources—can be overdone. Maintenance of a common goal that relates to the "whole economic process, the perfection of human persons who make up society," is necessary to ensure synchronization of the two.[81]

The concept of private property has drifted from the idea that resources should be proportionally allocated toward some common end. Contemporarily, property carries an almost purely legal connotation and is subject to contractual redefinition, often stimulated by financial innovation. The bundling of mortgages into mortgage-backed securities (MBSs) in the securitization process, for example, and the fragmentation of those securities through collateralized debt obligations, tranches, and other vehicles may well have facilitated the acceleration of capital flows and wider distribution of risk in the mortgage industry, but it has greatly complicated basic ownership rights, with significant implications for homeowners and other parties. Loss of holistic integrity in individual mortgages through securitization created situations where property ownership arrangements are so complex that there is little flexibility for modification of mortgage contracts in times of distress. For example, during the crisis a large number of Richmond, California's homeowners were underwater in their mortgages, many of which were so heavily embedded in mortgage securities that the fragmentation of ownership made renegotiation of terms difficult. In addition, the town's mayor, Gayle McLaughlin, complained of banks' unwillingness to renegotiate terms at all, prompting the city to craft an innovative relief plan. Richmond threatened to use its power of eminent domain to "persuade" investors in these mortgage securities to sell their holdings to the city at 80 percent of their present value, with the implied threat that the properties would be seized if mortgage investors refused to sell.[82]

This fragmentation of property associated with mortgage-backed securities and its loosened connection from the very people that property ostensibly should support—in this case, the families who live in the homes these mortgages represent—demonstrate the kind of inappropriate relationships between human beings and their capital warned against by Dempsey. As a significant driver of financialization, securitization has led to conditions that place division of property at odds with the human relationships it theoretically should support; in Dempsey's terms, such property divisions no longer support the "perfection of human persons." His thought is grounded in the idea that the primary purpose of "resources" of all kinds—the nonhuman factors of production—should be to facilitate human development. Separation of the two in the interest of efficiency or other considerations yields unpredictable, oftentimes negative cultural and ethical results. Overall, human participation in the mortgage market of consumers, underwriters, and mortgage analysts has remained relatively stable even as the asset component has exploded beyond control. In the MBS market as a whole, and in specific cases like Richmond, property has been divided so many times that it no longer represents the social relationships connected to it.

Dempsey observed a "paradox involved in 'property'" in that it is defined not only by proper use by the individual but also by its value to the common good.[83] He was convinced that ownership rights are not absolute, but that individual claims must be synchronized with the common interests of society. One of the enablers of financialization has been a conceptual evolution of property rights that has radically emphasized individual over common use even as it has dislodged any real connection between the two. When such asynchronous conditions develop, there may be a need for civil authority to resynchronize individual property rights with public interests, which leads Dempsey to quote Pius XI from *Quadragesimo Anno*:

> When the civil authority adjusts ownership to meet the needs of the public good it acts not as an enemy, but as the friend of private owners; for thus it effectively prevents the possessions of private property, intended by

> Nature's Author in His Wisdom for the sustaining of human life, from creating intolerable burdens and so rushing to its own destruction. It does not therefore abolish but protects private ownership, and, far from weakening the right of private property it gives it new strength.[84]

Pius's views on property suggest that governments grappling with the after effects of financial crises in which the securitization of mortgages, the explosion of derivatives, and other novel financial tools have factored heavily, must balance individual ownership rights with new forms of property to assess their impact on the common good. The benefits of enabling greater capital flows and distributing risks to investment should be balanced with the potential harm to traditional relationships, which serve not only to humanize the system but also, in cases like that of Richmond, sometimes help to untangle complex structures and reestablish stable ownership in the interests of sustainable growth.

Dempsey places particular emphasis on Catholic Social Teaching's principle of subsidiarity that insists "nothing should be done by a larger and more complex organization which can be done as well by a smaller and simpler organization."[85] He believes the broad application of subsidiarity offers a possible answer to many problems that have emerged in the modern economy. He traces the term to its Latin origin in the word *subsidium*, meaning "aid" or "assistance," and its essential connection to human welfare, asserting that "since man and his service are the sole purpose of all associations of men, every association must be designed for the service of the human persons who are its members."[86] Financialization contradicts the idea of *subsidium* because, as noted by O'Boyle, Solari, and Marangoni, "the financialization of the economy has resulted in the dominance of the logic of finance over the more substantive logic of production and a subordination of labor and community interests to capital."[87] This phenomenon defies a core principle of Catholic Social Teaching by essentially reversing the normative priority of productive inputs in which "capital strictly speaking is merely a means supportive to labor" to one in which financial capital, in particular, dominates all other forms in the interests of maximizing returns.[88] Dempsey understood this emerging reality in the 1950s as a reversal of what he saw as the "natural order" respecting the resources of production.

One potentially serious cultural change, reinforced by financialization but largely overlooked, is that one need not, but also increasingly cannot, know the social contribution of one's labor. Moreover, modes of money making have become a purely personal decision, considered to have few ramifications beyond the individual and those with whom she has immediate contact. Such attitudes run counter to the inherently communal nature of economy articulated by the Scholastics and revived by Dempsey. He believed that theologically grounded principles regarding labor, capital, usury, and other economic rudiments are not only relevant but also essential to preserving personalism and justice in the modern economy.

With regard to the financialized economy, the implication of Dempsey's Scholastic ethic is that the community holds a significant stake in the performance of work and the valuation of commodities. However much economic relations have become privatized, all activity takes place in social contexts and, just as economic practices draw on communal resources for their rational and normative content, so too the results of those practices have broader cultural consequences. Thus, value is inherently social. Betsy Jane Clary notes that in Dempsey's Scholastic view of economy,

> value is determined by a common evaluation and not by the special valuation of an individual. While each individual in the community has his own personal, subjective judgment concerning the value of a thing, the community estimate becomes the objective measure of value, on the condition that this valuation has not been unjustly arrived at.[89]

Price volatility associated with financialization, viewed through the Scholastic lens, suggests that its effects are not confined to those commodities, or the parties trading them, alone. Major price fluctuations resulting from speculative activity may have ripple effects impacting output, employment, interest rates, and other macro measures of economic performance.

This communal character of price determination has been lost in an era of economic subjectivism that encourages an affluent society to express itself through personalized consumption, ignoring the social consequences. Dempsey calls attention, however, to the unavoidable fact that "because exchange is socially necessary, money is socially necessary, and because both money and exchange are designed to serve the development of persons in community, the quantitative determination of price is necessarily social."[90] The "just price" facilitates the development of organic community in a natural social order that conforms to the Catholic principle of subsidiarity and prevents encroachments of the state into lower orders of responsibility.[91] It also assists in proper coordination of social functions by rewarding individuals for their proportionate contributions.

The social relevance of money was observed contemporarily in the mortgage crisis that, despite lessening effects, still continues to grip the country. Exuberance led to the dramatic escalation in housing prices over the past few decades and has now come home to roost with very real consequences for social groups (including American taxpayers) who had nothing to do with the original sales of these properties. "Innovative" mortgage relief programs led to charges of injustice by bondholders forced to bear the burdens of delinquencies and write downs that impact a secondary market forged by securitization. Dempsey's notion of the just price as taking into account the community's interest seems prescient in residential housing and other industries where the risks of significant price escalations extend to parties not part of the initial transactions.

Similarly, Dempsey advanced an expansive definition of usury, potentially enabling more comprehensive analysis of the ways in which modern financial methods go against Scholastic fundamentals. In some cases, creditors loan funds while retaining use of those funds; in others, funds are made available for loans to others without having resulted from actual production and in ways that often disrupt the savings-investment relationship. These situations constitute usury, according to Dempsey. Describing Dempsey's view of the harm caused by non-income-related loanable funds, Clary observes that when

> investment is made with funds which have never been income to anyone, the investment creates price disturbances. Such funds can be described as pure finance; they are pseudo-income, for they are not derived from the economic process of production. The funds give the borrower control over assets with no loss of control by others.[92]

Such arrangements may well be viewed as one of the benefits of modern financial innovation; indeed, it would seem the goal of many financial inventions. Yet Dempsey saw forms of gain without sacrifice as ultimately unstable and unsustainable. Price distortions enable situations where borrowers may receive "unearned" profits or where others benefit because of a borrower's misfortune in ways that are foreign to what he viewed as the "natural" operations of a market economy. Dempsey notes that regardless of who benefits from price disruptions brought about by these usurious practices,

> Somewhere in the economy, "windfall gains" will appear on someone's books; the economic process then has operated to produce a "gain from a loan" even though no person could be shown to have been guilty of usury. Again we have the effect of usury without the personal fault. The usury is institutional, or systemic.[93]

Much of the financial system as it has evolved likely would be seen by Dempsey as "institutional usury." Clary notes that one of Dempsey's major contributions is his extension of the Scholastic view of usury beyond a purely personal issue involving interest rates to a wider social one that has relevance even beyond the banking system.[94] Modern banking has evolved from the staid period of local institutions taking in deposits from customers and holding their mortgages for the duration into a highly concentrated yet amorphous industry dependent on the kinds of "unjustified gains" that Dempsey saw as exclusive of the production process, involving no real sacrifice by anyone. Making money by mastering financial complexity appears to have become a goal of banking and finance. The decline of real investment opportunities and the centrality of the Federal Reserve to the private banking system have altered the industry, enabling banks to charge interest well above what Dempsey would see as the "just rate" and to receive interest on reserves from the Fed that are kept out of circulation and allow banks to extract "a usurious 'liquidity premium' from taxpayers."[95]

Modern finance views innovations such as derivatives and securitized investment instruments as advances in economic understanding with enormous potential to increase wealth and development. Dempsey's sympathy with Scholastic principles makes it likely he would see such innovations as defying theologically grounded fundamentals, with inevitably adverse results, even as he might have viewed recent attempts to counteract the financial crisis as proliferating usurious gains and ignoring longer-term effects. Consider, for example, the moral hazard involved in massive bailouts of individuals and corporations. From these perspectives, modern financial techniques that expand money and credit with little to no sacrifice of existing resources and with no tie to savings are, by definition, usurious.

Preoccupation with financial capital at the expense of other factors of production has enabled certain innovations to proceed with little concern as to the cultural consequences. Finance is changing according to the dictates of reason while losing sight of the human element that for Dempsey, as for Röpke, should be the central focus of all economic activity.

Robert Solomon: bringing finance into conversation with virtue

The late University of Texas philosophy professor Robert Solomon is notable for his attempts to bring an "Aristotelian approach" to business ethics. His seminal *Ethics and Excellence* suggested that Milton Friedman got it all wrong when he declared, in 1970, that the social responsibility of the corporation is simply to increase its profits. By that logic, according to Solomon, Friedman must have viewed the Salamon Brothers trading floor as the "epitome of social responsibility" back in the late 1980s when its freshly minted MBAs were making "a travesty of the age-old business wisdom that only hard work and perseverance lead to success."[96] Solomon's sarcasm is obvious, but he makes an important point by showing the decline of traditional American business virtues, and that some industries are more damaging than others in that regard.

In Aristotelian style, Solomon strongly implies a hierarchy of goods (and professions) in the business world in which stock and commodity trading fall far down the list. He asks a simple question: "How did we so shift our attention from the classic business virtues of productivity and prosperity to the dubious virtues of the trading floor?"[97] Solomon quickly explains himself by noting that the yuppie financiers are not "amoral monsters"—"there were no congenital Midas-like symptoms evident in most of the trainee traders-to-be."[98] These were mostly kids fresh out of graduate school who took advantage of opportunities afforded them and did their jobs to the best of their abilities. But Solomon is also willing to state something that has become highly unfashionable since neoclassical economics became dominant: those young professionals do not earn their keep. He supports that bold claim with the confessions of the now-famous Michael Lewis, the author of *Liar's Poker* and *Flash Boys*, who today earns his money writing exposés about his former profession as a Wall Street trader. Concerning his time in high finance, Lewis writes, "I felt not like I was going to work but rather picking up my winnings at a lottery."[99] Lewis describes an environment in which greed and ego predominated; if a new trader "could make millions of dollars … he became the most revered of all species: a Big Swinging Dick.… Everyone wanted to be a Big Swinging Dick, even the women."[100] Solomon embellishes Lewis's description by saying that, in the Wall Street trading culture, "male high-school lockerroom sensibilities are elevated as golden keys to success" and "sentence-clogging profanity is employed as a mark of sophistication."[101] He attempts, apparently, to ease the concerns of any finance majors among his readers by stating that this brash, profit-crazed attitude is not unique to the trading floor but rather an extreme example of the wider culture's money obsession.

Solomon proposes to end what he calls "Cowboy Capitalism" by extending the ethics of virtue into the modern corporation. If the corporation will not come to Aristotle, Solomon will gladly bring Aristotle to the corporation. To do so requires basic changes in the culture of American business. Corporations adopting Aristotelian principles must be about more than profit; they must recognize their existence in community—not merely corporate culture but the wider culture of humanity—and they must engage teleology to exist for purposes that go beyond making profits.[102] Perhaps most important, the Aristotelian corporation must view business as a practice, as "a human institution in service to humans and not as a marvelous machine or in terms of the mysterious 'magic' of the market."[103]

Undoubtedly astonishing to those who accept Friedman's view of the corporation, Solomon dares to speak of it as a possible realm for human flourishing (*eudaemonia*), a place for self-actualization that brings happiness not from money making but rather from the development of character and integrity. In his view, these virtues are equally important traits for giant corporations as they are for individuals.[104] Much like Röpke, Solomon sees the power of narrative in the development of character and virtue:

> Aristotelian ethics is an ethics of virtue, an ethics in which personal and corporate integrity occupies the place of central concern and focus. But virtue and integrity are not to be found in a vacuum. They do not appear miraculously in the atomistic individual, they cannot be contracted or commissioned, nor are they the special province of saints.... A virtue has a place in a social context, in a human practice, and accordingly it is essentially part of a fabric that goes beyond the individual and binds him or her to a larger human network.[105]

Given the importance of human community even in the workplace, one might ask why so few have embraced this vision of a virtuous Aristotelian corporation. One answer Solomon provides is that powerful but often denigrating metaphors in business shape human attitudes such that higher aims seem unapproachable. "The pursuit of integrity is determined from the start," Solomon writes, "by such dangerous myths and metaphors about business, corporations, and the people who work for them."[106] Descriptions of corporations as "legal fictions" or "financial juggernauts" are, sadly, complemented by equally inhumane descriptions of individuals in economic theory such as "rational actors" and "utility maximizers." These harmful terms dash all hope for a more virtuous economy. Solomon recognizes just as Röpke and Dempsey that the symbols and language used to conduct business and describe economic relationships can do much damage even before the "game" (perhaps Solomon's most hated metaphor for business) has begun. Changing the discourse about business was, for Solomon, the first step toward nurturing an ethics of virtue so that it would take root in the financial field, which nourishes all others.

Conclusion

The question of human limits inevitably emerges in discussions of economy from religious and ethical perspectives. Theologian William Cavanaugh sees the problems that have arrived with financialization resulting not from greed and materialism so much as the human desire to transcend material boundaries. Recent excesses have been caused by vain attempts "to overcome the limits of the material world by making wealth multiply without any increase in real material production" (a form of *creatio ex nihilo*). Similarly, he sees the crisis emerging not from a failure of trust "but more fundamentally [from] the attempt to *overcome the necessity of trust*."[107] The explosion of derivatives that eclipsed $540 trillion in 2011,[108] exceeding by many times the value of global gross domestic product, resulted from denial of human limits and the application of human ingenuity in attempts to achieve an impossible security. The "dream" was an existence without need for reliance on human relationships beyond basic legal obligations. The tenuous connection of derivatives and other financial instruments with the "natural" world incites the human imagination, but it causes those who place great hope in them to lose sight of the appropriate ground for all economic relationships.

Perhaps the financial attitude most dissonant with Christian theology and ethics, in particular, stems from the heightened anxiety among not only professionals but also consumers and individual investors engendered by modern finance. The instructions in Matthew and Philippians to "Be not anxious" about wealth or the future are every day violated by our participation in the financialized society. Financial rhetoric furthers this anxiety with disquieting terms that forged the "crisis language" of the past decade and by simply overwhelming individuals with a vernacular that creates confusion in their daily lives.

Religious and ethical language can rebalance discourse to account for the rising influence of financial rhetoric. The voices of theologians and ethicists can inform business disciplines generally so they can better reflect the fullness of human beings and the communities in which they live. Yet theologians and ethicists must do the hard work of engaging financial issues directly, and, from the vantage points of their distinct traditions, uncover the limits of discourse and its outright distortions of what is real. In this regard, analysts and regulators are not likely to uncover the actual reasons for the financial crisis; discovering those reasons requires a deeper understanding of human failings and an appropriate conception of humanity's place in creation. Trust exists, for example, as a constraint in financial models, the need for which causes inefficiencies and limits the free flow of capital. Yet, from many religious and ethical perspectives, trust undergirds life in community and provides the moral basis for human action. Unfortunately, the recent crisis revealed that kind of trust to be deficient.

In addition to balancing financial rhetoric, religious leaders from across traditions need to develop theologies of scarcity, risk, money, and other concepts that help guide those who desire to express their values through capital.[109] Virtue must resume its conversation with finance, deconstructing damaging metaphors and replacing them with an upright vocabulary that inspires both those who work in the industry as well as those who profit from it. Considering the depths to which the financial industry recently has sunk, its potential is that much greater to reemerge, chastened yet revived. Indeed, the growing influence of the financial industry on American society as a whole suggests that an ethical revival in this sector may issue something grander: a more just society that rewards labor, reviles fraud, and smiles on those who ask a fair price.

Notes

1 Charles A. McDaniel, Jr., "Theology of the 'Real Economy': Christian Ethics in an Age of Financialization," *Journal of Religion and Business Ethics* vol. 2, no. 2 (2011); available at http://via.library.depaul.edu/cgi/viewcontent.cgi?article=1030&context=jrbe.

2 She defines performatives as "that which enacts or brings about what it names." De Goede notes how "understanding finance as a performative practice suggests that processes of knowledge and interpretation do not exist in addition to, or of secondary importance to, 'real' material financial structures, but are precisely *the way in which 'finance' materializes*" (emphasis De Goude's). See Marieke De Goede, *Virtue, Fortunes, and Faith: A Genealogy of Finance*, Borderlines series, vol. 24 (Minneapolis: University of Minnesota Press, 2005).

3 De Goede quotes Foucault that "we must produce truth in order to produce wealth in the first place"; in *Virtue, Fortunes, and Faith*, 9 (emphasis De Goede's).

4 De Goede writes about the power of "economic necessity" in shaping discourse in "Beyond Economism in International Political Economy," *Review of International Studies* 29, no. 1 (January 2003): 81.

5 Fabrizio Ferraro, Jeffrey Pfeffer, and Robert I. Sutton, "Economics Language and Assumptions: How Theories Can Become Self-Fulfilling," *Academy of Management Review* 30, no. 1 (January 2005), 12.

6 Ferraro, Pfeffer, and Sutton, "Economics Language and Assumptions," 12.

7 M. Rubenstein, "Nonparametric tests of alternative option pricing models using all reported trades and quotes on the 30 most active CBOE option classes from August 23, 1976 through August 31, 1978," *Journal of Finance* 40 (1985): 455–80; cited in Ferraro, Pfeffer, and Sutton, "Economics Language and Assumptions," 13.

8 Donald MacKenzie and Yuval Millo, "Negotiating a Market, Performing Theory: The Historical Sociology of a Financial Derivatives Exchange," *American Journal of Sociology*, 109, no. 1 (July 2003): 125–6.

9 MacKenzie and Millo, "Negotiating a Market, Performing Theory," 127.

10 Quoted in MacKenzie and Millo, "Negotiating a Market, Performing Theory," 121.

11 Donald MacKenzie, "Opening the Black Boxes of Global Finance," *Review of International Political Economy* 12, no. 4 (October 2005): 559.

12 MacKenzie, "Opening the Black Boxes of Global Finance," 559. He cites an article in *The Guardian* that offers an example of how the S&P500 Index dropped in September 2002 to a level that many of the chartists had established as a bottom and then reversed as being seen by many market watchers as evidence of chartism. See

Neil Hume, "Hocus Pocus Saves the Day," *The Guardian* September (2002) 6: 24; cited in MacKenzie, "Opening the Black Boxes of Global Finance," 559–60.

13 Klaus Schaeck, "Behavioral Finance, Behavioral Bias, and Market Anomalies: Implications for Bank Managers," *Corporate Finance Review*, vol. 9, no. 4 (January–February 2005): 11.

14 Schaeck, "Behavioral Finance, Behavioral Bias, and Market Anomalies," 5.

15 Steven Rattner, "The Dangerous Notion that Debt Doesn't Matter," *New York Times* (January 20, 2012); available at www.nytimes.com/2012/01/22/opinion/sunday/the-dangerous-notion-that-debt-doesnt-matter.html?_r=0.

16 Paul Krugman, "Nobody Understands Debt," *New York Times* (January 1, 2012); available at www.nytimes.com/2012/01/02/opinion/krugman-nobody-understands-debt.html?_r=0.

17 Nigel Thrift, "It's the Romance, not the Finance, that makes the Business Worth Pursuing," *Economy and Society*, 30 (2001): 430; quoted in Marieke De Goede, "Beyond Economism in International Political Economy."

18 Murray Davis, "That's Interesting! Towards a Phenomenology of Sociology and a Sociology of Phenomenology," *Philosophy of the Social Sciences* 1 (1971): 309–13.

19 For example, see Gary S. Becker, "Religions Thrive in a Free Market, Too," *Bloomberg Businessweek* [Businessweek Archives] (January 14, 1996); available at www.businessweek.com/stories/1996–01–14/religions-thrive-in-a-free-market-too.

20 "The Social Responsibility of Business is to Increase its Profits," *New York Times Magazine* (September 13, 1970). A copy of Friedman's article can be located at www.colorado.edu/studentgroups/libertarians/issues/friedman-soc-resp-business.html.

21 I teach a capstone class in my university's "interdisciplinary core" program that is commonly attended by business students. It has been revealing to encounter so many students who perceive Friedman's idea of the corporation to be "truth" rather than one among many possible interpretations. The force of Friedman's idea of the corporation is reaffirmed each semester that I teach that class.

22 Ferraro, Pfeffer, and Sutton, "Economics Language and Assumptions," 9.

23 Ferraro, Pfeffer, and Sutton, "Economics Language and Assumptions," 9.

24 Ferraro, Pfeffer, and Sutton, "Economics Language and Assumptions," 12.

25 Isaac Ehrlich, "The Deterrent Effect of Capital Punishment: A Question of Life and Death," *American Economic Review* vol. 65, no. 3 (June 1975): 397–417; cited in James Arnt Aune, *Selling the Free Market: The Rhetoric of Economic Correctness* (New York: The Guilford Press, 2001), 21.

26 Aune, *Selling the Free Market*, 77, 111, 135–6.

27 Aune, *Selling the Free Market*, 177 (emphasis Aune's).

28 De Goede, "Beyond Economism in International Political Economy," 81.

29 As described by Robert W. Kolb in "Ethical Implications of Finance," in *Finance Ethics: Critical Issues in Theory and Practice*, ed. John Boatright (Hoboken, NJ: John Wiley & Sons, 2010), 23.

30 Nelson cites Helena Norberg-Hodge, "Buddhism in the Global Economy," in *Mindfulness in the Marketplace: Compassionate Responses to Consumerism*, ed. A. H. Badiner. (Berkeley, Parallax Press, 2002). 15–27; Murray Bookchin, "What is Social Ecology?" in *Environmental Philosophy: From Animal Rights to Radical Ecology*, ed. M. E. Zimmerman, J. B. Callicot, K. J. Warren, I. J. Klaver, and J. Clark. (Upper Saddle River, Pearson Prentice Hall, 2005), 462–78; and David Watson, "Against the Megamachine: Empire and Earth," in *Environmental Philosophy: From Animal Rights to Radical Ecology*, ed. M. E. Zimmerman, *et al.*, 470–95; in Julie Nelson, "Poisoning the Well, or How Economic Theory Damages Moral Imagination," Global Development and Environment Institute, Working Paper No. 12–07 (October 2012), 6–7; available at http://ase.tufts.edu/gdae/Pubs/wp/12–07NelsonPoisoning-Well.pdf.

31 Jürgen Habermas, *The Theory of Communicative Action*. Boston, Beacon, 1981: cited in Nelson, "Poisoning the Well," 6.
32 Nelson, "Poisoning the Well," 6. Nelson concludes that "money and markets are thoroughly human and social creations." See Nelson, "Poisoning the Well," 6.
33 De Goede notes how "images of global finance as a predatory and immortal agency homogenize financial institutions and markets and assume unproblematic boundaries to this system." Scc "Beyond Economism," 82.
34 Willard Stawski II, *Kids, Parents & Money: Teaching Personal Finance from Piggy Bank to Prom* (New York: John Wiley and Sons, 2000); cited in Randy Martin, *Financialization of Daily Life* (Philadelphia: Temple University Press, 2002), 57–61.
35 Martin cites Carol Bosworth, "Teaching Children Money Habits for Life," http://outreach.missouri.edu/extensioninfoline/youth&family/money_habits4life.html; and Sharon Dawes and Tammy Dunrud, "Teaching Children Money Habits for Life," Children and Money Series, University of Minnesota Extension, 1997, p. 2, www.extension.umn.edu/distribution/youthdevelopment/DA6116.html; in *Financialization of Daily Life*, 64–5.
36 Edward M. Clift, "The Rhetoric of Economics," in *The SAGE Handbook of Rhetorical Studies*, eds. Andrea A. Lunsford, Kirt H. Wilson, and Rosa A. Eberly, (Thousand Oaks, CA: SAGE Publications, 2009), 210.
37 Denise Baden and Ian A. Harwood, "Terminology Matters: A Critical Exploration of Corporate Social Responsibility Terms," *Journal of Business Ethics* vol. 116, no. 3 (2013): 615.
38 MacKenzie, "Opening the Black Boxes of Global Finance," 555.
39 MacKenzie, "Opening the Black Boxes of Global Finance," 557.
40 See Charles McDaniel, "Theology of the 'Real Economy.'"
41 Baden and Harwood, "Terminology Matters," 619.
42 Max Haiven offers a Marxian perspective in suggesting that some critics of financialization do a disservice by implying that the powerful and sometimes destructive instruments and processes that have emerged are "entirely imaginary." Haiven believes that such descriptions deflect attention from the underlying economic inequalities that are the primary source of problems and lead us to desire a return to "normal," which he describes as the system of "gross economic inequality that caused the crisis in the first place." See Max Haiven, "Finance as Capital's Imagination? Reimagining Value and Culture in an Age of Fictitious Capital and Crisis," *Social Text* 108, 29, no. 3 (Fall 2011): 95.
43 Alan Perlman, "Forensic Linguistics: Financial Rhetoric and the Intent to Deceive," (n.d.); available at www.experts.com/Articles/Forensic-Linguistics-Financial-Rhetoric-Intent-to-Deceive-By-Alan-Perlman.
44 Jennifer Szalai, "The Banality of Avarice: Why the Finance Industry Never Had to Lie," *Harper's Magazine* (February 2012): 77.
45 Frederick B. Bird and James A. Waters, "The Moral Muteness of Managers," *California Management Review*, vol. 32, no. 1, (1989): 73–88; cited in Baden and Harwood, "Terminology Matters," 619.
46 Anthony Giddens, *Social Theory and Modern Sociology* (Cambridge: Polity Press, 1987); cited in Baden and Harwood, "Terminology Matters," 622.
47 Miller, D. T. (1999). "The Norm of Self-interest." *American Psychologist*. 54(12), 1053; quoted in Baden and Harwood, "Terminology Matters," 622. Baden and Harwood note how it is "clear from the literature that any term that does not explicitly denote a normative focus will tend to be co-opted by the dominant paradigm of instrumental economic rationality, with the ethical component becoming subservient to the economic component." See Baden and Harwood, "Terminology Matters," 624.
48 See http://thecolbertreport.cc.com/videos/d4hmi3/colbert-super-pac--stephen-colbert-occupies-occupy-wall-street-pt–1.

49 K. Heggen and S. Wellard, "Increased Unintended Patient Harm in Nursing Practice as a Consequence of the Dominance of Economic Discourses," *International Journal of Nursing Studies* 41 (2004): 296.

50 Heggen and Wellard, "Increased Unintended Patient Harm," 297.

51 Carol Cohn, "Slick Ems, Glick Ems, Christmas Trees and Cookie Cutters—Nuclear Language and How we Learned to Pat the Bomb," *Bulletin of the Atomic Scientists*, 43(5) (June 1987): 22.

52 Some scholars take exception to the association of moral dynamism with the Austrian School. Some classify Hayek as a conservative or even a traditionalist conservative despite his protests to the contrary in "Why I am not a Conservative" because Hayek emphasized competition among "traditions" as the foundation for social progress (See Edward Feser, "Hayek on Tradition," *Journal of Libertarian Studies* 17, no. 1 (Winter 2003): 17–56). Yet Hayek states that "conservatives are inclined to use the powers of government to prevent change or to limit its rate to whatever appeals to the more timid mind" (see "Why I am Not a Conservative"; excerpt from *The Constitution of Liberty*; available at http://press.uchicago.edu/books/excerpt/2011/hayek_constitution.html). Because of Hayek's statement that even traditional values—beyond property rights and the rule of law—are almost infinitely malleable, I accept Hayek's self-description as a liberal.

53 Röpke's holistic economic vision is best articulated in his most popular work, *A Humane Economy: The Social Framework of the Free Market* (Chicago: Henry Regnery Company, 1960).

54 Röpke, *The Moral Foundations of Civil Society* (New Brunswick, N.J.: Transaction Publishers, 2002 [Reprint of the 1996 edition]), 76.

55 Contemporarily, socialization of losses by large financial firms has regained public attention. Whether through political connections or other means, some market participants were able to do so by shifting risks to society as a whole, the most obvious examples being those "too big to fail" banks that engaged in highly risky investments with the backing of the federal government.

56 Röpke, *Economics of the Free Society*, trans. Patrick M. Boarman (Chicago: Henry Regnery Company, 1963), 237.

57 Röpke, *A Humane Economy*, 39–44.

58 Röpke, *A Humane Economy*, 93.

59 Röpke, *The Moral Foundations of Civil Society*, 31.

60 In "The Economic Necessity of Freedom," Röpke stated that the laws of market economics can only work "within a society that admits of the human virtues which issue in true service (not just 'service to the customer'), devotion, charity, hospitality, and in the sacrifices which genuine communities demand." See Röpke, *Economics of the Free Society*, 234.

61 Corporations such as AIG were bailed out from the consequences of their bad decisions even as many mortgage and credit companies were pressured by government to renegotiate loan terms that consumers had willingly accepted.

62 Röpke, *Economics of the Free Society*, 236.

63 Röpke, *A Humane Economy*, 149.

64 Röpke, *A Humane Economy*, 149.

65 Röpke, *The Social Crisis of Our Time* (Chicago: The University of Chicago Press, 1950), 94.

66 Röpke, *A Humane Economy*, 162.

67 Röpke, *The Moral Foundations of Civil Society*, 154.

68 Röpke, *The Social Crisis of Our Time*, 133.

69 Röpke, *The Moral Foundations of Civil Society*, 154.

70 Röpke, *The Social Crisis of Our Time*, 103.

71 Röpke, *Economics of the Free Society*, 63.

72 Röpke, *A Humane Economy*, 83.

73 Röpke, *The Moral Foundations of Civil Society*, 7.
74 Joseph Schumpeter, " Introduction," to Bernard Dempsey, *Interest and Usury* (Washington: American Council on Public Affairs, 1943), vii.
75 Bernard Dempsey, *The Functional Economy: The Bases of Economic Organization*, (Englewood Cliffs, N.J.: Prentice Hall, Inc., 1958), 189–95.
76 D. Stephen Long, "Bernard Dempsey's Theological Economics: Usury, Profit, and Human Fulfillment," *Theological Studies*, 57, no. 4, (1996): 700.
77 Dempsey, *Interest and Usury*, 41–62; and Long, "Bernard Dempsey's Theological Economics," 700.
78 Dempsey, *The Functional Economy*, 189.
79 Dempsey, *The Functional Economy*, 189.
80 Dempsey, *The Functional Economy*, 190.
81 Dempsey, *The Functional Economy*, 190.
82 Penelope Lemov, "Foreclosure and the Eminent Domain Solution Explained," *Governing the States and Localities*: *Public Money* (August 15, 2013); available at www.governing.com/columns/public-finance/col-foreclosure-eminent-domain-solution.html. The inability to modify mortgage loans has led to difficulties in resolving a significant component of the recent crisis and to a rather arbitrary shifting of burdens that appear to impose significant moral hazards in the process of homeownership. In a report to the Federal Reserve Bank of Chicago, researchers found

> bank-held loans … 26% to 36% more likely to be renegotiated than comparable securitized mortgages (4.2 to 5.7% in absolute terms). Also, modifications of bank-held loans are more efficient: conditional on a modification, bank-held loans have lower post-modification default rates by 9% (3.5% in absolute terms).
>
> S. Agarwal, *et al.*, (2011, January). "The Role of Securitization in Mortgage Renegotiation." Federal Reserve Bank of Chicago, working paper 2011–02. Retrieved from www.chicagofed.org/digital_assets/publications/working_papers/2011/wp2011_02.pdf

83 Dempsey, *The Functional Economy*, 191.
84 Quoted in Dempsey, *The Functional Economy*, 192.
85 David A. Bosnich, "The Principle of Subsidiarity," *Religion & Liberty*, vol. 6, no. 4 (July-August 1996); available at www.acton.org/pub/religion-liberty/volume-6-number-4.
86 Dempsey, *The Functional Economy*, 281.
87 E. J. O'Boyle, S. Solari, and G. Marangoni, "Financialization: Critical Assessment Based on Catholic Social Teaching," *International Journal of Social Economics*, vol. 37, no. 1 (2010): 6.
88 O'Boyle, Solari, and Marangoni, "Financialization," 9.
89 Betsy Jane Clary, "Institutional Usury and the Banks," *Review of Social Economy* vol. 69, no. 4 (December 2011): 423.
90 Dempsey, *The Functional Economy*, 421.
91 Dempsey, *The Functional Economy*, 424.
92 Clary, "Institutional Usury and the Banks," 429.
93 Dempsey, *Interest and Usury*, 207; cited in Clary, "Institutional Usury and the Banks," 429.
94 Clary, "Institutional Usury and the Banks," 429–30.
95 Clary, "Institutional Usury and the Banks," 436.
96 Robert C. Solomon, *Ethics and Excellence: Cooperation and Integrity in Business* (New York: Oxford University Press.1992), 13–21. Regarding Friedman's landmark declaration, see footnote 22.
97 Solomon, *Ethics and Excellence*, 15.
98 Solomon, *Ethics and Excellence*, 15.

99 Michael Lewis, *Liar's Poker* (New York: Norton, 1989), x; quoted in Solomon, *Ethics and Excellence*, 15.
100 Lewis, *Liar's Poker*, 46; quoted in Solomon, *Ethics and Excellence*, 17.
101 Solomon, *Ethics and Excellence*, 17.
102 Solomon, *Ethics and Excellence*, 103.
103 Solomon, *Ethics and Excellence*, 104.
104 Solomon, *Ethics and Excellence*, 105–6.
105 Solomon, *Ethics and Excellence*, 108–9.
106 Solomon, *Ethics and Excellence*, 109.
107 William Cavanaugh, "Only Christianity Can Save Economics," *ABC Religion and Ethics* (April 15, 2011); available at www.abc.net.au/religion/articles/2011/04/15/3192406.htm (emphasis Cavanaugh's).
108 A. Rashad Abdel Khalik, *Accounting for Risk, Hedging, and Complex Contracts* (New York: Routledge, 2014), xxiv.
109 McDaniel, "Theology of the 'Real Economy.'"

Bibliography

Agarwal, Sumit, Gene Amromin, Ben-David Itzhak, Souphala Chomsisengphet, and Douglas D. Evanoff. "The Role of Securitization in Mortgage Renegotiation." Working Paper 2011–02, Federal Reserve Bank of Chicago, 2011. www.chicagofed.org/digital_assets/publications/working_papers/2011/wp2011_02.pdf; accessed on April 1, 2015.

Aune, James Arnt. *Selling the Free Market: The Rhetoric of Economic Correctness*. New York: The Guilford Press, 2001.

Baden, Denise, and Ian A. Harwood. "Terminology Matters: A Critical Exploration of Corporate Social Responsibility Terms." *Journal of Business Ethics* 116, no. 3 (2013): 615–27.

Becker, Gary S. "Religions Thrive in a Free Market, Too." *Bloomberg Businessweek*, January 14, 1996. Businessweek Archives. www.businessweek.com/stories/1996-01-14/religions-thrive-in-a-free-market-too; accessed on September 14, 2014.

Bird, Frederick B., and James A. Waters. "The Moral Muteness of Managers." *California Management Review* 32, no. 1 (1989): 73.

Bookchin, Murray. "What Is Social Ecology?" In *Environmental Philosophy: From Animal Rights to Radical Ecology* edited by M. E. Zimmerman, J. B. Callicot, K. J. Warren, I. J. Klaver, and J. Clark, 462–78. Upper Saddle River, Pearson Prentice Hall, 2005.

Bosnich, David A. "The Principle of Subsidiarity." *Religion & Liberty* 6, no. 4 (August 1996): 9–10; available at www.acton.org/pub/religion-liberty/volume-6-number-4; accessed on January 6, 2015.

Cavanaugh, William. "Only Christianity Can Save Economics." *ABC Religion and Ethics*. www.abc.net.au/religion/articles/2011/04/15/3192406.htm; accessed September 16, 2014.

Clary, Betsy Jane. "Institutional Usury and the Banks." *Review of Social Economy* 69, no. 4 (December 2011): 419–38.

Clift, Edward M. "The Rhetoric of Economics." In *The SAGE Handbook of Rhetorical Studies*, edited by Andrea A. Lunsford, Kirt H. Wilson, and Rosa A. Eberly, 197–214. Thousand Oaks, CA: SAGE Publications, 2009.

Cohn, C. "Slick Ems, Glick Ems, Christmas Trees and Cookie Cutters—Nuclear Language and How We Learned to Pat the Bomb." *Bulletin of the Atomic Scientists* 43, no. 5 (1987): 17–24.

Colbert, Stephen. "Colbert Super PAC – Stephen Colbert Occupies Occupy Wall Street Pt. 1." *The Colbert Report*. Comedy Central, October 31, 2011. http://thecolbertreport.cc.com/videos/d4hmi3/colbert-super-pac—-stephen-colbert-occupies-occupy-wall-street-pt—1; accessed on April 15, 2014.
Davis, Murray S. "That's Interesting: Towards a Phenomenology of Sociology and a Sociology of Phenomenology." *Philosophy of the Social Sciences* 1, no. 4 (December 1971): 309–34.
Dempsey, Bernard. *Interest and Usury*. Washington: American Council on Public Affairs, 1943.
Dempsey, Bernard W. *The Functional Economy: The Bases of Economic Organization*. Englewood Cliffs, N.J.: Prentice Hall, 1958.
Ehrlich, Isaac. "The Deterrent Effect of Capital Punishment: A Question of Life and Death." *American Economic Review* 65, no. 3 (June 1975): 397–417.
Ferraro, Fabrizio, Jeffrey Pfeffer, and Robert I. Sutton. "Economics Language and Assumptions: How Theories Can Become Self-Fulfilling." *Academy of Management Review* 30, no. 1 (January 2005): 8–24.
Feser, Edward. "Hayek on Tradition." *Journal of Libertarian Studies* 17, no. 1 (Winter 2003): 17–56.
Friedman, Milton. "The Social Responsibility of Business Is to Increase Its Profits." *New York Times*, September 13, 1970. www.colorado.edu/studentgroups/libertarians/issues/friedman-soc-resp-business.html; accessed on September 30, 2014.
Giddens, Anthony. *Social Theory and Modern Sociology*. Cambridge: Polity Press, 1987.
Goede, Marieke De. "Beyond Economism in International Political Economy." *Review of International Studies* 29, no. 1 (January 2003): 79–97.
Goede, Marieke De. *Virtue, Fortunes, and Faith: A Genealogy of Finance*. Vol. 24. Borderlines Series. Minneapolis: University of Minnesota Press, 2005.
Habermas, Jürgen. *The Theory of Communicative Action*. Boston: Beacon, 1981.
Haiven, Max. "Finance as Capital's Imagination? Reimagining Value and Culture in an Age of Fictitious Capital and Crisis." *Social Text* 108, 29, no. 3 (Fall 2011): 93–124.
Hayek, Friedrich A. "Why I am Not a Conservative." In *The Constitution of Liberty: The Definitive Edition*, by F. A. Hayek. University of Chicago Press, 2011. http://press.uchicago.edu/books/excerpt/2011/hayek_constitution.html.
Heggen, K., and S. Wellard. "Increased Unintended Patient Harm in Nursing Practice as a Consequence of the Dominance of Economic Discourses." *International Journal of Nursing Studies* 41, no. 3 (March 2004): 293–98.
Hume, Neil. "Hocus Pocus Saves the Day." *Guardian*, September 6, 2002.
Khalik, A. Rashad Abdel. *Accounting for Risk, Hedging, and Complex Contracts*. New York: Routledge, 2014.
Kolb, Robert W. "Ethical Implications of Finance." In *Finance Ethics: Critical Issues in Theory and Practice*, edited by John Boatright, 23–42. Hoboken, NJ: John Wiley & Sons, 2010.
Krugman, Paul. "Nobody Understands Debt." *New York Times*, January 1, 2012; available at www.nytimes.com/2012/01/02/opinion/krugman-nobody-understands-debt.html?_r=0; accessed on September 14, 2014.
Lemov, Penelope. "Foreclosure and the Eminent Domain Solution Explained." *Governing the States and Localities*, August 15, 2013, Public Money edition; available at www.governing.com/columns/public-finance/col-foreclosure-eminent-domain-solution.html; accessed on November 1, 2013.
Lewis, Michael. *Liar's Poker*. New York: Norton, 1989.

Long, D. Stephen. "Bernard Dempsey's Theological Economics: Usury, Profit, and Human Fulfillment." *Theological Studies* 57, no. 4 (1996): 690–706.

MacKenzie, Donald. "Opening the Black Boxes of Global Finance." *Review of International Political Economy* 12, no. 4 (October 2005): 555–76.

MacKenzie, Donald, and Yuval Millo. "Negotiating a Market, Performing Theory: The Historical Sociology of a Financial Derivatives Exchange." *American Journal of Sociology* 109, no. 1 (July 2003): 107–45.

Martin, Randy. *Financialization of Daily Life*. Philadelphia: Temple University Press, 2002.

McDaniel, Charles A., Jr. "Theology of the 'Real Economy': Christian Economic Ethics in an Age of Financialization." *Journal of Religion and Business Ethics* 2, no. 2 (September 2011): 1–29. http://via.library.depaul.edu/cgi/viewcontent.cgi?article=1030&context=jrbe; accessed on January 8, 2015.

Miller, Dale T. "The Norm of Self-Interest." *American Psychologist* 54, no. 12 (1999): 1053–60.

Nelson, Julie. "Poisoning the Well, or How Economic Theory Damages Moral Imagination." Working Paper No. 12–07, Global Development and Environment Institute, 2012. http://ase.tufts.edu/gdae/Pubs/wp/12-07NelsonPoisoningWell.pdf; accessed on September 1, 2014.

Norberg-Hodge, Helena. "Buddhism in the Global Economy." In *Mindfulness in the Marketplace: Compassionate Responses to Consumerism*, edited by A. H. Badiner, 15–27. Berkeley: Parallax Press, 2002.

O'Boyle, Edward J., Stefano Solari, and GianDemetrio Marangoni. "Financialization: Critical Assessment Based on Catholic Social Teaching." *International Journal of Social Economics* 37, no. 1 (2010): 4–16.

Perlman, Alan. "Forensic Linguistics: Financial Rhetoric and the Intent to Deceive." *Experts.com*, (n.d.). www.experts.com/Articles/Forensic-Linguistics-Financial-Rhetoric-Intent-to-Deceive-By-Alan-Perlman; accessed on June 2, 2014.

Rattner, Steven. "The Dangerous Notion That Debt Doesn't Matter." *New York Times*, January 20, 2012. www.nytimes.com/2012/01/22/opinion/sunday/the-dangerous-notion-that-debt-doesnt-matter.html?_r=0; accessed on September 1, 2014.

Rubenstein, M. "Nonparametric Tests of Alternative Option Pricing Models Using All Reported Trades and Quotes on the 30 Most Active CBOE Option Classes from August 23, 1976 through August 31, 1978." *Journal of Finance* 40, no. 2 (June 1985): 455–80.

Röpke, Wilhelm. *Economics of the Free Society*. Translated by Patrick M. Boarman. Chicago: Henry Regnery Company, 1963.

Röpke, Wilhelm. *A Humane Economy: The Social Framework of the Free Market*. Chicago: Henry Regnery Company, 1960.

Röpke, Wilhelm. *The Moral Foundations of Civil Society*. New Brunswick, N.J.: Transaction Publishers, 2002.

Röpke, Wilhelm. *The Social Crisis of Our Time*. Chicago: The University of Chicago Press, 1950.

Schaeck, Klaus. "Behavioral Finance, Behavioral Bias, and Market Anomalies: Implications for Bank Managers." *Corporate Finance Review* 9, no. 4 (February 2005): 5–8, 10–18.

Schumpeter, Joseph. "Introduction." In *Interest and Usury*. by Bernard Dempsey, vii–x. Washington: American Council on Public Affairs, 1943.

Solomon, Robert C. *Ethics and Excellence: Cooperation and Integrity in Business*. New York: Oxford University Press, 1992.

Stawski, Willard, II. *Kids, Parents & Money: Teaching Personal Finance from Piggy Bank to Prom*. New York: John Wiley and Sons, 2000.

Szalai, Jennifer. "The Banality of Avarice: Why the Finance Industry Never Had to Lie." *Harper's Magazine*, February 2012.

Thrift, Nigel. "It's the Romance, Not the Finance, That Makes the Business Worth Pursuing." *Economy and Society* 30, no. 4 (November 2001): 412–32.

Watson, David. "Against the Megamachine: Empire and Earth." In *Environmental Philosophy: From Animal Rights to Radical Ecology*, edited by M. E. Zimmerman, B. Callicot, K. J. Warren, I. J. Klaver, and J. Clark, 462–78. Upper Saddle River: Pearson Prentice Hall, 2005.

Wuthnow, Robert. "The Crisis in the Churches." In *Financing American Religion*, edited by Mark Chaves and Sharon L. Miller, 67–78. Walnut Creek, CA: AltaMira Press, 1999.

Zimmerman, M. E., B. Callicot, K. J. Warren, I. J. Klaver, and J. Clark, eds. *Environmental Philosophy: From Animal Rights to Radical Ecology*. Upper Saddle River: Pearson Prentice Hall, 2005.

8 The goal

Mobilize civil society to civilize finance

Chapter 6 revealed that one area in which the term "American exceptionalism" seems unchallengeable is with respect to the dynamic development of voluntary associations that began around the turn of the nineteenth century, many of which responded to economic injustices. Social mobilizations in that time were not simply protests, however; they were culturally formative movements that provided needed cultural infrastructure as the nation expanded beyond the capabilities of its immature political institutions and the rigidity of its established religious traditions. The dynamic formation of American civil society not only facilitated the country's dramatic growth and the settling of a vast frontier, it also stirred citizen involvement in the social order to a degree arguably never before witnessed in history.

Given the problems of the past decade, it seems ironic that so much intellectual energy has been focused on "international" civil society solutions to financial problems in developing countries. Reviewing the scholarly literature, one is struck by how much of it pertains to the international arena and, in particular, to underdeveloped nations. Lacking knowledge of the recent financial calamity, one would be tempted to conclude that the U.S. and other economically advanced countries have their acts together and need only mentor those envious of what the "First World" has achieved. There have been calls for and even attempts at financial reform in the U.S., some of which are ongoing. However, "reform" is an overstatement; these efforts largely are regulatory "enhancements" hashed out by subject-matter experts of both government and industry, excluding other stakeholders and largely bypassing civil society, arguably the greatest of all American assets.

Some of the research for this chapter draws from the European experience in fostering civil society participation in global finance because much academic work has concentrated on the efforts of nongovernmental organizations (NGOs) working with International Financial Institutions (IFIs). Despite the sheer number of civil society organizations (CSOs) in the United States, and with due respect to the Occupy Movement, broader citizen mobilization in response to the financial crisis barely clipped the radar. Citizen apathy toward events that so dramatically impacted the public—putting it on the hook for the reckless and, in some cases, unethical acts of financial professionals—is hard to explain. Recent inaction also calls into question another of Alexis de Tocqueville's characterizations of the United States: "The great privilege enjoyed by the Americans is not only to be more enlightened than other nations but also to have the chance to make mistakes that can be retrieved [corrected]."[1] Reparation of faults must begin with their recognition and with robust debate. Contemporary Americans seem to have lost, if not the capacity to recognize the nation's faults, then the will to address them.

Little is likely to come from Dodd–Frank and other legislative initiatives because the parties most interested in the outcomes seem to desire no real reform of the system; rather, their involvement in reform efforts suggests that they desire at best to subtly reshape policy to secure their interests, consistent with Hayek's views of the motivations and behaviors of specialized interests.[2] Meanwhile, the financial system mushes on into evermore uncharted territory. The legislature applies (and often subsequently repeals) thousands of patchwork reforms, many of which will have unintended consequences while a major problem—the continuous growth in income inequality, much of which has been built upon manipulations of capital inaccessible to average Americans—proceeds unabated. One need not be a "liberal" to observe the unsustainable nature of this situation long term.

Present insecurities lead once again to the need to better articulate the kind of crisis or crises in which we have been involved. This book established at the outset that there are two distinct crises to consider. One is the immediate financial crisis beginning around 2008 and extending to 2012 or so that presumably has ended despite its continuing economic effects. The "financialization crisis" is the more intransigent predicament demonstrated in previous chapters, involving the rising dominance of financial values and decision making in all areas and the narrowing of the nation's diverse conceptions of flourishing to a singular obsession with monetary return. That crisis proceeds largely unrecognized by most Americans because of its ability to numb ethical senses and reshape values of those institutions within which the financial system should be embedded.

Financialization has dictated the "solution" to the more immediate financial crisis, promoting a continuation of the industry structure and regulatory regime that contributed to recent problems. A report in *The Nation* revealed how financial industry lobbyists outnumbered those associated with consumer groups by more than 20 to 1 and, by one estimate, had spent more than $1 billion to "defang" Dodd–Frank.[3] Insider access in the development of financial legislation and the disproportionate influence of industry groups vis-à-vis those representing private citizens are heightened by system complexity and broad information asymmetries characteristic of the financial sector.

Yet previous chapters have posited that the situation is even worse than it appears. Even those civil society organizations that might serve as countervailing powers and help balance financial industry interests are themselves becoming more financially interested. The larger financialization crisis dictates that the present system provides the solutions to the more immediate financial crises. This mechanistic response apparatus renders genuine reform of the system nearly impossible because industry insiders' privileged access overwhelms the few citizen groups that are able to get a seat at the table. Moreover, citizen groups feel the intense competitive pressure of financial survival themselves. This scenario begs the question of who is minding the store with respect to economic justice in the financial sector. It also calls into question whether the American Founders, in particular James Madison, were too hopeful concerning the virtue-sustaining characteristics of the novel liberal experiment that theoretically balances faction against faction.

Ironically, civil society's maturation in the international arena may position it to inform new conceptions of American social order. Much of what has been learned regarding global civil society is relevant to the possibility not only of including private organizations in the regulatory system but also in reorienting finance toward the individuals and organizations it should serve. This chapter offers some evidence to convey that potential and to provide some ideas for a new financial governance-regulatory paradigm and institutional structure to improve upon the present regime that has proven woefully deficient.

Civil society and finance

University of Warwick professor Jan Aart Scholte, who studies globalization and civil society, asks a provocative yet seemingly obvious question considering the events of the past decade. Given the changes in global finance that have impacted public interests—the greater volatility and "economic dislocations" originating in financial markets, the skewed nature of returns that have led to historic levels of income inequality, and the ethical transgressions of financial professionals—why have these markets "attracted relatively little effective civil society mobilization for change?"[4] Scholte attempts to answer his own question by combining (1) the approaches of scholars who see "actor circumstances" in the opaque, closed information networks that exist in finance as the primary problem with (2) the perspectives of scholars who emphasize social structures as the major obstacles to civil society activism.

Regarding the former impediments, which he attributes to "secrecy" in the financial industry, Scholte contends that "the public can often more easily discover the identities and strategies of military commanders than it can uncover the names and plans of financial chiefs."[5] Regarding social structures, he notes the entrenchment of powerful financial interests who want no disruptions to the present system of finance capital. But he also observes the resistance to civil society involvement by governments that depend on bonds and other instruments as they cling to solvency, political parties that "directly or indirectly" employ financial markets to fund their activities, and even religious authorities, which "have considerable assets bound up in financial markets."[6] This paralysis of self-interestedness leads to confusion about the broader goals of reform. "In short," Scholte writes, "public-interest civil society associations struggle to mobilise activism, to point it at the relevant targets, and to obtain effect when the object of their advocacy is highly elusive."[7]

Yet the role of CSOs is vital. Absent their involvement, finance becomes highly insular. Helmut Anheier notes how finance is permeated by "institutional voids" that often are

> accompanied by a normative weakness, even hollowness, as domain actors are alienated from social values and the civic awareness represented by diverse civil society groups. Increasingly, they operate under different norms, often rationalized as "logics," and the seemingly unquestionable system demands of global finance and the highly specialized professional groups involved—especially corporate lawyers, finance economists and accountants.[8]

Those institutional voids also limit the cognitive framework that should support the regulatory system. The agents of regulatory reform ignore the perspectives of many groups heavily impacted by financial operations. Technical and institutional sophistication within the confines of the industry itself exhausts intellectual resources, which reduces possibilities for effective governance. As has been seen, the reach of finance today means that almost everyone is affected by the ability of legislators and regulators to craft equitable and effective rules to guide the industry, but lack of input by many constituents means that those responsible for regulation operate with a very limited picture of the financial economy. Julia Black, pro director of research at the London School of Economics, cites an ideological influence that limits the regulatory paradigm. Black notes, in particular, how the efficient capital markets hypothesis (ECMH) developed by Eugene Fama in 1970 and the "neo-classical understanding of price formation" continue to dominate the industry and influence those who seek to regulate it.[9] She has called for a "social conception of financial markets, drawing on institutionalist theories, social network theories, and the sociology of science and technology, including technical systems" to better understand finance's components, the dynamics of the industry, and its regulatory imperatives.[10]

The assumptions of neoclassical models in finance can deceive regulators as to the best course of action just as they can persuade financial professionals to act in unsound ways. Neoclassical principles can convince both groups that excessive risk and collusive or unethical participants are effectively eliminated by "market means" without need for external authorities. In this regard, Black believes the capabilities of the pricing mechanism have been exaggerated. She sympathizes with Robert Shiller and others who observe that price often can be determined more by the "trading behavior" of participants in the market than by the products being traded. She writes,

> Contrary to the efficient markets hypothesis trading does not lead to price discovery, but to the creation of information feedback loops and "cascades" which in turn create patterns of behavior as individuals respond to the trading decisions of others, either on the basis of information, reputation or compensation effects.[11]

This herd mentality can lead to what Shiller, among others, has described as "irrational exuberance."[12]

Black views the financial crisis as evidence of the inadequacy of the ECMH and the many models based on its assumptions due to their lack of accounting for "organizational dynamics" within markets. She asserts,

> It was clear from the crisis that the incentives of key actors: banks, credit-rating agencies, and indeed investors, were fundamentally misaligned. At the level of organizational infrastructure, it became clear that internal systems, processes, and cultures were inadequate and/or inappropriate, and that there were significant weaknesses in the regulatory capacity of both regulators and firms.[13]

What is needed is a social conception of financial markets that bring institutions and a wider array of market players and other stakeholders with their many motivations into the picture. Absent a better understanding of how various actors react in different market contexts, the technical sophistication of financial models means little. Ignoring not only the behavior of individual actors but also the institutional complexity of markets in order to make reality "better fit the math" also can lead to assumptions that only financial professionals and government officials need be involved in industry regulation and governance.

The largely insider process by which the Dodd–Frank legislation was constructed (parts of which are presently being deconstructed) illustrates the proposition above. Robert Prasch, an economics professor at Middlebury College, has been highly critical of the Dodd–Frank reforms, noting their derailment by an attitude that conforms to what was described in previous chapters as the "Wall Street Rule":

> Any effort to tamper with the remarkable and intricate set of institutions collectively known as "Wall Street" risks the disruption or even permanent damage of this finely-honed, intricate, and invaluable source of job-creation. By inference, any effort to devise or impose better rules for the modern financial system would be an exercise of folly or stunning hubris. Unquestioned in the halls of power, these conclusions are rarely defended or even articulated publicly. It follows that, despite the size and severity of the financial crisis, little needs to be learned and even less needs to be done.[14]

Prasch is among those who observe Hayek's influence in contributing to the restrictive regulatory paradigm (and with respect to "real" reform, paralysis) that seems to foreshadow the next financial crisis. Hayek's principle concerning the impossibility of any single person or institution amassing the critical local knowledge necessary to avoid unintended consequences in collective action has led to what Prasch sees as a false inference: "that the best course of action is to do nothing."[15] Gretchen Morgenson reinforces Prasch's observation by noting how, four years after Congress ordered the SEC to construct a rule that would make it easier to recover executive compensation that was "earned improperly as a result of accounting shenanigans," there is no such rule despite broad support for it beyond the halls of Congress.[16] Morgenson quotes Dennis M. Kelleher, who lobbies on behalf of citizens in financial reform as head of the NGO Better Markets: "On the one hand, it's not a very complicated rule"; yet, "on the other hand, the industry and its lawyers have made it incredibly complicated. Anything that touches on compensation always generates a huge fight."[17] Thus, both practical and theoretical impediments to financial reform resist action by authorities: the simpler pragmatic objection is that people do not want government limiting activities that generate revenue and income while the theoretical objection asserts that any attempt to limit concentrations of market power will realize consequences even more inequitable and possibly more unstable than the status quo. The irony of American regulatory reticence is that a major problem resulting from the financial crisis stemmed from a massive unintended consequence itself—the rise of systemic risk that resulted from enormous growth in the derivatives and mortgage-backed securities markets, which arose with little regulation. Technically and institutionally complex markets commonly have their own unintended consequences. They can result from the kinds of "price cascades" Black observes along with the dynamic "private planning" in the financial industry that John Munkirs demonstrated with his Centralized Private Sector Planning model described in Chapter 3.[18] Even seemingly coordinated industry moves designed to enhance certainty but which do not account for institutional complexity can realize unpredictable outcomes.

When financial regulation is attempted in the U.S., it is subject to underfunding and "industry friendly" appointees and agency employees who "push to enact laws that are simultaneously more opaque and lenient." As Prasch observes, these underfunded agencies are not the result of responsible government attempts to corral the budget: "after all, the up-front cost of regulation is self-evidently trivial relative to expenses borne by society in the event of regulatory failure."[19] The attitude of "the less regulation the better" attends the neoliberal mindset that has developed a "large, concentrated, and essentially federally-guaranteed financial sector" that goes against the grain of American traditions; with regard to the financial sector as it has developed, Prasch notes how not only customers and borrowers are "better off without it," but "perhaps of overriding importance, our democracy is better off without it."[20] He references Louis Brandeis's 1914 book, *Other People's Money and How the Bankers Use It*, to make the case that participants in the Occupy Movement are not only correct to protest the threat of concentrated financial power to democracy and the rule of law, but also "are participating in a long and proud heritage."[21] Unfortunately, the Occupy Movement seems to lack the wide appeal or institutional structure needed to carry the load for civic involvement in the financial sector. A greater diversity of organizations is required to promote real change.

The variety of organizational participation, however, has been tempered in significant ways. Another major obstacle to civil society participation in the financial sector was observed in Chapters 4 and 5. Religious organizations and civic groups increasingly adopt the values and methods of for-profit companies, reducing institutional diversity and limiting possibilities for the kind of financial disinterestedness needed for reform and oversight of the industry. In this regard, Severyn T. Bruyn observes the thinning line between for-profit and nonprofit organizations as the latter come to accept the competitive paradigm of the former: "Nonprofit corporations are like 'for-profits' when they compete fiercely in their own market sectors. Nonprofit universities, churches, and hospitals contend for 'customers' and can become monopolistic in their own way."[22] This is occurring as nonprofits increasingly feel competitive pressure from for-profit firms in traditionally charitable and philanthropic fields.[23] Young, Salamon, and Grinsfelder describe the tensions that have formed in the American nonprofit sector caused by greater participation in competitive markets:

> The growing market involvement of nonprofit organizations is a complex and multifaceted phenomenon, with various strands interwoven into a rich tapestry. Nevertheless, a new reality is slowly coming into focus—a self-propelled, social problem-solving sector that has loosened its moorings to both traditional charity and government support and become much more tightly connected to the market system, while still trying to remain committed, however tenuously, to the pursuit of public benefit.[24]

Some blurring of lines among governmental, private for-profit, and private nonprofit sectors is inevitable and, in some cases, can benefit society. The social service and charitable activities of commercial enterprises, for example are important components of American philanthropy, though corporate philanthropy remains relatively small compared to individual giving. In 2013, American corporations gave almost $17 billion to charitable causes, though that figure pales in comparison to the more than $240 billion given by individuals (over 72 percent of total giving).[25] Likewise, nonprofits often engage in money-making activities to fund their missions. Section 501(c)(3) of the Internal Revenue Service (IRS) tax code allows these organizations to earn profit through certain functions so long as the proceeds do not go to individuals associated with the organization, though it allows employees to be paid "reasonable salaries." Nonprofit organizations are also limited as to the lobbying and other political activity in which they can engage.[26]

The phenomenon of "hybridization" is occurring rapidly among nonprofit and for-profit businesses, with the intent of enhancing the accomplishments of both. Relationships, for example, like those between Ralston Purina and the American Humane Association, McDonald's and the Environmental Defense Fund, or the Nature Conservancy and Georgia Pacific, seek to leverage the assets of each organization to maximize value for their firms and society at large.[27] In hybrid relationships, business corporations "polish their public images, gain access to special expertise or future talent, create demand for their products, and motivate their employees" to forms of community service while their nonprofit partners "gain access to substantial financial, personnel, and other corporate resources, obtain wider forums in which to broadcast their messages and appeals, and in some cases influence consumers in ways that directly support the nonprofit's mission."[28] Even the capital structures of nonprofits increasingly mimic those of their for-profit partners and competitors, as demonstrated in Chapter 4. Jed Emerson observes the gradual evolution toward a nonprofit capital market where portfolios are managed using risk/return logic, various combinations of capital instruments, and even rating services in assessing "social returns" on investments.[29]

A conception of "pure" civil society persists, however. The activities of these organizations "involve no quest for public office (so excluding political parties) and no pursuit of pecuniary gain (so excluding firms and the commercial mass media)."[30] This functional distinction is needed to overcome the confusion inherent in an institutionally complex society. Scholte sees such functional definitions as necessary in identifying those organizations that "involve conscious attempts to shape policies, norms, and structures in society at large."[31] Thus, while for-profits and nonprofits are increasingly similar operationally, their missions remain distinct, at least theoretically.

Scholte also sees the need to classify organizations according to their strategic missions vis-à-vis society, describing "conformist," "reformist," and "transformist" civil society associations. Conformist groups consist of business lobbies and professional associations, among other groups, that "seek to uphold and reinforce existing norms." Consumer associations and various human rights and relief groups constitute reformist groups, which seek to "correct what they see as flaws in existing regimes while leaving underlying social structures intact." Finally, anarchists, pacifists, radical feminists, and other groups make up transformist organizations, which "aim for a comprehensive change of the social order" by rigorously opposing the status quo in the belief that justice requires fundamental change.[32] Reflecting on the recent Occupy Movement, which arose largely in response to the global financial crisis, one observes the qualities of a transformist civil society organization that seeks an upwelling of those presently disenfranchised by the financial system and the "taking back" of society by the people who have been exploited by powerful interests. According to the Occupy Wall Street website, one informal leader of this professedly leaderless movement, Justine Alexandra Roberts Tunney, seeks a "world revolution, starting with a popular uprising against the financial executives who plunder society without contributing any social utility."[33]

Transformist movements like Occupy have their place. Attempts to suppress such grassroots mobilizations risk losing important voices in the debate on social justice in a financialized society in which economic rewards appear to have lost much connection to social contribution.[34] Financial anarchist websites have emerged since the crisis, with their sponsors/members often calling for radical reconstruction of the global financial system.[35] While these movements are likely to remain on the periphery, subject to scorn by elites and even much of mainstream society, their value lies in shocking Americans out of complacency regarding the direction of the global economy. They fulfill a well-established role in the American heritage by articulating how concentrations of financial power may threaten the very foundations of American democracy.[36]

Given the present disillusionment with American government, civil society has an opportunity to become a primary facilitator of collective self-determination and means for achieving social justice. American citizens are increasingly frustrated with the two-party system. A recent Harvard study showed that the percentage of American Millennials choosing to be identified as "independent" rather than Democrat or Republican has risen in recent years. Another survey conducted by the Harvard University Institute of Politics showed that among respondents between 18 and 29 years old, 80 percent answered "No" when asked the question: "Do you consider yourself to be politically engaged or politically active?"[37] Civil society provides an alternative means for collective action in a culture in which confidence in the political system is declining. A major question is whether "reformist" civil society movements will mobilize adequately to complement "transformist" movements, which commonly gain the most public attention.

Signs are positive for civil society involvement as political institutions and their leaders are increasingly seen as ineffective. In this regard, Scholte references scholars James Rosenau and Wolfgang Reinicke, who see not so much the erosion of territorial states but rather a decline in statism in the regulatory arena. He argues that "governance—a collectivity's steering, coordination, and control mechanisms—now clearly involves much more than the state."[38] The broadening of governance is natural with respect to the financial economy as the externalities of economic behavior grow. To the extent that financial outcomes impact more groups, they will have greater motivation to become involved in order to defend their interests. The question is whether they will have adequate channels for participation.

Greater disbursement of financial knowledge is necessary to bring civil society organizations into the realm of financial governance and regulation. Scholte contends that "widespread ignorance" does not imply the inability of "ordinary citizens" to comprehend financial concepts and instruments so much as the "failure of knowledge delivery."[39] Even in the education system, he notes the absence of studies of financialization in university economics programs, the emphasis in economics courses on "real" production over financial activity, and a similarly limiting emphasis on states as the sources of governance in political science curricula.[40] Moreover, most civil society literature on finance centers on underdeveloped countries, limiting exploration of new governance and regulatory structures in developed nations. Further, much research that focuses on global finance investigates how developing countries have adapted to policies prescribed by IFIs or implemented microfinance programs.[41] Lack of financial expertise in CSOs and their preoccupations with "state-centric conceptions of governance" lead to activism that focuses on international institutions that champion issue-specific agendas like debt relief—what Scholte describes as "barking at a few trees while the forest is left undisturbed." Scholte writes,

> Executives and boards at the large NGOs, FBOs and labor unions have generally not steered their organizations to address finance capital and its polycentric governance. Likewise, no philanthropic foundation has created a large program specifically to support civil society work to tame commercial financial markets (as distinct from the various projects to reform the IMF and multilateral development banks). Instead, funders of civil society activities have generally opted to emphasize traditional agendas on environmental conservation, human rights, peacebuilding and poverty reduction. Regarding financial markets, then, foundations have so far not proved to be dynamic innovative agents of change.[42]

The unimaginative, ineffectual character of civil society institutions with respect to finance appears to be exaggerated in the American context, even in relation to the rest of the financially developed world. One reason is that European financial governance seems less spellbound by market mystique. Across the Atlantic, the European Economic and Social Committee (EESC) bills itself as "a bridge between Europe and organized civil society." It promotes citizen involvement in the financial sector beyond simple investment, recognizing that the "representation of users versus providers is very unbalanced," to the detriment of the former.[43] The European Federation of Financial Services Users (EuroFinuse) attempts to give voice to what it sees as those marginalized users of financial services who function at a huge competitive disadvantage in relation to those who provide services. EuroFinuse has over 50 member organizations and approximately four million members worldwide. The organization's website describes its purpose:

> *EuroFinuse acts as an independent financial expertise center to the direct benefit of the European financial services users (shareholders, other investors, savers, pension fund participants, life insurance policy holders, borrowers, etc.) and other stakeholders of the European financial services who are independent from the financial industry.*[44]

Bridget M. Hutter, Joan O'Mahony, John Braithwaite, and Peter Drahos are among scholars who have investigated the role of civil society in industry and its potential for enhancing and effectively "democratizing" regulation. Their observations have potentially significant implications for the regulatory reform of American finance, given its present mire in the technologically deterministic insider paradigm. For example, Hutter and O'Mahony contend that the success of CSOs is critically dependent on "their ability to manage or 'frame' the issue at stake."[45] One example from 1995 was Greenpeace's successful intervention in Shell UK's decision (with the UK Government's approval) to dump its 14-thousand-ton Brent Spar oil platform into the North Sea. The success of Greenpeace in influencing Shell UK to reverse its decision resulted from the organization's ability to present "the disposal of waste as a normative issue rather than a purely scientific one."[46] Greenpeace reframed the debate, particularly among the German public, from a largely scientific discussion among experts over the environmental damage caused by platform dumping to a moral issue that transcended technical analysis.[47]

One may observe an analogy between Greenpeace's activism in the Brent Spar incident and debates over financial issues today. The financialized society tends to frame issues in ways such that experts dominate discourse. Such debates avoid normative discussions of how changes in finance may spawn moral hazards or generally reshape social ethics. Instead, economists and financial specialists speak in terms of benefit or harm, typically measured in monetary terms, which result from industry changes or government regulation. Proposals are based on whatever course of action is presumed to maximize economic benefits, with little regard for the equity of system rewards. The ability of CSOs to reframe financial debates in normative directions will be critical to enhancing their future roles in directing the financial economy. The relative scarcity of CSOs in this area, however, undoubtedly influences the largely technical debate (such that there is one) concerning the "future of finance."[48]

The traditionally narrow, issue-specific focus of many NGOs may also hinder their participation in the financial sector. In this regard, Lorenzo Fioramonti and Ekkehard Thümler make the case for CSO involvement in financial markets by asking two questions:

> Does it make sense to continue investing single-mindedly in social welfare initiatives, when the bursting of a financial bubble can easily plunge our countries into an economic recession threatening the very basic foundations of our societies? Shouldn't civil society become active in this field and learn from this experience so that it will not happen again?[49]

Yet the authors have found scant evidence of private foundation involvement with financial markets. They offer reasons for this reticence, including lack of industry knowledge, fear of controversy that involvement could entail, and preference for a narrow focus on more short-term, social-welfare issues.[50] Finally, private foundations that the authors surveyed reflect the kind of financial obsession combined with financial ignorance that was described among churches, NGOs, and other institutions in Chapters 4 and 5. One foundation respondent to the question of why they have limited involvement in finance stated that "while some change is under way, most foundations [still] aim to maximize investment income from their portfolios without giving attention to these important issues"; moreover, "the fact is that very few foundations pay much attention to how they get their own money, nor show a great interest in examining the financial and corporate sectors."[51] These responses seem puzzling given recent events, further supporting the thesis that civil society is itself becoming financialized.

Still, Fioramonti and Thümler see potential for a "Greenpeace moment" that might transform the industry and bring about the transparency and accountability called for by almost everyone. Admittedly, the inclusion of civil society in the financial economy is no guarantee against ethical transgressions, future financial bubbles, or further concentrations of power in financial markets. However, greater participation by less financially interested participants in the industry virtually assures improved transparency and governance.

Advantages of CSO participation in financial regulation

Hutter and O'Mahony note the enormous potential of civil society organizations to serve as "regulators" that promote the "development of ethics" and "norms of citizenship."[52] Bruyn goes even further, contending that such associations have "the potential to infuse the economy with a new morality, specifically calling nonprofit organizations the "twentieth-century equivalent to Smith's 'invisible hand' in which a non-profit's moral concern has matching power over a business interest."[53] The fine balancing of institutions was the great hope of James Madison and other Founders who recognized the potential for tyranny and general social decline, as some groups advance at the expense of others. While Elshtain is correct that the Constitution nowhere prescribes such organizations, they have been realized, even if feared for their potential divisiveness, in the most formative decades after the founding period. Many of these institutions put the greater good ahead of particular goods and were critical both to maintenance of the social order and to the moral development of American citizens.

In the global political context, Scholte has observed the potential positive effects of greater civil society participation in governance. They include "giving voice to stakeholders," enhancing "global governance through public education activities," fueling debate "in and about global governance," "increasing public transparency," and promoting democracy "by increasing the public accountability of regulatory agencies."[54] A logical question that emerges from Scholte's description of civil society's possible advantages in global governance is: Can these advantages be extended to financial governance in the American context?

Reflection on the recent crisis suggests that the needs are much the same both globally and domestically. Concerning the latter, certain stakeholders, in particular average American citizens, have little voice in a financial system that they ultimately underwrite. Citizens obviously need greater financial education to narrow the literacy gap and forums in which to voice their views on the purposes, practices, and regulatory policies of the American financial system. Finally, the need for greater transparency in the financial sector is one of the most discussed areas of reform, with greater accountability required not only of firms but also of regulatory agencies, credit rating agencies, and professional organizations.

The problem is the persistence of a monolithic approach to financial regulation that centers on the statist model. Policy development and enforcement focus on government agencies as singular avenues of implementation even as economists and financial professionals acknowledge the inefficiency and ineffectiveness of an old, tired regulatory regime that gives disproportionate voice to those regulated.[55]

The transition to a "mixed" regulatory structure involving state agencies, industry actors, and CSOs would offer a major paradigm shift and perhaps reenergize what was identified previously as the principal source of American exceptionalism—its religious and civic organizations. It also would revive an American first principle in the Madisonian balancing of factions in order to promote the common good. The more dynamic nature of civil society could yield more imaginative approaches to regulatory reform that better complement the dynamic aspects of the financial sector itself. In other words, more nimble private actors looking out for the public good could likely better respond to industry changes than state regulation controlled through a combination of legislatures and administrative agencies. Involvement of CSOs in financial regulation and governance would be more consistent with what Friedrich Hayek termed the "spontaneous order" and more capable of what Helmut Anheier terms "adaptive coping." In the adaptive coping model, "where institutions provide adequate rules and regulations, and the expectations and specifications set out by the institutional framework are implemented adequately, the interactions are stable and ordered among actors involved and the system rests in a state of equilibrium."[56] An idealistic vision, perhaps, but one worthy of an attempt given the present state of the financial industry and its regulatory structure.

Where regulatory institutions remain concentrated in government, they inevitably grow beyond the scale and complexity needed to "cope" with the environment. Anheier also notes how, after the onset of the crisis in 2008, the response was to heighten reporting requirements. In terms of truly reforming the global financial system, proposals "have aimed at establishing new agreements, statutes and committees without changing the overall institutional framework and to rationalize existing ones along altered macroeconomic conditions. In the end, such procedures merely add new layers of complexity."[57] Much the same could be said of attempts in the U.S. to reform finance. Chapter 2 described the complex of actors, including legislators, lobbyists, state bureaucrats, and financial professionals that have combined to produce new legislation such as the Dodd–Frank Bill, which, even in its attempts to break with the status quo, is now being softened by the political process. The present system seems a tragic waste of brainpower predisposed to add more layers of regulation while preserving its basic structure.

Anheier cites David Vogel in insisting that state-based regulatory regimes generally inspire a "race to the bottom" by establishing a system in which national regulators with ambiguous objectives and jurisdictions often work at cross purposes.[58] Instead, in the right conditions and often with CSOs reinforcing state authorities, there is a possibility for a "race to the top" in which reputational incentives inspire producers themselves to "self-impose" industry standards, minimizing the role of government.[59] Civil society institutions can act vitally not only to help verify and communicate producer reputation but also to establish appropriate institutional conditions and actor incentives for better societal outcomes—areas where the American regulatory framework, grounded in neoliberal ideology, typically is most lacking.

Internationally, there have been successes in promoting greater CSO participation in financial regulation. Johannes Petry notes how the top ten international banks realized approximately $14 billion in profit through commodity derivative trading in 2008 alone; yet he also cites Peter Gibbon's work in showing how such lucrative markets incentivize "regulatory capture"—where firms being regulated come to control the regulators, directing them to implement policies that benefit the firms themselves.[60] In the case of the commodity derivatives market, however, the formidable structure erected in the form of industry lobbying and other organizations has been effectively counterbalanced by a dynamically formed network of CSOs that brought to bear sufficient moral pressure and greatly limited regulatory capture. But not only financially oriented CSOs helped bring about this result. Petry shows how " 'finance' NGOs such as Finance Watch, SOMO [the Center for Research on Multinational Corporations], WEED [World Economy, Ecology & Development] and WDM [World Development Movement], that previously had not been very successful in preventing financial regulatory capture" teamed with organizations such as Oxfam, Welthungerhilfe, FoodWatch, and Friends of the Earth in highly effective ways. This NGO "team" thus connected what had largely been technical financial issues with the larger moral problem caused by volatility in food prices; it "turned the focus away from the discussion of technical standards towards a debate about the externalities and social costs created through commodity speculation."[61]

This CSO consortium reframed the issue effectively, bringing the social and moral effects of commodity derivatives to public attention and suggesting the potential of spontaneous, cross-sector mobilizations of civil society in other contexts. Importantly, similarly oriented CSOs also have great potential to reshape the regulatory mindset, extending accomplishments beyond disclosing the negative consequences associated with certain trading behaviors to reorienting the financial economy toward the development of individuals and communities. Financial firms seek their own interests, and government agencies exist primarily to limit abuses. CSOs, however, might help reposition finance as a servant of society rather than a master inclined to maximize returns for a few privileged players, ignoring the broader social consequences.[62]

More direct inclusion of such organizations in finance and its regulatory processes moves the global economy more toward "shared value," which counters the intense emphasis most companies have on profit at the expense of stakeholders' interests. Michael Porter and Mark Kramer define shared value as those "policies and operating practices that enhance the competitiveness of a company while simultaneously advancing the economic and social conditions in the communities in which it operates."[63] They note how economists have promoted the idea that corporations must *sacrifice* some of their "economic success" if they are to "provide societal benefits." This persistent attitude among not only for-profit companies but also governments and NGOs has resulted in an economic climate in which business and society are seen to be at odds respecting their basic motivations.[64] The negative consequences of such a mentality preclude a more social conception of markets and demonstrate reversion to the kind of zero-sum thinking most market enthusiasts left behind long ago.[65] Acting on the vision of shared value leads to conditions where "improving value in one area gives rise to opportunities in the others."[66]

Functional divisions will appear in the dynamic development of civil organizations to support financial regulation and governance. Some will be more naturally inclined to the enforcement of rules, serving as investor watchdogs or in other capacities that protect those interests easily exploitable by financial firms. These organizations are typical among the CSOs formed to date. In general, however, finance's lack of social embeddedness, with regard to other domains such as climate change and international trade, results in poor penetration of civil society into finance's regulatory framework.[67] Anheier notes how "civil society can act as a countervailing force to help fill the institutional void only if it can contribute towards embedding the finance sector within broader social norms and conventions."[68] The financialization of society poses a grave challenge here. Financialization does not so much resist embedding as much as it reshapes the normative structure within which the financial system *should be* embedded if society were to provide effective guidance and regulation. The potentially positive function of CSOs in identifying and promoting the social good of financial activity may be more difficult to derive because many CSOs themselves have become financially invested or have aligned themselves with firms that may compromise their missions, as Chapter 4 demonstrated.

CSO activism in this sector should make its principal goal the return of finance to the service of civilization. Acquiescence to the industry's technical complexity can become a huge problem in that regard. Many have come to believe that finance *should* become more technically complex because wealth and efficiency are often assumed to accompany rising complexity. The attitude that attends financialization results from a financial system that is, in one sense, "disembedded" from the social contexts it ostensibly supports and, in another sense, works to shape the norms and conventions of any social structure that seeks to embed it.[69]

In reflecting on the failure of Lehman Brothers, Emilios Avgouleas observes how "corporate complexity" contributes to the problems recently experienced. The "highly fragmented and labyrinthic" structure of large financial firms poses problems despite global integration of many of the firms' business functions.[70] This complexity reflects some unintended consequences of state regulation. Corporations commonly restructure themselves to compensate for forms of tax and regulatory arbitrage or, in other cases, to build firewalls between various entities in attempts to avoid the potential "spillover effects" of legal liability.[71] Such corporate repositioning represents yet another limitation of traditional statist approaches to financial regulation: in many cases, resource mobility in the global economy allows firms to "shop" for the regulatory system that best meets their "needs."

A major benefit of involving CSOs in financial regulation and governance is their inherent inclinations toward some vision or greater good that professional organizations or even government cannot easily advance. CSOs typically get involved because they possess some distinctive goal or social vision that provides socially desirable or altruistic benefits in the realms in which they are involved. Financial firms commonly advance proposals for "codes of ethics" or often initiate community outreach programs that, in some cases, can have significant benefits. Government regulation typically is designed to limit abuses or improve fairness among parties without trying to realize any particular "good." Neither of these contributions typically arises from social vision or altruistic motivation. CSOs, by contrast, have specific missions and statements of purpose that mobilize participants to achieve particular ends, to which government regulators, by "democratic design," are indifferent.

Limitations of CSO participation in financial regulation and governance

Greater involvement by CSOs in financial markets is no panacea either for limiting financial crises or addressing the broader, more intractable financialization crisis this book has described. CSOs will experience limitations and even ethical challenges to their participation either as watchdogs or in more constructive roles as they attempt to shape the overall direction and ethics of the sector. One limitation of CSOs extends from the very dynamism inherent in these organizations that makes them so effective. This book has premised that most CSOs that get involved would desire to help create a financial system of greater equity, transparency, and simplicity, to make wider participation possible. However, major vested interests in the industry, with the clout to persuade CSOs to their cause, may desire otherwise. Recall from the introduction Bill Ackman's attempts to take down Herbalife. Ackman's example was that of a major financier acting to win CSOs to his side in a billion-dollar derivative deal that may or may not serve to benefit American citizens or the industry as a whole. Even if Ackman is working for the betterment of society, others will attempt CSO capture for less noble purposes. The very nature of civil society entails that organizations will be employed to promote many positions on single issues, at times cancelling out their influence as they line up on opposing sides. "Civil society capture" is not always associated with governments; firms and elites will attempt to use their resources to channel CSOs to their benefit as well.

Hutter and O'Mahony note that just as with the potential for regulatory capture by banks and other financial firms, so the same possibility exists for CSOs as "capturers" of regulatory institutions.[72] CSOs, too, may attempt to shape the regulatory environment for their own purposes. For example, the simple act of lobbying to secure a more prominent seat at the table takes a step in that direction. The key is in knowing when the clout achieved is adequate to carry out the organization's mission and necessary functions and having the institutional discipline to decline unnecessary power or resources. That some might find the previous statement laughable demonstrates the difficulty and persistence of this challenge.

CSO participation in the financial sector faces other serious problems. Consider, for example, the tension between the independence of CSOs as social actors and their dependence on sources of funding. Since most voluntary and religious associations rely almost exclusively on donations, they must constantly seek out new sources of funding, yet they must remain leery of any entanglements such funding entails.[73] Even worse, the increasing financial interestedness of religious and civic organizations and the rising complexity of their environments make it difficult to discern appropriate "representative" CSOs for particular issues. Mission statements may deceive, and major donors whose interests deviate from the CSO's mission can subvert mission statements, attempting to use their clout to direct the organization to their own benefit. Reports have cited, for example, how the increased use of telemarketing in soliciting funds for charitable organizations has led to more cases of misrepresentation of organizations in attempts to acquire donations.[74] Furthermore, CSOs face the same limitations as all institutions—bureaucratization, opportunism, mission drift, and moral hazards can work to undermine CSO effectiveness.[75]

A new vision for the financial economy

Fioramonti and Thümler offer three ways in which private foundations (and presumably other CSOs) should become involved in the financial sector. First, "they should recognize the fundamental value of ethical investment," paying attention to their own organizations' endowments and capital. According to the authors, "it is no longer acceptable that foundations claiming to be concerned with the public good invest their resources in conventional (often high-risk) schemes."[76] In other words, they should exemplify financial integrity to the wider community. Second, they should pioneer "small-scale initiatives" by establishing a "neutral locus for interaction, networking and cooperation (at the national and international level)" in bringing together stakeholder parties in ways only such theoretically disinterested institutions can. Finally, more assertive organizations should become watchdogs over the financial sector to ensure greater transparency and accountability among all players.[77]

Participation of foundations and other CSOs broadens participation in the economy and potentially expands its benefits. Moreover, these benefits extend beyond income growth and return on investment; they include societal benefits of the kind Bruyn associates with a "civil economy," an alternative to the intensely competitive economic model that has been building over decades:

> In sum, the market develops a likeness to a "moral economy" when seen as a voluntary mutually-accountable system of competitive markets. It emerges through the creative play of countervailing powers and the integration of social (nonprofit) and (profit) economic values, by social inventions in the marketplace (e.g., intersectoral partnerships, civic banking, civil legislation, and social investments), by self-enforcing codes of conduct, by the practice of stakeholder mapping with an eye to finance and social accountability/investment.[78]

Some traditional forms of state-based regulation of the financial sector are always needed, however much the regulatory framework incorporates private organizations. Werner De Bondt lists some basic regulatory deficiencies observed in the recent crisis, a few of which have been addressed in Dodd–Frank and other legislation:

1 A systemic risk regulator as a "natural complement to the Federal Reserve's role in monetary policy";
2 Higher capital requirements "for all systemically significant financial service firms, including hedge funds, private equity funds, etc." to limit the amount of risk that can be undertaken by any single firm;
3 Restriction of commercial banks from proprietary trading (à la Glass–Steagall);
4 Greater transparency in the financial industry generally and, in particular, with respect to "esoteric derivatives" and other exotic instruments that are often "sold in the dark";
5 New compensation methods for traders to prevent individuals from "destroying wealth" and subsequently walking away with mega-bonuses and other excessive compensation packages;
6 A "consumer financial protection agency" to regulate product design and standards of performance for mortgages, credit cards, and other credit instruments; and
7 Reestaablishment of a principle of fiduciary duty such that conflicts of interest are eliminated wherever possible.[79]

Such reforms, while they can be helpful, largely reinforce the regulatory regime that has failed miserably in recent years. Simply erecting new rules or reinforcing existing ones within the entrenched paradigm that seek to restrain certain behaviors, the motivations for which remain largely in place, will be ineffectual. As Steve Mandis relates, the culture of Wall Street needs basic change, not simply the redefinition of legal boundaries. Based on his study of Goldman Sachs, Mandis concludes that employees of financial firms need financial interdependence. He seeks to develop a risk-reward system among these firms that more closely resembles their structure before they became publicly traded corporations. At that time, most Wall Street firms were private partnerships and managing directors were "financially interdependent with every other," receiving fixed percentages of an annual bonus pool and remaining "personally liable for other managing directors' actions."[80] Such a culture encourages greater self-regulation before external entities need be involved.

Mandis offers the example of the "London Whale" scandal at JPMorgan Chase, where the consequences of the massive trading loss were largely borne by (1) the company's shareholders along with those traders directly involved and (2) CEO Jamie Dimon, whose pay the company's board of directors reduced by more than half.[81] Had JPM operated from a general bonus pool with fixed percentages allocated to all managing directors, and had those directors been penalized for the actions of fellow employees, the corporate culture likely would have engaged in self-policing their trading behavior.

The need for cultural reform extends beyond banks and other financial firms to the regulatory framework itself. A major problem in achieving reform, however, is the persistent mindset, described in Chapter 2, that only experts can provide guidance and oversight. In a blog with the intriguing title, "Who Guards the Guardians of Monetary Stability and Financial Stability?" Rosa Lastra, a professor of international financial and monetary law at Queen Mary University in London, arrives at the disappointing conclusion that the supervisory failures of the recent crisis "were rooted in failures of 'how to supervise,' not in failures of 'who supervises.'" She opts for reworking the existing UK regulatory structure, with a tiered system that has the Bank of England reporting to a subcommittee appointed by Parliament, with members who "have the technical expertise required to deal with monetary matters."[82] Such "conformist reform" only perpetuates a system in which those with increasingly narrow and specialized knowledge (even if "MPs" or their committees) effectively form the universe of constituent expectations for the financial system. Lastra's conception is the very structure that made Hayek so dour concerning the long-term prospects of democracy in *The Road to Serfdom*; delegation of what is effectively political power to specialists only leads to competition among interest groups, which threatens liberty.

"Who supervises?" is an all-important question which guarantees the arrival of a technocratic order if one answers, "only experts." Thankfully, some are taking a broader view of the "Who supervises?" question. Mandis observes nascent steps in the direction of employee self-monitoring in a speech by New York Federal Reserve President William C. Dudley, who talked of compensation deferral for top bank employees and the need for some amount of the fines assessed to banks to be taken from the compensation pool.[83] That is a step in the direction of changing the culture of financial firms, but those firms exist within a wider culture in which stakeholders are heavily invested in the behaviors of those firms' employees. Thus, the logic of such changes should be extended. The pain being experienced by "average Americans," whether as shareholders, mortgage holders, or through unemployment caused by a financially inspired recession, has revealed that the "stakeholder theory" of ownership is not some abstract ideal but rather reflects a real, on-the-ground reality with significant ramifications for almost everyone on Main Street. Changing the culture of Wall Street begins with the understanding that many others are involved in financial outcomes beyond industry shareholders and employees. The price of concentration in the financial industry (the extreme being "too big to fail") must be the involvement of those who may lose their homes, retirement assets and/or jobs because of intensely self-interested, socially irresponsible, and untransparent activity for which state-based regulation inevitably lags behind.

The question, then, is "how" to give those impacted by high finance a voice in its governance. A starting point is convincing industry professionals that it is in their interests to seek out the involvement of stakeholders in order to avoid potentially more aggressive state intrusions into their businesses down the road. It is also in their interests in the sense that continued exclusion of constituent groups may prompt further efforts to bypass the established financial order.

Evidence in that regard is found in the remarkable development of the "off-economy" model of recent years in the form of services such as Airbnb, Uber, Bitcoin, and other attempts to bypass major industries. In his editorial, "The Evolution of Trust," *New York Times* columnist David Brooks has observed a nascent "peer-to-peer" economy in the development of Airbnb. Economic reality has combined with growing distrust of institutions[84] to inspire a rising alternative economic system that caters to younger consumers and makes cheap travel possible by letting people rent out rooms or take advantage of the discount prices of commercial hotels. Similarly, Uber is a ridesharing service that uses a SmartApp to help passengers contact drivers of vehicles for hire.

Brooks believes at least some of this nonmainstream economic behavior results from fundamental desires that the present economic order leaves unsatisfied. He sees "a personalistic culture in which people have actively lost trust in big institutions" and believes that "people are both hungrier for human contact and more tolerant of easy-come-easy-go relationships."[85] In one sense, these developments are encouraging in that people seem willing to oppose the rising impersonalism of the economic order as well as avoid the trappings of big institutions. In another sense, however, it is sad that the turn is so dramatic—people are becoming accustomed to what Brooks describes as "instant intimacy, or at least fast pseudo-intimacy."[86] So stark is the change, in fact, that one might reasonably suggest it cannot last. Similar to the radical anti-institutionalism of Occupy Wall Street, the new peer-to-peer economy that is trying to break free from the economic establishment appears to lack sufficient structure to endure over the long haul, perhaps because it inadequately addresses human relationship needs, one of the presumed goals of these movements. They are likely to remain on the fringe, important prophetic critiques of a system that has lost its way, but they are unlikely to promote the kind of change toward a more socially integrated, virtuous economy with real legs.

In Scholte's typology, Occupy Wall Street, Bitcoin, and Airbnb are important "transformist" attempts to break with established economic order. They call attention to injustices and mobilize segments of the population. Reformist attempts are needed to complement those efforts and provide institutional structures that have greater potential for persistent change to a financial system that seems unable or unwilling to reform itself.

A "reformist" model for civil society participation in the financial sector

The neoliberal bias that pervades the American business and regulatory cultures presents an inherent difficulty in putting forth a model for greater civil society involvement in the financial sector. Tapping the social imaginary is challenging in a society where rigid conceptual divisions exist between public and private, likewise where conceptualizations of the financial sector presume almost all institutions are not only private but for-profit. False dichotomies like these make the existence of intermediary institutions difficult to conceptualize in areas like finance, where profit is the dominant motivation. Nevertheless, almost all cultural spheres need civil society institutions to help achieve just, socially beneficial outcomes. A problem with including intermediary groups in the financial sector is the inaccessibility of its institutions and practices to those constituents it is designed to serve.

In his article, "Technocracy and Democracy in Monetary Institutions," John R. Freeman questions whether contemporary society may be experiencing a "crisis of imagination," observing "there are serious questions about the capability of today's citizens—even in the most advanced democracies—to comprehend and engage in monetary and other kinds of economic policymaking."[87] A similar limitation has been assumed in the construction and regulation of the present financial system, and the implications of that assumption have been evident both during the financial crisis and in subsequent recovery efforts to address the recession. Expertise is considered crucial; any nonexpert perspective on the financial system is largely excluded under the premise that financial issues either elude the understanding of most citizens or that any financial interests the average citizen may have are minor compared with those of larger, more critical institutions. This attitude reflects just one means by which the scale and complexity of the industry inhibits popular involvement in its direction and debate concerning how it *should* function.

From the standpoint of human capital, to neglect civil society involvement in financial governance leaves considerable resources on the table. While Freeman is correct that citizens may lack *general* knowledge to support economic and monetary policymaking, pockets of citizens have considerable knowledge and deserve to have their perspectives on the industry heard. For example, former industry professionals—Wall Street analysts and traders, bankers, insurance specialists, and others—who either have retired or left their former professions have expertise from which to draw.[88] In addition, MBAs have proliferated in the wider society[89] and some are involved in academia, NGOs, civic associations, and even religious organizations that might give them unique perspectives on banking and finance. Inadequate citizen involvement arguably has less to do with a lack of circulated knowledge than with the force of that neoliberal stamp which seals shut all thinking about possible alternatives to the present system. Former Citigroup CEO Sandy Weill's public announcement that it is time to resurrect regulation to separate commercial from investment banking (à la Glass–Steagall) shows that changes not only in economic conditions but also in the life perspectives of former industry professionals can inspire new insights otherwise neglected by the industry's artificially limited cohort of experts.[90]

Present discussions of where the financial system is headed overlook this kind of creative thinking. In fact, for the most part, there is no discussion. Analysts and investors hang on every word from the Federal Reserve concerning whether quantitative easing is in fact coming to an end and what its macroeconomic impacts will be in either case, but deliberations concerning where the financial system as a whole might be or *should be* in five or ten years in terms of participation, institutional composition, ethics, etc., are largely nonexistent. Despite the near financial implosion of recent memory, "fixing" the system still means not so much learning from its mistakes as taking immediate action to ensure its survival. "Financial reform" is a gross overstatement of what is more accurately described as "political maintenance." Critical repairs to the system took place, we are told, over eight crucial days in September 2008 when high-ranking public officials and banking executives decided to shutter some storied financial institutions and leave others to be gobbled up by competitors.[91] Perhaps this was the only solution, but it was done with little to no citizen participation or even the *idea* that citizens should have input on the kind of financial system that will support them, beyond what they are able to express with their deposits, credit cards, and mortgage loans.

The problem is that the financial gatekeepers view as manipulative any attempts to apply social imagination in constructing a more inclusive, equitable, and culturally sustainable financial economy. Even within the system, brilliant minds have expended much of their energy to maximize profits in the short term. Little opportunity exists to reflect on where the system is headed in terms of the inclusiveness or fairness of institutional structures—imagination is largely reserved for creating novelty for the purpose of profit, consistent with the spirit of financialization. One can agree that imagination finds no outlet within socialism or government bureaucracy while agreeing that it is also likely to starve in environments where there is no larger vision, regardless of the workings of "free" markets.

Americans have been forced in recent years, to entertain the idea that market-based healthcare in a mass society in which technological possibility creates the prospect of financial ruin may force us to make "collective" decisions about the kind of system desired. Other industries are so vital and universal in terms of demand that governments have recognized that resource allocation based purely on market determinations is inadequate. Telecommunication services are considered so critical to the safety and proper function of citizens that utility commissions were erected to mandate certain services, limit rates, require certain response levels on network troubles, and oversee other critical measures. Certain types of insurance are subject to similar oversight. More government regulatory agencies are not being proposed here; rather, the financial sector needs more inclusive forms of participation so that civil society institutions might provide critical services on behalf of citizens and even participate in financial industry governance and regulation in a complementary role to government.

The following model is designed to initiate discussion on new approaches to the financial economy. The paradigm for this model is articulated well by Anheier: "Civil society is the self-organization of society outside the stricter realms of state power and market interests, and, in the words of Gellner (1994), serves as a counterveiling force against the powers of both."[92] Anheier's concept of "institutional voids" in the present system also is a major impetus for what follows. The questions it attempts to answer are what will fill the voids and, at a high level, how those institutions might function.[93] The first step is to identify those functional areas in which voids are found.

I Functional areas for civil society involvement

Representation: standing for citizen financial rights to offset the significant underrepresentation of individual vis-à-vis institutional investors, representing citizen groups in consumer financial services policy issues, etc. Technical expertise can be drawn from among academics, banking/financial industry retirees, and former government officials, among others. Nonexpert public representatives should work alongside those with expertise.

Advocacy: promoting initiatives for financial reform; advocating goals of financial policy independent of industry and government objectives; representing citizen groups in class-action suits; working toward partnership among government and banking/financial firms; sponsoring various cross-sector initiatives; engaging government regulatory agencies on citizens' behalf.

Mobilization: fostering grassroots participation from the broader community; coordinating letter writing campaigns; sponsoring public protests; building coalitions with other civil society actors; recruiting financial expertise from the community; initiating media blitzes; forming delegations from among NGOs, religious organizations, and other groups; acquiring capital resources to support projects. Coordination with civil society groups beyond the financial sector will be critical to success.[94] Occupy Wall Street and Jubilee 2000 are obvious examples; a mix of grassroots and more structured forms of citizen mobilization is proposed to be most successful.

Policy: presenting citizen policy platforms for financial reform; enabling financial policy input from citizen groups; prioritizing policy issues/initiatives; disseminating policy ideas among constituents; producing policy briefs in response to legislation/regulation.

Governance: participating in financial governance bodies, both public and private; providing public members for governing boards of financial institutions; recruiting citizen representatives to serve on state regulatory agencies; developing surveillance teams to promote financial industry transparency; establishing local banking councils to facilitate information exchange between citizens and the banking community; monitoring compliance with regulation.

Standards/Certification: developing and coordinating nongovernmental *public* accreditation bodies; maintaining certification standards; working with professional organizations in finance on quality/accountability/ethics issues; developing and administering certification exams; staying abreast of standards/certification changes within the industry.

Communication: facilitating information exchange among citizens, government, and financial institutions; reporting to citizens concerning changes in financial policy, industry structure (mergers, consolidations, regulations, etc.); addressing information gaps and "rhetorical challenges" that limit public participation; establishing information clearinghouses and forming networks among constituents.

Education: coordinating financial literacy campaigns; instructing community leaders and concerned citizens in the structure of the financial industry, global economic institutions, and government regulatory structures; providing instruction in financial policy development and other critical functions that are today largely unknown by the general public; instigating personal finance education as a component of secondary schooling.

Consultation: working with both financial industry representatives and government officials on issues involving public finance, industry policy, mergers/consolidations, microfinance and small business development; working with banks and financial firms to provide citizen feedback on industry developments; providing policy development consultation.

Mediation: coordinating town hall and other meetings to gather citizen input concerning financial issues and goals for the financial system. In addition to performing a mediating function between citizens and financial organizations and government agencies, civil society groups can serve a vital function by mediating the demands/conflicts among citizens themselves, as objectives for civil society participation will vary.

Watchdog: performing oversight of financial institutions and government agencies; monitoring policy compliance of banks and financial firms; establishing website links with other watchdog organizations.[95]

II Filling institutional voids

Public Board Members in Financial Institutions: "voting" board members drawn from the public who are not financial professionals (goals: transparency, accountability)[96]

Consumer Financial Advocacy Groups: defend consumers against predatory lending and other practices (goal: consumer advocacy)[97]

Public Finance Liaisons: establish the "community voice" for issues of state and local budgets, bond elections, and other government expenditures; facilitate communication between citizens and controllers of the public purse (goal: monitor public spending)

Financial Industry-Community Relations Taskforces: citizen groups formed to meet with local finance and insurance professionals; facilitate Q&A with citizen groups (goal: establish "extra-market" communications between consumers-industry representatives)

Local Citizens Banking Councils: citizen groups established to foster communication between the local community and its banking institutions and representatives (goal: rebuild trust between citizens and the banking industry)

Potential Programs Sponsored by CSOs Involved in Finance

Financial Literacy Program: general education in financial vocabulary, concepts, statements; facilitate instructors working with local banks and investment firms to initiate cooperative public education programs.

Financial Counseling: for low-income families/individuals; instruction in budgeting, saving, investment, etc.

"Financial Town Hall": facilitation of citizen meetings with representatives of financial institutions and government officials involved in the financial industry

Financial Industry-Community Relations Taskforce: promotion of meetings/Q&A with local leaders of banking and finance

Student Loan Debt Relief: consultation with students on loan acquisition and debt; provision of debt relief services

Mortgage-financing Consultation: education on types of mortgage instruments and the process of securing a mortgage, refinance procedures

Consumer-Credit Accountability Training: advisement on establishing credit, use of credit cards, debt relief counseling

Microfinance/Small Business Development: consultation with small business owners on acquisition of startup capital, grant programs for small business, etc.

Youth Financial Education Program: basic financial education for teenagers and young adults

Faith-Group Financial Forums: facilitate religious and theological dialogue on financial ethics/practices; develop faith-based statements on financial issues

Alternative Financial Economy Awareness: public information on nonmainstream financial developments (i.e., Crowdsourcing, Bitcoin, Airbnb)

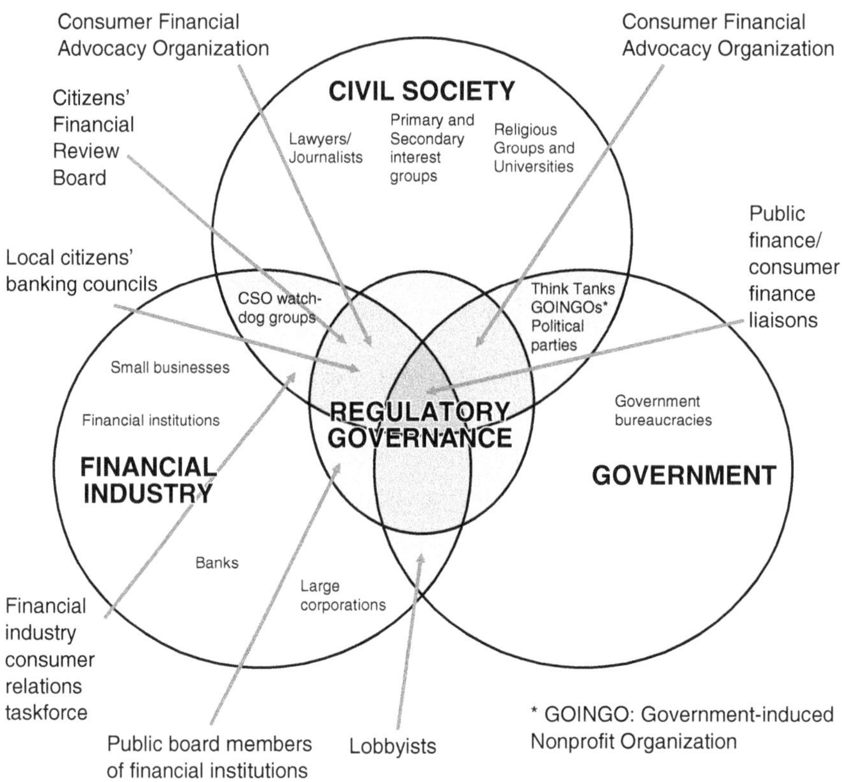

Figure 8.1 Proposed schematic for civil society involvement in finance.[98]

This model seeks primarily to start a conversation. As it is, the financial sector suffers from a dearth of ideas and, in particular, a lack of organizations addressing citizen involvement in the financial economy. Because organizations such as those proposed above would have potential for "civil society capture" by the financial industry, organization charters should be formed with this in mind. Restrictions are advised concerning funding, governance, and representation/participation by professionals from the financial industry.

The model proposed is not intended as a "collectivist" answer to present financial problems. Rather, it proposes that nongovernmental institutions can serve critical mediating roles between financial organizations and citizens without need for government interference. The emerging financial technocracy described in Chapter 2 involves a mix of public- and private-sector specialists who possess enormous control and lack key perspectives in their decision-making processes. The inclusion of civil society in the ongoing evolution of financial governance/regulation would provide a critical point of access for individuals, civic groups, and religious organizations to weigh in on the financial concerns that affect their lives in much deeper ways than the present political system allows.

Conclusion

The final section of this chapter in no way seeks to minimize the roles presently played by American CSOs such as Better Markets, Public Citizen, and Americans for Financial Reform. These groups provide critical functions, including the sponsorship of symposia, facilitating communication between citizens and their representatives, keeping legislator voting record scorecards on financial issues, providing technical analysis of financial policy/legislation, and, in the case of Americans for Financial Reform, coordinating more than 200 nonpartisan nonprofits from various sectors (civil rights, faith groups) who are demanding financial reform.[99] The work of these groups is essential; however, much of their work focuses on the watchdog function and centers on issues of national importance.

The proposed model presented in this chapter envisions the formation of community groups to facilitate personalized involvement in local financial economies. Citizen activism through national nonprofits can accomplish much, but it cannot substitute for local, grassroots organization of the kind that, virtually from the nation's founding, has distinguished American society. The financialization of American society promotes processes and instruments at the expense of relationships. Involvement of local CSOs is a principal way of countering that effect and better empowers Americans to choose their financial futures.

Emilios Avgouleas observes that even global markets call for governance structures based on shared values at some level. However, his emphasis on building "supranational regulatory structures"[100] still implies a top-down structure that will confront the past limitations of similar approaches in which rights more than values were the primary consideration. Local efforts are needed to complement these other movements, defending not only citizen rights but also expressing citizen values. In the American context, such mobilizations might also reenergize a civil sphere that, for reasons about which scholars will disagree, no longer provides the vital center to American democracy that is its legacy. A final quotation from Alexis de Tocqueville provides the ultimate justification for the "localization" of civil society:

> Local institutions are to liberty what primary schools are to science; they put it within the people's reach; they teach people to appreciate its peaceful enjoyment and accustom them to make use of it. Without local institutions a nation may give itself a free government, but it has not got the spirit of liberty.[101]

Local CSOs are today critical to the defense of liberty not only against intrusions by the state but also the dominance by a financial economy that has grown well beyond boundaries appropriate to any balanced conception of progress. The involvement of intermediary organizations focused on the public good in financial regulation and governance can help reestablish more comprehensive and integrated growth that encourages long-term stability and ethical development—a gift to future generations to offset the fiscal deficit they will inherit.

Notes

1 Quotation taken from Alexis de Tocqueville, *Democracy in America*, 3rd edn, vol. 1, edited by J. P. Mayer, translated by George Lawrence (Garden City, NY: Anchor Books, 1969), 225.
2 For example, see David Dayen, "Wall Street Is Dismantling Financial Reform Piece by Piece," *The New Republic* (December 19, 2014); available at www.newrepublic.com/article/120606/volcker-rule-delayed-how-wall-street-dismantling-financial-reform.
3 Gary Rivlin, "How Wall Street Defanged Dodd–Frank: Battalions of Regulatory Lawyers Burrowed Deep in the Federal Bureaucracy to Foil Reform," *The Nation* (May 20, 2013); available at www.thenation.com/article/174113/how-wall-street-defanged-dodd-frank. A *Bloomberg* report by Robert Schmidt and Jesse Hamilton in 2012 cited emails obtained through the Freedom of Information Act that offered insight into the network of lawyers and lobbyists involved in the Dodd–Frank Bill that ultimately comprised more than 2,300 pages. Sources acknowledged the revolving door that exists between the Securities and Exchange Commission (and other government agencies) and private industry while denying that the system privileges any particular groups. See Robert Schmidt and Jesse Hamilton, "Top Bank Lawyer's E-Mails Show Washington's Inside Game," *Bloomberg.com* (September 5, 2012); available at www.bloomberg.com/news/2012–09–05/top-bank-lawyer-s-e-mails-show-washington-s-inside-game.html.
4 Jan Aart Scholte, "Civil Society and Financial Markets: What is Not Happening and Why," Essay for the Project "Citizens versus Markets," Centre for Social Investment, University of Heidelberg (n.d.); available at http://wrap.warwick.ac.uk/53095; 2.
5 Scholte, "Civil Society and Financial Markets," 15–16.
6 Scholte, "Civil Society and Financial Markets," 22.
7 Scholte, "Civil Society and Financial Markets," 16.

8 Helmut K. Anheier, "Institutional Voids and the Role of Civil Society: The Case of Global Finance," *Global Policy* vol. 5, no. 1 (February 2014): 27.

9 Black references Fama's landmark "Efficient Capital Markets: A Review of Theory and Empirical Work," *Journal of Finance* 25, no. 2 (1970): 383; in "Seeing, Knowing, and Regulating Financial Markets," London School of Economics: Law, Society, and Economy Working Papers 24/2013 (n.d.): 1–2; available at www.lse.ac.uk/collections/law/wps/WPS2013–24_Black.pdf.

10 Black, "Seeing, Knowing, and Regulating Financial Markets."

11 Black cites Robert Shiller, *Market Volatility* (Cambridge, MA: MIT Press, 1988); Shiller, *Irrational Exuberance* (Princeton, NJ: Princeton University Press, 2000); Shiller, "From Efficient Market Theory to Behavioral Finance," *Journal of Economic Perspectives* 17, no. 1 (2003): 83; and John Kay, *The Kay Review of Equity Markets and Long Term Decision Making* (BIS, London, 2012), paras. 5.10–5.30; in "Seeing, Knowing, and Regulating Financial Markets," 9. Price "cascades" are precipitous and "self-reinforcing" price movements that seem to occur independently of basic supply and demand forces, pointing to investor behavior as a primary causal factor. See C. L. Osler, "Stop-Loss Orders and Price Cascades in Currency Markets"; available at www.newyorkfed.org/research/staff_reports/sr150.pdf.

12 Shiller, *Irrational Exuberance.*

13 Black, "Seeing, Knowing, and Regulating Financial Markets," 24. Black says that markets

> should be understood as complex adaptive *systems*, and not necessarily as a series of bilateral transactions which simply lead to aggregate effects.... Multiple transactions can create externalities but also a network of relationships and a system of interlocking rights and obligations.

Therefore, regulators need to view markets as "systems supported by institutional, social and technological infrastructures, not as a series of unconnected exchanges." See Black, "Seeing, Knowing, and Regulating Financial Markets, 45 (emphasis Black's).

14 Robert E. Prasch, "The Dodd–Frank Act: Financial Reform or Business as Usual?" *Journal of Economic Issues* 46, no. 2 (June 2012): 550.

15 Prasch, "The Dodd–Frank Act," 550.

16 Gretchen Morgenson, "A Blank Page in the S.E.C. Rule Book, Four Years Later," *New York Times* (November 8, 2014); available at www.nytimes.com/2014/11/09/business/a-blank-page-in-the-sec-rule-book-four-years-later.html?_r=0.

17 Quoted in Morgenson, "A Blank Page in the S.E.C. Rule Book."

18 See Chapter 3 of this book, pp. 80–82, 94n72.

19 Prasch, "The Dodd–Frank Act: Financial Reform or Business as Usual?" 551.

20 Prasch, "The Dodd–Frank Act: Financial Reform or Business as Usual?" 555.

21 Prasch cites Louis Brandeis, *Other People's Money and How the Bankers Use It* (New York: F. A. Stokes, 1914); in "The Dodd–Frank Act: Financial Reform or Business as Usual?" 555.

22 Severyn T. H. Bruyn, "The Moral Economy," *Review of Social Economy* LVII, no. 1 (March 1999), 36.

23 Dennis R. Young, Lester M. Salamon, and Mary Clark Grinsfelder, "Commercialization, Social Ventures, and For-Profit Competition," in *The State of Nonprofit America*, 2nd edition, ed. Lester M. Salamon (Brookings Institution Press, 2012), 524–5.

24 Young, Salamon, and Grinsfelder, "Commercialization, Social Ventures, and For-Profit Competition," 529.

25 See "Giving USA: Americans Gave $335.17 Billion to Charity in 2013; Total Approaches Pre-Recession Peak JUN 17, 2014"; available at www.philanthropy.iupui.edu/news/article/giving-usa-2014#sthash.7ABlmO7g.dpuf; accessed on November 5,

2014. See also "Charitable Giving Statistics"; available at www.nptrust.org/philanthropic-resources/charitable-giving-statistics/; accessed on November 5, 2014. Both reports cite Giving USA, whose reports can be purchased at www.givingusareports.org/.

26 Digital Media Project, "Nonprofit Organization"; available at www.dmlp.org/legal-guide/nonprofit-organization; accessed on November 5, 2014.

27 Young, Salamon, and Grinsfelder, "Commercialization, Social Ventures, and For-Profit Competition," 536.

28 Young, Salamon, and Grinsfelder, "Commercialization, Social Ventures, and For-Profit Competition," 536.

29 Jed Emerson, "The U.S. Nonprofit Capital Market: An Introductory Overview of Developmental Stages, Investors, and Funding Instruments," in *Social Purpose Enterprises*, vol. 2: 187–216; Michael E. Porter and Mark R. Kramer, "Philanthropy's New Agenda: Creating Value," *Harvard Business Review* 77 (November–December 1999): 121–30. See also Lester M. Salamon, ed., *New Frontiers of Philanthropy*, New York: Oxford University Press, 2014 which develops the contept of the foundation as a "philanthropic bank"; cited in Young, Salamon, and Grinsfelder, "Commercialization, Social Ventures, and For-Profit Competition," 539.

30 Jan Aart Scholte, "Civil Society and Democracy in Global Governance," *Global Governance* vol. 8, no. 3 (July–September 2002): 283.

31 Scholte, "Civil Society and Democracy in Global Governance," 284.

32 Scholte, "Civil Society and Democracy in Global Governance," 284.

33 OccupyWallStreet, "About"; available at http://occupywallst.org/about/; accessed on November 5, 2014.

34 I am indebted to my colleague, Dr. Sam Perry, for our many conversations on the impact of financialization and especially its effects on the reciprocality of individual and social goods, commonly ascribed to Adam Smith's "invisible hand." Of all financialization's deleterious effects, the undermining of this principle of exchange is potentially the most harmful in damaging the credibility of the market system as a whole.

35 There has also been some mainstream reporting and even support of these websites/movements. See Kimberley Thorpe, "The Financial Anarchist's Cookbook: Some of Steven Katz's Tips for Driving Creditors Crazy," *Mother Jones* (January/February 2011); available at www.motherjones.com/politics/2011/01/tips-to-avoid-creditors; and Thorpe, "50 Ways to Leave Your Banker," *Mother Jones* (January/February 2011); available at www.motherjones.com/politics/2011/01/steven-katz-credit-card-debt.

36 Prasch, "The Dodd–Frank Act: Financial Reform or Business as Usual?" 554–5.

37 Casey Given, "Harvard Survey Reveals Libertarian Streak Among Youth," *The Hill* (May 15, 2014); available at http://thehill.com/blogs/congress-blog/politics/206120-harvard-survey-reveals-libertarian-streak-among-youth. See also "Survey of Young Americans' Attitudes toward Politics and Public Service," Harvard Fall Poll 2014 (October 30, 2014); available at http://tcjlpac.com/2014/10/survey-of-young-americans-attitudes-toward-politics-and-public-service/.

38 Scholte cites J. N. Rosenau, "Governance in the Twenty-First Century," *Global Governance* 1, no. 1 (Winter 1995): 13–43; Commission on Global Governance: *Our Global Neighborhood* (Oxford: Oxford University Press, 1995); W. Reinicke, *Global Public Policy: Governing Without Government?* (Washington, DC: Brookings Institution, 1998); M. Henson and T. Sinclair, eds., *Approaches to Global Governance Theory* (Albany: State University of New York Press, 1999); in "Civil Society and Democracy in Global Governance," 288, n. 11.

39 Scholte, "Civil Society and Financial Markets," 16.

40 Scholte, "Civil Society and Financial Markets," 16. Scholte also observes how "the popular mass media gives scant attention to financial capital and its governance,

while the financial press mainly directs itself at narrow insider audiences." See Scholte, "Civil Society and Financial Markets," 16.

41 A search on the journal archive JSTOR using the search term "civil society and finance," for example, yielded references to more than 82,000 articles. Of the first 25 articles in that list, only one, which related to civil society and NAFTA, involved either the United States or a Western European country. Regarding articles involving civil society and IFIs, see for example Ngaire Woods, "Making the IMF and the World Bank More Accountable," *International Affairs* (Royal Institute of International Affairs 1944–), vol. 77, no. 1 (January 2001): 83–100; and Jonathan Murphy, "The World Bank, INGOs, and Civil Society: Converging Agendas? The Case of Universal Basic Education in Niger," *Voluntas: International Journal of Voluntary and Nonprofit Organizations*, vol. 16, no. 4 (December 2005): 353–74.

42 Scholte, "Civil Society and Financial Markets," 17–18. Both the World Bank and IMF have made certain advances in establishing networks with civil society groups that are worth exploring for possible application in the context of American finance. The IMF, for example, has an extensive website showcasing resources dedicated to working and networking with CSOs, including a robust conference schedule, workshops, economic forums, and other events designed to facilitate its interaction with private associations dedicated to global issues in political economy. It also sponsors research for scholars investigating such issues. See www.imf/org/external/np/exr/cs/.

43 See www.eesc.europa.eu/?i=portal.en.the-committee.

44 Statement in EuroFinuse's "Response to the Consultation on the Regulation of Indices: Reply of the European Federation of Financial Services Users," (EuroFinuse; emphasis in the original) 29 November 2012; available at http://ec.europa.eu/internal_market/consultations/2012/benchmarks/registered-organisations/eurofinuse_en.pdf.

45 Bridget M. Hutter and Joan O'Mahony, "The Role of Civil Society Organizations in Regulating Business," Economic & Social Research Council, The London School of Economics and Political Science, Discussion Paper No. 26 (September 2004): 7.

46 Hutter and O'Mahony, "The Role of Civil Society Organizations in Regulating Business," 7. See also "1995—Shell Reverses Decision to Dump the Brent Spar: Background," (September 13, 2011); available at www.greenpeace.org/international/en/about/history/Victories-timeline/Brent-Spar/.

47 G. Jordan, *Shell, Greenpeace and the Brent Spar* (Basingstoke, UK: Palgrave, 2002); and Boris Holzer, *Transnational Subpolitics and Corporate Discourse: A Study of Environmental Protest and the Royal Dutch/Shell Group*, PhD Thesis, London School of Economics and Political Science Department of Sociology (2002); cited in Hutter and O'Mahony, "The Role of Civil Society Organizations in Regulating Business," 7.

48 This statement is in no way intended to diminish the importance of CSOs such as Better Markets, Public Citizen, American Citizens for Financial Reform and other groups involved in financial reform and the industry generally; it simply recognizes their paucity relative to the scale of the industry and magnitude of recent problems. For an interesting (though largely technical) discussion in this regard, see the *Wall Street Journal*'s "Future of Finance" special section that offers perspectives on major financial players in government and industry; available at http://online.wsj.com/public/page/future-of-finance.html.

49 Lorenzo Fioramonti and Ekkehard Thümler, "A Civil Society Watchdog for Financial Markets: Where Private Foundations Stand," *openEconomy* (February 24, 2011): 1; available at https://www.opendemocracy.net/openeconomy/lorenzo-fioramonti-ekkehard-th%C3%BCmler/watchdog-for-financial-markets-foundations. Fioramonti is Director of the Centre for the Study of Governance Innovation at the University of Pretoria and an associate professor in the University's Department of Political Sciences. In addition, he is a senior fellow at the University of Heidelberg's Centre for Social Investment

and an associate fellow at the United Nations University Institute on Comparative Regional Integration Studies (UNU-CRIS).

50 Fioramonti and Thümler, "A Civil Society Watchdog for Financial Markets."

51 Fioramonti and Thümler, "A Civil Society Watchdog for Financial Markets."

52 Hutter and O'Mahony, "The Role of Civil Society Organizations in Regulating Business," 8.

53 Severyn T. H. Bruyn, "The Moral Economy," 30; quoted in Hutter and O'Mahony, "The Role of Civil Society Organizations in Regulating Business," 8.

54 Scholte, "Civil Society and Democracy in Global Governance," 293–4.

55 A recent positive sign in this regard was a November 21, 2014 hearing by the U.S. Senate Committee on Banking, Housing, and Urban Affairs titled "Improving Financial Institution Supervision: Examining and Addressing Regulatory Capture." See www.banking.senate.gov/public/index.cfm?FuseAction=Hearings.Hearing&Hearing_ID=ba1c89dc-817b-4c-ad-9e16–514fd6e6a489.

56 Anheier, "Institutional Voids and the Role of Civil Society," 25.

57 Anheier, "Institutional Voids and the Role of Civil Society," 24.

58 Anheier cites David Vogel, *Trading Up: Consumer and Environmental Regulation in a Global Economy* (Cambridge, MA: Harvard University Press, 1995), 18; in "Institutional Voids and the Role of Civil Society," 24.

59 Tanja A. Börzel, *et al.*, "Racing to the Top? Regulatory Competition Among Firms in Areas of Limited Statehood," in *Governance without a State? Policies and Politics in Areas of Limited Statehood*, ed. Thomas Risse (New York: Columbia University Press, 2011), 122–46.

60 Peter Gibbon and Jakob Vestergaard, "Commodity Derivatives: Financialization and Regulatory Reform," Danish Institute for International Studies, DIIS Working Paper 2013:12 Copenhagen; cited in Johannes Petry, "Regulatory Capture, Civil Society & Global Finance in Derivative Regulation: An Analysis of Commodity Derivative Regulation in Europe," ECPR Standing Group on Regulatory Governance, 5th Biennial Conference, 25–27 June 2014, Barcelona, Spain; available via the Social Science Research Network at http://papers.ssrn.com/sol3/papers.cfm?abstract_id=2450644.

61 Petry states that "although the interests of these different groups were diverse, they were united by the idea of curbing speculation." See Petry, "Regulatory Capture, Civil Society & Global Finance in Derivative Regulation," 18.

62 For an informative perspective on the "servant" role of finance, see Paul H. Dembinski, *Finance: Servant or Deceiver? Financialization at the Crossroads* (New York: Palgrave, 2009).

63 Michael E. Porter and Mark R. Kramer, "Creating Shared Value: How to Reinvent Capitalism—and Unleash a Wave of Innovation and Growth," *Harvard Business Review* (January–February 2011): 66.

64 Porter and Kramer, "Creating Shared Value," 64, 72–73.

65 Porter and Kramer reject that thinking by insisting that individual "companies can create economic value by creating societal value" in three distinct ways: "by reconceiving products and markets, redefining productivity in the value chain, and building supportive industry clusters at the company's locations." See Porter and Kramer, "Creating Shared Value," 67.

66 Porter and Kramer, "Creating Shared Value," 67.

67 Anheier, "Institutional Voids and the Role of Civil Society," 30. In speculating on possible reasons why civil society actors "are underrepresented in the financial sector," Anheier notes that "finance is a 'dry affair' and more emotionally charged issues like peace, human rights or the environment offer easier affective attachment." Also, "the abstract nature of banking and finance doesn't help either, which makes the hurdle separating passive animosity and frustration from active involvement relatively high." See Anheier, "Institutional Voids and the Role of Civil Society," 31.

68 Anheier, "Institutional Voids and the Role of Civil Society," 31.
69 Anheier, "Institutional Voids and the Role of Civil Society," 31.
70 Emilios Avgouleas, "Effective Governance of Global Financial Markets: An Evolutionary Plan for Reform," *Global Policy* vol. 4, suppl. 1 (July 2013): 78.
71 Avgouleas cites R. Herring and J. Carmassi, "The Corporate Structure of International Financial Conglomerates, Complexity and Its Implications for Safety and Soundness," in A. N. Berger, P. Molyneux, and J. Wilson, eds., *Oxford Handbook of Banking* (Oxford: Oxford University Press, 2010), 195–229; and the Basel Committee on Banking Supervision, "Report and Recommendations of the Cross-Border Bank Resolution Group," (September 2009): 14–16; in "Effective Governance of Global Financial Markets," 78.
72 Hutter and O'Mahony, "The Role of Civil Society Organizations in Regulating Business," 9.
73 Hutter and O'Mahony, "The Role of Civil Society Organizations in Regulating Business," 9–10.
74 Naomi T. Tacuyan, "Disclosure for Charitable Solicitors," *Responsive Philanthropy* (Spring 2005): 12–15.
75 For an interesting discussion of NGOs' successes and failures in the global arena, see Steve Charnovitz, "Two Centuries of Participation: NGOs and International Governance," *Michigan Journal of International Law* vol. 18, no. 2 (1997): 183–286.
76 Fioramonti and Thümler, "A Civil Society Watchdog for Financial Markets."
77 Fioramonti and Thümler, "A Civil Society Watchdog for Financial Markets."
78 Bruyn, "The Moral Economy," 44.
79 With respect to the principle of fiduciary duty, De Bondt references William O. Douglas, *Democracy and Finance* (New Haven: Yale University Press, 1940); John C. Bogle, *The Battle for the Soul of Capitalism* (London: Yale University Press, 2005); and Bogle, "Restoring Faith in Financial Markets," *Wall Street Journal* (March 26, 2010); in "The Crisis of 2008 and Financial Reform," *Qualitative Research in Financial Markets* 2, no. 3 (2010): 147–8.
80 Mandis notes that "at Goldman there was the added restriction that partners could not pull out their capital until after they retired (a far cry from the three-to-five year vesting that bankers complain about today)." See Steven G. Mandis, "What It Will Take to Change the Culture of Wall Street," *Harvard Business Review* Blog Network (October 24, 2014); available at http://blogs.hbr.org/2014/10/what-it-will-take-to-change-the-culture-of-wall-street/.
81 Mandis, "What It Will Take to Change the Culture of Wall Street."
82 Rosa Lastra, "Who Guards the Guardians of Monetary Stability and Financial Stability? That is the Key Question Behind the Debate about the Accountability of the Bank of England" (August 19, 2011); available at http://eprints.lse.ac.uk/38143/.
83 Cited in Mandis, "What It Will Take to Change the Culture of Wall Street."
84 See Pew Forum, "Millennials in Adulthood: Detached from Institutions, Networked with Friends," (March 7, 2014); available at www.pewsocialtrends.org/2014/03/07/millennials-in-adulthood/.
85 David Brooks, "The Evolution of Trust," *New York Times* (June 30, 2014); available at www.nytimes.com/2014/07/01/opinion/david-brooks-the-evolution-of-trust.html?_r=0.
86 David Brooks, "The Evolution of Trust."
87 John R. Freeman, "Technocracy and Democracy in Monetary Institutions," *International Organization*, vol. 56, no. 4 (Autumn 2002): 907.
88 Interesting in this regard was a proposal of Federal Reserve Board Vice Chairman Preston Martin in response to bank failures in the 1980s. He recommended "surveillance boards" staffed by retired bankers and certified public accountants for early detection of bank failures. He also recommended that the banking industry develop a code of ethics. See "Fed's Martin Proposes Self-Policing by Banks," *Los Angeles*

Times (AP Report) (December 4, 1985); available at http://articles.latimes.com/1985–12–04/business/fi-677_1_bank-failures.

89 A *Fortune* article reported that in 2011–2012, 191,571 students received advanced business degrees from American colleges and universities and that the MBA has become the most popular graduate degree. Presumably, most of these programs require advanced courses in economics and finance. See John A. Byrne, "Why the MBA has become the most popular master's degree in the U.S." *Fortune* (May 31, 2014); available at http://fortune.com/2014/05/31/mba-popular-masters-degree/.

90 Kevin Wack, "Weill Puts Glass–Steagall Back on Washington's Agenda," *American Banker* (July 25, 2012); available at www.americanbanker.com/issues/177_143/sandy-weill-puts-glass-steagall-back-on-washingtons-agenda-1051271–1.html.

91 James B. Stewart, "Eight Days: The Battle to Save the American Financial System," *New Yorker* (September 21, 2009); available at www.newyorker.com/magazine/2009/09/21/eight-days.

92 Anheier cites E. Gellner, *Conditions of Liberty: Civil Society and its Rivals* (New York: Allen Lane, 1994); in "Institutional Voids and the Role of Civil Society," 26.

93 The ideas that follow are derived from my own "social imaginary" as well as from outlines and models of scholars such as Scholte, Anheier, and others who have offered other high-level outlines of civil society involvement in aspects of economic governance. According to Scholte's typology of civil society elements, what follows should likely be classified as falling somewhere between "reformist" agenda—in that it wishes to correct flaws in the existing regime while principally "leaving underlying social structures intact," and a "transformist" one—in the sense of desiring a broad social movement among citizens to take back considerable oversight responsibility for their financial system. For more, see Scholte, "Civil Society and Democracy in Global Governance," 284.

94 Petry, "Regulatory Capture, Civil Society & Global Finance in Derivative Regulation."

95 In all these areas, acting "locally" is critical to avoid the elitism that often accompanies civil society action at high levels. See Lisa Jordan, "Civil Society's Role in Global Policymaking," *Global Policy Forum* (March 2003); available at www.globalpolicy.org/component/content/article/177/31621.html.

96 An advocacy organization might well lobby for a law requiring public members on the governing boards of all publicly traded financial institutions.

97 Some groups like this exist at the national level.

98 This diagram was contributed by my colleague and research assistant Dresden McGregor, whose assistance on this project was invaluable.

99 See the Americans for Financial Reform website at http://ourfinancialsecurity.org/; and the Public Citizen website at www.citizen.org/Page.aspx?pid=183.

100 Avgouleas, "Effective Governance of Global Financial Markets," 83.

101 Tocqueville, *Democracy in America*, 63.

Bibliography

Anheier, Helmut K. "Institutional Voids and the Role of Civil Society: The Case of Global Finance." *Global Policy* 5, no. 1 (February 2014): 23–35.

Avgouleas, Emilios. "Effective Governance of Global Financial Markets: An Evolutionary Plan for Reform." *Global Policy* 4, no. suppl. 1 (July 2013): 74–84.

Black, Julia. "Seeing, Knowing, and Regulating Financial Markets." Law, Society, and Economy Working Papers 24/2013, London School of Economics, (n.d.). www.lse.ac.uk/collections/law/wps/WPS2013-24_Black.pdf; accessed on November 10, 2014.

Bogle, John C. *The Battle for the Soul of Capitalism*. London: Yale University Press, 2005.

Bogle, John C. "Restoring Faith in Financial Markets." *Wall Street Journal*, March 26, 2010.

Bondt, Werner de. "The Crisis of 2008 and Financial Reform." *Qualitative Research in Financial Markets* 2, no. 3 (2010): 137–56.

Brandeis, Louis. *Other People's Money and How the Bankers Use It*. New York: F. A. Stokes, 1914.

Brooks, David. "The Evolution of Trust." *New York Times*, June 30, 2014. www.nytimes.com/2014/07/01/opinion/david-brooks-the-evolution-of-trust.html?_r=0; accessed on November 12, 2014.

Bruyn, Severyn T. H. "The Moral Economy." *Review of Social Economy* LVII, no. 1 (March 1999): 25–46.

Byrne, John A. "Why the MBA Has Become the Most Popular Master's Degree in the U.S." *Fortune*, May 31, 2014. http://fortune.com/2014/05/31/mba-popular-masters-degree/; accessed on December 31, 2014.

Börzel, Tanja A., Adrienne Heritier, Nicole Kranz, and Christian R. Thauer. "Racing to the Top? Regulatory Competition Among Firms in Areas of Limited Statehood." In *Governance without a State? Policies and Politics in Areas of Limited Statehood*, edited by Thomas Risse, 144–70. New York: Columbia University Press, 2011.

Charnovitz, Steve. "Two Centuries of Participation: NGOs and International Governance." *Michigan Journal of International Law* 18, no. 2 (1997): 183–286.

Commission on Global Governance. *Our Global Neighborhood*. Oxford: Oxford University Press, 1995.

Dayen, David. "Wall Street Is Dismantling Financial Reform Piece by Piece." *New Republic*, December 19, 2014. www.newrepublic.com/article/120606/volcker-rule-delayed-how-wall-street-dismantling-financial-reform; accessed on January 2, 2015.

Dembinski, Paul H. *Finance: Servant or Deceiver? Financialization at the Crossroads*. New York: Palgrave Macmillan, 2008.

Digital Media Project. "Nonprofit Organization." *DMLP.org*, February 3, 2009. www.dmlp.org/legal-guide/nonprofit-organization.

Douglas, William O. *Democracy and Finance*. New Haven, CT: Yale University Press, 1940.

Emerson, Jed. "The U.S. Nonprofit Capital Market: An Introductory Overview of Developmental Stages, Investors, and Funding Instruments." *Social Purpose Enterprises* 2, chap. 10: 187–216.

EuroFinuse. "Response to the Consultation on the Regulation of Indices: Reply of the European Federation of Financial Services Users." *EC.europa.eu*, November 29, 2012. http://ec.europa.eu/internal_market/consultations/2012/benchmarks/registered-organisations/ eurofinuse_en.pdf; accessed on November 3, 2014.

Fama, Eugene. "Efficient Capital Markets: A Review of Theory and Empirical Work." *Journal of Finance* 25, no. 2 (1970): 383–417.

Fioramonti, Lorenzo, and Ekkehard Thümler. "A Civil Society Watchdog for Financial Markets: Where Private Foundations Stand." *openEconomy*, February 24, 2011; available at www.opendemocracy.net/openeconomy/lorenzo-fioramonti-ekkehard-th%C3%BCmler/watchdog-for-financial-markets-foundations; accessed on November 10, 2014.

Freeman, John R. "Technocracy and Democracy in Monetary Institutions." *International Organization* 56, no. 4 (Autumn 2002): 889–910.

Gellner, E. *Conditions of Liberty: Civil Society and Its Rivals*. New York: Allen Lane, 1994.

Gibbon, Peter, and Jakob Vestergaard. "Commodity Derivatives: Financialization and Regulatory Reform." DIIS Working Paper 2013:12 Copenhagen, Danish Institute for International Studies, 2013.

Given, Casey. "Harvard Survey Reveals Libertarian Streak among Youth." *The Hill*, May 15, 2014. http://thehill.com/blogs/congress-blog/politics/206120-harvard-survey-reveals-libertarian-streak-among-youth; accessed on November 5, 2014.

Giving USA. "Giving USA: Americans Gave $335.17 Billion to Charity in 2013; Total Approaches Pre-Recession Peak JUN 17, 2014." *Philanthropy.iupui.edu*, June 17, 2014. www.philanthropy.iupui.edu/news/article/giving-usa-2014#sthash.7ABlmO7g.dpuf; accessed April 1, 2015.

Greenpeace. "1995—Shell Reverses Decision to Dump the Brent Spar: Background," (September 13, 2011); www.greenpeace.org/international/en/about/history/Victories-timeline/Brent-Spar/; accessed on November 3, 2014.

Harvard University Institute of Politics. "Survey of Young Americans' Attitudes toward Politics and Public Service," October 30, 2014, Harvard Fall Poll, 2014 edition. http://tcjlpac.com/2014/10/survey-of-young-americans-attitudes-toward-politics-and-public-service/; accessed on November 5, 2014.

Henson, M., and T. Sinclair, eds. *Approaches to Global Governance Theory*. Albany: State University of New York Press, 1999.

Herring, R. and J. Carmassi. "The Corporate Structure of International Financial Conglomerates, Complexity and Its Implications for Safety and Soundness." In *Oxford Handbook of Banking*, edited by A. N. Berger, P. Molyneux, and J. Wilson, 195–229. Oxford: Oxford University Press, 2010.

Holzer, B., and London School of Economics and Political Science Department of Sociology. *Transnational Subpolitics and Corporate Discourse: A Study of Environmental Protest and the Royal Dutch/Shell Group*. UK: UMI Dissertations Publishing, 2001.

Hutter, Bridget M., and Joan O'Mahony. "The Role of Civil Society Organizations in Regulating Business." Discussion Paper No. 26, The London School of Economics and Political Science, 2004.

Jordan, G. *Shell, Greenpeace and the Brent Spar*. Basingstroke: Palgrave, 2001.

Jordan, Lisa. "Civil Society's Role in Global Policymaking." *Global Policy Forum*, March 2003. www.globalpolicy.org/component/content/article/177/31621.html; accessed on December 31, 2014.

Kay, John. *The Kay Review of Equity Markets and Long Term Decision Making*. London: BIS, 2012.

Lastra, Rosa. "Who Guards the Guardians of Monetary Stability and Financial Stability? That Is the Key Question behind the Debate about the Accountability of the Bank of England." *EPrints.lse.ac.uk*, August 19, 2011. http://eprints.lse.ac.uk/38143/; accessed on November 10, 2014.

Los Angeles Times. "Fed's Martin Proposes Self-Policing by Banks," *Los Angeles Times* (AP Report) (December 4, 1985); available at http://articles.latimes.com/1985–12–04/business/fi-677_1_bank-failures; accessed on December 12, 2014.

Mandis, Steven G. "What It Will Take to Change the Culture of Wall Street." *Harvard Business Review* Blog Network, October 24, 2014. http://blogs.hbr.org/2014/10/what-it-will-take-to-change-the-culture-of-wall-street/; accessed on November 12, 2014.

Morgenson, Gretchen. "A Blank Page in the S.E.C. Rule Book, Four Years Later." *New York Times*, November 8, 2014. www.nytimes.com/2014/11/09/business/a-blank-page-in-the-sec-rule-book-four-years-later.html?_r=0: accessed on November 12, 2014.

Murphy, Jonathan. "The World Bank, INGOs, and Civil Society: Converging Agendas?

The Case of Universal Basic Education in Niger." *Voluntas: International Journal of Voluntary and Nonprofit Organizations* 16, no. 4 (December 2005): 353–74.
National Philanthropic Trust. "Charitable Giving Statistics." *NPTrust.org*, (n.d.). www.nptrust.org/philanthropic-resources/charitable-giving-statistics; accessed on April 1, 2015.
OccupyWallStreet. "About." *OccupyWallSt.org*, (n.d.). http://occupywallst.org/about/.
Osler, C. L. "Stop-Loss Orders and Price Cascades in Currency Markets." *NewYorkFed.org*, (n.d.). www.newyorkfed.org/ research/staff_reports/sr150.pdf; accessed on January 2, 2015.
Petry, Johannes. "Regulatory Capture, Civil Society & Global Finance in Derivative Regulation: An Analysis of Commodity Derivative Regulation in Europe." In *ECPR Standing Group on Regulatory Governance*. Barcelona, Spain, 2014. http://papers.ssrn.com/sol3/ papers.cfm?abstract_id=2450644.
Pew Forum, "Millennials in Adulthood: Detached from Institutions, Networked with Friends," (March 7, 2014); www.pewsocialtrends.org/2014/03/07/millennials-in-adulthood/; accessed on October 7, 2014.
Porter, Michael E., and Mark R. Kramer. "Creating Shared Value: How to Reinvent Capitalism—and Unleash a Wave of Innovation and Growth." *Harvard Business Review* 89, no. 1–2 (January–February 2011): 62–77.
Porter, Michael E., and Mark R. Kramer. "Philanthropy's New Agenda: Creating Value." *Harvard Business Review* 77, no. 6 (November–December 1999): 121–30.
Prasch, Robert E. "The Dodd–Frank Act: Financial Reform or Business as Usual?" *Journal of Economic Issues* XLVI, no. 2 (June 2012): 549–56.
Reinicke, W. *Global Public Policy: Governing Without Government*? Washington, DC: Brookings Institution, 1998.
Rivlin, Gary. "How Wall Street Defanged Dodd–Frank: Battalions of Regulatory Lawyers Burrowed Deep in the Federal Bureaucracy to Foil Reform." *Nation*, May 20, 2013. www.thenation.com/article/ 174113/how-wall-street-defanged-dodd-frank; accessed on November 3, 2014.
Rosenau, James N. "Governance in the Twenty-First Century." *Global Governance* 1, no. 1 (Winter 1995): 13–43.
Salamon, Lester M., ed. *New Frontiers of Philanthropy*. New York: Oxford University Press, 2014.
Schmidt, Robert, and Jesse Hamilton. "Top Bank Lawyer's E-Mails Show Washington's Inside Game." *Bloomberg.com*, September 5, 2012. www.bloomberg.com/news/2012-09-05/top-bank-lawyer-s-e-mails-show-washington-s-inside-game.html; accessed on November 1, 2014.
Scholte, Jan Aart. "Civil Society and Democracy in Global Governance." *Global Governance* 8, no. 3 (September 2002): 281–304.
Scholte, Jan Aart. "Civil Society and Financial Markets: What Is Not Happening and Why." Essay for the Project "Citizens versus Markets," University of Heidelberg, (n.d.) http://wrap.warwick.ac.uk/53095/; accessed on November 3, 2014.
Shiller, Robert. *Irrational Exuberance*. Princeton, NJ: Princeton University Press, 2000.
Shiller, Robert. *Market Volatility*. Cambridge, MA: MIT Press, 1988.
Shiller, Robert J. "From Efficient Markets Theory to Behavioral Finance." *Journal of Economic Perspectives* 17, no. 1 (Winter 2003): 83–104.
Stewart, James B. "Eight Days: The Battle to Save the American Financial System." *New Yorker*, September 21, 2009. www.newyorker.com/magazine/2009/09/21/eight-days; accessed on August 10, 2014.

Tacuyan, Naomi T. "Disclosure for Charitable Solicitors." *Responsive Philanthropy* (Spring 2005): 12–15.

Thorpe, Kimberley. "50 Ways to Leave Your Banker." *Mother Jones*, January/February 2011. www.motherjones.com/politics/2011/01/steven-katz-credit-card-debt.

Thorpe, Kimberley. "The Financial Anarchist's Cookbook: Some of Steven Katz's Tips for Driving Creditors Crazy." *Mother Jones*, January/February 2011. www.motherjones.com/politics/2011/01/tips-to-avoid-creditors.

Tocqueville, Alexis de. *Democracy in America*, 3rd edition, vol. 1. Edited by J. P. Mayer, translated by George Lawrence. Garden City, NY: Anchor Books, 1969.

Vogel, David. *Trading Up: Consumer and Environmental Regulation in a Global Economy*. Cambridge, MA: Harvard University Press, 1995.

Wack, Kevin. "Weill Puts Glass–Steagall Back on Washington's Agenda." *American Banker*, July 25, 2012. www.americanbanker.com/issues/177_143/sandy-weill-puts-glass-steagall-back-on-washingtons-agenda-1051271-1.html; accessed on November 10, 2014.

Woods, Ngaire. "Making the IMF and the World Bank More Accountable." *International Affairs (Royal Institute of International Affairs 1944–)* 77, no. 1 (January 2001): 83–100.

Young, Dennis R., Lester M. Salamon, and Mary Clark Grinsfelder. "Commercialization, Social Ventures, and For-Profit Competition." In *The State of Nonprofit America*, edited by Lester M. Salamon, 2nd edition, 521–48. Washington, DC: Brookings Institution Press, 2012.

9 Conclusion

Despite much popular anger toward Wall Street chicanery and the flood of books and legislation in response to the recent financial crisis, little real change has taken place. How does one explain that the incentives of market participants as well as the structural and, to a considerable extent, regulatory components of the financial system are not much different than they were prior to 2008? Little has been done to effect real improvement because, for the most part, American society has skirted the basic social and moral questions at the heart of financial dysfunction.

Most efforts to "correct finance" have been technical attempts to put us back on track after our recent derailment, without considering the *cultural* implications of finance's ubiquitous reach and its influence on formative institutions. The essential yet incorrigible nature of the financial industry cajoles Americans into turning a blind eye to its transgressions, as much as its arcane techniques, because it exists as a lifeline in which many are invested. This dependence enables a dispassionately rational, bottom-line thinking to penetrate deep into American consciousness and into those core establishments that constitute the nation's identity. "Return" and "efficiency" dominate decision making in many areas, from the "church shopping" that shapes our religious lives to the length of our hospital stays and, with the exploding cost of college education, the number of children a family brings into this world.

Some undoubtedly contend that this extreme financial orientation has been essential to the American economic miracle. The United States has continued a course of reasonable economic growth even as other nations have struggled mightily with fiscal problems often caused by financial excesses that jeopardize national solvency. With stock markets rising and capital flowing again, the nation's economy no longer teeters on the brink of collapse as it did a couple of years ago. Yet, the spell of complacency beguiles Americans once again. Such rationalization, no matter how enchanting, discounts the bigger picture of finance as a socially integral institution with enormous power to reshape values and attitudes as much as bank accounts. Despite the recent resurgence of the U.S. economy, events in recent years have turned the traditional good of financial intermediation in matching not only savers with investors but also capital with social purpose into a form of finance that damages our sense of humanity and community.

Finance is unrivaled in its radical information asymmetry, concentration of market power, ubiquitous reach of influence, and criticality to economic well-being. Almost every household and firm in the United States (and increasingly the world) is involved in the financial economy in some way. Nevertheless, the knowledge gap between industry professionals on the one hand and investors and consumers on the other makes abuses of trust more likely in finance than in other industries.

These unique characteristics make some form of industry regulation inevitable. Justin O'Brien claims that the "appropriate first order question ... is not *how* we regulate, but *for what specific purpose*?" The problem in answering O'Brien's question is that dominance of the neoclassical mindset in mainstream economics greatly limits such teleological inquiries—markets determine purpose; regulators exist to enforce rules. Regulatory reform is taking place, however, if for no other reason than the magnitude of recent problems, several of which O'Brien observes:

> Three interlinked global phenomena are at play: flawed governance mechanisms, including remuneration incentives skewed in favor of short-term profit-taking and leverage; flawed models of financing, including, in particular, the dominant originate-and-distribute model of securitization, which promoted a moral hazard-culture; and regulatory structures predicated on micro-institutional risk reduction which created incentives for capital arbitrage and paid insufficient attention to systemic macro-credit risk. These factors combined to create an architectural blueprint for economic growth in which innovation trumped security.[1]

One would hope, however, that the present "round" of regulatory reform in this seemingly unending cycle would be wiser in embracing the institutional context of the environment regulated. The first step is reviving "proper mechanisms for the transmission of institutional memory."[2] Lacking knowledge of the human motivations and institutional structures that led to past problems, we are fated to revisit them. And it is likely that the material and ethical consequences of our repeated missteps will be pitched on higher levels.

The present indecision as to how regulation should proceed offers an interesting possibility as we look to *reform the greatest economic machine of history*. The previous statement captures the bizarre conundrum facing American society. In Henry Adams' strange but brilliant book, *The Degradation of Democratic Dogma*,[3] he theorizes that the vital organizing energy of civilization may have crested and that society may be dissipating into disorder. His application of the Second Law of Thermodynamics, "entropy," to history and social structures has renewed relevance today. Despite the long stretch of robust economic growth and the expansion of technical systems to almost every aspect of life, "order" seems simultaneously to be eroding. In this regard, financial problems have become a bellwether signaling both our cultural imbalance and the limitations of rationalism; they also increasingly appear to be the engine of social entropy. The challenge is to mobilize the social and moral capital to prove Adams wrong and demonstrate that we can tame the sector, initiating true ethical reform that only *begins* with finance.

A virtuous economy requires a vibrant civil society. Reassessing the dynamic development of voluntary associations in the nation's early history that supported its fledgling political and economic order can be instructive. The subtler and more intransigent financialization crisis described in this book would seem to require a similar civic energy for resolution. The kind of reform being worked out in Washington only repositions the train back on the original tracks, with the likelihood that a future derailment could inflict more damage than the last one. What is envisioned here is more in line with Robert Solomon's vision of a business culture and economic system capable of forming individual virtue alongside material development. Such paradigmatic change ideally would begin with banking and finance because, being so central to the nation's development and so demonstrably vulnerable to moral drift, the sector also offers an opportunity for broader cultural reform.

A shift both in industry governance and in its regulatory framework to include greater involvement of civil society could have significant positive byproducts that extend well beyond the industry. These changes are also proposed to promote a genuine "democratization of finance," one that more equitably distributes its benefits and involves citizens in its oversight. The hopeful message is that the pervasive reach of finance can become morally transformative if we learn to harness its techniques and steer the industry toward more virtuous outcomes. The participation of ethicists, theologians, and philosophers is needed to counter the insular nature of the industry and to help re-embed its institutions in the wider society it is meant to serve.

Perhaps offering some justification for the involvement of theologians in financial reform, author and financial market analyst Satyajit Das, appearing in the PBS Frontline documentary "Money, Power, and Wall Street," summarized global society's decisive turn to finance as a panacea:

> We now somehow believe that finance sort of drives everything. The crisis was an opportunity to change that, to ask questions like, "What is the role of finance in our economy? What is the role of banks?"
>
> But I suspect it's very hard because it's very difficult to change gods. And in the modern age, our god was finance, except it's (*sic*) turned out to be a very cruel and destructive god.[4]

Das's comment implies that a critical opportunity has been missed. Indeed, the revelations from the recent calamity, in some ways, are less concerning than the realization of just how quickly American society has adapted to the "new normal" of this financially driven economy. Paul Dembinski, director of the Observatoire de la Finance in Geneva, states that the financial paradigm "has gradually permeated and transformed behavior patterns, mechanisms and structures, and extended its control over society to the point where it is now one of its main organizing principles, or indeed the dominant one."[5] Some might suggest that present inequalities, ethical transgressions, and lack of transparency are the best for which we can hope in our modern, mass society, but the extension of financial ways of thinking and acting to such a broad array of institutions is likely to have even more significant social and ethical consequences for future generations. One might be more optimistic than Das, however, in believing that the "moment" for reflection on the financial system has not passed completely. There is opportunity to establish a more humane economy; yet *genuine* ethical reform is essential.

Despite seeming ethical problems that have been associated with the rising dominance of finance, some argue that greed has been oversold as a source of the recent crisis. Philip Booth notes how "governments and monetary authorities have created incentives for banks to behave recklessly," stimulating imprudent behavior.[6] He dismisses the potential for ethics reform "unless self-interest in financial markets runs with the grain of the interests of society."[7] In Booth's view, government incursions into markets will have generally negative implications for social ethics, and thus we must allow individual self-interest to synchronize with collective interests as the best path to ethical reform. A limiting factor to his solution, however, is the general assumption that synchronization of self-interest and society's interests are accomplished through the market or not at all. The market system is a vital component of both ethical reform and the harmonizing of interests but inadequate alone to bear the load.

Human ingenuity and technology, moreover, have added to the moral challenge Booth describes. They have enabled opportunistic behaviors even as they have provided cover for those who profit from financial "innovation." O'Brien demonstrates how the "originate-distribute-relocate model of financial engineering significantly emaciated corporate responsibility precisely because it distanced institutional actors at every stage of the process from the consequences of their actions."[8] Ultimately, the dynamics of finance allow almost everyone to take refuge in ignorance, but that is what makes the ethics problem associated with the ongoing financialization crisis so persistent. The "compartmentalization" of knowledge, and the ethical free-play it enables, is available to chief executive officers and low-level analysts alike. Even investors can take advantage of insider information, often beyond public purview.

Philosophical and theological exploration of our financial culture—reflective examination of what finance is for—could be valuable in reestablishing the true purpose of finance and ending the reign of purely calculative reason over an industry that offers so much more. Chapter 5 criticized some of the Catholic Church's financial practices, including accounting shenanigans employed to cover up clerical abuse. Recently, however, there have been positive signs in the Church's Vatican Bank reforms and in encyclical pronouncements that the financial world must change. In 2009, Pope Benedict XVI published the encyclical *Caritas in Veritate* ("*Charity in Truth*") to rearticulate many of the ideas expressed in Paul VI's *Populorum Progressio* ("*On Human Development*") four decades earlier. Benedict's encyclical, however, was more than a tribute to a predecessor; it also responded to monumental changes in the financial aspect of human development. While Benedict acknowledges the expansion of the global economy "that has lifted billions of people out of misery," he expresses concern about "the damaging effects on the real economy of badly managed and largely speculative financial dealing" and the exploitation of both human and natural resources that have resulted.[9] He references a time when finance was integral to social and moral formation. The lender-borrower relationship involved more than capital transferred and debt owed; it forged the basis for meaningful community and made individuals dependent upon one another in the best way. The encyclical demonstrates Benedict's awareness that the form of poverty is changing with significant shifts in the world economy. While acknowledging global wealth increases "in absolute terms," there are renewed concerns about the inequalities that intensely financial forms of growth entail.[10]

Benedict laments the modern idea of development that has caused much of the world to turn away from supporting institutional networks that offer services for the poor.[11] He implores the world to put away financial games that enrich some but offer little real development for the many; such manipulative growth forgets the need for charity in the hope that finance can craft some kind of magic bullet for the social problem. He also notes how changes in the financial system are narrowing the scope of business to a singular focus on the return to shareholders. That myopic vision leads to "a speculative *use of financial resources* that yields to the temptation of seeking only short-term profit, without regard for the long-term sustainability of the enterprise" even as it deters "further economic initiatives in countries in need of development."[12] Here, Benedict unmistakably connects an element of financialization (speculation to maximize shareholder wealth) to the neglect of impoverished nations that need real, sustainable growth.

Charity in Truth recognizes how even those who benefit monetarily from speculative dealings are diminished because such practices strain solidarity and obscure meaning in society. The encyclical advocates what might be considered an absurd goal from the perspective of contemporary finance: "to launch financial initiatives in which the humanitarian dimension predominates."[13] Benedict clearly sees this proposal not as something new but as one that seeks to return to finance's noble past. He knows that state enforcement alone cannot accomplish it; a humanitarian economy requires ethical commitments by financial professionals and their associations, investor groups, and even consumers, who have a responsibility to become educated in their choices.

Recently, Pope Francis has taken up the financial reform mantle, blaming corruption and the deregulation of markets for inspiring a "cult of money" that has led to rising income inequality. He notes how this "imbalance is due to ideologies promoting markets' absolute freedom and financial speculation, which prevent governments from exercising their right to control [of financial institutions] for the common good."[14] Markets are being granted freedom rather than people—a perverse twist of means and ends that elevates the wellbeing of economic systems over that of the communities they are designed to serve. In this respect, theologian William Cavanaugh states that what is needed is "a substantive account of the ends of earthly life and creation, so that we may enter into particular judgments of what kinds of exchanges are free and what kinds are not."[15] He describes the consumerism of contemporary culture in a way analogous to the financialization of capitalism in stating that consumerism "is not so much about having *more* as it is about having *something else*."[16] This condition reflects a spiritual restlessness with material possessions resulting from the global economy's disposition to make everything a commodity, even the most personal and sacred elements of life. In such an economic climate, new possibilities for exploitation abound.[17]

Cavanaugh's concern with consumerism has much to do with the alienation of consumers from the products they purchase and even from the work that funds their purchases.[18] The shift to increasingly complex financial instruments has contributed similarly to alienation of investors and ambivalence toward the objects of investment. These conditions taken together result in a kind of economic anomie, impoverishing the spirit in consumption and investment in ways that transcend the income spectrum. Even those privileged with wealth often no longer care for what they own because, in many cases, they no longer understand what they own, much as consumers remain aloof from the Byzantine processes that supply our retail goods.

Libertarian economist William Niskanen criticizes *Caritas in Veritate* for making excessive demands of the "human spirit" and, in particular, the Pope's contention that improvement of humanity necessitates "solidarity ... a sense of responsibility on the part of everyone with regard to everyone."[19] For Niskanen, such an effervescence of social concern led to the massively expensive "Ponzi schemes" of Social Security and Medicare that threaten the nation's solvency. He sees the ethics of capitalism as "undemanding" because it stems from "the abundant supply of self-interest" and depends only minimally on the "awesome instruments of threat" available to government.[20] Niskanen believes "good" can result from the lack of personal caring in modern capitalist economies because it enables more specialized divisions of labor that, in turn, lead to "a higher level of output and income for most everyone."[21] Moreover, he is skeptical of ideas like those of Benedict that a global economic system can be reformed around principles of social responsibility, respect for workers' rights and dignity, robust international organizations, etc., that draw on an "inherently limited supply of caring."[22] The obvious problem, however, is that Niskanen's views represent the status quo, which not only exhibits a lack of solidarity and caring but, recently, economic instability as well.

The Roman Catholic Church's recent steps to get its own financial house in order as well as to speak out on those qualities of the global financial system that have fostered an unsustainable distribution of wealth demonstrate it's recognition of the financial system's threats to nation-states, corporations, and families. Other religious and civic groups should help return finance and the capital it marshals to the service of society. In the American context, the policy recommendations of the preceding chapter offer possible groundwork for employing the nation's greatest asset—its civil society—to reshape social attitudes and restructure institutions for the kind of genuine financial reform needed. This book also has suggested that counter voices are required to offset the steady incursion of financial discourse and logic into the civil and religious spheres, reestablishing an appreciation for "real production" over pure money making and insisting on the primacy of social and economic vision. Ethics cannot exist without intentionality. Neither can ethics effectively inform a society where the "allure" of the technocratic approach and the "dominance of technique" radically eclipse other economic visions.[23]

As noted in the introduction, the American pragmatist philosopher John Dewey wrote about the challenges of American democracy in 1939. He observed that "ways of life and institutions which were once the natural, almost inevitable, product of fortunate conditions have now to be won by conscious and resolute effort" in a way that "puts a heavier demand on human creativeness."[24] Dewey was responding to the transformation of the American frontier from a physical to a moral one. The moral challenge that Dewey saw to democracy in his day is the challenge of capitalism in ours. Like democracy, capitalism needs creativity, but not only the kind of creativity that yields productive innovations. Capitalism needs the creativity to reenvision and nurture institutions for virtuous, sustainable growth. Creative capitalism, like the creative democracy of which Dewey wrote, insists that in the right contexts human beings can thrive socially and morally, as well as materially. It acknowledges the autonomous human person but also enriches that view with the perspective of history and the continuity of tradition to promote flourishing, both of human beings and the social groups they form.

More recently, another notable American philosopher, Daniel Bell, observed how the demand for a return to civil society "is the demand for a return to a manageable scale of social life, particularly where the national economy has become embedded in an international frame and the national polity has lost some degree of its independence."[25] Importantly, Bell recognized the particularly American form of civil society that has contributed, as much as any single American quality, to the nation's identity:

> The actual existence of civil society … has been distinctively American, shaped initially by the varied impulses of rugged individualism and radical populism. Yet to the extent that a renewed appreciation for the virtues of civil society is again required in order to define a new kind of social order that limits the State and enhances individual and group purposes … it is also one more twist to the long tale of American exceptionalism.[26]

A new appreciation for civil society is once again necessary. Americans seem to have lost the understanding both of its necessity and its potency in directing the nation's progress. The financialized society encourages isolation and an illusory self-sufficiency that also limits civil society as a counterforce. The first step is for religious and civic organizations to dislodge themselves from relationships that can compromise their integrity. The formation of "Church-PACs" and the co-optation of civic groups by hedge funds to help the latter profit from derivative deals take these intermediary institutions in the wrong direction. Altruistic and financially disinterested forms of civil society must remain alive to point to something nobler than self-interest and for the reason that social idealism is indispensable to ethical debate. The admittedly idealistic model presented in the previous chapter is intended primarily to start a conversation and, hopefully, to stimulate social imagination. Involvement of religious and civic organizations in a financial economy that increasingly reshapes the society it ostensibly serves is essential to secure the kind of balanced progress supportive of societal, not just individual, flourishing.

Notes

1 Justin O'Brien, "The Future of Financial Regulation: Enhancing Integrity through Design," *Sydney Law Review* vol. 32, no. 1 (March 2010): 67.
2 Alan Montefiore, "Integrity: A Philosopher's Introduction," in Alan Montefiore and David Vines, eds., *Integrity in the Public and Private Domains* (New York: Routledge, 1999), 10, quoted in O'Brien, "The Future of Financial Regulation," 69. See also J. Patrick Dobel, "Public Trusteeship: The Responsibilities of Transparency and Legacy," in Justin O'Brien, ed., *Governing the Corporation: Regulation and Corporate Governance in an Age of Scandal and Global Markets* (Wiley, 2005), 317.
3 Henry Adams, *The Degradation of Democratic Dogma* (New York: The Macmillan Company, 1919).
4 PBS Frontline, "Money, Power, and Wall Street," Part Four; transcript available at www.pbs.org/wgbh/pages/frontline/business-economy-financial-crisis/money-power-wall-street/transcript-19/.
5 Paul H. Dembinski, *Finance: Servant or Deceiver? Financialization at the Crossroads* (New York: Palgrave Macmillan, 2008), 6.
6 Philip Booth, "Ethics Alone Will Not Prevent Financial Crises," *Financial Times* [London (UK)]. (November 13, 2009): 17.
7 Booth, "Ethics Alone Will Not Prevent Financial Crises," 17.
8 O'Brien, "The Future of Financial Regulation," 75.
9 Benedict, *Caritas in Veritate*, #21.
10 Benedict, *Caritas in Veritate*, #36, #45, #65.
11 Benedict, *Caritas in Veritate*, #27.
12 Benedict, *Caritas in Veritate*, #27 (emphasis Benedict's).
13 Benedict, *Caritas in Veritate*, #65.
14 Quoted in Umberto Bacchi, "Pope Francis Blames Global Cult of Money for Rising Poverty," *International Business Times* (May 16, 2013). Available online at www.ibtimes.co.uk/articles/468288/20130516/pope-francis-finance-markets-rome.htm.
15 William Cavanaugh, "The Unfreedom of the Market"; available at www.jesusradicals.com/uploads/2/6/3/8/26388433/unfreedom.pdf, p. 1. The article also appeared in *Wealth, Poverty, and Human Destiny*, eds. Doug Bandow and David L. Schindler (Wilmington, DE: ISIBooks, 2003), [103–28].
16 Cavanaugh, "When Enough is Enough: Why God's Abundant Life Won't Fit in a Shopping Cart, and Other Mysteries of Consumerism," *Sojourners* (May 1, 2005): 8.
17 Cavanaugh, "When Enough is Enough," 8.
18 Cavanaugh, "When Enough is Enough," 12.
19 Benedict, *Caritas in Veritate*, #38; quoted in William A. Niskanen, "The Undemanding Ethics of Capitalism," *Cato Journal* 29(3): 562. Niskanen, senior economist and

chairman emeritus of the Cato Institute, states that "blaming a financial crisis on greed is like blaming airplane crashes on gravity." See Niskanen, "The Undemanding Ethics of Capitalism," 559.

20 Niskanen, "The Undemanding Ethics of Capitalism," 562–3.

21 Niskanen, "The Undemanding Ethics of Capitalism," 561.

22 Niskanen, "The Undemanding Ethics of Capitalism," 561, 564.

23 Geoffrey M. Hodgson, "The Great Crash of 2008 and the Reform of Economics," *Cambridge Journal of Economics*, vol. 33, no. 6 (November 2009): 1209–12.

24 John Dewey, "Creative Democracy—The Task Before Us," in *John Dewey: The Later Works, 1925–1953, vol. 14: 1939–1941*, ed. Jo Ann Boydston, textual ed. Anne Sharp (Carbondale and Edwardsville, Ill: Southern Illinois University Press, 1988); available at www.faculty.fairfield.edu/faculty/hodgson/Courses/progress/Dewey.pdf. First published in *John Dewey and the Promise of America*, Progressive Education Booklet No. 14 (Columbus, Ohio: American Education Press, 1939), from an address read by Horace M. Kallen at the dinner in honor of Dewey in New York City on 20 October 1939; reprinted in *The Later Works, vol. 14*. (1939).

25 Daniel Bell, "'American Exceptionalism' Revisited: The Role of Civil Society," in *The Essential Civil Society Reader: The Classic Essays*, ed. Don E. Eberly (Lanham, MD: Rowman & Littlefield, 2000), 388.

26 Bell, "'American Exceptionalism' Revisited," 388.

Bibliography

Adams, Henry. *The Degradation of Democratic Dogma*. New York: The Macmillan Company, 1919.

Bacchi, Umberto. "Pope Francis Blames Global Cult of Money for Rising Poverty." *International Business Times*, May 16, 2013. www.ibtimes.co.uk/ articles/468288/20130516/pope-francis-finance-markets-rome.htm; accessed on October 12, 2014.

Bell, Daniel. "'American Exceptionalism' Revisited: The Role of Civil Society." In *The Essential Civil Society Reader: The Classic Essays*, edited by Don E. Eberly, 373–89. Lanham, MD: Rowman & Littlefield, 2000.

Benedict XVI. *Caritas in Veritate*, (2009). www.vatican.va/holy_father/benedict_xvi/encyclicals/documents/hf_ben-xvi_enc_20090629_caritas-in-veritate_en.html; accessed on September 10, 2014.

Booth, Philip. "Ethics Alone Will Not Prevent Financial Crises." *Financial Times* [London (UK)], November 13, 2009.

Cavanaugh, William. "The Unfreedom of the Market." In *Wealth, Poverty, and Human Destiny*. Edited by Doug Bandow and David L. Schindler, 103–28. Wilmington, DE: ISIBooks, 2003. www.jesusradicals.com/uploads/2/6/3/8/26388433/unfreedom.pdf. accessed September 16, 2014.

Cavanaugh, William. "When Enough Is Enough: Why God's Abundant Life Won't Fit in a Shopping Cart, and Other Mysteries of Consumerism." *Sojourners*, May 1, 2005.

Dembinski, Paul H. *Finance: Servant or Deceiver? Financialization at the Crossroads*. New York: Palgrave Macmillan, 2008.

Dewey, John. "Creative Democracy—The Task Before Us." In *John Dewey: The Later Works, 1925–1953, vol. 14: 1939–1941*, edited by Jo Ann Boydston, textual editor Anne Sharp. Carbondale and Edwardsville, Ill: Southern Illinois University Press, 1988. www.faculty.fairfield.edu/faculty/hodgson/Courses/progress/Dewey.pdf; accessed on September 5, 2014.

Dobel, J. Patrick. "Public Trusteeship: The Responsibilities of Transparency and Legacy." In *Governing the Corporation: Regulation and Corporate Governance in an Age of Scandal and Global Markets*, by Justin O'Brien, 317–38. Wiley, 2005.

Hodgson, Geoffrey M. "The Great Crash of 2008 and the Reform of Economics." *Cambridge Journal of Economics* 33, no. 6 (November 2009): 1205–21.
Montefiore, Alan. "Integrity: A Philosopher's Introduction." In *Integrity in the Public and Private Domains*, edited by Alan Montefiore and David Vines, 2–17. New York: Routledge, 1999.
Niskanen, William A. "The Undemanding Ethics of Capitalism." *Cato Journal* 29, no. 3 (n.d.): 559–65.
O'Brien, Justin. "The Future of Financial Regulation: Enhancing Integrity through Design." *Sydney Law Review* 32, no. 1 (March 2010): 63–85.
Smith, Martin and Marcela Gaviria. "Money, Power, and Wall Street." PBS Frontline (n.d.) www.pbs.org/wgbh/pages/frontline/business-economy-financial-crisis/money-power-wall-street/transcript-19/ on July 5, 2012.

Index

For Product Safety Concerns and Information please contact our EU
representative GPSR@taylorandfrancis.com
Taylor & Francis Verlag GmbH, Kaufingerstraße 24, 80331 München, Germany

www.ingramcontent.com/pod-product-compliance
Ingram Content Group UK Ltd.
Pitfield, Milton Keynes, MK11 3LW, UK
UKHW022219190926
475702UK00003B/442

* 9 7 8 1 1 3 8 8 8 5 6 9 1 *